AF722236

# AI-Augmented Creativity in Learning Analytics

Stavroula Kalogeras
https://orcid.org/0000-0002-5028-0413
*Heriot-Watt University, UAE*

Sepideh Samadi
https://orcid.org/0000-0002-1689-5596
*Heriot-Watt University, UAE*

Hamed Nozari
https://orcid.org/0000-0002-6500-6708
*Independent Researcher, Australia*

IGI Global
Scientific Publishing
Publishing Tomorrow's Research Today

Vice President of Editorial — Melissa Wagner
Director of Acquisitions — Mikaela Felty
Director of Book Development — Jocelynn Hessler
Production Manager — Mike Brehm
Cover Design — Jose Rosado

Published in the United States of America by
IGI Global Scientific Publishing
701 East Chocolate Avenue
Hershey, PA, 17033, USA
Tel: 717-533-8845 | Fax: 717-533-7115
Website: https://www.igi-global.com E-mail: cust@igi-global.com

Copyright © 2026 by IGI Global Scientific Publishing. All rights reserved. No part of this publication may be reproduced, stored or distributed in any form or by any means, electronic or mechanical, including photocopying, without written permission from the publisher. Use of this publication to train generative artificial intelligence (AI) technologies is expressly prohibited. The publisher reserves all rights to license its use for generative AI training and machine learning model development.

Product or company names used in this set are for identification purposes only. Inclusion of the names of the products or companies does not indicate a claim of ownership by IGI Global Scientific Publishing of the trademark or registered trademark.

Library of Congress Cataloging-in-Publication Data

Names: Kalogeras, Stavroula editor | Samadi, Sepideh, 1985- editor | Nozari, Hamed, 1984- editor
Title: AI-augmented creativity in learning analytics / Edited by Stavroula Kalogeras, Sepideh Samadi, Hamed Nozari.
Description: Hershey, PA : IGI Global Scientific Publishing, [2026] | Includes bibliographical references and index. | Summary: "This book explores and explains the role of artificial intelligence in enhancing human creativity in the field of learning analytics"-- Provided by publisher.
Identifiers: LCCN 2025028484 (print) | LCCN 2025028485 (ebook) | ISBN 9798337351179 hardcover | ISBN 9798337351186 paperback | ISBN 9798337351193 ebook
Subjects: LCSH: Artificial intelligence--Educational applications | Creative ability | Education--Research--Statistical methods
Classification: LCC LB1028.43 .A383 2026 (print) | LCC LB1028.43 (ebook)
LC record available at https://lccn.loc.gov/2025028484
LC ebook record available at https://lccn.loc.gov/2025028485
British Cataloguing in Publication Data
A Cataloguing in Publication record for this book is available from the British Library.

All work contributed to this book is new, previously-unpublished material.
The views expressed in this book are those of the authors, but not necessarily of the publisher.
This book contains information sourced from authentic and highly regarded references, with reasonable efforts made to ensure the reliability of the data and information presented. The authors, editors, and publisher believe the information in this book to be accurate and true as of the date of publication. Every effort has been made to trace and credit the copyright holders of all materials included. However, the authors, editors, and publisher cannot assume responsibility for the validity of all materials or the consequences of their use. Should any copyright material be found unacknowledged, please inform the publisher so that corrections may be made in future reprints.

# Table of Contents

# Detailed Table of Contents

of blockchain, smart contracts, and analytics opens up new horizons for assessment, digital trust, and personalized learning.



With a generation of technological advancements, AI, AR and VR are the hotspots of a paradigm shift in the interactions between the brands and the consumer. In this chapter, the technology of engaging the consumers in some new forms and ways using these emerging technologies is discussed, where the traditional experiences of a brand are turning to innovative immersive experiences. The key driver in the process, AI fits perfectly into these strategies, boosting data-driven personalization, predictive storytelling, and emotional connection with avatars, chatbots, and recommendation engines. At the same time, the immersive worlds which are fuelled by the technologies of AR and VR are redefining consumer behaviour. This chapter discusses important ethical dilemmas that include data privacy, algorithm bias, and digital fatigue that provide future outlook on metaverse, spatial computing, and digital twins. Overall, the study offers comprehensive road guide the brands can use in walking with the immersive brand experiences in the future.



The integration of Large Language Models (LLMs) into Creative Project-Based Learning (CPBL) enhances student engagement and creativity. This chapter proposes a framework embedding LLMs within CPBL using the Double Diamond model, guiding students through Discover, Define, Develop, and Deliver. LLMs serve as cognitive tools for idea generation, refining problem statements, and articulating outputs. The framework highlights prompt engineering, ethical considerations, and educator guidance to maintain student agency and ensure responsible AI use. The integration is evaluated using quantitative methods (Ennis' taxonomy, modified Torrance Test of Creative Thinking) and qualitative methods (interviews, prompt

# Preface

The technological evolution of recent decades, especially in the field of artificial intelligence, has shifted the boundaries of knowledge, creativity, and learning in an unprecedented way. In such an era, analytical learning is no longer limited to collecting behavioral data; it has become a platform for discovering hidden patterns, understanding the learner experience more deeply, and designing personalized learning paths. In the meantime, the emerging concept of "AI-enhanced creativity" has found a key position in the transformation of education and learning design. A new perspective that not only takes the accuracy of educational data analysis to a higher level, but also enables the creation of innovative and inspiring solutions that were previously beyond the power of humans or traditional algorithms.

This book is an attempt to explore new paths for combining analytical learning with artificial intelligence. This work attempts to go beyond the conventional view of educational data analysis to address the question of how learning experiences can be designed to be more personalized, engaging, and data-driven by utilizing the capabilities of artificial intelligence. An approach that does not seek to replace humans, but rather seeks to enhance the power of analysis and creativity in educational processes.

This book offers a fresh look at the intersection of data, creativity, and technology in the field of education and attempts to respond to the needs of researchers, instructors, instructional designers, content developers, and educational policymakers. Those who are concerned about how to build a better future for education by relying on data and creativity. A future in which technology is not a threat to learning, but a tool for enriching it.

Undoubtedly, what is presented in this collection is not a complete answer to all existing questions, but it can be a starting point for new and inspiring conversations in the field of combining artificial intelligence and analytical learning. It is hoped that this book can contribute to the ideas and actions that will transform the path of education in the coming decades.

Dr. Hamed Nozari

# Chapter 1
# Machine Learning for Predictive Learning Analytics

**Agnieszka Szmelter-Jarosz**
*Faculty of Economics, University of Gdańsk, Poland*

## ABSTRACT

*This research examines the role of machine learning in predictive learning analytics and its applications in educational settings. The main focus has been on how to prepare data, select and train machine learning models, evaluate and validate them, and finally, effectively integrate these models into educational systems. The findings show that combining data-driven analytics with machine learning algorithms can help improve the quality of learning, personalize education, and enhance educational interventions. In addition to technical requirements, this approach requires attention to ethical, social, and educational policy considerations in order to serve as an effective tool in education.*

## 1. INTRODUCTION

In recent decades, the digital transformation in education has led to the accumulation of a vast amount of data related to teaching and learning processes. Data that previously remained in the form of traditional teacher-student interactions or limited educational activities is now recorded and stored in a structured manner with the spread of virtual learning environments, learning management systems (LMS), massive online courses (MOOCs), and personalized learning platforms (Sghir et al., 2023). This change has not only provided new opportunities for more accurate monitoring and analysis of the learning process, but also made it possible

DOI: 10.4018/979-8-3373-5117-9.ch001

ght © 2026, IGI Global Scientific Publishing. Copying or distributing in print or electronic forms without written permission of IGI Global Scientific Publishing is prohibited. Use of this chapter to generative artificial intelligence (AI) technologies is expressly prohibited. The publisher reserves all rights to license its use for generative AI training and machine learning model development.

to predict learner behaviors and educational outcomes. In this regard, a new field called Learning Analytics has emerged that analyzes learning data with the aim of extracting patterns, better understanding learning processes, and improving educational decision-making (Nozari, Szmelter-Jarosz, & Ghahremani-Nahr, 2022).

Among the various branches of learning analytics, predictive learning analytics has gained a special place due to its ability to predict academic performance, identify educational risks, and optimize interventions. Predictive analytics, unlike descriptive and diagnostic analytics, goes beyond observing the past and attempts to predict future events based on existing data (Mubarak et al., 2021). Applying this type of analytics in education can play an effective role in preventing academic failure, dropout, or reduced learner engagement, and at the same time, it enables the design of personalized learning paths (Guryanova et al., 2020).

Meanwhile, machine learning, as one of the most important sub-branches of artificial intelligence, plays a key role in implementing predictive analytics. Machine learning's ability to discover hidden patterns in data, identify complex relationships between learning variables, and generate models that can generalize to new data has made it a powerful tool for learning analytics (Nozari, Ghahremani-Nahr, & Szmelter-Jarosz, 2024). Machine learning algorithms, whether classifiers to predict learning outcomes or regressions to predict continuous values, have been widely used in various fields of education (Samanpour et al., 2017).

One of the most important advantages of using machine learning models in learning analytics is their ability to be applied in adaptive learning environments and personalized learning systems. Such models can continuously analyze data on learner interactions, performance changes, or learning behaviors to adjust the learning path in real time to suit the individual needs of each user (Nozari, Tavakkoli-Moghaddam, & Dolgui, 2024). This feature is especially important in open learning environments, such as massively online courses or self-paced e-learning, where teachers or course designers cannot directly interact with each learner (Alam & Mohanty, 2022).

However, implementing machine learning-based predictive learning analytics is not without its challenges. One of the main obstacles is the quality and structure of educational data. Data obtained from educational systems often have characteristics such as heterogeneity, class imbalance, incomplete data, or noise, which can affect the accuracy and reliability of predictive models (Nozari, Ghahremani-Nahr, & Szmelter-Jarosz, 2023). On the other hand, choosing the right algorithm, tuning model parameters, and interpreting the outputs also require technical knowledge and a deep understanding of the nature of educational data (Hlosta et al., 2022).

Another important challenge is the ethical and social considerations associated with educational data analytics. Learning analytics, especially in its predictive form, often deals with sensitive student and user data, which can raise serious concerns about privacy, information security, and even the social consequences of inaccurate or discriminatory analytics (Sciarrone, 2018). This highlights the need to pay attention to the principles of Responsible AI in the design and implementation of learning analytics models. It is necessary to take advantage of technical capabilities, as well as social implications, model transparency, and stakeholder engagement (Aliahmadi & Nozari, 2023).

At the same time, the growth of new technologies such as Digital Twin in education has opened up new horizons for the development of predictive learning analytics. Digital Twin in the educational context means building a living and dynamic virtual model of the learner that can simultaneously represent his or her behaviors, performance, and interactions (Kurilovas, 2019). This technology, when connected to machine learning models, enables simulation, prediction, and even targeted intervention in the learning process (Nozari, Tavakkoli-Moghaddam, Ghahremani-Nahr, & Najafi, 2023). In other words, combining Digital Twin with predictive analytics models can lead to the formation of a new generation of intelligent and adaptive learning systems in which not only the past and present, but also the future of learning is managed in a data-driven manner (Bujang et al., 2021).

With this perspective in mind, the present study aims to examine the role of machine learning in the framework of predictive learning analytics, introduce the main algorithms and approaches, and express the opportunities, challenges, and practical applications of this technology in educational environments. The focus of this study is to show how machine learning can play a role as a key element in the evolution of data-driven education and personalized learning beyond a mere tool. Finally, future research directions will be discussed, with an emphasis on combining machine learning, Digital Twin, and social responsibility principles in educational analytics.

## 2. FOUNDATIONS OF PREDICTIVE LEARNING ANALYTICS

Predictive learning analytics, as a key subfield of learning analytics, has received significant attention in educational research and data science in recent years. This approach attempts to identify hidden patterns in data from learners' activities in educational environments and use them to predict future behaviors, performances, or outcomes. Due to its forward-looking nature, this type of analysis can help instructional designers, teachers, educational administrators, and even learners themselves make smarter decisions and implement more timely interventions to improve learning (Najafi, Nozari, & Edalatpanah, 2022).

A fundamental understanding of predictive learning analytics requires a thorough understanding of the nature of educational data and its structure. Educational data often includes a wide range of information that comes from direct learner interactions with e-learning systems, assessment activities, social interactions in educational environments, data related to academic achievement, and sometimes even physiological or emotional data (Mathrani et al., 2021). Unlike other areas of data analysis that focus on structured and uniform data, in the field of educational analytics, data is diverse, multi-source, and of variable quality. This characteristic has made predictive learning analytics a challenging yet rewarding field (Nozari & Chobar, 2024).

Educational data can usually be classified into several general categories. Transactional data refers to user interactions with educational systems, which includes information such as login time, duration of attendance, access to educational content, participation in online activities, and use of learning tools. Performance data from tests, projects, assignments, and continuous assessments are considered important indicators of academic performance. Contextual data include demographic information, educational background, and environmental conditions of the learner, which play a significant role in interpreting learning behavior. In addition, data from social interactions, participation in learning groups, peer communication, and other interactive activities constitute an important part of the data sources in this area (Herodotou et al., 2019).

Predictive learning analysis is based on extracting meaningful patterns from data, selecting key indicators, and designing appropriate predictor variables. In this regard, indicators such as academic success, participation rate, progress in learning courses, or the probability of dropping out of school are considered as predicted outcomes in the models. Accurate identification of these indicators not only helps to improve the performance of predictive models, but also determines the direction of educational interventions (Fallah & Nozari, 2021).

The concept of feature engineering has a special place in this field. Feature engineering refers to the process of extracting, selecting, and transforming variables in a way that provides the most information possible to predictive models. This process may include data cleaning, incomplete data management, normalization, dimensionality reduction, or even combining different features to create more complex profiles. In fact, the success of machine learning models in predictive learning analysis largely depends on the quality of feature engineering and the way the input data is processed (Nozari, Abdi, Szmelter-Jarosz, & Motevalli, 2024).

Figure 1 shows the conceptual framework of predictive learning analysis based on machine learning. In this framework, data from various educational sources are collected and, after going through the cleaning and preprocessing stages, they enter the modeling stage using machine learning algorithms. The output of this process is predictions that can be presented to stakeholders in the form of analytical reports, educational alerts, or adaptation suggestions. This model not only structures the prediction process, but also helps integrate data flow with educational decisions and provides a suitable platform for timely interventions (Ghahremani-Nahr, Nozari, & Aliahmadi, 2023).

*Figure 1. Conceptual framework of machine learning-based predictive learning analytics*

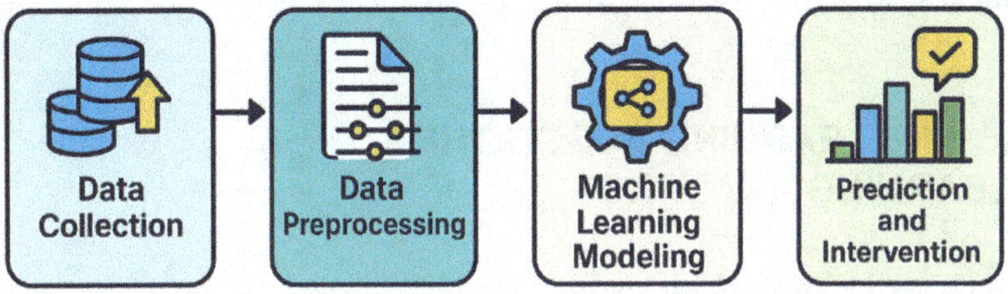


One of the most important functions of this framework is to support effective and evidence-based educational interventions. For example, in an online learning environment, if a predictive model predicts a high probability of a student's academic failure based on past behavioral patterns and performance, this prediction can be the basis for actions such as suggesting additional educational resources, changing teaching approaches, or even inviting them to counseling sessions. In this way, predictive analytics is not just an analytical tool, but becomes part of the educational decision-making system (Nozari, Rahmaty, Foukolaei, Movahed, & Bayanati, 2025).

However, predictive learning analytics faces serious challenges, including the quality of educational data. Incomplete, inconsistent, or biased data can have a direct impact on the accuracy of predictions. Also, the complexity of learner behaviors and the influence of various cultural, social, and individual factors on the learning process make the task of prediction more difficult and require the use of more advanced and flexible models (Aliahmadi, Nozari, Ghahremani-Nahr, & Szmelter-Jarosz, 2022).

Another important challenge in this area is the issue of model transferability. Models that have shown good performance in one educational setting may not produce similar results in other conditions and for different populations. For this reason, the issue of adjusting and adapting models for different educational settings is of great importance and requires serious attention from researchers and educational system designers (Nozari, 2025a).

A final but crucial point is to pay attention to the ethical dimensions of predictive learning analysis. Educational data analysis, especially when it leads to the prediction of individual behaviors, faces sensitive issues of privacy and social justice. Using the results of the analysis to judge students or make important educational decisions must be done with the principles of transparency, impartiality, and accountability in order to prevent unintended consequences.

Overall, predictive learning analysis, despite its challenges and considerations, is a powerful tool for improving the quality of education and promoting data-driven decision-making. Combining technical knowledge of machine learning with a deep understanding of learning processes and attention to ethical requirements can lead to the development of solutions that contribute to the transformation of contemporary educational systems, both scientifically and practically.

## 3. MACHINE LEARNING ALGORITHMS FOR LEARNING ANALYTICS

The application of machine learning in predictive learning analytics represents the intersection of data science, education, and artificial intelligence. Machine learning algorithms, as tools for discovering hidden patterns in educational data, are capable of analyzing complex relationships between variables and can provide accurate predictions about learners' performance, behavior, and future trajectories. In learning analytics, the use of these algorithms not only helps to improve the accuracy of predictions, but also enables the application of targeted interventions and the development of adaptive learning (Weng, 2020).

Machine learning is generally divided into two main groups: supervised learning and unsupervised learning. In predictive learning analytics, supervised learning is most widely used because in this approach, the training data is labeled and the learning model attempts to predict expected output values based on the input features. This method has been widely used to predict academic performance, probability of success, or risk of academic failure (Nozari, Fallah, Szmelter-Jarosz, & Krzemiński, 2021).

Classification algorithms are one of the most widely used supervised learning algorithms in learning analytics. These algorithms try to place inputs into predefined categories. Among them, decision trees have been proposed as a basic algorithm in many studies due to their high interpretability and ease of implementation. Random Forest models also increase prediction accuracy by combining multiple decision trees and using reinforcement methods and are more resistant to overfitting (Theng & Theng, 2020). The Support Vector Machine (SVM) algorithm uses geometric concepts to try to find an optimal boundary between classes and shows acceptable performance in classifying complex data. This algorithm performs well, especially when the number of features is high (Nozari & Rahmaty, 2023).

Deep learning models have also entered the field of learning analytics in recent years. Artificial neural networks, especially their deep variants, have great power in analyzing complex and nonlinear data, with the ability to extract high-level features from raw data. Convolutional neural networks (CNN) and recurrent networks (RNN) play an important role, especially in cases where multimodal data such as text, image or audio data are used. However, high complexity, the need for extensive data for training and difficulty in interpretation are among the limitations of using these models in educational environments (Lotfi, Najafi, & Nozari, 2016).

Along with classification algorithms, regression algorithms also play an important role in predicting continuous values such as final score, average performance or time remaining to the end of the course. Linear regression, as the simplest model, forms the basis of many early analyses. More advanced regression models, such as Ridge and Lasso regression, help improve accuracy and prevent overfitting by adding penalty coefficients to the regression equation (Nozari, Rahmaty, & Szmelter-Jarosz, 2024). For more complex problems, nonlinear regression and boosting models such as XGBoost or Gradient Boosting can provide better performance.

In some applications, especially when the goal is to identify hidden patterns in the data, clustering algorithms and unsupervised learning are used. The K-Means algorithm can help identify different groups of learners by grouping data into clusters with similar characteristics. These clusterings may be the basis for designing personalized learning paths or analyzing collaborative behaviors (Joseph-Richard et al., 2021). The DBSCAN method is also used in some cases due to its ability to identify irregularly shaped clusters and its robustness to noise.

Figure 2 shows a schematic view of the types of machine learning algorithms used in learning analytics. This figure divides the algorithms into three main categories: classification, regression, and clustering algorithms. Each category is accompanied by examples of its most commonly used algorithms to provide a clear picture of the structure of machine learning models in this field. This framework can be a basis for selecting the appropriate method based on the type of data and the analytical goal (Uskov et al., 2021).

*Figure 2. Classification of machine learning algorithms in predictive learning analytics*

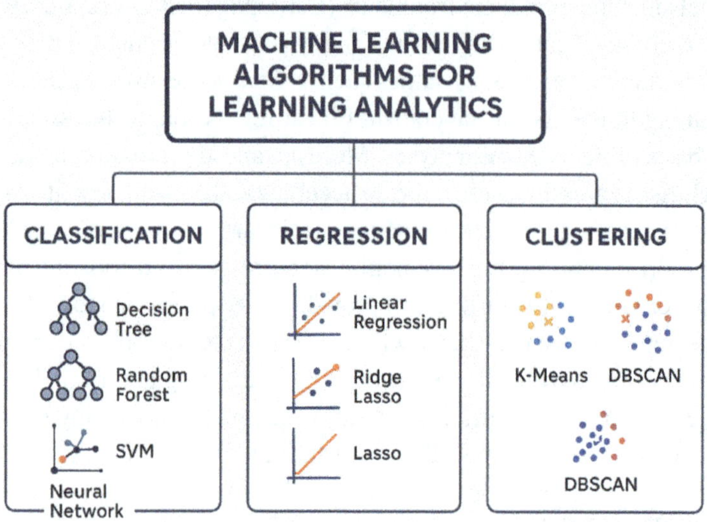


Despite the diversity and power of machine learning algorithms, selecting the most appropriate model for a specific application in learning analytics requires a thorough understanding of the data characteristics, the prediction goal, and environmental considerations. For example, in situations where the interpretation of results is of great importance to teachers or educational administrators, the use of models with high explanatory power, such as decision trees or linear regression, will be preferred over more complex models, such as neural networks. In contrast, when the goal is to achieve maximum prediction accuracy in large and complex data, models based on deep learning or reinforcement algorithms will be a better choice (Nozari, Najafi, Jafari-Eskandari, & Aliahmadi, 2016).

Another issue in the use of machine learning algorithms is parameter tuning, or the so-called Hyperparameter Tuning process. This process involves selecting optimal values for model parameters in order to increase prediction accuracy and avoid problems such as overfitting. For this purpose, methods such as Grid Search or Random Search are used. In recent years, algorithms based on automatic optimization such as Bayesian Optimization have also been developed for this purpose (Shridharan et al., 2018).

Finally, it should be noted that the success of machine learning algorithms in learning analysis is not limited to their technical capabilities alone. The issue of interpretability, reliability of results, and social acceptance of models in educational environments is of great importance. Developing models that have high accuracy, transparency, and explainability is one of the main research axes in the field of predictive learning analysis. Combining machine learning approaches with explainable artificial intelligence (XAI) principles can provide a suitable path to respond to this need (Nozari, 2025b).

Overall, machine learning algorithms, as the backbone of predictive learning analysis, play a fundamental role in identifying patterns, predicting behaviors, and improving educational decisions. The diversity of these algorithms and their adaptability to different situations have enabled learning analytics to establish its place not only at the level of academic research, but also in practical and commercial applications. The intelligent use of these algorithms requires a combination of technical knowledge, educational understanding, and a commitment to ethical principles in working with sensitive educational data (Mohammadi et al., 2015).

## 4. DATA PREPROCESSING AND FEATURE ENGINEERING

As a fundamental pillar of predictive learning analytics and machine learning-based modeling, data preprocessing and feature engineering play a critical role in ensuring the accuracy and efficiency of results. Due to their complex, heterogeneous, and multi-source nature, training data are often not suitable for use in machine learning models in their raw state and require preliminary processing to transform them into modeling-ready data (Nozari, 2024a). Data preprocessing is a set of targeted actions that clean, modify, integrate, and standardize data with the aim of improving their quality and compatibility with analytical models.

One of the most important challenges observed in training data is the existence of incomplete data. This defect can be caused by non-recording of interactions, technical errors in training systems, or even the absence of learners. Incomplete data management, if not done properly, can lead to model bias and reduced prediction accuracy. The most common solutions to deal with incomplete data include deleting incomplete records, replacing them with median or mean values, and in more advanced cases, using techniques for estimating missing values based on the similarity of data patterns (Poh & Khor, 2024). The choice of the appropriate method for managing this data should be made considering the volume of available data and the sensitivity of the variables.

Another problem in training data is the presence of outliers or anomalies. These data, which usually appear as values that are very large or small compared to the mean or unexpected values in the data set, can severely affect the performance of predictive models. Identifying and managing outliers through methods such as statistical tests, image analysis, or automated anomaly detection algorithms is considered a key step in data preprocessing (Movahed, Aliahmadi, Parsanejad, & Nozari, 2023). In some cases, it is justified to remove outliers, while in others, it is recommended to replace them with more reasonable values or re-check the data for correctness.

Another essential step in preprocessing is data normalization and scaling. Many machine learning algorithms, especially those that work on distance or gradient, are sensitive to the scale of the data. Data normalization, by converting values to a specific interval or standardizing them to have a mean of zero and a variance of one, helps models perform optimally without affecting the scale of the variables (Ghahremani-Nahr, Nozari, Rahmaty, Zeraati Foukolaei, & Sherejsharifi, 2023). This step is especially important in training data where there are variables with different scales, such as grades, activity time, or login times.

After the preprocessing steps, the feature engineering process begins, which is one of the most important parts of predictive learning analytics. Feature engineering is the process of identifying, extracting, modifying, and creating variables that can enhance the predictive power of a model. The goal of this process is to reduce the irrelevant dimensions of the data, focus on meaningful variables, and improve the performance of machine learning models (Candelieri & Archetti, 2019).

In many learning analytics projects, it is important to identify key variables that are directly related to the predicted outcome. For example, in predicting academic performance, variables such as participation in virtual classes, frequency of access to resources, duration of interaction with educational content, and assessment records play a key role in enhancing the model's performance. The correct selection of these variables based on statistical analysis, correlation tests, or feature selection algorithms helps the model to discard unnecessary information and focus on effective features (Nozari & Edalatpanah, 2023).

Feature transformation is another feature engineering technique that involves applying changes to the data to improve its predictive power. These changes may include constructing new features from combinations of other variables, applying mathematical transformations, grouping continuous values into discrete categories, or even encoding text data as numbers. A common example of this process is converting date and time into analyzable features such as day of the week, hour, or time period that can better represent learner behavior patterns (Doss et al., 2024).

In some cases, reducing the dimensionality of the data through methods such as principal component analysis (PCA) or feature selection techniques based on feature importance can help simplify the model and reduce processing time. This is especially important when dealing with large training data or multi-source data that contains hundreds of initial features (Nozari, Irani, & Rahmaty, 2023).

Figure 3 depicts the overall process of data preprocessing and feature engineering in the form of a sequential chain. This chain starts with data collection, then moves on to data cleaning, normalization, and standardization. Next, the feature engineering process is performed through feature identification, extraction, transformation, and reduction, and finally the prepared data is fed into machine learning models. This framework clearly shows how the success of any predictive learning analytics project depends on the quality of the initial data processing steps (Movahed, Movahed, & Nozari, 2024a).

*Figure 3. Data preprocessing and feature engineering process in predictive learning analytics*

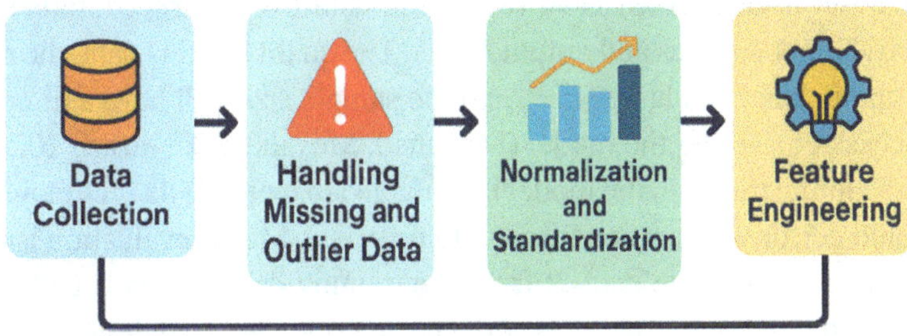


One important aspect of this process is the concurrency and matching of data with analytical models. Especially in learning analytics projects based on time-series data, data synchronization is of great importance in order to correctly understand the sequence of events and avoid temporal interference. Although many machine learning algorithms can handle non-sequential data, in analyzing learner behavior over time, maintaining the temporal sequence of events is essential to achieve accurate predictions (Nozari, 2024b).

Finally, the process of data preprocessing and feature engineering is not only a technical step, but also a strategic part of predictive learning analytics that requires a deep understanding of the data, the project goals, and how the analytical models work. The choices made at this stage have a direct impact on the quality, accuracy, and generalizability of the machine learning models. For this reason, this process must be followed carefully, sensitively, and in close interaction with educational and research goals in order to be the foundation for success in data-driven learning analytics (Razali et al., 2022).

## 5. MODEL TRAINING, EVALUATION, AND VALIDATION

The process of training, evaluating, and validating models in predictive learning analytics is one of the most important steps in the development of intelligent systems based on machine learning. The main goal of this step is to build a model that can learn the hidden patterns in the training data in a way that performs well not only on the trained data but also on new and unseen data. This goal will only be possible by following a rigorous and systematic framework for training, evaluation, and validation (Szmelter-Jarosz & Nozari, 2025). Model training in machine learning refers to the process by which the selected algorithm uses the training data set to adjust the weights, parameters, and relationships between features. In this step, the model attempts to achieve an optimal pattern of the data by minimizing an error function or optimizing an objective measure. In predictive learning analytics, the training dataset usually consists of real-world data from learner interactions that have specific input features and output labels. The quality of this data, the degree of diversity and balance of classes in it, and the sample size will have a direct impact on the success of training the model (Movahed, Movahed, & Nozari, 2024b).

After the initial training, the model is evaluated to measure its accuracy, generalizability, and performance when faced with new data. Model evaluation is typically performed using a separate dataset from the training data, which is called the test or evaluation data. At this stage, various metrics are used to measure the model's performance, the choice of which depends on the type of problem and the type of model output. In classification problems, metrics such as Accuracy, Precision, Recall, and F1 score are used. In regression problems, metrics such as mean square error (MSE), mean absolute error (MAE), and coefficient of determination ($R^2$) are used (Nozari, Tavakkoli-Moghaddam, Rohaninejad, & Hanzalek, 2023). The careful selection of these metrics helps the researcher to gain a better understanding of the strengths and weaknesses of the model in different situations. One of the common dangers in training machine learning models is the phenomenon of overfitting. In this case, the model adapts to the training data in such a way that it loses its ability to generalize to new data. Conversely, in underfitting conditions, the model cannot function properly even on the training data and does not learn the real structure of the data well. To deal with these problems, one of the most important methods is to use cross-validation techniques. In cross-validation, the dataset is divided into several parts and the model is trained on one part of the data and evaluated on another part. This process helps to expose the model to a variety of data and to measure its generalization ability in a more realistic way (Seyedtabib, Najafi-Vosough, & Kamyari, 2024).

Another widely used technique in the evaluation phase is the use of hold-out validation. In this method, the data is divided into two or three parts: a training set, an evaluation set, and if necessary, a final test set. In this approach, the model is trained on the training data, adjusted on the evaluation data, and finally, its actual performance is measured on the test data. This method can provide reliable results and avoid the risk of unrealistic evaluation, especially when a large amount of data is available (Rahmaty & Nozari, 2023).

Figure 4 illustrates the overall framework of the model training, evaluation, and validation process in predictive learning analytics. This figure shows that the initial data, after preprocessing and feature engineering, enters the model training phase. Next, the model performance is checked using the evaluation data and, if necessary, the model parameters are adjusted. Finally, the validated model is ready for deployment in operational environments using the final test data.

*Figure 4. Model training, evaluation, and validation framework in predictive learning analytics*

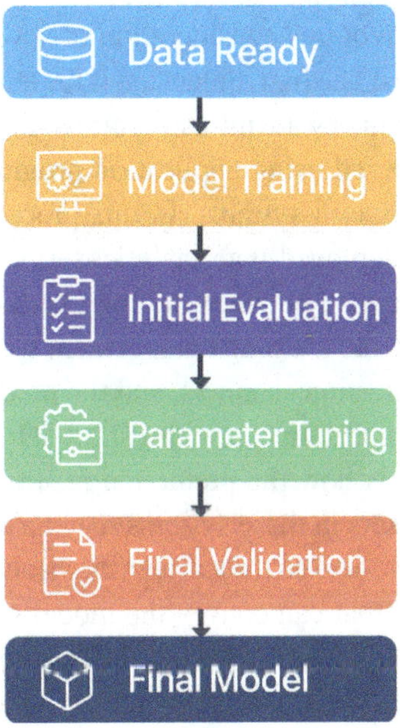


The importance of this process is that, while ensuring the technical performance of the model, it helps to ensure the reliability of the results in real educational environments. Using these evaluation frameworks allows for the identification of model weaknesses, improvement of its performance, and prevention of incorrect decisions in learning environments. Also, by following these processes, the possibility of problems arising from data bias, misinterpretation of results, or misconceptions about the model's performance is minimized.

In general, model training, evaluation, and validation in predictive learning analytics is a multi-stage and rigorous process that encompasses not only technical aspects, but also ethical, operational, and applied aspects of educational analytics.

## 6. INTEGRATION WITH EDUCATIONAL SYSTEMS AND PLATFORMS

Integrating machine learning-based predictive learning analytics models with educational systems and digital learning platforms is a key step in the practical application of these models in educational settings. While the development of analytical models can be done in research settings, the true value of these models is revealed when they are seamlessly integrated into educational platforms such as learning management systems (LMS), personalized learning systems, or online learning platforms (Yordanova & Nozari, 2025).

Successful integration requires consideration of several technical, operational, and educational dimensions. The first dimension is the technical integration between the analytical model and the software infrastructure of the educational systems. This integration is usually achieved using application programming interfaces (APIs), microservices, or module-based systems. In this process, a separately developed machine learning model is deployed as an analytics service alongside the educational system, enabling data exchange between the two platforms. For example, learner behavioral data recorded in the learning management system is sent to the analytics model via secure communication channels, and the prediction results are provided to the educational system in real time or with a short delay (Nithya & Ilango, 2017).

The second dimension is how the prediction results are presented to different users of the system. End users in these systems may be educational administrators, teachers, academic advisors, or even the learners themselves. It is important to design the user interface in a way that can convey the model's outputs to the audience in a clear, understandable, and technically complex manner. Analytical dashboards, visual reports, alert notifications, and personalized recommendations are among the tools that can effectively present these results to end users. This is especially important when one of the main goals of learning analytics is to facilitate informed decision-making in educational settings (Nozari, 2023).

The third dimension is the alignment of analytical models with educational policy and implementation requirements. Each educational system operates within a specific cultural, legal, and organizational context that may influence how data is collected, processed, and analytical results are presented. For example, data privacy laws, information security policies, or ethical requirements may impose limitations on how predictive analytics can be used. Therefore, the integration of analytical models should be done with a full understanding of these considerations, not only to ensure the effectiveness of the system but also to ensure its social acceptance (Nozari, Ghahremani-Nahr, & Najafi, 2023).

Figure 5 illustrates the conceptual framework for integrating predictive models into educational systems. In this framework, raw learner data is sent to the prediction module through the learning platforms and, after processing and analysis, the results are provided to users in the form of real-time feedback, analytical reports or educational recommendations. This process is not only a one-way data flow, but also an interactive and feedback loop in which analytical outputs can lead to learning path readjustments, educational interventions or policy improvements.

*Figure 5. Framework for integrating predictive learning analysis models with educational systems*

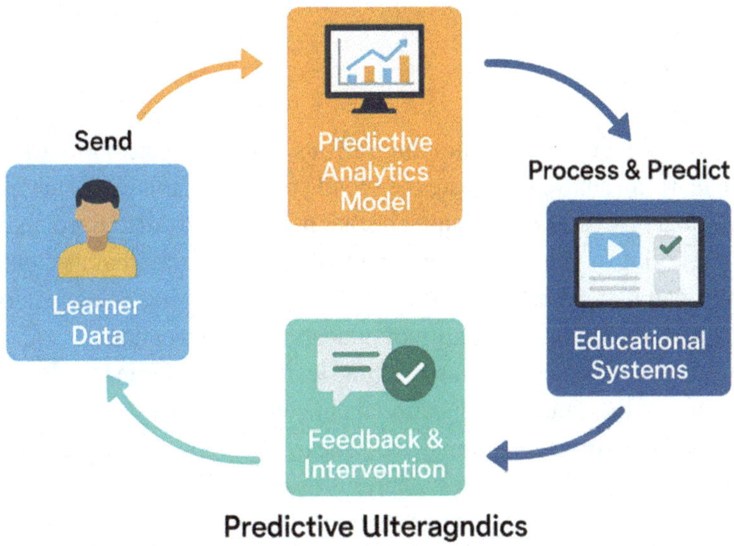


In addition, the integration of learning analysis models with educational systems should be such that their scalability and flexibility are maintained over time. Given the dynamics of learning environments, changes in educational needs, or changes in the target population, analytical models and how they are integrated must also be able to adapt to these developments. This feature requires the design of analytical modules with an open structure, the ability to be continuously updated, and the ability to be customized based on environmental needs.

Another issue that arises in this regard is the ability to monitor and track the performance of integrated models over time. Integrating machine learning models with educational systems should not be considered as a static process. Rather, it requires continuous monitoring infrastructures to ensure the accuracy of predictions, identify changes in the quality of input data, and periodically update models based on new data. Establishing such monitoring mechanisms can help maintain the quality and effectiveness of learning analytics in the long term (Movahed, Movahed, & Nozari, 2024c).

Ultimately, the successful integration of learning analytics models into educational systems requires close collaboration between technical developers, educational professionals, system administrators, and policymakers. Only by effectively interacting with these groups can we ensure that analytics models are properly developed, appropriately implemented in educational contexts, and effectively used. Such synergy between technical and educational aspects can transform predictive learning analytics from a theoretical concept into an effective tool for improving the quality of teaching and learning.

## 7. CONCLUSION

The results obtained from examining various aspects of machine learning-based predictive learning analysis indicate the broad potential of this approach in improving educational processes and learning decision-making. As discussed in this study, predictive learning analysis is not only a mere analytical tool, but as a data-driven approach, it can play an effective role in optimizing learning paths, personalizing education, and improving the quality of educational interventions.

The basis for success in applying machine learning for learning analysis is a deep understanding of the nature of educational data and the processes of preprocessing and feature engineering. Educational data, due to its diversity of sources, interactive nature, and heterogeneity, requires a careful process of cleaning, standardization, and extraction of meaningful features. Only by going through these steps can machine learning models extract reliable and meaningful patterns from the data and provide effective predictions. These prerequisites double the need to invest in data infrastructure and develop data analysis capacities in educational institutions.

On the other hand, the correct selection and implementation of machine learning algorithms in the learning analysis process plays a decisive role in the quality and effectiveness of the outputs. As examined in this study, each of the classification, regression, and clustering algorithms has its own applications and limitations, depending on the nature of the data and the analytical goals. The conscious use of these algorithms, along with the optimal adjustment of parameters and the selection of appropriate evaluation criteria, can increase the reliability of predictive analytics and provide more practical results for educational decision-makers.

The stages of training, evaluation, and validation of models, as a bridge between model development and its practical application, play a fundamental role in the success of predictive learning analytics. These steps, while avoiding common pitfalls such as overfitting or underfitting, ensure that the developed models can perform reliably and consistently when faced with real-world data. The use of techniques such as cross-validation, supervised evaluation, and monitoring model performance in real-world environments are among the factors that directly affect the generalizability and applicability of models in educational settings.

One of the most important achievements of this research was the emphasis on the importance of integrating predictive learning analytics models with educational systems and digital learning platforms. This integration, beyond a simple technical attachment, requires alignment between technology infrastructure, educational goals, and social considerations. Analytical models can be effective when they are integrated seamlessly into educational processes, their results are made available to users in a transparent and understandable manner, and organizational policies facilitate their use. In this regard, collaboration between technical, educational, and management teams will be essential for achieving successful and sustainable integration.

Another key point emphasized in this study is the need to pay attention to the ethical and legal aspects of learning analytics. The use of educational data, especially in predictive analytics that can lead to labeling or decision-making about learners, requires adherence to principles such as privacy, transparency in algorithms, and respect for the rights of stakeholders. Adherence to these principles is essential not only for the social acceptance of analytical models, but also has a direct impact on user trust and the ultimate effectiveness of these technologies.

Given the findings of this study, it can be concluded that predictive learning analytics, at the intersection of data-driven technologies, machine learning algorithms, and educational processes, is one of the most promising new approaches to improving teaching and learning. However, effective use of this approach requires a comprehensive and interdisciplinary perspective that pays sufficient attention not only to technical aspects, but also to human, social, and organizational dimensions.

Finally, it is important to emphasize that the path of development and application of predictive learning analytics is a dynamic and evolving one. With the continuous advancement of data and machine learning technologies, along with developments in learning theories and changes in educational needs, new opportunities for innovation in this area will arise. Educational researchers and policymakers can use these capacities to improve the quality of education, increase learner participation, and support teaching-learning processes in different environments with a responsible and scientific approach. This will require investment in applied research, development of data capacities, and upgrading the level of specialized knowledge in the field of learning analytics and artificial intelligence in education.

## REFERENCES

Alam, A., & Mohanty, A. (2022, December). Predicting students' performance employing educational data mining techniques, machine learning, and learning analytics. In International Conference on Communication, Networks and Computing (pp. 166-177). Cham: Springer Nature Switzerland.

Aliahmadi, A., & Nozari, H. (2023, January). Evaluation of security metrics in AIoT and blockchain-based supply chain by Neutrosophic decision-making method. In Supply chain forum: an international journal (Vol. 24, No. 1, pp. 31-42). Taylor & Francis. DOI: 10.1080/16258312.2022.2101898

Aliahmadi, A., Nozari, H., Ghahremani-Nahr, J., & Szmelter-Jarosz, A. (2022). Evaluation of key impression of resilient supply chain based on artificial intelligence of things (AIoT). arXiv preprint arXiv:2207.13174.

Bujang, S. D. A., Selamat, A., & Krejcar, O. (2021, February). A predictive analytics model for students grade prediction by supervised machine learning. []. IOP Publishing.]. *IOP Conference Series. Materials Science and Engineering*, *1051*(1), 012005. DOI: 10.1088/1757-899X/1051/1/012005

Candelieri, A., & Archetti, F. (2019). Global optimization in machine learning: The design of a predictive analytics application. *Soft Computing*, *23*(9), 2969–2977. DOI: 10.1007/s00500-018-3597-8

Doss, A. N., Krishnan, R., Karuppasamy, A. D., & Sam, B. (2024). Learning analytics model for predictive analysis of learners behavior for an indigenous MOOC platform (tadakhul system) in Oman. *International Journal of Information and Education Technology (IJIET)*, *14*(7), 961–967. DOI: 10.18178/ijiet.2024.14.7.2123

Fallah, M., & Nozari, H. (2021). Neutrosophic mathematical programming for optimization of multi-objective sustainable biomass supply chain network design. *Computer Modeling in Engineering & Sciences*, *129*(2), 927–951. DOI: 10.32604/cmes.2021.017511

Ghahremani-Nahr, J., Nozari, H., & Aliahmadi, A. (2023). Contract Design for Return Products in a Cooperative Closed-Loop Supply Chain. *Global Business Review*. DOI: 10.1177/09721509221148892

Ghahremani-Nahr, J., Nozari, H., Rahmaty, M., Zeraati Foukolaei, P., & Sherejsharifi, A. (2023). Development of a novel fuzzy hierarchical location-routing optimization model considering reliability. *Logistics (Basel)*, *7*(3), 64. DOI: 10.3390/logistics7030064

Guryanova, L. S., Yatsenko, R., Dubrovina, N. A., & Babenko, V. O. (2020). Machine learning methods and models, predictive analytics and applications. Academic Press.

Herodotou, C., Rienties, B., Boroowa, A., Zdrahal, Z., & Hlosta, M. (2019). A large-scale implementation of predictive learning analytics in higher education: The teachers' role and perspective. *Educational Technology Research and Development*, *67*(5), 1273–1306. DOI: 10.1007/s11423-019-09685-0

Hlosta, M., Herodotou, C., Papathoma, T., Gillespie, A., & Bergamin, P. (2022). Predictive learning analytics in online education: A deeper understanding through explaining algorithmic errors. *Computers and Education: Artificial Intelligence*, *3*, 100108. DOI: 10.1016/j.caeai.2022.100108

Joseph-Richard, P., Uhomoibhi, J., & Jaffrey, A. (2021). Predictive learning analytics and the creation of emotionally adaptive learning environments in higher education institutions: A study of students' affect responses. *The International Journal of Information and Learning Technology*, *38*(2), 243–257. DOI: 10.1108/IJILT-05-2020-0077

Kurilovas, E. (2019). Advanced machine learning approaches to personalise learning: Learning analytics and decision making. *Behaviour & Information Technology*, *38*(4), 410–421. DOI: 10.1080/0144929X.2018.1539517

Lotfi, F. H. Z., Najafi, S. E., & Nozari, H. (Eds.). (2016). *Data envelopment analysis and effective performance assessment*. IGI Global.

Mathrani, A., Susnjak, T., Ramaswami, G., & Barczak, A. (2021). Perspectives on the challenges of generalizability, transparency and ethics in predictive learning analytics. *Computers and Education Open*, *2*, 100060. DOI: 10.1016/j.caeo.2021.100060

Mohammadi, H., Ghazanfari, M., Nozari, H., & Shafiezad, O. (2015). Combining the theory of constraints with system dynamics: A general model (case study of the subsidized milk industry). *International Journal of Management Science and Engineering Management, 10*(2), 102-108.

Movahed, A. B., Aliahmadi, A., Parsanejad, M., & Nozari, H. (2023). A systematic review of collaboration in supply chain 4.0 with meta-synthesis method. *Supply Chain Analytics*, *4*, 100052. DOI: 10.1016/j.sca.2023.100052

Movahed, A. B., Movahed, A. B., & Nozari, H. (2024a). Opportunities and challenges of smart supply chain in Industry 5.0. Information Logistics for Organizational Empowerment and Effective Supply Chain Management, 108-138.

Movahed, A. B., Movahed, A. B., & Nozari, H. (2024b). Marketing 6.0 Conceptualization. In Advanced Businesses in Industry 6.0 (pp. 15-31). IGI Global Scientific Publishing.

Mubarak, A. A., Cao, H., & Ahmed, S. A. (2021). Predictive learning analytics using deep learning model in MOOCs' courses videos. *Education and Information Technologies*, *26*(1), 371–392. DOI: 10.1007/s10639-020-10273-6

Najafi, S. E., Nozari, H., & Edalatpanah, S. A. (2022). Investigating the key parameters affecting sustainable IoT-based marketing. In *Computational Intelligence Methodologies Applied to Sustainable Development Goals* (pp. 51–61). Springer International Publishing. DOI: 10.1007/978-3-030-97344-5_4

Nithya, B., & Ilango, V. (2017, June). Predictive analytics in health care using machine learning tools and techniques. In *2017 International Conference on Intelligent Computing and Control Systems (ICICCS)* (pp. 492-499). IEEE. DOI: 10.1109/ICCONS.2017.8250771

Nozari, H. (Ed.). (2023). *Building Smart and Sustainable Businesses with Transformative Technologies*. IGI Global. DOI: 10.4018/979-8-3693-0210-1

Nozari, H. (2024a). Green supply chain management based on artificial intelligence of everything. *Journal of Economics and Management*, *46*, 171–188. DOI: 10.22367/jem.2024.46.07

Nozari, H. (2024b). Supply chain 6.0 and moving towards hyper-intelligent processes. In *Information logistics for organizational empowerment and effective supply chain management* (pp. 1–13). IGI Global Scientific Publishing.

Nozari, H. (2025a). NeuroTwinceutics™ as a Neuromorphic Digital Twin Model for Predictive and Personalized Pharmacotherapy. *Transformative Science*, *1*(1), 1–8.

Nozari, H. (2025b). Cognitive Targeting and Neuromarketing Applications in AI-Driven Digital Advertising. *Applied Innovations in Industrial Management*, *5*(2), 52–58. DOI: 10.63630/aiim.52.52

Nozari, H., Abdi, H., Szmelter-Jarosz, A., & Motevalli, S. H. (2024). Design of dual-channel supply chain network based on the internet of things under uncertainty. *Mathematical & Computational Applications*, *29*(6), 118. DOI: 10.3390/mca29060118

Nozari, H., & Chobar, A. P. (2024). The Dimensions and Components of Marketing 5.0: Introduction to Marketing 6.0. In Advanced Businesses in Industry 6.0 (pp. 75-86). IGI Global Scientific Publishing.

Nozari, H., & Edalatpanah, S. A. (2023). Smart systems risk management in IoT-based supply chain. In *Advances in reliability, failure and risk analysis* (pp. 251–268). Springer Nature Singapore. DOI: 10.1007/978-981-19-9909-3_11

Nozari, H., Fallah, M., Szmelter-Jarosz, A., & Krzemiński, M. (2021). Analysis of security criteria for IoT-based supply chain: a case study of FMCG industries. Central European Management Journal, 29(4).

Nozari, H., Ghahremani-Nahr, J., & Najafi, E. (2023). The role of Internet of things and Blockchain in the development of agile and sustainable supply chains. In Digital Supply Chain, Disruptive Environments, and the Impact on Retailers (pp. 271-282). IGI Global. DOI: 10.4018/978-1-6684-7298-9.ch015

Nozari, H., Ghahremani-Nahr, J., & Szmelter-Jarosz, A. (2023). A multi-stage stochastic inventory management model for transport companies including several different transport modes. *International Journal of Management Science and Engineering Management*, *18*(2), 134–144. DOI: 10.1080/17509653.2022.2042747

Nozari, H., Ghahremani-Nahr, J., & Szmelter-Jarosz, A. (2024). AI and machine learning for real-world problems. [). Elsevier.]. *Advances in Computers*, *134*, 1–12. DOI: 10.1016/bs.adcom.2023.02.001

Nozari, H., Irani, H. R., & Rahmaty, M. (2023, November). Investigating Critical Success Factors in IoT-Based Marketing Systems. In International Conference on Optimization and Data Science in Industrial Engineering (pp. 259-271). Cham: Springer Nature Switzerland.

Nozari, H., Najafi, S. E., Jafari-Eskandari, M., & Aliahmadi, A. (2016). Providing a model for virtual project management with an emphasis on IT projects. In *Strategic Management and Leadership for Systems Development in Virtual Spaces* (pp. 43–63). IGI Global Scientific Publishing. DOI: 10.4018/978-1-4666-9688-4.ch003

Nozari, H., & Rahmaty, M. (2023). Modeling the make-to-order problem considering the order queuing system under uncertainty. *International Journal of Industrial Engineering*, *34*(4), 1–20.

Nozari, H., Rahmaty, M., Foukolaei, P. Z., Movahed, H., & Bayanati, M. (2025). Optimizing Cold Chain Logistics with Artificial Intelligence of Things (AIoT): A Model for Reducing Operational and Transportation Costs. *Future Transportation*, *5*(1), 1. DOI: 10.3390/futuretransp5010001

Nozari, H., Rahmaty, M., & Szmelter-Jarosz, A. (2024). A framework for AIoT-based smart sustainable marketing system. In *Artificial Intelligence of Things for Achieving Sustainable Development Goals* (pp. 255–271). Springer Nature Switzerland. DOI: 10.1007/978-3-031-53433-1_13

Nozari, H., Szmelter-Jarosz, A., & Ghahremani-Nahr, J. (2022). Analysis of the challenges of artificial intelligence of things (AIoT) for the smart supply chain (case study: FMCG industries). *Sensors (Basel)*, *22*(8), 2931. DOI: 10.3390/s22082931 PMID: 35458916

Nozari, H., Tavakkoli-Moghaddam, R., & Dolgui, A. (2024, September). Analysis of Critical Success Factors of Sustainable and Resilient Aioe-based Supply Chain in Industry 5.0. In IFIP International Conference on Advances in Production Management Systems (pp. 76-90). Cham: Springer Nature Switzerland. DOI: 10.1007/978-3-031-65894-5_6

Nozari, H., Tavakkoli-Moghaddam, R., Ghahremani-Nahr, J., & Najafi, E. (2023). A conceptual framework for Artificial Intelligence of Medical Things (AIoMT). In Computational Intelligence for Medical Internet of Things (MIoT) Applications (pp. 175-189). Academic Press.

Nozari, H., Tavakkoli-Moghaddam, R., Rohaninejad, M., & Hanzalek, Z. (2023, September). Artificial intelligence of things (AIoT) strategies for a smart sustainable-resilient supply chain. In IFIP International Conference on Advances in Production Management Systems (pp. 805-816). Cham: Springer Nature Switzerland. DOI: 10.1007/978-3-031-43670-3_56

Poh, Z. X., & Khor, E. T. (2024). Predictive Analytics for Student Online Learning Performance Using Machine Learning and Data Mining Techniques. In International Journal on E-Learning (pp. 269-283). Association for the Advancement of Computing in Education (AACE). DOI: 10.70725/686437bpltsf

Rahmaty, M., & Nozari, H. (2023). Optimization of the hierarchical supply chain in the pharmaceutical industry. *Edelweiss Applied Science and Technology*, *7*(2), 104–123. DOI: 10.55214/25768484.v7i2.376

Razali, M. N., Zakariah, H., Hanapi, R., & Rahim, E. A. (2022, May). Predictive model of undergraduate student grading using machine learning for learning analytics. In 2022 4th International Conference on Computer Science and Technologies in Education (CSTE) (pp. 260-264). IEEE. DOI: 10.1109/CSTE55932.2022.00055

Samanpour, A. R., Ruegenberg, A., & Ahlers, R. (2017). The future of machine learning and predictive analytics. In *Digital marketplaces unleashed* (pp. 297–309). Springer Berlin Heidelberg.

Sciarrone, F. (2018, April). Machine learning and learning analytics: Integrating data with learning. In 2018 17th International conference on information technology based higher education and training (ITHET) (pp. 1-5). IEEE.

Seyedtabib, M., Najafi-Vosough, R., & Kamyari, N. (2024). The predictive power of data: Machine learning analysis for Covid-19 mortality based on personal, clinical, preclinical, and laboratory variables in a case–control study. *BMC Infectious Diseases*, *24*(1), 411. DOI: 10.1186/s12879-024-09298-w PMID: 38637727

Sghir, N., Adadi, A., & Lahmer, M. (2023). Recent advances in Predictive Learning Analytics: A decade systematic review (2012–2022). *Education and Information Technologies*, *28*(7), 8299–8333. DOI: 10.1007/s10639-022-11536-0 PMID: 36571084

Shridharan, M., Willingham, A., Spencer, J., Yang, T. Y., & Brinton, C. (2018, March). Predictive learning analytics for video-watching behavior in MOOCs. In 2018 52nd Annual Conference on Information Sciences and Systems (CISS) (pp. 1-6). IEEE. DOI: 10.1109/CISS.2018.8362323

Szmelter-Jarosz, A., & Nozari, H. (2025). AI-Driven Decision Intelligence and Human-AI Collaboration in Economic Systems. In Dynamic and Safe Economy in the Age of Smart Technologies (pp. 171-190). IGI Global Scientific Publishing.

Theng, D., & Theng, M. (2020, July). Machine learning algorithms for predictive analytics: A review and new perspectives. In Conf. High Technol. Lett (Vol. 26, No. 6, pp. 536-545).

Uskov, V. L., Bakken, J. P., Putta, P., Krishnakumar, D., & Ganapathi, K. S. (2021, June). Smart education: predictive analytics of student academic performance using machine learning models in Weka and Dataiku systems. In International KES Conference on Smart Education and Smart E-Learning (pp. 3-17). Singapore: Springer Singapore. DOI: 10.1007/978-981-16-2834-4_1

Weng, W. H. (2020). Machine learning for clinical predictive analytics. In *Leveraging data science for global health* (pp. 199–217). Springer International Publishing. DOI: 10.1007/978-3-030-47994-7_12

Yordanova, Z., & Nozari, H. (2025). Harnessing Cyber-Physical Systems and Digital Twins for Industrial Innovation and Economic Resilience. In Dynamic and Safe Economy in the Age of Smart Technologies (pp. 33-48). IGI Global Scientific Publishing. DOI: 10.4018/979-8-3693-4369-2.ch003

# Chapter 2
# AI-Augmented Creative Assessment:
## From Static Tests to Dynamic Insight Generation

**Hamed Nozari**
http://orcid.org/0000-0002-6500-6708
*Azad University UAE, Dubai, UAE*

## ABSTRACT

*This research examines the conceptual and technological evolution of creativity assessment in educational contexts using artificial intelligence. Emphasizing the transition from static tests to the generation of dynamic insights, the role of AI in analyzing cognitive processes, providing adaptive feedback, and personalizing assessments is explained. Ethical challenges, algorithmic transparency, and the risk of reducing creativity to quantitative values are also analyzed. The research shows that artificial intelligence can transform assessment from a purely measurement tool to a factor for fostering creativity and learner self-regulation.*

## 1. INTRODUCTION

In recent decades, the concept of assessment in education has faced fundamental challenges, the most important of which is the inability of traditional tests to measure complex and high-level cognitive skills such as creativity. Although standardized assessments have been widely used to measure rote knowledge and analytical skills, such assessments are largely limited to predetermined responses and cannot accurately reveal the creative capacities of learners. In a world that is rapidly moving towards a knowledge-based economy and an innovative society,

DOI: 10.4018/979-8-3373-5117-9.ch002

ght © 2026, IGI Global Scientific Publishing. Copying or distributing in print or electronic forms without written permission of IGI Global Scientific Publishing is prohibited. Use of this chapter to generative artificial intelligence (AI) technologies is expressly prohibited. The publisher reserves all rights to license its use for generative AI training and machine learning model development.

ignoring the element of creativity in educational assessment systems is tantamount to ignoring one of the most important indicators of individual and social success (Chen, Brandimarte, & Susarla, 2024).

Contrary to popular belief, creativity is not an innate and mysterious phenomenon that occurs only in certain minds, but rather a cognitive and nurtured process that finds meaning in interaction with the environment, experience, and feedback. However, assessing this process requires tools that go beyond linear questions and answers. This is where AI, as a transformative technology, can provide new opportunities to rethink assessment systems (Eager & Brunton, 2023).

AI in education has not only been used to personalize content or analyze performance, but has also gradually become an important tool in creating more dynamic, interactive, and intelligent assessments. The use of natural language processing algorithms to analyze written responses, deep learning models to recognize creative patterns in artwork, and adaptive systems to suggest creative activities based on the cognitive style of the learner are just some of the capabilities of AI in this area (Nozari, Tavakkoli-Moghaddam, Rohaninejad, & Hanzalek, 2023). What distinguishes these applications from traditional assessment is not only their high processing power, but also the ability to generate deep insights into the learning process, not just its output.

Artificial intelligence-enhanced creative assessment is an answer to the fundamental question of how to measure creativity in educational settings in a way that motivates further learning and new discoveries. Unlike traditional tests that are limited to final results and correct answers, dynamic creativity assessment using AI focuses on the process of idea generation, problem-solving paths, and divergent thinking patterns (Ou, Thajchayapong, & Joyner, 2024). By engaging learners in open-ended and multifaceted activities, this approach not only provides a better understanding of their mental capacities, but can also serve as a tool for developing creativity.

Also, the shift from static assessment to dynamic analysis provides opportunities for creating meaningful learning environments. When AI can analyze learner interactions in real time and provide intelligent and personalized feedback, assessment becomes a tool for empowerment rather than just measurement (Nozari, Szmelter-Jarosz, & Ghahremani-Nahr, 2021). This transformation is moving the education system from a surveillance space to a creative, self-regulating learning environment, where learners gain a better understanding of their own development by analyzing their own data.

However, this approach also comes with challenges. These include concerns about the transparency of algorithms, data-driven biases, misinterpretations of creativity in different cultural contexts, and the risk of turning creativity into a quantitative, scoreable category without regard to its depth and context (Koon, 2025). Therefore, designing AI-assisted creative assessment systems requires an interdisciplinary, context-sensitive, and ethically-driven approach.

The aim of this chapter is to explore the role of AI in the evolution of creative assessment in educational settings, focusing on the transition from static tests to dynamic insights.

## 2. THEORETICAL FOUNDATIONS OF CREATIVE ASSESSMENT

A proper understanding of the theoretical foundations of creativity assessment requires an exploration of the concept of creativity in the context of education, an understanding of its cognitive and psychological dimensions, and a distinction between different types of creative assessment. Creativity is defined as a multidimensional process, encompassing the ability to generate new, diverse, and meaningful ideas in the face of educational problems or stimuli. Unlike rote learning or the reproduction of knowledge, creativity is a generative, nonlinear, and context-dependent process in which the learner makes new connections between existing information. This multifaceted and open-ended nature creates fundamental challenges for its measurement, as it cannot be properly assessed with the quantitative and standardized measures used for established knowledge (Najafi, Nozari, & Edalatpanah, 2022a).

In cognitive models, creativity is often divided into two main components: divergent and convergent thinking. Divergent thinking refers to the generation of diverse, original, and flexible ideas, while convergent thinking is concerned with selecting the appropriate solution from among available options. In education, divergent thinking is most closely associated with creative activities. Assessing this dimension of creativity requires tools that pay attention not only to the number of responses but also to their quality and variety. For example, seemingly unusual but meaningful responses can be an indicator of originality, while varied but superficial responses are not necessarily considered creative (Zhou et al., 2024).

Various approaches to measuring creativity in education have been proposed, ranging from structured tests to qualitative and open-ended assessments. Structured tests typically involve short tasks with specific stimuli and limited time, and attempt to quantify creativity using standardized measures. Although these tests are applicable in large-scale environments, they often fail to detect the depth of creativity and are prone to cultural and linguistic biases. In contrast, open-ended assessments such as art analysis, creative writing, or design projects allow for observation of the creative process and active participation of the learner. However, these approaches suffer from challenges in reliability and scalability due to their heavy reliance on human judgment (Aliahmadi & Nozari, 2023).

In recent years, some hybrid frameworks have attempted to strike a balance between quantitative and qualitative assessment. These frameworks attempt to assess different dimensions of creativity simultaneously by defining indicators such as fluency, flexibility, originality, and elaboration. Each of these components also has characteristics that can be modeled and analyzed by intelligent systems. For example, fluency refers to the number of responses in a given time and can be easily measured, while originality requires comparing the response to a database of common and rare examples. These features have paved the way for the introduction of artificial intelligence algorithms in assessment (Ghorbani et al., 2025).

Meanwhile, the structure of creative assessment is highly dependent on the cultural and educational context. What is considered creative in one culture may be considered unfamiliar or even inappropriate in another. Also, learning styles and creative expression differ among age, gender, and language groups. This makes the design of a creative assessment system require cultural sensitivity, adaptability, and high flexibility. Therefore, many experts emphasize that creative assessment should focus on the process of idea generation and analyze the learner's interaction with the problem, rather than focusing solely on the output (Bathaee, Nozari, & Szmelter-Jarosz, 2023).

With the growth of digital tools, it has become possible to analyze the learning process and creative production in real time. This development has paved the way for a new approach to assessment called "dynamic assessment," in which intelligent systems analyze the learner's problem-solving paths, choices, mistakes, and corrections rather than focusing on the final product. In such an approach, the learner becomes part of the process of measuring and recreating knowledge rather than being merely assessed (Singh, Kaunert, Lal, & Arora, 2025). This type of assessment is particularly useful in areas such as creative writing, engineering design, and visual arts, and can pave the way for a constructive integration of artificial intelligence with creativity assessment.

At the end of this section, the conceptual structure of creativity assessment can be outlined in a framework that combines cognitive components, measurement dimensions, and technological capabilities. Figure 1 shows this framework, which depicts the interaction between creativity components, types of assessment methods, and AI-based analytical tools.

*Figure 1. Conceptual framework for assessing creativity in smart learning platforms*

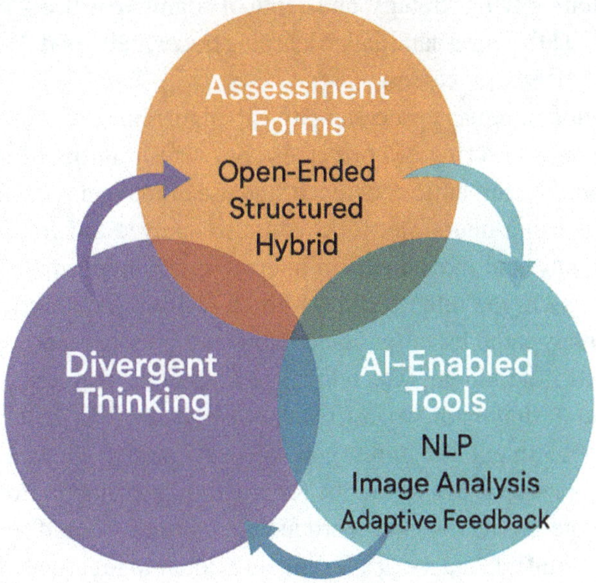


As seen in Figure 1, creativity assessment in smart learning platforms is the result of the interaction of three key components that must be designed and analyzed in an integrated manner.

## 3. THE ROLE OF AI IN REIMAGINING ASSESSMENT PARADIGMS

The evolution of educational assessment systems in the digital age cannot be achieved without considering the increasing role of artificial intelligence. By entering traditional assessment structures, AI has enabled assessments to be not only more accurate and faster, but also to reflect the nature of the learning process, individual cognitive styles, and creative capacities. In this direction, reinventing assessment models means moving from static, standardized, and score-based tests to dynamic systems in which learner data is continuously and intelligently analyzed and deeper insights into educational performance are generated (Najafi, Nozari, & Edalatpanah, 2022b).

The first step in rethinking assessment models is to recognize the ability of AI to analyze complex, multi-layered data from the learning process. Unlike traditional assessments that focus only on the final answer, AI technologies can analyze data such as mouse movement, time spent on each question, order of clicks, text editing, or multimedia interaction style and extract patterns that reflect the learner's creative thinking, problem-solving strategy, and depth of cognitive processing (Vadisetty & Polamarasetti, 2024). These data, called learning traces, help model learner behavior and understand mental processes.

Through natural language processing (NLP) algorithms, AI can analyze written responses, not only in terms of correctness but also in terms of aspects such as structural innovation, semantic coherence, and use of metaphorical language. Deep learning models using neural networks can also analyze images designed by the learner or even physical movements in interactive activities and identify signs of creative thinking. On the other hand, AI-based recommender systems can design suggested learning paths based on the cognitive, emotional, and behavioral characteristics of each individual, which enables adaptive assessment of creativity in dynamic contexts (Aliahmadi, Nozari, Ghahremani-Nahr, & Szmelter-Jarosz, 2022).

In modern assessment structures, generative AI models play an important role in the creation of content and scenarios for creative assessment. For example, systems that generate innovative and reproducible questions based on initial student input, or provide unfinished stories for the individual to creatively complete. This type of interaction activates higher cognitive levels and provides conditions in which creativity can manifest itself in a more organic and personalized way (Gupta, Epiphaniou, & Maple, 2023).

The integration of AI with creative assessment is not limited to data analysis alone, but also includes the generation of interactive feedback. Systems have been designed to provide adaptive, descriptive, and motivational feedback in real time. For example, if a learner wrote a response that was strong in terms of language but weak in terms of originality, the system could provide suggestions for increasing creativity, or display more creative examples from the same domain. This feedback, which is formed within the framework of assessment-learning, not only measures performance, but also becomes a factor in cognitive growth (Fallah & Nozari, 2021).

From the perspective of educational systems architecture, the introduction of AI requires the design of platforms that can analyze data in real time, machine learn from previous behaviors, and provide personalized feedback. This requires infrastructures such as educational data mining, dynamic learning models, and explainable algorithms. Especially in the field of creativity education, the use of AI should be accompanied by mechanisms that take into account cultural, linguistic, and cognitive style diversity in the analysis to prevent creativity from becoming stereotyped patterns (Grabill et al., 2024).

In designing future assessment systems, the interaction between teacher, learner, and intelligent systems will take the form of a dynamic triangle. The teacher's role will no longer be that of a mere evaluator or observer, but rather a facilitator of the interpretation of learning data. The learner will not be merely a test taker, but an active actor in the learning and assessment process. AI, meanwhile, as a mediator and analyst, will transform data into meaningful insights that can be effective in educational decision-making (Nozari, Fallah, Szmelter-Jarosz, & Krzemiński, 2021).

To better understand this new structure, Figure 2 depicts the conceptual architecture of AI-based creative assessment. In this model, multifaceted data from learner activities enters the system, is processed by different AI layers, and leads to dynamic feedback, creativity analysis, and learning path improvement.

*Figure 2. Architecture of AI-based creativity assessment*

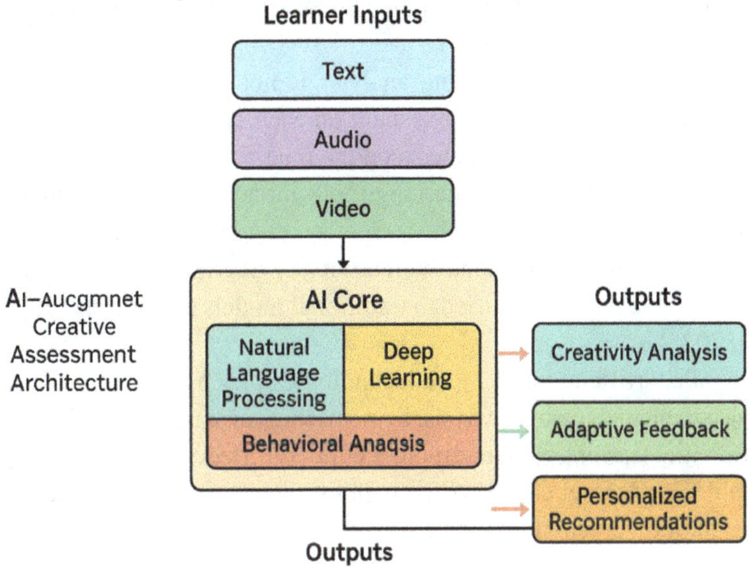


This architecture outlines a new paradigm of assessment in which artificial intelligence plays a role not as a substitute for the teacher, but as a complement to improve the quality and depth of creativity assessment.

## 4. FROM STATIC TESTS TO DYNAMIC INSIGHT GENERATION

The shift from static tests to dynamic insights in educational assessment is one of the most profound developments in the philosophy and technology of education. Traditional tests, based on static assessments, usually focus on final answers and often aim to determine the extent to which a particular content has been learned at a given point in time. These tests not only ignore the learner's creativity and thought process, but also provide a limited and reduced picture of the individual's true capabilities. On the other hand, the new approach of "dynamic insights" focuses on analyzing the learning process, continuous interactions, and deeper understanding of intellectual and creative mechanisms (Klein et al., 2020).

In the traditional model, learner success is defined by a numerical score based on correct or incorrect answers to a few questions. This approach lacks sensitivity to cognitive diversity, problem-solving styles, and the degree of creativity in responding. Also, static tests are very ineffective in the face of the complexity of modern learning environments that include multimedia content, high interactivity, and continuous data flow. As a result, there is a need for a system that can monitor, analyze, and interpret the entire learning path instead of judging based on the result (Lotfi, Najafi, & Nozari, 2016).

In the insight-based model, data analysis is not limited to the final answer, but also includes examining the time spent on each question, response variations, movement sequences, marginal notes, and the type of interaction with the content. This approach, often known as "learning footprint analysis" or learning analytics, provides a platform for extracting the learner's mental patterns. Through these patterns, it is possible to achieve signs of creativity, cognitive flexibility, and cognitive stability that could not be identified in traditional models (Sahibzada, Malik, Nasir, & Lodhi, 2025).

Meanwhile, artificial intelligence technologies play a key role in moving from static assessment to dynamic analysis. Systems that can analyze learning data in real time can identify learning paths and more accurately reflect strengths and weaknesses. For example, if a learner changes their path to solve a math problem several times, this is a sign of divergent thinking and an attempt to find creative solutions. AI can process such data through time series algorithms, behavioral analysis, and deep learning, and provide interpretable insights to the teacher or the learner (Movahed, Aliahmadi, Parsanejad, & Nozari, 2023).

Adaptive assessment models designed based on AI use information obtained from learner interactions to adjust subsequent content. This means that assessment is not a discrete event, but part of the learning and cognitive improvement process in the moment. In this case, feedback is personalized and accurate, and tailored to the cognitive style and real needs of the individual. These types of systems are able to establish connections between learner interactions, types of errors, and mental strategies and draw a unique pattern of learning (Lekan & Pardos, 2025).

In order to implement dynamic creative assessments, one of the important innovations is the design of open-ended and multi-path tasks. Unlike multiple-choice questions that have only one correct answer, open-ended tasks allow for multiple paths to be taken, generating diverse responses, and presenting individual perspectives. These types of tasks become more valuable when AI systems can dynamically analyze the response generation process and evaluate its quality in terms of creativity, depth of analysis, and structural logic. In fact, the goal is to produce "learning insights" rather than "raw scores" (Movahed, Movahed, & Nozari, 2024a).

In modern models, dashboards are designed for teachers, instructors, or even learners themselves, where not only scores are visible, but also indicators such as the variety of solutions, the level of linguistic creativity, the structural complexity of the answers, and the development of problem-solving strategies. These dashboards are decision-making tools for improving learning, not just assessment tools. In addition, they can provide alerts for intelligent educational interventions; for example, identifying a gradual decline in analytical thinking or a decrease in the variety of answers as a sign of cognitive fatigue or reduced motivation (Inaganti, Ravichandran, Nersu, & Muppalaneni, 2021).

To make this development clearer, Figure 3 shows an example of the fundamental difference between static and insight-based assessment. On the left, we see the traditional test structure, which consists of questions and answers, and the output is a final score. On the right, the insight-driven structure is shown, which includes multi-stage interactions, process analysis, real-time feedback, and analytical report generation of the learning pattern. At the center, AI technology acts as the processing engine of this transformation.

*Figure 3. The transition from static assessment to dynamic insights in AI-based learning environments*

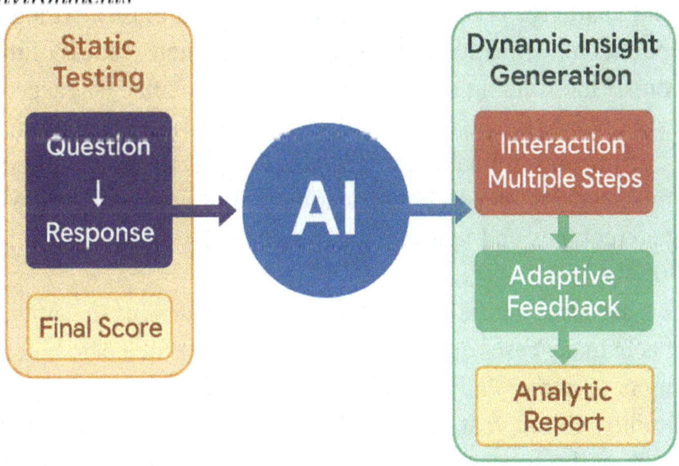


This transformation is not simply a technological change, but rather a reflection of a rethinking of the philosophy of learning. In this approach, assessment, rather than being a judgment on the learner, will be an opportunity to understand him/her more deeply and develop his/her hidden potential.

## 5. CHALLENGES AND ETHICAL CONSIDERATIONS

The use of AI in assessing creativity not only promises to revolutionize traditional methods of assessment, but also raises profound theoretical, technical, and ethical challenges that, if ignored, could reduce not only the effectiveness of assessment systems but also the legitimacy of the entire process. The complexity of the issue lies in the fact that creativity assessment is inherently associated with uncertainty, cultural diversity, and individual characteristics, and its combination with intelligent systems that operate on data and mathematical models can create a tension between technical accuracy and the human depth of the assessment process (Nozari & Edalatpanah, 2023).

One of the most important challenges in this area is the issue of the interpretability of algorithms. In many machine learning systems, especially deep models, the decision-making process is carried out in hidden layers, and the final output is presented to human users without a clear explanation. In a field such as creativity assessment, where the results can have a direct impact on the learner's self-concept, motivation, and educational trajectory, the lack of transparency of decisions can lead to distrust, confusion, or even psychological harm (Rahmaty & Nozari, 2023). Therefore, the development of explainable AI algorithms and the design of interfaces that interpret the model's output in a language that is understandable to the teacher and the student are inevitable.

The second challenge is related to the issue of data biases. AI algorithms are highly dependent on the quality, diversity, and comprehensiveness of the data they are trained on. If the training data is limited to a particular language, culture, or style of creative thinking, learning models will inadvertently ignore alternative perspectives or unconventional creative styles or treat them as outliers. This, especially in multicultural and global educational environments, carries the risk of reproducing stereotypes and ignoring indigenous creativity (Movahed, Movahed, & Nozari, 2024b).

A further issue concerns the transformation of creativity into quantity. The nature of creativity is in many cases qualitative, contextual and subject to human interpretation. Attempts to numerically score creativity using criteria such as originality, variety or fluidity, although at first glance seem scientific and standard, may lead to the reduction of the concept of creativity to a fixed formula. There is a risk that teachers, learners and educational policy makers will be influenced by smart scores and see creativity not as a complex process but as a gradeable outcome (Nozari, 2023).

Another important issue is data privacy and security. In AI-based assessments, especially those involving audio, image or video analysis, a large amount of personal data of learners is recorded and stored. Managing this data without security, encryption, and clear privacy policies can lead to abuse, data leakage, or even discrimination at later levels of education or employment. This challenge is exacerbated when assessment systems are implemented online and in the cloud, and data is stored in cross-border infrastructures (Nozari, Ghahremani-Nahr, & Najafi, 2023).

Alongside these technical issues, a philosophical challenge also arises: the extent to which AI should interfere with human creativity. Should AI only play the role of observer and analyst, or can it also intervene in the creative production process? The line between facilitating creativity and over-directing it is very thin. If AI systems take control of the creative process by constantly suggesting, structuring responses, or providing overly precise feedback, there is a risk that the learner will start producing responses that conform to algorithmic preferences rather than nurturing personal creativity (Movahed, Movahed, & Nozari, 2024c).

Finally, the issue of educational equity in AI contexts also needs to be carefully examined. Unequal access to technology, differences in infrastructure, internet connectivity quality, and familiarity with digital tools can create new gaps in assessment and learning. If a student in a disadvantaged area has access to a low-quality or unsupported AI system, their creative performance is likely not to be properly recorded or analyzed, and they may receive unfair grades or feedback. This not only reduces educational opportunities, but also turns assessment systems into tools for reproducing inequality (Movahed, Movahed, & Nozari, 2024c).

To conclude this section, Figure 4 depicts a conceptual map of the challenges and ethical considerations in assessing AI-based creativity. The map shows the connections between technical, psychological, and social challenges in color to provide a comprehensive and systematic view of the risks and possible solutions.

*Figure 4. Concept map of ethical challenges and considerations in AI-based creative evaluation*

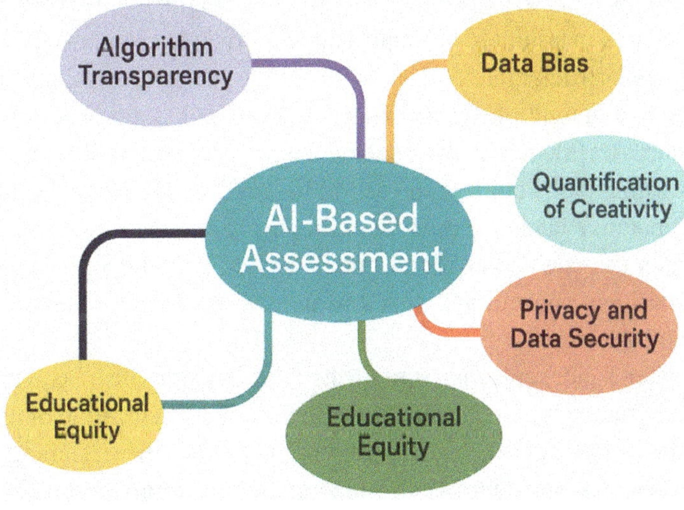

As seen in Figure 4, the technical and ethical challenges of AI-based assessment operate in an intertwined manner and require an integrated and context-sensitive approach.

## 6. CONCLUSION

In the last decade, education and assessment have undergone an unprecedented transformation; a transformation that has been manifested not only in tools but also in conceptual foundations and assessment philosophies with the introduction of artificial intelligence. Among them, creativity assessment, as one of the most challenging areas, is of particular importance because it is not only related to the complex mental and cognitive dimensions of humans, but also directly affects the motivational, personality development, and creative path of the learner. Therefore, using artificial intelligence to analyze and enhance this aspect is considered a unique opportunity to recreate the concept of assessment in contemporary education.

Traditional assessment has in most cases sought to measure established knowledge, recall concepts, or select the correct answer; while creativity, unlike these models, is formed in an uncertain, context-dependent, and multi-path space. Accordingly, attempts to measure creativity with static methods have always faced profound conceptual and technical limitations. The AI-Augmented Assessment approach, relying on the power of data analysis, machine learning, and real-time processing, has made it possible to not only see, but also recognize, interpret, and nurture the creative process in learning. This perspective is a starting point for changing the dominant paradigm from "assessing the final product" to "recognizing learning processes."

A review of the theoretical dimensions of creativity assessment showed that this field relies on concepts such as divergent thinking, originality, fluidity, and extension that were less measurable in traditional contexts. However, using educational data mining and artificial intelligence technologies, these dimensions can now be analyzed live and in multiple layers. This development has not only contributed to more accurate assessment, but also enabled the personalization of feedback and the design of learning paths tailored to each individual's cognitive style. In addition, the use of generative language models, neural networks, machine vision, and sentiment analysis has enabled artificial intelligence to gain a deeper understanding of learners' written, spoken, and visual responses; And without being limited to predetermined answers.

On the other hand, replacing static tests with dynamic insights, especially in interactive environments, is a turning point in the conceptualization of assessment. The raw score is no longer the end of the road, but rather the beginning of a cycle of analysis, feedback, self-regulation, and learning correction. In such a model, the teacher finds the role of a guide, the learner becomes responsible for his or her own cognitive path, and the intelligent system, as an analytical mediator, transforms complex information into understandable insights. This redefinition of the assessment function transforms education into an intelligent, creative, and responsive space.

However, the path to establishing this new paradigm is not without challenges. As discussed in the section on ethical considerations, issues such as algorithmic transparency, data bias, the threat of over-quantification of creativity, and privacy concerns are fundamental issues that, in the absence of rigorous theoretical and operational frameworks, can distort the functions of this technology. Especially in the assessment of creativity, which is personal, cultural, and dependent on subtle individual differences, the slightest bias or incorrect analysis can lead to an unfair and frustrating experience for the learner. Therefore, the development of AI systems must be accompanied by the ethical principles of education, educational justice, and respect for cognitive and cultural diversity.

Strategically, the future of creativity assessment relying on AI depends on designing systems that have both high analytical and predictive power, and can interact with humans in a transparent, explainable, and reliable way. These systems must go beyond mere assessment to become tools for inspiration, fostering self-expression, and facilitating creative flows in learning. In other words, AI will act not as an arbiter but as a cognitive assistant. In this direction, the connection between algorithm designers, educational experts, and learners themselves will be crucial so that systems grow and mature not in a technical vacuum, but in the real context of education.

In conclusion, it can be said that the concept of assessment in education no longer means measuring the past, but has become a predictive tool for learner growth. If AI can properly play its role in this change, then the education of the future will not only be more accurate and intelligent, but also more humane, as it recognizes and strengthens hidden capacities, diverse learning styles, and personal paths to creativity. The future of creative assessment is one in which the learner is not a score on a scale, but a dynamic model of their cognitive and creative capabilities.

## REFERENCES


Aliahmadi, A., & Nozari, H. (2023, January). Evaluation of security metrics in AIoT and blockchain-based supply chain by Neutrosophic decision-making method. In Supply chain forum: an international journal (Vol. 24, No. 1, pp. 31-42). Taylor & Francis. DOI: 10.1080/16258312.2022.2101898

Aliahmadi, A., Nozari, H., Ghahremani-Nahr, J., & Szmelter-Jarosz, A. (2022). Evaluation of key impression of resilient supply chain based on artificial intelligence of things (AIoT). arXiv preprint arXiv:2207.13174.

Bathaee, M., Nozari, H., & Szmelter-Jarosz, A. (2023). Designing a new location-allocation and routing model with simultaneous pick-up and delivery in a closed-loop supply chain network under uncertainty. *Logistics (Basel)*, *7*(1), 3. DOI: 10.3390/logistics7010003

Chen, J., Brandimarte, L., & Susarla, A. (2024). Does Increasing Reliance on Artificial Intelligence Boost Creativity? Assessing AI-Augmented Creativity with Large Language Models. Assessing AI-Augmented Creativity with Large Language Models (July 17, 2024).

Eager, B., & Brunton, R. (2023). Prompting higher education towards AI-augmented teaching and learning practice. *Journal of University Teaching & Learning Practice*, *20*(5), 1–19. DOI: 10.53761/1.20.5.02

Fallah, M., & Nozari, H. (2021). Neutrosophic mathematical programming for optimization of multi-objective sustainable biomass supply chain network design. *Computer Modeling in Engineering & Sciences*, *129*(2), 927–951. DOI: 10.32604/cmes.2021.017511

Ghorbani, J., Aghdasi, S., Nazem, M., McCartney, J. S., & Kodikara, J. (2025). Augmented intelligence framework for real-time ground assessment under significant uncertainty. *Engineering with Computers*, 1–22. DOI: 10.1007/s00366-025-02108-0

Grabill, N., Wang, S., Olayinka, H. A., De Alwis, T. P., Khalil, Y. F., & Zou, J. (2024). AI-augmented failure modes, effects, and criticality analysis (AI-FMECA) for industrial applications. *Reliability Engineering & System Safety*, *250*, 110308. DOI: 10.1016/j.ress.2024.110308

Gupta, S., Epiphaniou, G., & Maple, C. (2023). AI-augmented usability evaluation framework for software requirements specification in cyber physical human systems. *Internet of Things : Engineering Cyber Physical Human Systems*, *23*, 100841. DOI: 10.1016/j.iot.2023.100841

Inaganti, A. C., Ravichandran, N., Nersu, S. R. K., & Muppalaneni, R. (2021). AI-Augmented Workforce Planning: Leveraging Predictive Analytics for Talent Acquisition and Retention. *Artificial Intelligence and Machine Learning Review, 2*(1), 10–20.

Klein, M., Carpentier, T., Jeanclaude, E., Kassab, R., Varelas, K., de Bruijn, N., & Aligne, F. (2020, September). AI-augmented multi function radar engineering with digital twin: Towards proactivity. In *2020 IEEE Radar Conference (RadarConf20)* (pp. 1-6). IEEE. DOI: 10.1109/RadarConf2043947.2020.9266455

Koon, S. (2025). A Beautiful Mind: Principles and Strategies for AI-Augmented Human Reasoning. arXiv preprint arXiv:2503.15530.

Lekan, K., & Pardos, Z. A. (2025). AI-Augmented Advising: A Comparative Study of GPT-4 and Advisor-Based Major Recommendations. *Journal of Learning Analytics, 12*(1), 110–128. DOI: 10.18608/jla.2025.8593

Lotfi, F. H. Z., Najafi, S. E., & Nozari, H. (Eds.). (2016). *Data envelopment analysis and effective performance assessment*. IGI Global.

Movahed, A. B., Aliahmadi, A., Parsanejad, M., & Nozari, H. (2023). A systematic review of collaboration in supply chain 4.0 with meta-synthesis method. *Supply Chain Analytics, 4*, 100052. DOI: 10.1016/j.sca.2023.100052

Movahed, A. B., Movahed, A. B., & Nozari, H. (2024). Opportunities and challenges of smart supply chain in Industry 5.0. Information Logistics for Organizational Empowerment and Effective Supply Chain Management, 108-138.

Movahed, A. B., Movahed, A. B., & Nozari, H. (2024). Marketing 6.0 Conceptualization. In Advanced Businesses in Industry 6.0 (pp. 15-31). IGI Global.

Najafi, S. E., Nozari, H., & Edalatpanah, S. A. (2022a). Investigating the key parameters affecting sustainable IoT-based marketing. In *Computational Intelligence Methodologies Applied to Sustainable Development Goals* (pp. 51–61). Springer International Publishing. DOI: 10.1007/978-3-030-97344-5_4

Najafi, S. E., Nozari, H., & Edalatpanah, S. A. (2022b). Artificial Intelligence of Things (AIoT) and Industry 4.0–Based Supply Chain (FMCG Industry). A roadmap for enabling industry 4.0 by artificial intelligence, 31-41.

Nozari, H. (Ed.). (2023). *Building Smart and Sustainable Businesses with Transformative Technologies*. IGI Global. DOI: 10.4018/979-8-3693-0210-1

Nozari, H., & Edalatpanah, S. A. (2023). Smart systems risk management in IoT-based supply chain. In *Advances in reliability, failure and risk analysis* (pp. 251–268). Springer Nature Singapore. DOI: 10.1007/978-981-19-9909-3_11

Nozari, H., Fallah, M., Szmelter-Jarosz, A., & Krzemiński, M. (2021). Analysis of security criteria for IoT-based supply chain: a case study of FMCG industries. Central European Management Journal, 29(4).

Nozari, H., Ghahremani-Nahr, J., & Najafi, E. (2023). The role of Internet of things and Blockchain in the development of agile and sustainable supply chains. In Digital Supply Chain, Disruptive Environments, and the Impact on Retailers (pp. 271-282). IGI Global. DOI: 10.4018/978-1-6684-7298-9.ch015

Nozari, H., Szmelter-Jarosz, A., & Ghahremani-Nahr, J. (2021). The ideas of sustainable and green marketing based on the internet of everything—The case of the dairy industry. *Future Internet*, *13*(10), 266. DOI: 10.3390/fi13100266

Nozari, H., Tavakkoli-Moghaddam, R., Rohaninejad, M., & Hanzalek, Z. (2023, September). Artificial intelligence of things (AIoT) strategies for a smart sustainable-resilient supply chain. In IFIP International Conference on Advances in Production Management Systems (pp. 805-816). Cham: Springer Nature Switzerland. DOI: 10.1007/978-3-031-43670-3_56

Ou, C., Thajchayapong, P., & Joyner, D. (2024, July). Open, collaborative, and AI-augmented peer assessment: Student participation, performance, and perceptions. In Proceedings of the Eleventh ACM Conference on Learning@ Scale (pp. 496-500).

Rahmaty, M., & Nozari, H. (2023). Optimization of the hierarchical supply chain in the pharmaceutical industry. *Edelweiss Applied Science and Technology*, *7*(2), 104–123. DOI: 10.55214/25768484.v7i2.376

Sahibzada, S., Malik, F. S., Nasir, S., & Lodhi, S. K. (2025). AI-Augmented Turbulence and Aerodynamic Modelling: Accelerating High-Fidelity CFD Simulations with Physics-informed Neural Networks. *International Journal of Innovative Research in Computer Science and Technology*, *13*(1), 91–97. DOI: 10.55524/ijircst.2025.13.1.14

Singh, B., Kaunert, C., Lal, S., & Arora, M. K. (2025). Enhancing AI-Augmented Classrooms: Teacher-Centric Integration of Intelligent Tutoring Systems and Adaptive Learning Environments. In Fostering Inclusive Education With AI and Emerging Technologies (pp. 99-130). IGI Global.

Vadisetty, R., & Polamarasetti, A. (2024, December). AI-Augmented Skill Development Roadmaps: Tailoring 12-Month Learning Paths for Future-Ready Careers in Education 4.0 and Industry 4.0. In 2024 13th International Conference on System Modeling & Advancement in Research Trends (SMART) (pp. 655-661). IEEE.

Zhou, C., Liu, X., Yu, C., Tao, Y., & Shao, Y. (2024). Trust in AI-augmented design: Applying structural equation modeling to AI-augmented design acceptance. *Heliyon*, *10*(1), e23305. DOI: 10.1016/j.heliyon.2023.e23305 PMID: 38192792

Chapter 3
# Design of Emotionally-Aware Digital Twin Models for Socio-Affective Learning Analysis

**Hossein Abdi**
*Islamic Azad University, UAE*

## ABSTRACT

*This research designs an emotion-based digital twin model for analyzing social-emotional learning in the context of smart education. The proposed model, using multimodal data including facial expressions, voice, physiological signals, and behavioral interactions, identifies the emotional and social state of the learner in real time and provides adaptive educational interventions based on that. The three-layer structure of the system architecture includes data collection, social-emotional analysis, and real-time decision-making. The results show that this model can help improve the learning experience, increase participation, and maintain the psychological well-being of learners.*

## 1- INTRODUCTION

In recent decades, technological advances in education have fundamentally transformed the traditional structure of learning. The development of smart learning environments, along with the rapid growth of artificial intelligence, the Internet of Things, and educational data mining, has provided a new platform for personaliza-

DOI: 10.4018/979-8-3373-5117-9.ch003

ght © 2026, IGI Global Scientific Publishing. Copying or distributing in print or electronic forms without written permission of IGI Global Scientific Publishing is prohibited. Use of this chapter to generative artificial intelligence (AI) technologies is expressly prohibited. The publisher reserves all rights to license its use for generative AI training and machine learning model development.

tion, adaptability, and interactivity; but at the heart of these advances, one of the fundamental and sometimes overlooked components, namely the emotional and social dimension of the learner, still requires deep and systematic attention. Understanding emotions, motivations, and social relationships in the learning process not only plays a supporting role, but also affects the depth of understanding, the persistence of information, and the active participation of the learner (Longhi & Behar, 2024).

In such a context, the concept of the digital twin has entered the field of education as one of the newest technological approaches. Essentially a real-time digital representation of a physical entity, the digital twin has grown significantly in industry and engineering and is now entering more human-oriented fields such as health and education (Nozari, Abdi, & Jahangard, 2025). In the context of education, this concept means creating a dynamic model of the cognitive, behavioral, and emotional state of a learner that is continuously fed with real-time data and guides instructional decisions in real time (Longhi, Behar, & Machado, 2024). What distinguishes this model from other learning analytics systems is its ability to simultaneously adapt to the individual's behavioral and emotional changes and reflect them in the learning environment.

However, the main challenge in designing such twins is to accurately model emotions and social interactions in dynamic learning environments. Emotions play a crucial role in regulating learner behavior, selecting cognitive strategies, and persevering in the learning process. When learners are faced with difficult content, emotional states such as anxiety, anger, or confusion may lead to disengagement or reduced learning quality. In contrast, emotions such as curiosity, trust, and satisfaction can increase cognitive engagement and deepen interaction (Movahed, Movahed, & Nozari, 2024). This means that advanced learning systems must be able to identify, interpret, and respond to these emotions in order to optimize the learning experience at the individual level.

On the other hand, social interaction analysis is also an integral part of modern education, especially in virtual or collaborative environments. Learners' relationships with each other, group participation styles, and social dynamics can be important indicators of the level of emotional engagement, social support, and group cohesion, all of which should be reflected in the digital twin model (Nozari, Abdi, & Szmelter-Jarosz, 2025). Therefore, designing a comprehensive model that accurately models both the emotional dimension and social interactions is a serious necessity for the next generation of personalized learning systems.

In order to address this need, the present study focuses on designing an emotion-based digital twin for analyzing social-emotional learning. In this model, a combination of multimodal data including facial expressions, speech patterns, physiological signals, and behavioral interactions is used to identify the emotional and social state of the learner in real time. This information is then stored in the digital model in the form of structured emotional profiles and used in the decision-making process to provide feedback, adapt content, and adjust activities. The goal is to not only optimize the learner's cognitive performance, but also to maintain their psychological well-being and social participation (Andronie, Lăzăroiu, Iatagan, Hurloiu, & Dijmărescu, 2021).

One of the key innovations of this research is the design of a three-layer conceptual architecture for the digital twin, which includes a data collection layer, social-emotional analysis, and adaptive feedback. This structure is designed to be scalable, interoperable with different educational infrastructures, and adaptable to real-time changes in the learner. The system is also evaluated using rigorous scientific criteria, including emotion recognition accuracy, improved learning outcomes, and human acceptance, to measure not only its technical effectiveness but also its practical value in real-world educational settings (Andronie, Lăzăroiu, tefănescu, U ă, & Dijmărescu, 2021).

Overall, this chapter attempts to provide a new model for understanding and responding to learners' emotional and social states, drawing on theoretical foundations from educational psychology, data science, and cognitive engineering. It is hoped that this approach can serve as a starting point for the development of a new generation of intelligent learning systems that care not only about what learners know but also about what they feel.

## 2- THEORETICAL FOUNDATIONS

In recent years, the concept of digital twins has expanded beyond industry and engineering to the field of education, where a digital representation of the cognitive, behavioral, and emotional characteristics of a learner is created dynamically and in real time. In this context, a digital twin is not only a reflection of the learner's physical or interactive state, but also provides the capacity to model his or her mental state, emotional engagement, and individual needs (Nozari, 2025). This model can provide an intelligent picture of the learner's state in real time by interpreting behavioral and multimodal data such as facial expressions, interaction patterns with educational content, speech, and even physiological signals (Guaña-Moya et al., 2023).

On the other hand, learning analytics is defined as the process of collecting, measuring, and analyzing data generated by learners, with the aim of understanding and optimizing learning environments. In recent years, a branch of this field called Socio-Affective Learning Analytics has emerged, which focuses on analyzing the emotional, motivational, and social components of the learning process (Nozari, 2023). This approach is based on the assumption that learning is not only a cognitive process, but also an emotional and social phenomenon, and its accurate modeling requires identifying and responding to the learner's emotions.

To design an emotion-aware digital twin, it is essential to properly understand cognitive-emotional theories that address the role of emotions in information processing and educational decision-making. Theories such as the PAD (Pleasure-Arousal-Dominance) model or the OCC model (which classifies emotions based on cognitive appraisals of situations) are key frameworks for profiling emotions in educational contexts (Guaña-Moya et al., 2023). Self-determination theory, emphasizing fundamental psychological needs such as autonomy, competence, and relatedness, can also play a vital role in interpreting learner emotions and motivation (Szmelter-Jarosz & Nozari, 2025).

Combining these three domains, a conceptual model is designed in which the digital twin simulates the learner's emotional-social state using multimodal real-time data and provides the educational system with this information to adapt the educational content, feedback, and interactions accordingly. Figure 1 shows this conceptual architecture. In this structure, the first layer is dedicated to data collection through software and hardware sensors, the second layer is responsible for processing and analyzing emotional and social data, and the third layer is dedicated to modeling decision-making and educational feedback according to the emotional state (Kraftl et al., 2022).

*Figure 1. Conceptual model of emotion-aware digital twin design in social-emotional learning analysis*

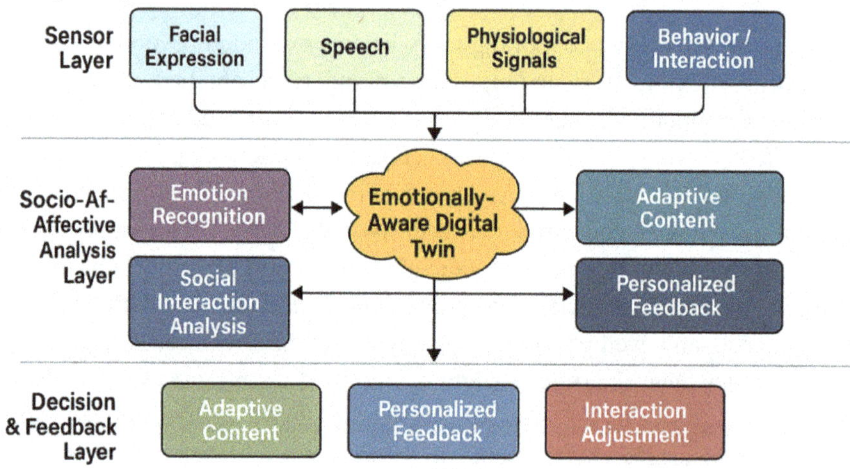


As this diagram illustrates, the process of emotion modeling and its connection to learning analytics requires a coherent, real-time, and ethically-driven system that incorporates not only technical rigor but also a deep understanding of the emotional context of learning. This framework is the foundation for developing systems that can elevate learning from a static, impersonal level of interaction to an empathetic, dynamic, and adaptive experience.

## 3- EMOTION DETECTION AND REPRESENTATION IN DIGITAL TWIN

The section "Emotion Recognition and Representation in Digital Twins" examines in detail the processes by which raw data from learner interactions are transformed into processed emotional information and incorporated into the digital twin framework. In this direction, the goal is not only to detect momentary emotional states, but also to represent them in a structured and interpretable form in a digital model of the learner; a model that allows educational systems to make adaptive decisions and make the learning experience dynamic and intelligent based on the individual's emotional state.

The emotion recognition process in a digital twin system usually begins with the receipt of multimodal data. This data includes facial features, vocal expressions, physiological signals such as heart rate and skin conductance changes, as well as interactive behaviors such as clicks, response latency, and content selection (Nozari, Abdi, & Rafiei, 2025). Importantly, none of these sources alone can provide a complete picture of an individual's emotional state; therefore, advanced systems use data fusion techniques to create a multidimensional and multisensory view of the learner's emotions (Rodríguez & Marquínez, 2024).

After receiving the data, the second step occurs in the processing layer, where the extracted features are presented to emotion recognition algorithms. These algorithms are usually based on machine learning, neural networks, or hybrid models that are trained to classify emotions into specific classes such as happiness, anxiety, anger, or confusion. Some of the most commonly used frameworks in this phase are continuous models such as PAD (pleasure-arousal-dominance) and discrete models such as OCC, which allow for a semantic and processable representation of emotions at the system level (Sandre, 2022).

The third layer is dedicated to the representation of emotions; That is, transforming the detected emotions into forms that can be stored and understood in the digital twin model. These representations can be presented in the form of temporal vectors, emotional profiles, cognitive maps, or even emotional icons in visual dashboards. Depending on the level of arousal and the type of emotion detected, the system makes various adjustments, such as changing the difficulty of the content, the type of feedback, or even the time of interaction (Nozari & Samadi, 2025). Figure 2 shows a more detailed view of this three-step process.

*Figure 2. The process of detecting, processing, and representing emotions in the digital twin model*

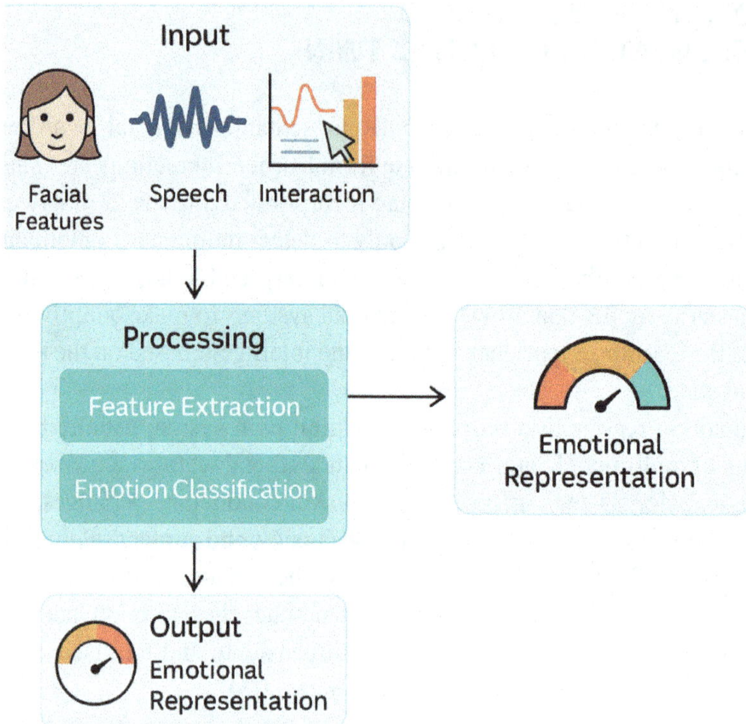


As shown in Figure 2, the sensor layer collects inputs such as face, voice, and biosignals. Then, this data is analyzed through the feature extraction and emotion classification module, and the result is stored in the form of an emotional representation. Finally, the output of this module is passed to the decision engine, and the training is adaptively changed according to the current emotional state. It is worth noting that this process must not only be carried out with high technical precision, but also be designed in a way that is ethically defensible and respects the emotional privacy of the learner (Movahed, Movahed, & Nozari, 2024).

In summary, emotion recognition and representation in digital twins is the beating heart of emotion-based intelligent education systems, where accurate emotion analysis can lead to meaningful interactions, empathetic decision-making, and deeper learning. This approach takes education beyond a static and one-sided level and provides a platform for more human, effective learning based on real emotional needs.

## 4- ARCHITECTURE OF AN EMOTIONALLY-AWARE DIGITAL TWIN

The architecture of an emotion-based digital twin for social-emotional learning analysis should be designed to provide a good overlap between technical, cognitive, and human layers. This architecture should be capable of receiving and processing multimodal data, analyzing the learner's emotional state, and adapting instructional responses in real time. The proposed structure consists of three main layers that are designed hierarchically and with real-time communication: the data collection layer, the social-emotional analysis layer, and the decision-making and feedback layer.

At the first level, the data collection layer, the system is connected to software and hardware sensors that record data such as facial expressions, voice pitch, physiological signals such as heart rate or palm sweating, as well as interactive behaviors in the learning environment (Nozari, Ghahremani-Nahr, & Najafi, 2023). This layer uses application programming interfaces (APIs) or IoT edge devices to send data to the analytics core with minimal latency. The most important feature of this layer is its flexibility to add new data sources and its resistance to momentary disruptions.

At the second level, there is the social-emotional analytics layer, which forms the cognitive core of the architecture. The received data is first processed by the feature extraction module and translated into specific vectors of emotional features. These vectors are then presented to emotion classification algorithms to detect the emotional state of the learner, such as fatigue, apathy, or cognitive engagement. In parallel with this process, the social interaction analytics module also examines patterns of cooperation, participation, or isolation. The results of the analyses of these two paths are fed into the digital twin model to form a comprehensive and dynamic representation of the individual's state (Yordanova & Nozari, 2025).

The third layer is dedicated to decision-making and feedback. The digital twin model, in interaction with the decision engine, compares the current situation with the optimized patterns and then issues suggestions for changing the content, type of activity, or type of feedback accordingly. For example, if signs of cognitive fatigue are detected, the system may change the current activity to a lighter exercise or recommend a break. In cases where a decrease in motivation is detected, the learning content is combined with motivational elements such as competition or gamification (Nozari & Edalatpanah, 2023).

Figure 3 shows the complete architecture of this system. In this diagram, the relationship between the different layers and the components of each of them is clearly and systematically specified and the data flow from multisensory inputs to adaptive decision-making is outlined.

*Figure 3. Conceptual architecture of an emotion-centric digital twin for social-emotional learning analysis*

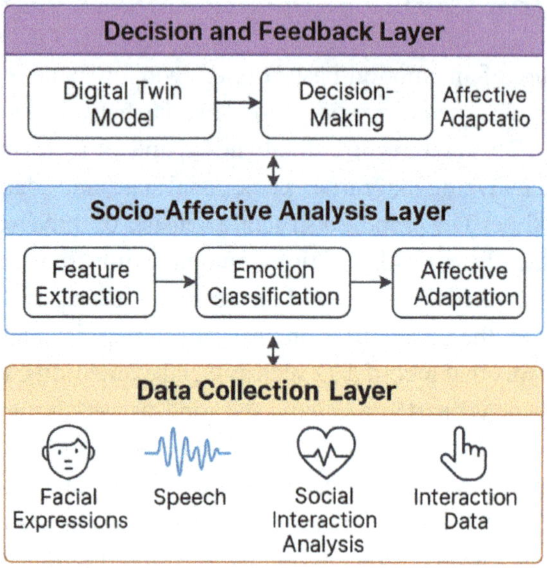


This architecture is designed to not only optimize system performance in virtual and physical learning environments, but also to be ethically responsible. The secret to its success lies in the integration of intelligent emotion processing, real-time personalization, and emotional data privacy (Carella & Conte, 2024). The proposed architecture provides an extensible model for broader applications in adaptive learning, digital mental health, and even organizational behavior analysis.

## 5- SOCIO-AFFECTIVE LEARNING CONTEXTS AND USE CASES

Understanding and analyzing the contexts of social-emotional learning and identifying practical applications of emotion-based digital twins is a fundamental necessity for the successful design and implementation of such systems in smart education. The contexts in which this technology can be applied range from formal educational environments to virtual education systems, serious games, and augmented reality-based classrooms. What these contexts have in common is the presence of learners who are influenced by cognitive, emotional, and social factors involved in learning, and who require adaptive responses from the educational system.

In a smart classroom environment, the physical presence of the learner alongside digital tools such as smart boards and computer systems provides a good opportunity to measure emotions, attention, and engagement levels. By continuously monitoring movement data, voice patterns, and facial expressions, the digital twin can model the emotional state of each student in a personalized way and accordingly suggest the level of difficulty of the activity or the type of teacher feedback (Nozari, Najafi, Jafari-Eskandari, & Aliahmadi, 2016). In such an environment, human interaction is maintained, but decisions are richer and more informed by data.

In distance learning, challenges such as learner isolation, apathy, and reduced social interaction can hinder effective learning. By monitoring digital behaviors such as response timing, click patterns, and even analyzing voice and facial microbiota via webcam, the digital twin in this space estimates the learner's emotional and social state and implements interventions such as sending motivational messages, changing the content format, or suggesting interactions with classmates (Attanasio, Mazza, Le Donne, Nigri, & Valenti, 2024). In effect, the twin model acts as a silent observer, constantly monitoring the quality of the learner's experience and, if necessary, making intelligent adjustments to the learning path.

In the context of game-based learning, the digital twin system can play an effective role in adjusting the difficulty of challenges, matching rewards to emotional state, and maintaining active participation. For example, if signs of anxiety or stress are identified, the game can slow down or create a calmer atmosphere, transforming the learning experience from a threat to an opportunity. Also, in augmented reality-based learning, the digital twin uses location data, gaze direction, and sound to analyze not only the level of cognitive engagement but also the emotional coordination with the environment and design more realistic scenarios for learning (Nozari, 2024).

Figure 4 shows an example of three different application scenarios in which the emotion-based digital twin actively participates in analysis, decision-making, and intervention suggestions. These scenarios demonstrate the high flexibility of the technology in different learning contexts.

*Figure 4. Application scenarios of the emotion-based digital twin model in different educational contexts*

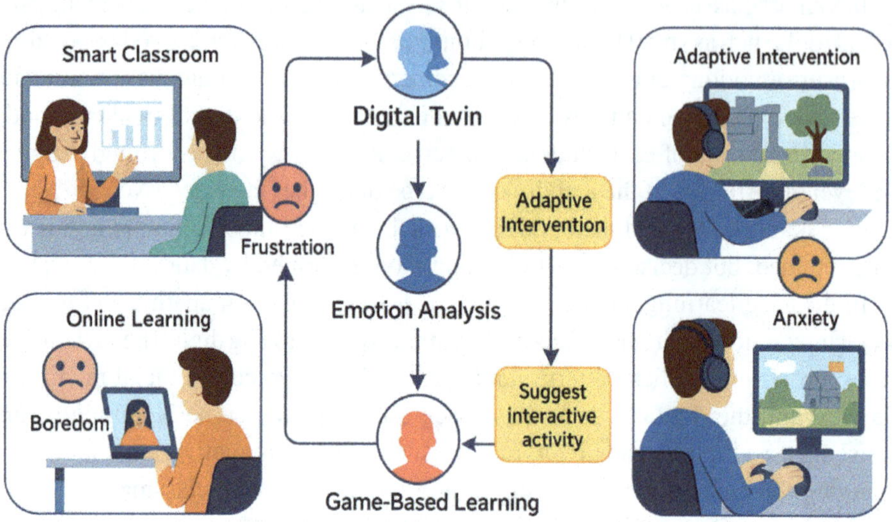


As shown in the figure, the data flow from the learner to the system, and from the system to the adaptive intervention, is clearly depicted. In each scenario, different data sources, their own analysis algorithms, and the type of response appropriate to the situation of that context are used. On the other hand, the common feature of all these applications is the need to observe ethical principles, maintain privacy, and transparency in sentiment analysis, which are requirements for the design and implementation of such systems in a real context (Movahed, Aliahmadi, Parsanejad, & Nozari, 2023).

## 6- EVALUATION METHODS AND METRICS

Evaluation of an emotion-based digital twin model requires a combination of quantitative and qualitative methods that can measure both the technical accuracy of the system and the educational effectiveness and learning experience. Since such models detect and interpret learner behaviors and emotions in real time, their evaluation should go beyond the accuracy of the classification algorithms to measure the quality of adaptive interventions, human acceptance, and cognitive performance improvement.

One of the most important indicators is the accuracy of emotion recognition, which is usually determined by comparing the system output with standard labels or human judgments. Metrics such as overall accuracy, sensitivity, specificity, and

F1 index are widely used to evaluate emotion recognition algorithms (Marciano et al., 2025). For this purpose, laboratory data with induced emotions can be used to measure the accuracy of identifying states such as anger, apathy, or anxiety. However, high accuracy alone does not guarantee the success of the system.

In the next step, the effectiveness of the educational adaptation should be assessed. This assessment is carried out by a comparative analysis between the experimental group and the control group, one of which was trained with and without a digital twin. Indicators such as improved academic performance, retention, cognitive engagement, and active participation are among the most important measures of intervention effectiveness (Rahmaty & Nozari, 2023). Also, the time spent on each activity, the number of re-interactions, or the dropout rate can be used as complementary behavioral indicators.

On the other hand, measuring the user experience and acceptance of the system is also important. Through standard questionnaires such as SUS or technology acceptance scales, learners' views on usefulness, ease of use, trust in the digital twin model, and overall satisfaction can be measured. This section is particularly effective in assessing the ethical and psychological dimensions of system use (Movahed, Movahed, & Nozari, 2024). Combining objective and subjective results can provide a complete picture of the success of the system in the field of application.

Figure 5 depicts an integrated model of assessment methods and associated key indicators. This diagram shows the assessment flow path from the emotion recognition level to the measurement of the learner experience.

*Figure 5. Emotion-based digital twin performance evaluation framework in smart educatıon*

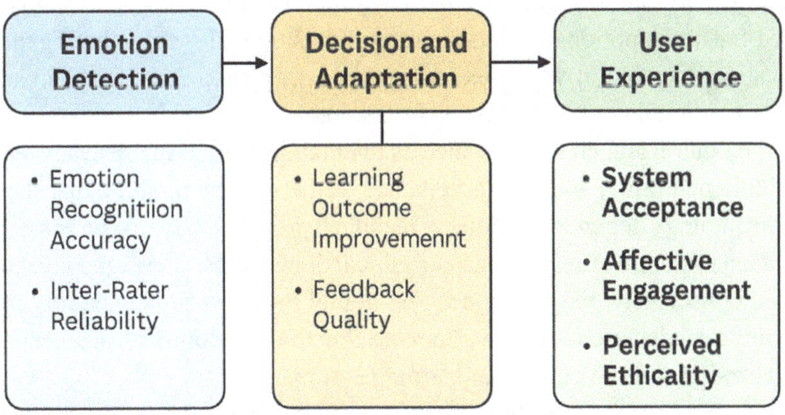

In this framework, each layer of the system is evaluated with its own indicators. The detection layer includes algorithmic accuracy and interpersonal validation. The decision-making and adaptation layer is measured with indicators such as learning effectiveness and feedback quality. Finally, the user experience layer includes system acceptance, emotional engagement, and ethical perception. This evaluation structure provides a combination of biological, interaction, and psychometric data that together provide a comprehensive view of the performance and sustainability of the digital twin model (Viswanath & Weber, 2024).

In short, the success of the emotion-based digital twin does not depend only on technical accuracy, but also on the effective interaction between emotional modeling, educational feedback, and human acceptance. Multi-layered and continuous evaluation is the condition for this sustainable interaction.

## 7- CONCLUSION

In conclusion, it can be seen that the design and implementation of emotion-based digital twins in smart education has not only revolutionized the methods of learning analysis, but also deepened and structured our understanding of the role of emotions in the learning process. In a world where educational interactions are becoming increasingly complex and personalized, the presence of a dynamic system that can identify, interpret, and respond to the emotional state of the learner in real time is no longer a luxury or an accessory, but a fundamental requirement.

The models presented in this chapter showed that by combining emotion analysis technologies, social-cognitive constructs, and real-time digital twin architectures, the learning path can be guided in such a way that the learner is not only cognitively engaged, but also emotionally feels seen and understood. This empathetic experience of education is the point where technology goes beyond a mere tool and achieves the role of an intelligent educational companion.

On the other hand, challenges such as maintaining emotional privacy, ensuring algorithmic neutrality, and user acceptance of the system all show that the future of this technology depends not only on technical progress, but also on the degree to which it pays attention to its human and ethical dimensions. If designed responsibly and used consciously, the emotion-based digital twin can fundamentally improve the quality of education and pave the way for the development of deeper, more personalized, and more emotional learning systems.

However, this path has only just begun. Future research should expand towards designing self-learning systems, optimizing emotion representation models, and deeper integration of this technology with new interactive platforms such as the metaverse, mixed reality, and conversational interactions. With such an approach, we can expect the digital twin to become an integral part of the future education ecosystem; An ecosystem that not only pays attention to the individual's knowledge, but also respects their state and feelings.

## REFERENCES


Andronie, M., Lăzăroiu, G., Iatagan, M., Hurloiu, I., & Dijmărescu, I. (2021). Sustainable cyber-physical production systems in big data-driven smart urban economy: A systematic literature review. *Sustainability (Basel), 13*(2), 751. DOI: 10.3390/su13020751

Andronie, M., Lăzăroiu, G., tefănescu, R., U ă, C., & Dijmărescu, I. (2021). Sustainable, smart, and sensing technologies for cyber-physical manufacturing systems: A systematic literature review. *Sustainability (Basel), 13*(10), 5495. DOI: 10.3390/su13105495

Attanasio, M., Mazza, M., Le Donne, I., Nigri, A., & Valenti, M. (2024). Salience Network in Autism: Preliminary results on functional connectivity analysis in resting state. *European Archives of Psychiatry and Clinical Neuroscience*, •••, 1–14. DOI: 10.1007/s00406-024-01949-y PMID: 39673625

Carella, G., & Conte, M. (2024). Supporting Problem-Solving skills through Strategic Design tools: an exploratory study. In *ICERI2024 Proceedings* (pp. 3937-3945). DOI: 10.21125/iceri.2024.0997

Guaña-Moya, J., Ballesteros-Casco, T., Arteaga-Alcívar, Y., Antamba-Guasgua, J., Lutsak, E. V. A., & Morales, J. C. (2023, June). The New Educational Models Based on Information and Communication Technology and Education 4.0. In International Conference in Information Technology and Education (pp. 267-277). Singapore: Springer Nature Singapore. DOI: 10.1007/978-981-99-5414-8_26



Guaña-Moya, J., Ballesteros-Casco, T., Arteaga-Alcívar, Y., Antamba-Guasgua, J., Lutsak, E. V. A., & Morales, J. C. (2023, June). The New Educational Models Based on Information and Communication Technology and Education 4.0. In International Conference in Information Technology and Education (pp. 267-277). Singapore: Springer Nature Singapore. DOI: 10.1007/978-981-99-5414-8_26



Kraftl, P., McKenzie, M., Gulson, K., Accioly, I., Blackmore, J., Burke, C., & Wood, A. (2022). Learning spaces: built, natural and digital considerations for learning and learners. In *Education and the learning experience in Reimagining education: The International Science and Evidence based Education Assessment* (pp. 452–547). UNESCO MGIEP. DOI: 10.56383/KWAW2002

Longhi, M. T., & Behar, P. A. (2024). Socio-Affective Competence in Virtual Learning Environments: A View from the Empathetic. In Creative Approaches to Technology-Enhanced Learning for the Workplace and Higher Education: Proceedings of 'The Learning Ideas Conference'2024, Volume 2 (Vol. 2, p. 350). Springer Nature. DOI: 10.1007/978-3-031-73427-4_34

Longhi, M. T., Behar, P. A., & Machado, L. S. R. (2024, June). Socio-Affective Competence in Virtual Learning Environments: A View from the Empathetic Subject. In The Learning Ideas Conference (pp. 350-362). Cham: Springer Nature Switzerland. DOI: 10.1007/978-3-031-73427-4_34

Marciano, L., Dubicka, B., Magis-Weinberg, L., Morese, R., Viswanath, K., & Weber, R. (2025). Digital Media, Cognition, and Brain Development in Adolescence. In *Handbook of Children and Screens* (pp. 21–29). Springer. DOI: 10.1007/978-3-031-69362-5_4

Movahed, A. B., Aliahmadi, A., Parsanejad, M., & Nozari, H. (2023). A systematic review of collaboration in supply chain 4.0 with meta-synthesis method. *Supply Chain Analytics*, *4*, 100052. DOI: 10.1016/j.sca.2023.100052

Movahed, A. B., Movahed, A. B., & Nozari, H. (2024). Opportunities and challenges of smart supply chain in Industry 5.0. Information Logistics for Organizational Empowerment and Effective Supply Chain Management, 108-138.

Movahed, A. B., Movahed, A. B., & Nozari, H. (2024). Marketing 6.0 Conceptualization. In Advanced Businesses in Industry 6.0 (pp. 15-31). IGI Global.

Movahed, A. B., Movahed, A. B., & Nozari, H. (2024). Opportunities and challenges of marketing 5.0. Smart and Sustainable Interactive Marketing, 1-21.

Nozari, H. (Ed.). (2023). *Building Smart and Sustainable Businesses with Transformative Technologies*. IGI Global. DOI: 10.4018/979-8-3693-0210-1

Nozari, H. (2024). Green Supply Chain Management based on Artificial Intelligence of Everything. *Journal of Economics and Management*, *46*, 171–188. DOI: 10.22367/jem.2024.46.07

Nozari, H. (2025). Cognitive Targeting and Neuromarketing Applications in AI-Driven Digital Advertising. *Applied Innovations in Industrial Management*, *5*(2), 52–58. DOI: 10.63630/aiim.52.52

Nozari, H., Abdi, H., & Jahangard, S. (2025). Quantum Cognitive Intelligence Network Q-CIN as a Transformative Framework for Industry 6.0. *ALL Bioscience*, *1*(1), 27–37.

Nozari, H., Abdi, H., & Rafiei, K. (2025). Edge Computing and Marketing in the Smart Economy: Processing Consumer Data in Real-Time. In Dynamic and Safe Economy in the Age of Smart Technologies (pp. 191-208). IGI Global Scientific Publishing.

Nozari, H., Abdi, H., & Szmelter-Jarosz, A. (2025). A Neuromorphic and Bio-Inspired Framework for Optimization in Multi-Echelon Supply Networks. *Transformative Science*, *1*(1), 9–17.

Nozari, H., & Edalatpanah, S. A. (2023). Smart systems risk management in IoT-based supply chain. In *Advances in reliability, failure and risk analysis* (pp. 251–268). Springer Nature Singapore. DOI: 10.1007/978-981-19-9909-3_11

Nozari, H., Ghahremani-Nahr, J., & Najafi, E. (2023). The role of Internet of things and Blockchain in the development of agile and sustainable supply chains. In Digital Supply Chain, Disruptive Environments, and the Impact on Retailers (pp. 271-282). IGI Global. DOI: 10.4018/978-1-6684-7298-9.ch015

Nozari, H., Najafi, S. E., Jafari-Eskandari, M., & Aliahmadi, A. (2016). Providing a model for virtual project management with an emphasis on IT projects. In *Strategic Management and Leadership for Systems Development in Virtual Spaces* (pp. 43–63). IGI Global Scientific Publishing. DOI: 10.4018/978-1-4666-9688-4.ch003

Nozari, H., & Samadi, S. (2025). Digital Twin-Enhanced Sentiment Analysis for Targeted Marketing Optimization. In Dynamic and Safe Economy in the Age of Smart Technologies (pp. 121-138). IGI Global Scientific Publishing. DOI: 10.4018/979-8-3693-4369-2.ch008

Rahmaty, M., & Nozari, H. (2023). Optimization of the hierarchical supply chain in the pharmaceutical industry. *Edelweiss Applied Science and Technology*, *7*(2), 104–123. DOI: 10.55214/25768484.v7i2.376

Rodríguez, S. P. L., & Marquínez, O. P. B. (2024). Empathic Interactions in Multigrade Schools: A Strategy for Developing a Didactic Subject of Learning. *Migration Letters : An International Journal of Migration Studies*, *21*(S2), 180–206.

Sandre, A. (2022). *From risk to illness: Examining familial and environmental pathways to the development of depression via neural response to socio-affective information*. McGill University.

Szmelter-Jarosz, A., & Nozari, H. (2025). AI-Driven Decision Intelligence and Human-AI Collaboration in Economic Systems. In Dynamic and Safe Economy in the Age of Smart Technologies (pp. 171-190). IGI Global Scientific Publishing.

Viswanath, K., & Weber, R. (2024). Digital Media, Cognition, and Brain Development. Handbook of Children and Screens: Digital Media, Development, and Well-Being from Birth Through Adolescence, 21.

Yordanova, Z., & Nozari, H. (2025). Harnessing Cyber-Physical Systems and Digital Twins for Industrial Innovation and Economic Resilience. In Dynamic and Safe Economy in the Age of Smart Technologies (pp. 33-48). IGI Global Scientific Publishing. DOI: 10.4018/979-8-3693-4369-2.ch003

# Chapter 4
# Evaluating the Role of Artificial Intelligence in Learning Analytics

**Maryam Rahmaty**
http://orcid.org/0000-0003-3772-4216
*Department of Management, Islamic Azad University, Chalus, Iran*

## ABSTRACT

*This chapter examines the role of artificial intelligence in learning analytics, exploring its theoretical, technical, interdisciplinary, and institutional dimensions. First, the cognitive and data-driven foundations of the field are introduced, and then the capabilities of AI in personalizing learning, providing real-time feedback, and educational decision-making are analyzed. Interdisciplinary applications are then examined, with an emphasis on the connection with cognitive science, linguistics, and UX design. The scalability challenges and institutional impacts of learning analytics at the educational policy level are also discussed. The conclusion shows that the effective use of AI requires synergy between humans, technology, and institutional structures.*

## 1- INTRODUCTION

In recent years, the field of education has undergone a fundamental transformation; a transformation that, with the emergence of data-driven technologies and artificial intelligence, has crossed the traditional boundaries of learning and has confronted classical concepts of education with new questions. One of the important consequences of this transformation is the emergence of a new branch called Learning Analytics; a branch that is based on the collection, processing, and interpretation of

DOI: 10.4018/979-8-3373-5117-9.ch004

ght © 2026, IGI Global Scientific Publishing. Copying or distributing in print or electronic forms without written permission of IGI Global Scientific Publishing is prohibited. Use of this chapter to generative artificial intelligence (AI) technologies is expressly prohibited. The publisher reserves all rights to license its use for generative AI training and machine learning model development.

data related to the behavior and performance of learners and its goal is to optimize the teaching-learning process (Movahed, Movahed, & Nozari, 2024). In such an environment, the entry of artificial intelligence as a powerful analytical engine seems not only inevitable but also mandatory. Artificial intelligence makes it possible to extract meaningful patterns from the mass of learning data; patterns that would be difficult or impossible for humans to understand alone.

The convergence between learning analytics and artificial intelligence has emerged in response to two fundamental needs in education: first, the need for a deeper and more accurate understanding of each individual's learning path; Second, the need for evidence-based educational decision-making, not just intuition. If we consider education to be a complex and multifaceted process that depends on cognitive, psychological, social, and contextual factors, then understanding and analyzing it also requires tools that can model and manage this complexity. Artificial intelligence plays a facilitating and interpretive role in this, especially when combined with machine learning algorithms, neural networks, or educational recommender systems (Nozari & Ghahremani-Nahr, 2023).

However, before we explore the capabilities of AI in learning analytics, it is necessary to review the fundamental concepts of both fields. Learning analytics, simply put, is the process of using learning data to better understand learner behavior, improve content, predict performance, and provide targeted feedback. This data may be extracted from a variety of sources, such as virtual learning environments, learning management platforms, online tests, or even social interactions in the digital space (Movahed, Movahed, & Nozari, 2024). In contrast, artificial intelligence is a set of technologies and algorithms designed to simulate human cognitive abilities. When these two fields come together, a platform is provided in which education moves from a static and general state to a dynamic, personalized and adaptable process.

One of the main reasons for addressing the role of artificial intelligence in learning analytics is the shift in the paradigm of education from static models to adaptive learning approaches. Today, one can no longer expect the same output from the same curriculum for all learners. Instead, new approaches seek to design flexible and data-driven learning paths; paths that can adapt to the needs and individual abilities of the learner through continuous analysis of his performance. In such a model, the role of AI goes beyond mere data analysis and is elevated to the level of making recommendations, supporting decision-making and even designing learning paths (Nozari, Szmelter-Jarosz, & Ghahremani-Nahr, 2021).

Furthermore, the shift in the education landscape from traditional education to lifelong learning has made the need for intelligent analytics more pressing. In environments where learners learn independently and within self-directed pathways, human supervision and support will be difficult and limited. This is where AI can play a key role in supporting learners by analyzing learning trends, identifying performance gaps, and providing real-time feedback (Ghahremani-Nahr et al., 2023). Even at the policy level, data extracted from learning analytics can inform macro-planning, resource allocation, and evaluation of the efficiency of the education system.

Despite these capabilities, important questions arise about the validity, interpretability, and efficacy of AI-based analytics. Can machine learning algorithms be trusted to predict academic success? Is data collected based on digital interaction truly representative of learners' cognitive or motivational behavior? How can we avoid false generalizations, algorithmic biases, or ignoring individual differences? These are the questions that this chapter attempts to address with a critical, evidence-based perspective.

The aim of this chapter is to provide a multidimensional assessment of the role of AI in learning analytics. It then attempts to present a comprehensive picture of this technological synergy by reviewing the theoretical foundations, examining the technical capabilities, analyzing the tools and approaches used, and finally analyzing the institutional and interdisciplinary impacts. In the end, the reader should be able to answer the key question of to what extent AI can play a role as a credible, ethical, and effective analyst in the context of data-driven education.

## 2- THEORETICAL FOUNDATIONS

Understanding the role of AI in learning analytics requires a thorough understanding of the theoretical foundations of these two fields, as their connection is not based solely on technology or engineering applications, but rather on a deep theoretical foundation that draws on educational science, data science, cognitive psychology, and complex systems theory. In this section, we will examine the key theoretical concepts that underlie the interaction between AI and learning analytics, from understanding the nature of learning as a data-driven phenomenon to the place of intelligent systems in cognitive and educational processes.

One of the first steps in theorizing about learning analytics is to explain the nature of learning from a data-driven perspective. In classical models of education, learning was usually considered a subjective and internal phenomenon that could only be measured through external assessments such as tests. However, with the spread of digital technologies, it has become possible to track and record behavioral data during the learning process; Data that includes not only outcomes but also learning paths, timing, repetition patterns, and individual interactions (Nozari, Ghahremani-Nahr, & Szmelter-Jarosz, 2024). In such a context, learning is no longer defined simply as "what the learner knows" but as "what the learner does." This shift in perspective has shifted the theoretical foundation of learning analysis toward action-oriented and behavioral models.

On the other hand, modern cognitive theories, especially those based on processivism and constructivism, emphasize that learning is not the result of information accumulation, but rather the result of active interaction with the environment. These theories align well with learning analytics, as data obtained from digital learning environments can reflect such interactions (Tavakkoli-Moghaddam et al., 2024). For example, analysis of clickstreams, participation in class discussions, or the number of visits to educational resources are considered indicators of how learners construct knowledge in the context of learning. This theoretical link justifies the use of artificial intelligence, since intelligent algorithms are able to process such data on a large scale and reveal their hidden patterns.

Another important point in the theoretical foundation of this field is the concept of self-regulated learning; a concept that emphasizes the learner's conscious control and guidance of his or her own learning process. In this framework, learning analytics and artificial intelligence can be tools for increasing cognitive transparency; that is, by providing accurate feedback, visualizing progress, and suggesting alternative paths, the learner can help better manage the learning process (Nozari, Ghahremani-Nahr, & Szmelter-Jarosz, 2023). The theoretical explanation for this is based on models of self-monitoring, metacognition, and learner reflection, which have gained a prominent place in effective learning research today.

From the perspective of the philosophy of science, the combination of AI with learning analytics represents a shift from descriptive to predictive science. Previously, educational analytics were largely limited to examining the past, but with the use of machine learning models, it is now possible to predict future trends with high accuracy; for example, the probability of academic failure, test success, or the need for educational intervention (Aliahmadi, Movahed, & Nozari, 2024). This theoretical shift is a shift from static to dynamic analysis and from a posteriori assessment to a priori intervention. In this process, intelligent modeling plays a facilitating role, transforming data from a passive state into an agent of change.

The concept of complex adaptive systems also provides a suitable theoretical framework for explaining the functioning of AI in educational environments. In this view, a learning environment can be considered as a dynamic system consisting of human actors (students, teachers, administrators), technologies (digital platforms, AI tools), and data. The behavior of this system arises from the nonlinear interaction of its components. Complex systems theory believes that overall learning patterns arise not from individual components, but from the overall dynamics of the system (Nozari & Sadeghi, 2021). In this space, artificial intelligence is not only an analytical tool, but also an active element in shaping the behavior of the entire system; because it becomes a direct intervener in the dynamics of the system by offering feedback, modifying learning paths, and allocating educational resources.

The link between learning analytics and open systems theories is also noteworthy. In these theories, learning is considered as a non-isolated process influenced by continuous input data. Thus, learning analytics can provide a model for continuous optimization of the educational process by examining these continuous inputs and outputs (Darvishi et al., 2022). This view also provides a theoretical framework for using AI to design adaptive systems; systems that not only react to data, but also learn from it and modify their behavior over time.

Finally, another theoretical aspect should be considered that is less discussed in the conventional education literature: the relationship between algorithms and human interpretation. Many researchers believe that learning analytics cannot be based solely on numerical processing, but also requires “situational understanding” and contextual interpretation. This is where AI must be combined with hybrid human-machine approaches to ensure that the results of the analysis are not only accurate, but also understandable, reliable, and actionable (Szmelter-Jarosz, Ghahremani-Nahr, & Nozari, 2021). Interpretive theories, especially in the field of qualitative data analysis, remind us that meaning does not emerge from data alone, but rather is the product of the intersection of data, context, and the analyst’s perspective.

In summary, the theoretical foundation of AI-based learning analytics is a fusion of cognitive concepts, complex systems, self-regulation models, and data-driven theories. This theoretical fusion allows for the creation of environments in which learning is not only measured, but also understood and enhanced, with the help of AI acting not as an arbiter but as an advisor and companion.

## 3- CAPABILITIES OF AI IN LEARNING ANALYTICS

In addition to the theoretical consideration of the role of AI in learning analytics, it is essential to consider its real-world and practical capabilities in educational settings. What distinguishes AI from other data analytics tools is not simply its ability to process data faster or more accurately, but rather its power to extract complex patterns, predict future behaviors, and suggest adaptive solutions in real time. In educational settings, these capabilities are manifested at various levels of interaction with the learner, the teacher, and the educational content.

One of the most important capabilities of AI in learning analytics is the ability to predict the future performance of learners based on behavioral and cognitive data. These predictions can include the probability of success on a test, the risk of academic failure, or even the level of mental engagement with the content. Machine learning models can estimate the probability of a specific educational event by using historical data from learners, such as the timing of access to resources, previous grades, and interaction patterns with the educational system (Nozari, Ghahremani-

Nahr, & Najafi, 2023). This capability allows educational administrators to plan for intervention before a problem reaches a critical point.

In addition to prediction, AI has a high ability to analyze personalized learning patterns. Unlike traditional education models that are designed based on the same curriculum for everyone, AI is able to identify the learning style, speed of progress, level of understanding of concepts, and even individual interests of each learner and design personalized learning paths based on them (Aliahmadi & Nozari, 2023). This personalization not only increases the efficiency of the learning process, but also improves the learning experience. In other words, by continuously observing the learner's performance, intelligent algorithms automatically adjust learning paths to suit the individual's cognitive and psychological state.

Other key capabilities of AI in this area include analyzing emotions and recognizing the mental states of learners. Using methods such as natural language processing, facial analysis, and voice processing, AI-based educational systems can identify emotions such as anxiety, confusion, or apathy (Salas-Pilco, Xiao, & Hu, 2022). This information can help teachers better understand the emotional state of the class and take appropriate supportive measures. Intelligent systems can also automatically adapt educational content or presentation style to the emotional state of the learner.

Another capability that has received attention in recent years is the design of educational recommendation systems. Similar to what is done in online stores to recommend products, these systems analyze past behaviors and overall preferences to recommend educational content tailored to the individual's needs and learning style. These recommendations may include new resources, study paths, or even suitable groups for collaborative learning (Najafi, Nozari, & Edalatpanah, 2022). Such systems prevent confusion in content selection by creating a continuous learning flow and help to better guide the educational path.

AI also plays an important role in providing real-time and accurate feedback. In the past, feedback was usually provided by the teacher in a delayed and general manner, but now analytical systems can provide immediate, targeted, and personalized feedback based on each learner's action. This feedback can include suggestions for error correction, further explanation, or alternative learning paths (Cukurova, 2025). Such a feature increases inclusive self-regulation and enhances a sense of control over the learning process.

At a higher level, AI can act as a decision-making engine for teachers and educational administrators. By collecting and analyzing data related to the classroom, student performance, educational content, and other environmental factors, intelligent analytical systems provide recommendations for improving the curriculum, choosing teaching methods, and setting educational goals. These recommendations can be displayed in the form of visual dashboards or analytical reports that help decision-makers identify the strengths and weaknesses of the educational system (Bathaee, Nozari, & Szmelter-Jarosz, 2023).

The above capabilities can be depicted in the form of a hierarchical model that shows the different levels of AI functions in learning analytics. In this model, three main levels are considered: Personal, Interactive, and Systemic. At each level, the type of data, tools, and type of AI intervention are different.

*Figure 1. AI functional levels in learning analytics*

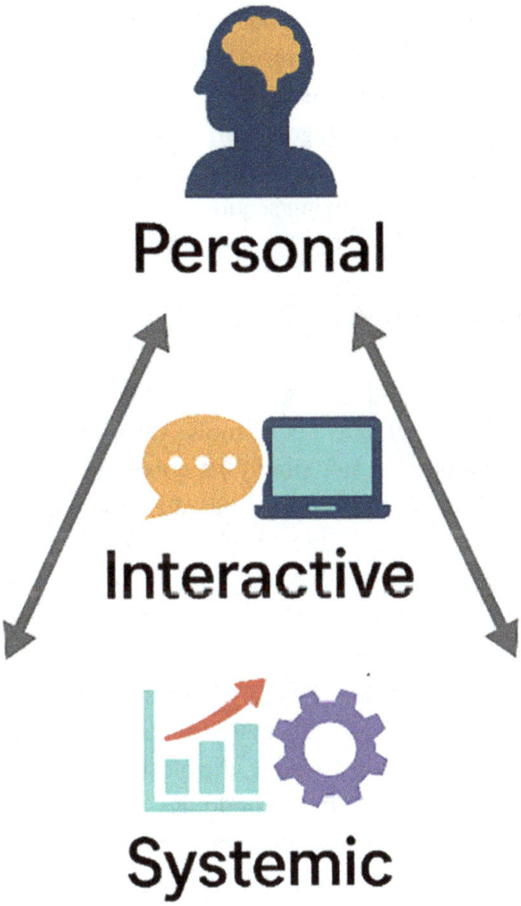


At the individual level, the focus is on analyzing learner behavior, progress, and preferences. At this level, AI is tasked with identifying individual patterns and suggesting appropriate learning paths. At the interaction level, AI analyzes interactions between learners, or between learners and content. This level includes recommender systems, discussion participation analysis, and interactive assessment. Finally, at the system level, data is analyzed on a large scale to help with institutional decision-making, course design, and policy-making.

It is noteworthy that all of these capabilities depend on the quality of the data, the technical infrastructure, and the compatibility of the algorithms with the educational environment. AI algorithms, however powerful, will not be able to provide valid analyses if they are fed with incomplete or biased data (Nozari et al., 2023). Therefore, the success of AI applications in learning analytics depends to a large extent on careful design, human supervision, and implementation tailored to the cultural and educational context.

In general, it can be said that AI has opened up a new perspective for improving the quality of learning by offering a diverse range of capabilities. These capabilities have not only made educational processes faster and more accurate, but also enabled personalized, responsive, and intelligent learning. However, the full realization of these capacities requires coherent theoretical, technical, and ethical frameworks, which we will discuss in the following sections of the chapter.

## 4- METHODOLOGIES AND TOOLS

To effectively utilize AI in learning analytics, it is essential to be familiar with the methodologies used and the available tools. What distinguishes the use of AI in educational environments is not simply its computational power, but also the adaptability of the methods and tools to the educational context, the behavioral characteristics of learners, and the nature of the learning data. This section examines the common analytical methods and software tools used in AI-based learning analytics. The goal is to provide a clear picture of the path to operationalizing this technology in the learning process.

The first step in using AI is to correctly define the educational problem and determine the type of analysis expected. Analytics based on educational data can be divided into several categories: descriptive, diagnostic, predictive, and prescriptive. Each of these levels requires a specific methodology. Descriptive analytics uses more basic statistical methods to understand the current situation. However, for diagnostic analysis, algorithms such as clustering and classification are used to reveal hidden patterns and classifications in the data (Aliahmadi, Ghahremani-Nahr, & Nozari, 2023). In predictive analytics, regression models, decision trees, artificial neural networks, and ensemble algorithms are used to predict future learner behavior or performance based on historical data. Prescriptive analytics goes a step further and aims to provide suggestions for action. This type of analysis is usually associated with optimization algorithms, reinforcement learning, and recommender systems.

The nature of the data also plays a key role in choosing an analytical method. Educational data is usually a combination of numerical, textual, audio, or visual data and is collected from sources such as learning management systems, online classroom activities, content interactions, test results, and even physiological sensors. For example, if the data consists of student-generated texts, natural language processing techniques such as sentiment analysis or semantic feature extraction are necessary (Nozari, 2024). If the data is sequential or temporal, such as sequential learner activities, algorithms such as LSTM or Hidden Markov Models perform better.

Algorithmically, three main families of machine learning are used in educational analytics: supervised learning, unsupervised learning, and reinforcement learning. Supervised learning is used when labeled data (such as grades or performance level classifications) are available. In this case, the model attempts to learn the relationship between features and labels in order to predict new examples (Najafi, Nozari, & Edalatpanah, 2022). Unsupervised learning is used to discover hidden structures in unlabeled data and is particularly useful in analyzing unknown behaviors or classifying learners. Reinforcement learning is also used in scenarios where the system needs to learn the optimal strategy in a dynamic environment, receiving feedback from the results of its actions. This approach is very effective for designing adaptive intelligent systems that perform better over time.

In addition to methods, software tools also play a vital role in implementing and analyzing AI models. Among open-source tools, Python has a prominent position. Libraries such as Scikit-learn for classical modeling, TensorFlow and PyTorch for deep neural networks, and NLTK or spaCy for natural language processing provide extensive facilities to researchers and educational developers (Nozari & Szmelter-Jarosz, 2024). In addition, analytical environments such as RapidMiner and KNIME, which have graphical interfaces, allow people with less coding knowledge to run analytical models.

In addition to technical tools, there are also platforms specifically designed for learning analytics. Systems such as Moodle Analytics, OpenLAP or EduLMS not only enable the collection and analysis of educational data, but also provide teachers and educational administrators with interactive dashboards, enabling continuous monitoring and real-time decision-making. Some of these platforms are equipped with recommender systems that suggest personalized learning paths, while others have the ability to connect to external algorithms.

In practical scenarios, the implementation of AI-based learning analytics is carried out in several stages. First, raw data is collected from various sources and, after filtering and preprocessing (such as removing incomplete data, normalization and feature extraction), it is fed into analytical models. After training and evaluating the models, the results are presented in the form of reports, graphs, alerts or recommendations. This cycle is usually repeated continuously to improve the system with new data (Aliahmadi et al., 2022).

Figure 2 shows a conceptual view of the complete AI-based learning analytics cycle, from data collection to final action and model update, with the role of each tool or method in the process outlined.

*Figure 2. AI-based learning analytics cycle*

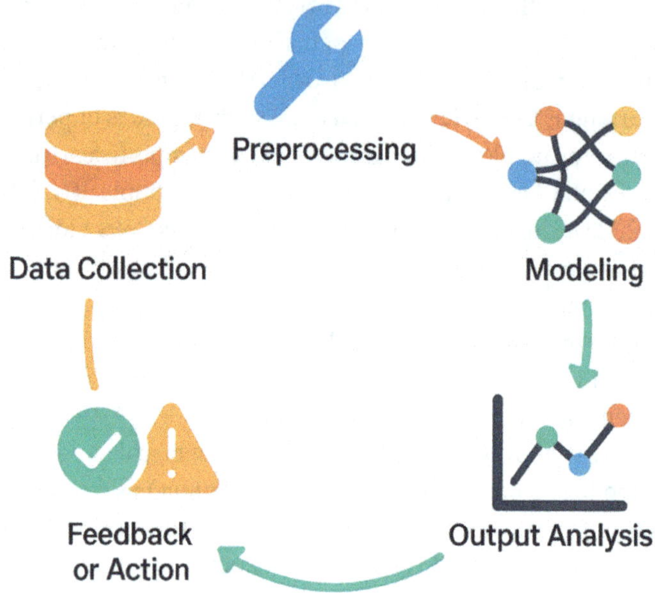


It is worth noting that the performance of models depends on the quality of the preprocessing stage and the careful design of features. In many studies, a large share of the success of the model is not due to the algorithm, but to the skill in designing appropriate features. For this reason, some researchers prefer to use automated methods such as feature learning or deep learning, in which the system extracts feature from raw data instead of receiving ready-made features.

In terms of evaluating the performance of analytical models, criteria such as accuracy, sensitivity, specificity, F1 score, and AUC are used. However, in the field of education, aspects such as interpretability, scalability, and cultural adaptability are also of great importance. An algorithm that works successfully in one environment may provide misleading results in a different cultural context. Therefore, despite the use of advanced technologies, learning analytics must always be accompanied by contextual awareness and human review (Nozari, 2023).

At the end of this section, we can conclude that AI-based learning analytics is not a single tool, but an ecosystem of methods, algorithms, and software tools that must be carefully selected, designed, and implemented. Success in this direction requires synergy between technical expertise, pedagogical understanding, and interdisciplinary approaches. With this view institutionalized, we can expect AI as a transformative force to transform education from a one-sided structure to a dynamic, adaptive, and data-driven platform.

## 5- CROSS-DISCIPLINARY APPLICATIONS

The interdisciplinary application of AI-based learning analytics provides a platform in which traditional boundaries between scientific fields are removed and the education system is more deeply integrated with new knowledge. This convergence not only increases the accuracy and efficiency of educational analytics, but also enables the creation of systems that take into account the human, cognitive, and social context of the learning process. In this section, the role of various sciences in strengthening and expanding the capabilities of learning analytics is examined; focusing on how this field is linked to cognitive psychology, neuroscience, linguistics, data science, and the design of adaptive learning systems.

The first important link in this field is made between learning analytics and cognitive psychology. Understanding how learners receive, process, store, and retrieve information is a key element in the design of intelligent analytical systems. Data obtained from users' interactions with digital learning environments reflect cognitive processes such as attention, working memory, cognitive load, and schema formation (Fallah & Nozari, 2021). For example, the duration of focus on a content, the sequence of activities performed, or the rate of revisiting a topic are all indirect indicators of how information is cognitively processed. Combining these indicators with cognitive theoretical models allows for a deeper analysis of learner behavior.

In conjunction with psychology, neuroscience has also found a special place as an emerging field in education. Using physiological data such as heart rate, brain wave patterns, or even facial muscle contractions, it is possible to identify pervasive mental and emotional states during learning. These data, especially when combined with machine learning algorithms, can lead to instantaneous and real-time analyses of the learner's cognitive state (Tiukhova et al., 2024). For example, systems have been designed that, based on EEG fluctuations, detect moments of attention lapses or cognitive overload and adjust the content accordingly. This approach, defined within the framework of "neuroanalytics," is a bridge between learning analytics and neuroscience.

On the other hand, computational linguistics also plays a significant role in the development of learning analytics tools. Much educational data is in the form of writing, speech, or linguistic interactions; therefore, the ability to analyze natural language plays an important role in interpreting this data. Analyzing student writing, examining questions asked in class, or analyzing sentiment in text messages are all made possible using natural language processing (NLP) methods (Nozari, Fallah, Szmelter-Jarosz, & Krzemiński, 2021). These methods are able to automatically analyze writing style, linguistic complexity, level of critical thinking, or even the level of general comprehension and adapt them to analytical models. In addition, the use of more advanced techniques such as deep language models and transformers also allows for more precise semantic analysis and learner intent detection.

A further link is made to the field of data science, which is at the heart of all AI-based analytics. Methods such as clustering, classification, predictive modeling, social network analysis, and data visualization all have their roots in advanced data mining and machine learning techniques. But what makes this field unique in the context of education is how the methods adapt to the specific characteristics of learning data; data that is usually unbalanced, noisy, heterogeneous, and constantly changing (Alfredo et al., 2024). Therefore, there is a need to design special-purpose algorithms and flexible analytical frameworks. For example, algorithms that can simultaneously process current data and adapt to pervasive cognitive or behavioral changes are among the interdisciplinary achievements of this field.

Designing adaptive intelligent systems is another interdisciplinary convergence point, particularly in the combination of learning analytics with user experience (UX) design. An effective analytical system is only successful when it can be presented in a format that is understandable, interactive, and consistent with the needs of users. Therefore, the design of user interfaces, visual feedback, alert systems, and personalized structures should be consistent with the principles of cognitive psychology, human-machine interaction, and cognitive design (Lotfi, Najafi, & Nozari, 2016). For example, dashboards presented to teachers or learners should provide not only accurate information, but also an intuitive and easy-to-understand representation of the learning process, weaknesses, and suggestions for improvement.

Learning analytics can also be integrated with educational sciences and educational management in curriculum planning and educational policy design. Big data collected from learners' performance can be used to make institutional decisions, optimize resources, design new courses, or even measure the effectiveness of educational policies. In this way, learning analytics goes beyond the individual level and extends to the structural and systemic level. This extension itself requires interaction between data analysts, educational administrators, learning specialists, and policy makers (Simbeck, 2024).

Figure 3 shows a conceptual map of the interdisciplinary applications of AI-based learning analytics. The map shows the relationship between different domains in the form of an interconnected network, each serving a dimension of learning analytics.

*Figure 3. Interdisciplinary applications of AI-based learning analytics*

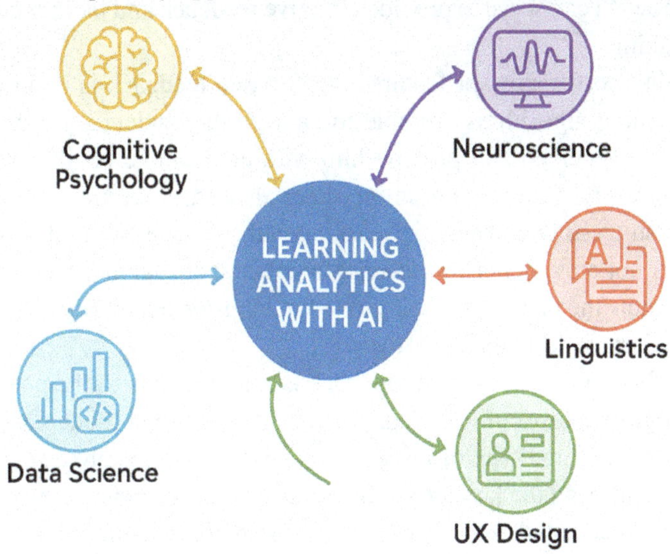


This diagram shows that AI-based learning analytics is not a single field, but rather a core at the center of several scientific disciplines that all contribute to a better understanding of learning, improving the quality of education, and optimizing educational decision-making processes.

In conclusion, it can be said that interdisciplinary applications of learning analytics not only emphasize the inherent complexity of learning, but also provide new paths for the transformation of education. By leveraging cognitive insights, linguistic tools, advanced data mining, and human-centered design, systems can be designed that, instead of providing static analytics, take a dynamic, personalized, and multifaceted approach to learning. This convergence is the starting point for a new generation of data-driven education and informed decision-making.

## 6- AI-AUGMENTED FEEDBACK AND DECISION MAKING

One of the transformative aspects of AI in education is its ability to enhance feedback systems and intelligent decision-making; dimensions that together form the core of data-driven education. Feedback has always played a vital role in learning and is recognized as one of the most effective elements of improving student performance. In traditional education systems, feedback was usually provided in a general, delayed, and sometimes only quantitative manner; but with the advent of AI, this trend has been upgraded to immediate, accurate, personalized, and based on multi-layered analytics. This section examines this fundamental transformation and shows how AI can serve to provide effective feedback and facilitate educational decision-making.

One of the most important features of AI-based feedback is its instant nature. Machine learning algorithms are able to analyze the student's performance data as soon as it is received and provide him with an accurate result. This feedback may take the form of correcting an incorrect answer, providing a supplementary resource, or suggesting a change in learning path. Precise and real-time timing of this feedback not only increases the learner's mental engagement with the content, but also prevents the error from being fixed in long-term memory (Nozari, Najafi, Jafari-Eskandari, & Aliahmadi, 2016).

Another feature of this type of feedback is that it adapts to the needs, learning style, and cognitive level of each learner. Unlike traditional models where all students received the same type of feedback, AI-based systems provide personalized feedback by analyzing the learner's behavioral, cognitive, and even emotional data. This feedback is adjusted not only to previous performance but also to future goals, creating a kind of learning guidance (Rerhaye et al., 2021). For example, if the algorithm detects that the learner is struggling to understand a particular concept, the feedback is designed to reinforce prerequisite concepts and reconstruct the learner's learning path.

In addition to feedback, the role of AI in educational decision-making has also become increasingly prominent. Teachers and educational administrators are faced with a huge amount of data related to student performance, progress, participation, and learning behaviors every day. Analyzing this data manually is not only difficult, but sometimes impossible. Intelligent analytical algorithms with the ability to process it quickly and find hidden patterns provide decision-making tools that help decision-makers design and implement the right educational interventions at the right time (Mohammadi et al., 2015).

One of the most common applications of AI decision-support is the design of analytical dashboards for teachers. These dashboards visually display the current state of the classroom, key performance indicators, the risk of academic failure, student engagement levels, and other educational variables. The analytics behind these dashboards are not only data-driven, but also highly dynamic and adaptive. In fact, systems can even make suggestions for action, from changing teaching strategies to reassigning learners to group activities (Nozari, 2024).

A more advanced example of these systems are educational recommendation engines. These engines analyze a student's learning trajectory, cognitive style, and interests to provide suggestions for content, practice, or interaction. For example, a student with a visual learning style might be recommended specific instructional videos, while another student with an analytical style might be given priority over problem-based exercises. These suggestions are not based on human intuition, but on algorithms that have analyzed thousands of past successful and unsuccessful patterns (Movahed, Aliahmadi, Parsanejad, & Nozari, 2023).

An important point here is the place of humans in the decision-making loop. Although AI can analyze, predict, and suggest, the final decision must still be made by the teacher or administrator. For this reason, in the design of feedback and intelligent decision-making systems, human-in-the-loop models are used, in which humans are not only users, but also observers and correctors of the system. This approach is more reassuring from both an ethical and an efficient perspective (Nozari, Rahmaty, & Szmelter-Jarosz, 2024).

Another important capability is the ability of AI to provide indirect and inter-level feedback. For example, an algorithm can analyze performance in several consecutive activities to reach deeper patterns of motivation loss, cognitive fatigue, or lack of self-regulation. Feedback at this level may include warnings to the teacher, suggestions for a break for the learner, or recommendations for thc use of alternative learning strategies. This type of feedback, which goes beyond the direct level of performance, helps to better understand the overall state of the learner and forms the connection point between data, cognition, and action.

Figure 4 depicts the conceptual framework for providing feedback and decision-making with the help of AI. In this model, the data path from the moment of collection to providing feedback and final decision-making is designed hierarchically and with the participation of humans and machines.

*Figure 4. Hybrid framework for feedback and educational decision support based on artificial intelligence*

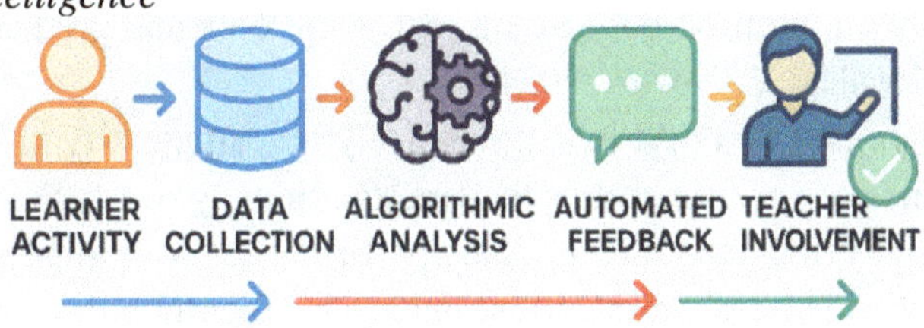


As can be seen in this diagram, the feedback and decision-making process in an intelligent educational system is not a linear and simple process; rather, it is an open and interactive cycle in which data, analysis, feedback, and action continuously reinforce each other. The human role in this cycle, as observer, refiner, and final decision-maker, is still preserved, and this combination allows for the safe and effective use of artificial intelligence in the educational context.

In conclusion, it can be said that artificial intelligence has provided a new platform for intelligent education by improving the quality of educational feedback and strengthening human decision-making capabilities. This technology not only analyzes information, but also translates it into targeted and effective actions. However, the full realization of this capacity requires the design of systems that, while utilizing the computational power of artificial intelligence, also take into account human interaction, educational ethics, and cultural context.

## 7- INSTITUTIONAL IMPACT AND SCALABILITY

Implementing AI-based learning analytics is not just about the classroom or individual interaction between teacher and learner; its institutional dimensions play a crucial role in the success or failure of such systems. Universities, schools, distance learning institutions, and online learning platforms can only benefit from the true potential of AI if they can integrate it into their organizational structure, macro-policymaking, resource management, and educational strategy development. This section examines the institutional impacts of learning analytics and the challenges and opportunities for scaling it.

At the institutional level, one of the most important developments resulting from the use of AI-based learning analytics is the change in the way educational macro-decisions are made. Instead of relying on general reports or traditional surveys, it is now possible to analyze more precisely educational behaviors, trends, and critical points. These analyses help administrators and policymakers make decisions about curriculum design, resource allocation, staffing, or review of assessment methods based not only on intuition but also on real-world data and predictive algorithms (Movahed, Movahed, & Nozari, 2024).

In particular, the use of AI in learning analytics can identify hidden patterns in the performance of specific groups that are traditionally overlooked. For example, an institution may find that students from a particular social or linguistic background systematically underperform in certain units. This identification not only leads to targeted interventions but also to redesigning the macrostructure of courses and support practices (Susnjak, 2024).

On the other hand, implementing learning analytics at the institutional level also comes with challenges. The first challenge is related to the data infrastructure. For AI algorithms to be effective, they need high-quality, structured, up-to-date, and integrated data. This requires the creation of interoperable, highly secure, and scalable educational databases. In many institutions, learner data is stored in separate and incompatible systems, from learning management systems to grading and enrollment systems. Lack of data integration undermines the performance of algorithms and can lead to incomplete or inaccurate analyses (Nozari & Edalatpanah, 2023).

The next challenge is the human dimension. Adoption of analytics technologies by teachers, administrators, and even students themselves requires a change in attitude and trust. If users feel that these technologies are used solely to monitor or evaluate them, we may encounter resistance or even compensatory behaviors. Therefore, in addition to technical implementation, it is necessary to include culture building, continuous training, and stakeholder engagement (Owan et al., 2023). Transparency in how data is used, explaining analytical goals, and ensuring confidentiality of information are key elements in building this institutional trust.

Scalability of learning analytics is also an important concern at the institutional level. A system that works well in a classroom with 30 students will not necessarily be effective at the level of a university with thousands of students. Increasing scale creates the need for faster processing, more robust algorithms, and methods for analyzing heterogeneous and multi-source data. In the meantime, the use of cloud technologies, microservice architectures, and distributed data mining frameworks can enable horizontal and vertical scalability (Rahmaty & Nozari, 2023).

One successful model in this regard is the creation of an "institutional learning analytics unit"; An interdisciplinary team of data scientists, educationists, psychologists, and IT professionals who are responsible for designing, implementing, and reviewing analytics processes at the organizational level. These teams provide a platform for continuous improvement by creating feedback loops between data, policy, and practice. The role of such teams is not only technical, but also serves as a bridge between technology and the operational realities of education.

In addition to structures, financial and legal models for learning analytics need to be defined at the institutional level. Issues of data ownership, privacy policies, transparent and interpretable algorithms, and how analytics results are used all need to be defined within institutional regulations. Many educational institutions will first need to review internal regulations and policies to move toward widespread use of learning analytics (Ghahremani-Nahr, Najafi, & Nozari, 2022).

The Figure 5 shows a view of the institutional impacts and scalability components of AI-based learning analytics. This diagram is designed in layers and shows how, from the data level to the policy level, a set of technical, human, and structural elements must work together to institutionalize the use of learning analytics.

*Figure 5. Multi-layered structure of institutional impact and scalability of AI-based learning analytics*

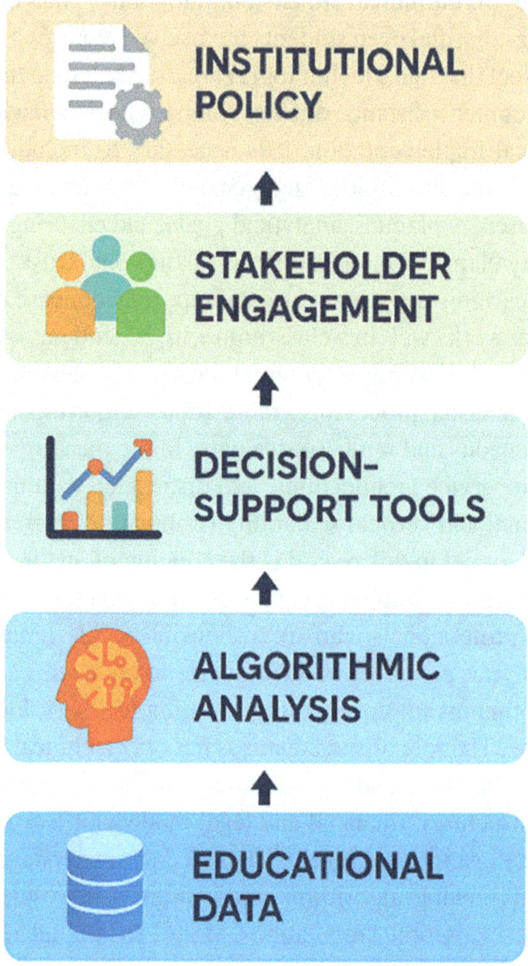


The diagram above clearly shows that none of the levels will be effective without coordination with the other. The existence of data, without appropriate analytical tools or organizational acceptance, will not lead to change. Similarly, the formulation of upstream policies without relying on reliable and analyzed data remains at best recommendation-based. What makes learning analytics a lever for institutional transformation is the continuous, data-driven, and interactive connection between these layers.

At the end of this section, we can conclude that AI-based learning analytics is not just a technical innovation, but a deeply institutional process that requires a review of organizational culture, decision-making structures, and educational management practices. The successful scalability of these systems depends on the availability of technological infrastructure, ethical frameworks, human capacity, and the will of policymakers. When these elements come together, learning analytics can be expected to play its role in improving educational quality and equity as the backbone of modern education.

## 8- CONCLUSION

By the end of this chapter, what becomes clear is that the role of AI in learning analytics is not a fleeting technological trend, but a profound transformation in the foundations of teaching and learning; a transformation whose scope of influence begins with the momentary interactions of learners with content and extends to the level of institutional policy-making and futures studies of education. Learning analytics, using intelligent algorithms, can now understand and improve not only what is learned, but also the how, why, and effectiveness of learning.

In the path outlined in this chapter, an attempt was first made to outline the theoretical foundations of this convergence; where cognitive theories, concepts of self-regulation, complexity models, and data-driven structures were introduced as the main pillars of understanding learner behavior. These theoretical foundations not only provide the philosophical and psychological underpinnings of learning analytics, but also provide a framework for interpreting data that would otherwise be considered merely dry statistics. In this way, the role of AI has been elevated from a mere numerical processor to a semantic interpreter.

The practical capabilities of AI in learning analytics were then explained. It was found that this technology is able to personalize the learning path, provide real-time feedback, analyze emotions and motivations, and even recommend appropriate content. Such capabilities have been realized through the use of machine learning models, natural language processing, image analysis, and neural network algorithms. But what makes these capabilities valuable is not their technical complexity, but their educational function in empowering learners and teachers.

A point that was particularly highlighted in the middle sections of the chapter is the importance of an interdisciplinary perspective in the development and application of AI-based learning analytics. Education, unlike many other fields, is not a purely technological or purely human phenomenon. Rather, in its interweaving of cognitive, affective, social, and cultural elements, it requires an approach that draws on cognitive science and psychology, linguistics and user experience design, and data science and intelligent systems. Without this interdisciplinary connection, learning analytics will remain at best a tool for ranking learners; but with this connection, it can become a tool for individual and collective growth.

From a strategic perspective, the discussion of feedback and decision-making was also emphasized as one of the fundamental functions of AI in learning analytics. It became clear that feedback is no longer a one-sided and static concept, but has become personal, dynamic, and data-driven with the smartization of processes. Teachers and educational administrators are now faced with tools that not only display information, but also facilitate informed decision-making by analyzing that information. This transformation in the concept of feedback is itself a reflection of the transformation in the concept of education; education that is increasingly moving away from the "transmission" model and towards "accompaniment" and "data-driven guidance."

In the final sections, the institutional impact of learning analytics was addressed; where this technology, instead of being used only at the individual or classroom level, becomes a tool for planning, policymaking, and structural transformation. The issue of scalability, the need for data infrastructure, the challenges of organizational acceptance, and the necessity of defining legal and ethical frameworks were among the institutional dimensions of this technology. What was highlighted here is that the success of AI-based learning analytics is not only a function of technical capability, but also depends on institutional maturity, culture, and coordination between the human and technological components of the educational system.

Following these studies, it can be concluded that the effective use of artificial intelligence in learning analytics requires a combination of three factors: first, the existence of theoretical and philosophical frameworks that make sense of data; second, the design and implementation of algorithms and tools that have the ability to process, interpret, and act; and third, institutions that provide the capacity to accept, adapt, and apply this technology in real educational contexts. This triad will be the basis for the realization of smart, fair, and sustainable education.

It should not be forgotten that although artificial intelligence has provided possibilities that seemed impossible a few decades ago, education still remains a human, relationship-oriented, and ethical phenomenon. Learning data, although valuable, only becomes meaningful when it serves to improve the human experience of learning. Therefore, the use of AI in this context should not lead to the elimination of the human factor, but should be aimed at strengthening it. Algorithms can analyze, but it is humans who make decisions, empathize, and connect.

Ultimately, the future of education lies in the hands of those institutions that can build a lasting bridge between technology and humans, between data and understanding, and between analysis and meaning. AI-powered learning analytics, if properly understood and carefully implemented, could be the starting point for such a future; a future in which each learner follows their own unique path, teachers play the role of facilitators, and education becomes an adaptive, data-driven, and more human experience.

## REFERENCES


Alfredo, R., Echeverria, V., Jin, Y., Yan, L., Swiecki, Z., Gašević, D., & Martinez-Maldonado, R. (2024). Human-centred learning analytics and AI in education: A systematic literature review. Computers and Education: Artificial Intelligence, 100215.

Aliahmadi, A., Ghahremani-Nahr, J., & Nozari, H. (2023). Pricing decisions in the closed-loop supply chain network, taking into account the queuing system in production centers. *Expert Systems with Applications*, *212*, 118741. DOI: 10.1016/j.eswa.2022.118741

Aliahmadi, A., Movahed, A. B., & Nozari, H. (2024). Collaboration analysis in supply chain 4.0 for smart businesses. In *Building Smart and Sustainable Businesses With Transformative Technologies* (pp. 103–122). IGI Global Scientific Publishing.

Aliahmadi, A., & Nozari, H. (2023, January). Evaluation of security metrics in AIoT and blockchain-based supply chain by Neutrosophic decision-making method. In Supply chain forum: an international journal (Vol. 24, No. 1, pp. 31-42). Taylor & Francis. DOI: 10.1080/16258312.2022.2101898

Aliahmadi, A., Nozari, H., Ghahremani-Nahr, J., & Szmelter-Jarosz, A. (2022). Evaluation of key impression of resilient supply chain based on artificial intelligence of things (AIoT). arXiv preprint arXiv:2207.13174.

Bathaee, M., Nozari, H., & Szmelter-Jarosz, A. (2023). Designing a new location-allocation and routing model with simultaneous pick-up and delivery in a closed-loop supply chain network under uncertainty. *Logistics (Basel)*, *7*(1), 3. DOI: 10.3390/logistics7010003

Cukurova, M. (2025). The interplay of learning, analytics and artificial intelligence in education: A vision for hybrid intelligence. *British Journal of Educational Technology*, *56*(2), 469–488. DOI: 10.1111/bjet.13514

Darvishi, A., Khosravi, H., Sadiq, S., & Gašević, D. (2022). Incorporating AI and learning analytics to build trustworthy peer assessment systems. *British Journal of Educational Technology*, *53*(4), 844–875. DOI: 10.1111/bjet.13233

Fallah, M., & Nozari, H. (2021). Neutrosophic mathematical programming for optimization of multi-objective sustainable biomass supply chain network design. *Computer Modeling in Engineering & Sciences*, *129*(2), 927–951. DOI: 10.32604/cmes.2021.017511

Ghahremani-Nahr, J., Najafi, S. E., & Nozari, H. (2022). A combined transportation model for the fruit and vegetable supply chain network. *Journal of Optimization in Industrial Engineering*, *15*(2), 131–145.

Ghahremani-Nahr, J., Nozari, H., Rahmaty, M., Zeraati Foukolaei, P., & Sherejsharifi, A. (2023). Development of a novel fuzzy hierarchical location-routing optimization model considering reliability. *Logistics (Basel)*, *7*(3), 64. DOI: 10.3390/logistics7030064

Lotfi, F. H. Z., Najafi, S. E., & Nozari, H. (Eds.). (2016). *Data envelopment analysis and effective performance assessment*. IGI Global.

Mohammadi, H., Ghazanfari, M., Nozari, H., & Shafiezad, O. (2015). Combining the theory of constraints with system dynamics: A general model (case study of the subsidized milk industry). International journal of management science and engineering management, 10(2), 102-108.

Movahed, A. B., Aliahmadi, A., Parsanejad, M., & Nozari, H. (2023). A systematic review of collaboration in supply chain 4.0 with meta-synthesis method. *Supply Chain Analytics*, *4*, 100052. DOI: 10.1016/j.sca.2023.100052

Movahed, A. B., Movahed, A. B., & Nozari, H. (2024). Opportunities and challenges of smart supply chain in Industry 5.0. Information Logistics for Organizational Empowerment and Effective Supply Chain Management, 108-138.

Movahed, A. B., Movahed, A. B., & Nozari, H. (2024). Marketing 6.0 Conceptualization. In Advanced Businesses in Industry 6.0 (pp. 15-31). IGI Global.

Movahed, A. B., Movahed, A. B., & Nozari, H. (2024). Opportunities and challenges of marketing 5.0. Smart and Sustainable Interactive Marketing, 1-21.

Najafi, S. E., Nozari, H., & Edalatpanah, S. A. (2022). Investigating the key parameters affecting sustainable IoT-based marketing. In *Computational Intelligence Methodologies Applied to Sustainable Development Goals* (pp. 51–61). Springer International Publishing. DOI: 10.1007/978-3-030-97344-5_4

Najafi, S. E., Nozari, H., & Edalatpanah, S. A. (2022). Artificial Intelligence of Things (AIoT) and Industry 4.0–Based Supply Chain (FMCG Industry). A roadmap for enabling industry 4.0 by artificial intelligence, 31-41.

Nozari, H. (Ed.). (2023). *Building Smart and Sustainable Businesses with Transformative Technologies*. IGI Global. DOI: 10.4018/979-8-3693-0210-1

Nozari, H. (2024). Green Supply Chain Management based on Artificial Intelligence of Everything. *Journal of Economics and Management, 46*, 171–188. DOI: 10.22367/jem.2024.46.07

Nozari, H. (2024). Supply chain 6.0 and moving towards hyper-intelligent processes. In *Information logistics for organizational empowerment and effective supply chain management* (pp. 1–13). IGI Global.

Nozari, H., & Edalatpanah, S. A. (2023). Smart systems risk management in IoT-based supply chain. In *Advances in reliability, failure and risk analysis* (pp. 251–268). Springer Nature Singapore. DOI: 10.1007/978-981-19-9909-3_11

Nozari, H., Fallah, M., Szmelter-Jarosz, A., & Krzemiński, M. (2021). Analysis of security criteria for IoT-based supply chain: a case study of FMCG industries. Central European Management Journal, 29(4).

Nozari, H., & Ghahremani-Nahr, J. (2023). A comprehensive strategic-tactical multi-objective sustainable supply chain model with human resources considerations. *Supply Chain Analytics, 4*, 100044. DOI: 10.1016/j.sca.2023.100044

Nozari, H., Ghahremani-Nahr, J., & Najafi, E. (2023). The role of Internet of things and Blockchain in the development of agile and sustainable supply chains. In Digital Supply Chain, Disruptive Environments, and the Impact on Retailers (pp. 271-282). IGI Global. DOI: 10.4018/978-1-6684-7298-9.ch015

Nozari, H., Ghahremani-Nahr, J., & Szmelter-Jarosz, A. (2023). A multi-stage stochastic inventory management model for transport companies including several different transport modes. *International Journal of Management Science and Engineering Management, 18*(2), 134–144. DOI: 10.1080/17509653.2022.2042747

Nozari, H., Ghahremani-Nahr, J., & Szmelter-Jarosz, A. (2024). AI and machine learning for real-world problems. [). Elsevier.]. *Advances in Computers, 134*, 1–12. DOI: 10.1016/bs.adcom.2023.02.001

Nozari, H., Najafi, S. E., Jafari-Eskandari, M., & Aliahmadi, A. (2016). Providing a model for virtual project management with an emphasis on IT projects. In *Strategic Management and Leadership for Systems Development in Virtual Spaces* (pp. 43–63). IGI Global Scientific Publishing. DOI: 10.4018/978-1-4666-9688-4.ch003

Nozari, H., Rahmaty, M., & Szmelter-Jarosz, A. (2024). A framework for AIoT-based smart sustainable marketing system. In *Artificial Intelligence of Things for Achieving Sustainable Development Goals* (pp. 255–271). Springer Nature Switzerland. DOI: 10.1007/978-3-031-53433-1_13

Nozari, H., & Sadeghi, M. E. (2021). Artificial intelligence and Machine Learning for Real-world problems (A survey). *International Journal of Innovation in Engineering, 1*(3), 38–47.

Nozari, H., & Szmelter-Jarosz, A. (2024). An analytical framework for smart supply chains 5.0. In *Building Smart and Sustainable Businesses With Transformative Technologies* (pp. 1–15). IGI Global Scientific Publishing.

Nozari, H., Szmelter-Jarosz, A., & Ghahremani-Nahr, J. (2021). The ideas of sustainable and green marketing based on the internet of everything—The case of the dairy industry. *Future Internet, 13*(10), 266. DOI: 10.3390/fi13100266

Nozari, H., Tavakkoli-Moghaddam, R., Rohaninejad, M., & Hanzalek, Z. (2023, September). Artificial intelligence of things (AIoT) strategies for a smart sustainable-resilient supply chain. In IFIP International Conference on Advances in Production Management Systems (pp. 805-816). Cham: Springer Nature Switzerland. DOI: 10.1007/978-3-031-43670-3_56

Owan, V. J., Abang, K. B., Idika, D. O., Etta, E. O., & Bassey, B. A. (2023). Exploring the potential of artificial intelligence tools in educational measurement and assessment. *Eurasia Journal of Mathematics, Science and Technology Education, 19*(8), em2307. DOI: 10.29333/ejmste/13428

Rahmaty, M., & Nozari, H. (2023). Optimization of the hierarchical supply chain in the pharmaceutical industry. *Edelweiss Applied Science and Technology, 7*(2), 104–123. DOI: 10.55214/25768484.v7i2.376

Rerhaye, L., Altun, D., Krauss, C., & Müller, C. (2021, July). Evaluation methods for an AI-supported learning management system: quantifying and qualifying added values for teaching and learning. In *International Conference on Human-Computer Interaction* (pp. 394-411). Cham: Springer International Publishing. DOI: 10.1007/978-3-030-77857-6_28

Salas-Pilco, S. Z., Xiao, K., & Hu, X. (2022). Artificial intelligence and learning analytics in teacher education: A systematic review. *Education Sciences, 12*(8), 569. DOI: 10.3390/educsci12080569

Simbeck, K. (2024). They shall be fair, transparent, and robust: Auditing learning analytics systems. *AI and Ethics, 4*(2), 555–571. DOI: 10.1007/s43681-023-00292-7

Susnjak, T. (2024). Beyond predictive learning analytics modelling and onto explainable artificial intelligence with prescriptive analytics and ChatGPT. *International Journal of Artificial Intelligence in Education, 34*(2), 452–482. DOI: 10.1007/s40593-023-00336-3

Szmelter-Jarosz, A., Ghahremani-Nahr, J., & Nozari, H. (2021). A neutrosophic fuzzy optimisation model for optimal sustainable closed-loop supply chain network during COVID-19. *Journal of Risk and Financial Management, 14*(11), 519. DOI: 10.3390/jrfm14110519

Tavakkoli-Moghaddam, R., Nozari, H., Bakhshi-Movahed, A., & Bakhshi-Movahed, A. (2024). A Conceptual framework for the Smart Factory 6.0. In *Advanced Businesses in Industry 6.0* (pp. 1–14). IGI Global. DOI: 10.4018/979-8-3693-3108-8.ch001

Tiukhova, E., Vemuri, P., Flores, N. L., Islind, A. S., Óskarsdóttir, M., Poelmans, S., Baesens, B., & Snoeck, M. (2024). Explainable Learning Analytics: Assessing the stability of student success prediction models by means of explainable AI. *Decision Support Systems, 182*, 114229. DOI: 10.1016/j.dss.2024.114229

Chapter 5

# Personalizing Learning Pathways Through Deep Learning Models and Educational Data Analytics

**Sepideh Samadi**
http://orcid.org/0000-0002-1689-5596
*Heriot-Watt University, UAE*

**Stavroula Kalogeras**
*Heriot-Watt University, UAE*

## ABSTRACT

*The aim of this research is to investigate the role of deep learning and educational data analysis in personalizing learning paths. Relying on the capacity of deep learning models to identify behavioral patterns and predict learner performance, it is possible to design learning paths that meet individual needs. In this context, educational data analysis not only helps to improve the quality of education, but also paves the way for the development of adaptive and intelligent learning systems. The research also addresses the technical challenges, ethical considerations, and implementation limitations of this approach and offers solutions for the responsible use of new technologies in education.*

DOI: 10.4018/979-8-3373-5117-9.ch005

ght © 2026, IGI Global Scientific Publishing. Copying or distributing in print or electronic forms without written permission of IGI Global Scientific Publishing is prohibited. Use of this chapter to generative artificial intelligence (AI) technologies is expressly prohibited. The publisher reserves all rights to license its use for generative AI training and machine learning model development.

## 1- INTRODUCTION

The rapid growth of new technologies in recent decades has brought about significant changes in the field of education and learning. The emergence of digital tools and advances in data analysis and artificial intelligence have provided opportunities to improve the quality of learning and transform educational methods. In the meantime, deep learning, as one of the important achievements of artificial intelligence, has become an effective tool in analyzing complex data and identifying hidden patterns (Naseer, Khan, Tahir, Addas, & Aejaz, 2024). Along with the expansion of e-learning and the development of virtual learning environments, the need to more accurately understand the behavior of learners and provide educational paths tailored to individual needs has become more important than ever (Aliahmadi & Nozari, 2023).

Personalization of education has become one of the key approaches in modern educational systems in recent years. This approach is based on understanding individual differences among learners and adapting learning processes to their unique needs, preferences, and characteristics. The learning experience is most effective when the content, timing, structure of the learning path, and delivery style are designed to suit the unique characteristics of each learner. In contrast to traditional models of education that emphasize the integration of content and teaching style for everyone, the personalized approach focuses on providing a dynamic, interactive experience tailored to individual circumstances and needs (Nozari & Chobar, 2024).

Educational data analytics, as one of the central tools in realizing personalization, plays a fundamental role. By collecting and processing data from learners' interactions with educational systems, valuable information can be obtained about learning styles, behavioral trends, cognitive engagement, and academic progress. This data, which often remains in the form of digital footprints in online learning environments, is a rich and potential resource for use in designing personalized learning experiences (Dwivedi, Mahanty, & Dwivedi, 2024). Analyzing this data enables informed decision-making at different levels of education and can lead to optimization of the learning process.

Deep learning, with its high processing power and big data analysis capabilities, has gained a prominent position in the field of educational data analysis. Unlike traditional methods based on simple models, deep learning models have the ability to understand and analyze nonlinear and complex relationships between educational data. Deep neural networks, using multilayer structures, are able to extract hidden information and high-level features from raw data and identify meaningful behavioral patterns (Bathaee, Nozari, & Szmelter-Jarosz, 2023). This capability has enabled the development of educational recommender systems, predicted the path of learners' progress, and designed learning paths tailored to individual needs.

One of the prominent applications of deep learning in this field is the development of intelligent recommender systems in learning environments. By continuously analyzing learner behavior, these systems are able to update educational content, learning activities, and suggested paths according to the characteristics of each individual. Also, deep learning-based models can predict the academic progress trend, identify the strengths and weaknesses of each learner, and help improve the learning process. In the meantime, the possibility of early intervention to prevent academic decline or improve performance is an important advantage.

Despite these achievements, there are also challenges in applying deep learning to personalize learning paths. The quality and diversity of educational data, ethical considerations regarding user privacy, and the need for high computational resources are among the important obstacles in this path. Despite these challenges, the high capabilities of deep learning models in processing and analyzing educational data have provided unique opportunities to enhance the learning experience and optimize educational processes.

Overall, personalizing learning paths by relying on educational data analysis and utilizing deep learning models is recognized as one of the effective approaches in the transformation of digital educational systems. This approach can not only improve the quality of education and learner experience, but also pave the way for the development of adaptive and intelligent learning environments. Combining data analysis capacities and deep model capabilities allows for the provision of unique learning paths based on the real needs of each learner; a path that can lead to the realization of more effective and sustainable learning.

## 2- THEORETICAL FOUNDATIONS OF PERSONALIZED LEARNING

Personalized learning, as one of the key approaches in the evolution of contemporary educational systems, is based on the principle that each learner has unique needs, preferences, abilities, and learning styles. This approach, which, unlike traditional education models, moves with the approach of standardizing education for all learners, attempts to design the learning process in a way that is most aligned with the individual characteristics of learners. Accordingly, personalization is understood as adjusting the content, pace, sequence, presentation style, and level of educational support based on the specific characteristics and needs of each learner (Patil, 2025).

The concept of personalization in the educational literature has traditionally been linked to the ideas of individualized learning and adaptive teaching. In these approaches, instead of following a standard educational path, the learning path is formed based on real data from the learner's performance and interaction. Such an approach, in addition to paying attention to individual differences, also allows the development of evidence-based learning strategies. In fact, personalization transforms education from a static process into a dynamic, interactive, and adaptive experience (Ning, Ma, Yao, Wang, & Zhang, 2025).

One of the most important theoretical aspects of personalization is its connection to the concepts of self-regulated learning and self-directed learning. Theories related to self-regulation show that learners will perform better when they can consciously choose and manage their own learning path, goals, and strategies. By providing a suitable platform for self-regulation, personalization allows the learner to take more responsibility for their learning process and actively participate in the construction of knowledge. Accordingly, personalization is not limited to adapting content only, but also emphasizes creating conditions in which the learner is recognized as an active agent in the learning process (Aliahmadi, Ghahremani-Nahr, & Nozari, 2023).

From the perspective of learning psychology, personalization can lead to improved motivation, cognitive engagement, and learner satisfaction. When the content and learning path are aligned with individual interests, abilities, and goals, the learner's level of active participation increases and the learning process becomes more effective. This is especially important in digital learning environments where there are more opportunities for providing adaptive content and diverse interactions. Providing immediate feedback, different learning paths, and appropriate challenge levels are important aspects that should be considered in the design of personalized systems (Taylor, Fakhimi, Ioannou, & Spanaki, 2024).

With the expansion of online learning environments and e-learning systems, the field for the practical realization of the concept of personalization has become more prepared than ever before. Learning management systems, interactive educational platforms, and digital learning tools have made it possible to continuously collect and analyze learning data and, based on it, educational decisions can be made automatically and in real time. This situation has provided a suitable platform for the development of educational recommender systems and analytical models that can recommend educational content, learning tasks, and even the sequence of topics based on individual data. In such a system, each individual's learning experience will be unique and dynamic, and the learning process will be continuously aligned with the characteristics and performance of the learner (Nozari, Tavakkoli-Moghaddam, & Dolgui, 2024).

Adaptive learning is one of the concepts related to personalization, which is known in the educational literature as a process for adjusting the level of difficulty of content and providing feedback based on the learner's performance. In adaptive learning, instead of providing a fixed path, the educational system uses data from previous interactions to adjust the learning path in a way that has the greatest impact on the learner's progress. This process can be done automatically by using machine learning and deep learning algorithms, and as a result, learning systems will move towards true intelligence and personalization (Aliahmadi, Nozari, Ghahremani-Nahr, & Szmelter-Jarosz, 2022).

From an operational perspective, personalizing learning paths using educational data and advanced analytics tools requires designing precise mechanisms for data collection, analyzing behavioral patterns, and implementing adaptive strategies. In this path, data related to academic performance, online interactions, learning styles, and individual interests are used as input to analytical models. Based on the results obtained from analyzing this data, educational systems will be able to design paths that meet the specific needs of each learner and help develop effective learning. Meanwhile, the use of advanced machine learning and deep learning models has provided new opportunities for more accurate data analysis and intelligent suggestions (Yekollu, Bhimraj Ghuge, Sunil Biradar, Haldikar, & Farook Mohideen Abdul Kader, 2024).

Despite the vast potential, implementing personalized learning also comes with challenges. The most important of these challenges include the quality and quantity of educational data, the protection of learner privacy and information security, and the need for computational resources to analyze complex data. Also, designing analytical models that can accurately identify individual differences and implement them in practice requires theoretical rigor and technical expertise. Therefore, the successful realization of personalized learning paths will require constructive interaction between educational theorists, data experts, and intelligent system designers.

Finally, personalized learning as an interdisciplinary approach can pave the way for a transformation in the quality of person-centered education by integrating educational concepts, data science, and information technology. This approach not only improves the learning experience for each individual but can also lead to increased efficiency of educational systems and the development of learning equity in educational environments. The future of education is moving towards smart and adaptive learning in light of the utilization of personalization capacities and advanced analytical technologies.

## 3- ANALYZING EDUCATIONAL DATA AND IDENTIFYING LEARNING PATTERNS

Educational data analysis, as one of the new approaches to improving the quality of education, plays a fundamental role in understanding learner behavior and optimizing the learning process. Today, with the expansion of virtual learning systems, extensive data on learner interactions in educational environments is recorded and stored. This data, which includes academic performance, participation in course activities, interaction with educational content, and cognitive engagement, is a valuable source for analyzing learning processes (Xia, Shin, & Shin, 2024).

Analyzing this data provides an opportunity to better understand individual differences, predict future behaviors, and optimize educational interventions. Data-driven approaches have made it possible to identify learner behavior patterns and paved the way for the development of adaptive education. Instead of relying on traditional methods, educational data analysis using data mining and machine learning techniques has made it possible to recognize hidden patterns in learner behavior (Nozari, Fallah, Szmelter-Jarosz, & Krzemiński, 2021).

In this regard, data mining algorithms such as classification, clustering, and regression analysis play an important role in grouping learners based on common characteristics and performance levels. The results of these analyses can be used to design personalized educational content, determine suggested learning paths, and improve educational interventions. In particular, learning path analysis helps teachers and designers identify effective and ineffective paths and, as a result, redesign educational content and activities in a way that matches the real needs of learners (Yuan, Hou, Feng, & Rahman, 2025).

One of the emerging technologies that has revolutionized educational data analysis is deep learning. Models based on deep neural networks with the ability to process big data and identify nonlinear relationships have enabled more accurate analysis of learner behavior and prediction of learning outcomes. These models are able to identify complex behavioral patterns and extract meaningful information from raw data. Especially in e-learning environments, this capability has greatly contributed to the development of intelligent recommender systems, predictive performance assessment, and optimization of personalized learning paths (Nozari, 2023).

*Figure 1. The process of analyzing educational data and identifying learning patterns*

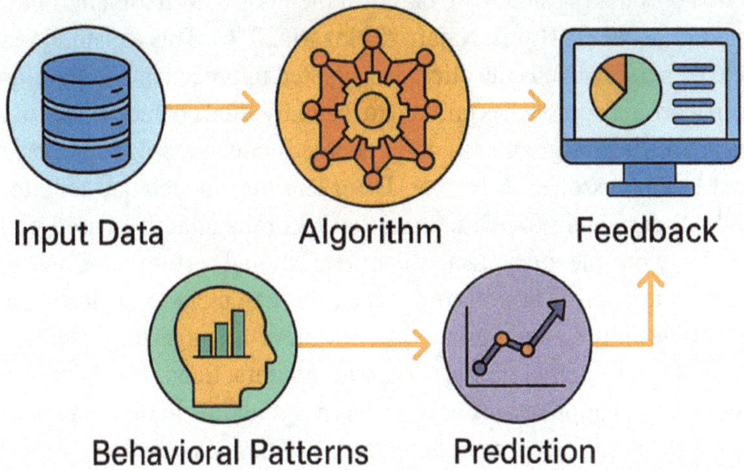


In this figure, the process of analyzing educational data is depicted as a dynamic cycle. Input data from learner interactions is fed into analytical algorithms, after algorithmic analysis, behavioral patterns are identified, predictive models are used, and finally, the analysis results are provided as feedback to the teacher or educational system to optimize the learning path.

Despite these capabilities, educational data analysis also faces challenges, including data quality, accuracy of analyses, and ethical considerations, especially privacy. In the analysis process, paying attention to the quality of the collected data and using valid analytical methods is of great importance. Also, observing ethical principles in the use of learners' personal data is a requirement of any educational analysis (Sumathy & Navamani, 2024).

Overall, analyzing educational data and identifying learning patterns has opened up new horizons for the development of intelligent, personalized, and adaptive education. This approach not only helps improve the quality of learning, but also paves the way for creating data-driven and adaptive learning environments where each learner will have an experience tailored to their needs and capabilities.

## 4- APPLICATION OF DEEP LEARNING MODELS IN PERSONALIZING LEARNING PATHS

In recent decades, advances in the field of deep learning have had a significant impact on the methods of analyzing educational data and developing intelligent learning systems. Deep learning, as a subset of machine learning, has provided the ability to analyze complex data, identify hidden patterns, and predict future behaviors in a way that was not possible with classical methods by utilizing multilayer structures of neural networks (Lotfi, Najafi, & Nozari, 2016). This capability, especially in the field of personalized education, has created unprecedented opportunities for developing learning approaches tailored to the individual characteristics of learners.

Personalizing learning paths requires a detailed understanding of the performance, needs, and behaviors of each learner. Deep learning models are able to identify behavioral patterns and provide educational recommendations based on them by processing large volumes of interactive data, educational performance, and contextual information of learners. These recommendations can include suggesting appropriate content, determining appropriate difficulty levels, suggesting specific learning activities, and even optimal timing for learning interactions (Reddy et al., 2015).

One of the main applications of deep learning models in this field is the development of educational recommender systems. These systems use deep learning algorithms to analyze and predict educational needs using data obtained from the previous behavior of learners. Recommender models based on deep neural networks can highly accurately recommend educational content in a way that is consistent with the level of knowledge and interests of each individual. This helps to increase cognitive engagement and improve the learning experience (Nozari, 2024).

On the other hand, academic performance prediction models based on deep learning are able to estimate the level of learner success in the future based on interaction data. These predictions allow teachers and educational systems to make timely interventions, tailor learning content, and prevent academic failure. In such an approach, deep models, by considering sequential data and time trends, provide predictions that are more accurate and precise than traditional linear models (Movahed, Aliahmadi, Parsanejad, & Nozari, 2023).

Another important application of deep learning in personalizing learning paths is the identification of individual learning styles and preferences. By analyzing interaction data, study patterns, how different content is used, and educational feedback, deep models are able to identify each individual's dominant learning style and adjust educational suggestions accordingly. This allows the learning process to be adjusted in a way that brings the highest level of effectiveness and motivation to the learner (Ghahremani-Nahr, Nozari, & Aliahmadi, 2023).

*Figure 2. Conceptual model of the application of deep learning in personalizing learning paths*

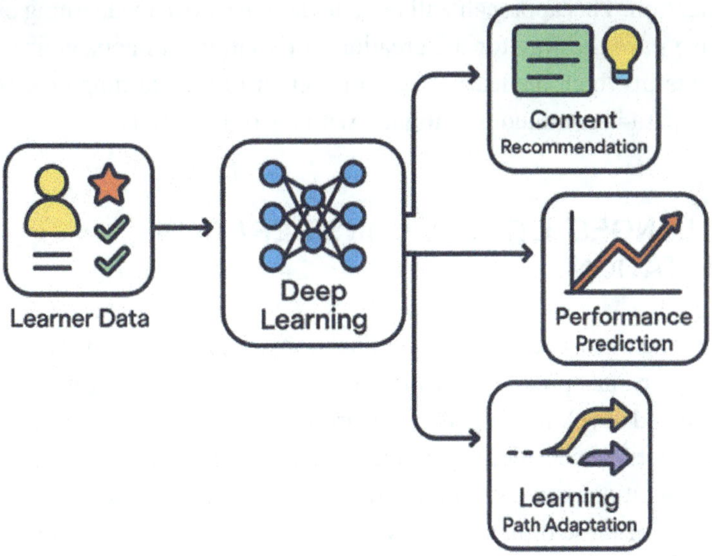


In this figure, the process of personalizing learning paths using deep learning models is depicted. Data from learner interactions is fed into deep models, and after analysis, three main outputs are sent as feedback to the educational system, including content recommendations, performance predictions, and learning path adjustments. In this cycle, deep learning algorithms are at the heart of the analysis process, and each step from data to output is based on intelligent and continuous analysis.

From a technical perspective, one of the main advantages of deep learning models in this area is the ability to process unstructured data such as text, images, and audio. This feature allows educational systems to include a variety of data, including learner notes, conversations, interactions in educational networks, and even non-verbal activities, in the analysis and personalization process. As a result, deep learning-based recommendation and analysis models can provide a more comprehensive and realistic picture of learner behavior and educational needs (Baleja, 2024).

Despite these extensive capabilities, the use of deep learning models in personalizing education also comes with challenges. One of the most important of these is the need for a large volume of high-quality data to train the models. In addition, the interpretability of deep model results and ensuring ethical considerations in the use of learner data are among the sensitive issues in this area. Therefore, the proper design of analytical frameworks, compliance with ethical principles, and ensuring data protection are undeniable necessities in implementing this approach.

Finally, the use of deep learning models in personalizing learning paths has opened a new window towards the development of intelligent, adaptive, and data-driven education. This approach will not only help improve the learning experience but will also pave the way for the creation of dynamic and personalized learning environments in which the learner is at the center of the learning process and the educational path is continuously aligned with his or her needs.

## 5- CHALLENGES, ETHICAL CONSIDERATIONS, AND LIMITATIONS

The growing use of deep learning in educational data analysis and personalization of learning paths has provided significant opportunities for improving the quality of education and developing intelligent learning systems. However, the use of these technologies without considering the challenges, ethical considerations, and technical and social limitations can have unintended consequences. In this regard, a detailed understanding of these dimensions is essential for any sustainable development in the field of data-driven education.

One of the fundamental challenges in the application of deep learning models in education is the strong dependence of these models on extensive and high-quality data. Deep learning, by its nature, requires a large volume of diverse and accurate educational data for training and optimizing models. In many cases, access to such data in educational environments is difficult, and the available data may be incomplete, scattered, or unbalanced (Nozari & Edalatpanah, 2023). This can lead to reduced accuracy of models, introducing unwanted biases, and reducing the generalizability of results to real-world environments.

Another issue is the technical complexity of deep learning models. These models often require powerful computational infrastructures, high processing resources, and extensive storage capacity. Providing such infrastructure is challenging, especially in underserved educational environments or public education systems, and can create operational and cost barriers to deploying intelligent educational systems (Ullah, Hashim, Bandeali, & Akbar, 2025).

From an ethical perspective, one of the main concerns is the issue of protecting learner privacy. In the process of collecting, storing, and analyzing educational data, sensitive and personal information of learners is exposed to processing, especially in online environments. Failure to comply with ethical principles and privacy standards can lead to violations of individual rights, loss of user trust, and even legal consequences. For this reason, ensuring data security and obtaining informed consent from learners before using their information is a fundamental requirement of any analytics project in the field of education (Nozari, Szmelter-Jarosz, & Rahmaty, 2024).

In addition to privacy, the issue of transparency and interpretability of deep learning models is another serious ethical consideration. Due to their complex and nonlinear structure, deep models are often considered black boxes, whose decision-making process is difficult for end users or even developers to understand. This is especially important in the field of education, where decisions based on data analysis can affect the academic fate and educational opportunities of individuals. The lack of transparency in the performance of models can lead to a decrease in the trust of teachers, parents, and learners themselves in intelligent educational systems (Rahmaty & Nozari, 2023).

*Figure 3. Challenges, ethical considerations, and limitations of using deep learning in education*

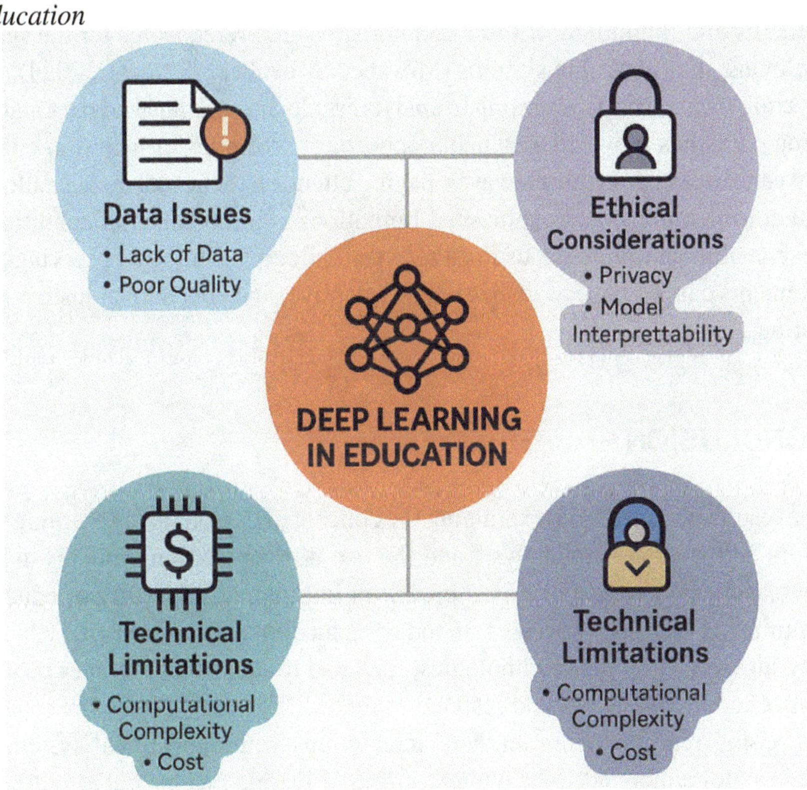


This figure graphically illustrates three main challenges: data issues including data scarcity and poor quality, technical constraints including computational complexity and cost, and ethical considerations including privacy and model interpretability. Each of these challenges is represented by a colored icon in the diagram, highlighting their relevance to the application of deep learning in education.

In addition to the aforementioned, another important limitation is the issue of algorithmic bias in deep learning models. Training data often reflects social, cultural, or institutional biases, and deep learning models may reinforce these biases in their learning process. As a result, the outputs of these models may unintentionally reproduce existing inequalities and create unequal educational opportunities. Addressing this challenge requires designing bias-sensitive models and employing bias-correction methods in the algorithm training process (Stasolla et al., 2025).

Finally, the issue of user acceptance and trust in deep learning-based systems is also a major challenge. Learners, teachers, and educational administrators may resist the use of data analytics and personalized recommender systems due to lack of familiarity with the technology or concerns about possible consequences. Creating a data-driven culture in educational systems, educating users, and clearly explaining the benefits and limitations of these technologies are prerequisites for the success of deploying smart learning systems (Movahed, Movahed, & Nozari, 2024).

Overall, the use of deep learning in analyzing educational data and personalizing learning paths has provided a valuable opportunity for transformation in contemporary educational systems. However, paying attention to the technical challenges, ethical considerations, and operational limitations is a fundamental condition for the responsible and effective use of these technologies. Only by observing these requirements can we hope to realize smart, adaptive, and educational justice-based education.

## 6- CONCLUSION

The results obtained from examining the concept of personalizing learning paths based on educational data analysis and the use of deep learning models indicate the increasing importance of this approach in improving the quality of education and optimizing learning processes. In today's educational environments, which are heavily influenced by new technologies, the need to understand learner behavior, recognize individual needs, and respond to their differences is felt more than ever before. Using real data from learners' interactions with educational systems not only allows for a more accurate understanding of learning paths, but also creates a platform for designing timely and effective educational interventions.

Deep learning, as one of the most important tools for analyzing complex data, has demonstrated unparalleled capacity in identifying behavioral patterns, predicting learner performance, and providing personalized educational recommendations. The ability of these models to process big data, analyze nonlinear relationships, and infer from diverse data has led them to be used as the core of many intelligent educational systems. Deep learning models are able to extract learning behaviors from raw data, identify hidden trends, and based on them, suggest optimal educational decisions. This ability, especially in online and virtual learning environments, plays a key role in improving the effectiveness of education and increasing learner motivation.

One of the important achievements of this research is to clarify the synergistic effect of educational data analysis and deep models in the development of personalized learning systems. Analyzing learner behavioral data along with the use of deep learning can lead to the formation of unique learning paths for each individual; a path that is not only tailored to their individual capabilities and needs, but is also dynamically and continuously updated during the learning process. This view is a far cry from traditional approaches to education, where all learners are guided within a fixed, predetermined framework.

At the same time, the analyses conducted in this study show that the effective implementation of personalized deep learning-based systems requires facing serious challenges in technical, data, and ethical dimensions. The quality and quantity of educational data is a critical factor in the proper functioning of deep learning models. Incomplete or biased data can lead to inaccurate results and, in some cases, even reproduce educational inequalities. For this reason, ensuring data quality and applying rigorous analytical approaches is essential to ensure the correct functioning of these systems.

On the other hand, ethical considerations, especially in the area of protecting learner privacy, have become one of the main concerns in the use of data-based technologies. The collection, analysis, and use of educational data must be carried out within the framework of specific rules, with the informed consent of learners, and in compliance with standards of transparency and interpretability. If these principles are not observed, user trust in intelligent educational systems will decrease and the adoption of these technologies will face serious resistance.

Also, the study conducted on the technical limitations of deep learning shows that the need for advanced computational infrastructure, processing costs, and the complexity of implementing models can create obstacles to the widespread use of these approaches in some educational environments, especially in underserved areas. Therefore, the development of technological infrastructure and the adoption of cost-effective solutions are considered essential for the sustainable implementation of these approaches.

In summary, it can be concluded that personalizing learning paths based on educational data analysis and deep learning not only provides an opportunity to improve the quality of teaching and learning, but also paves the way for the creation of smart and adaptive educational environments. But fully realizing these capacities requires a combination of technical knowledge, ethical approaches, and appropriate infrastructure. The future of smart education depends on the responsible, informed, and scientific use of data and new technologies; a future in which the learner is not recognized as a passive unit but as the main axis of the learning process, and all components of the educational system will be designed and guided to respond to his or her real needs.

## REFERENCES


Aliahmadi, A., Ghahremani-Nahr, J., & Nozari, H. (2023). Pricing decisions in the closed-loop supply chain network, taking into account the queuing system in production centers. *Expert Systems with Applications*, *212*, 118741. DOI: 10.1016/j.eswa.2022.118741

Aliahmadi, A., & Nozari, H. (2023, January). Evaluation of security metrics in AIoT and blockchain-based supply chain by Neutrosophic decision-making method. In Supply chain forum: an international journal (Vol. 24, No. 1, pp. 31-42). Taylor & Francis. DOI: 10.1080/16258312.2022.2101898

Aliahmadi, A., Nozari, H., Ghahremani-Nahr, J., & Szmelter-Jarosz, A. (2022). Evaluation of key impression of resilient supply chain based on artificial intelligence of things (AIoT). arXiv preprint arXiv:2207.13174.

Baleja, K. (2024, July). Exploring the Efficacy of Personalized Learning Pathways Utilizing Artificial Intelligence in Education. In EdMedia+ Innovate Learning (pp. 157-161). Association for the Advancement of Computing in Education (AACE).

Bathaee, M., Nozari, H., & Szmelter-Jarosz, A. (2023). Designing a new location-allocation and routing model with simultaneous pick-up and delivery in a closed-loop supply chain network under uncertainty. *Logistics (Basel)*, *7*(1), 3. DOI: 10.3390/logistics7010003

Dwivedi, D. N., Mahanty, G., & nath Dwivedi, V. (2024). The role of predictive analytics in personalizing education: tailoring learning paths for individual student success. In Enhancing Education With Intelligent Systems and Data-Driven Instruction (pp. 44-59). IGI Global Scientific Publishing.

Ghahremani-Nahr, J., Nozari, H., & Aliahmadi, A. (2023). Contract Design for Return Products in a Cooperative Closed-Loop Supply Chain. *Global Business Review*, •••, 09721509221148892. DOI: 10.1177/09721509221148892

Lotfi, F. H. Z., Najafi, S. E., & Nozari, H. (Eds.). (2016). *Data envelopment analysis and effective performance assessment*. IGI Global.

Movahed, A. B., Aliahmadi, A., Parsanejad, M., & Nozari, H. (2023). A systematic review of collaboration in supply chain 4.0 with meta-synthesis method. *Supply Chain Analytics*, *4*, 100052. DOI: 10.1016/j.sca.2023.100052

Movahed, A. B., Movahed, A. B., & Nozari, H. (2024). Marketing 6.0 Conceptualization. In Advanced Businesses in Industry 6.0 (pp. 15-31). IGI Global Scientific Publishing.

Naseer, F., Khan, M. N., Tahir, M., Addas, A., & Aejaz, S. H. (2024). Integrating deep learning techniques for personalized learning pathways in higher education. *Heliyon, 10*(11), e32628. DOI: 10.1016/j.heliyon.2024.e32628 PMID: 38961899

Ning, J., Ma, Z., Yao, J., Wang, Q., & Zhang, B. (2025). Personalized learning supported by learning analytics: A systematic review of functions, pathways, and educational outcomes. *Interactive Learning Environments*, •••, 1–23. DOI: 10.1080/10494820.2025.2478437

Nozari, H. (Ed.). (2023). *Building Smart and Sustainable Businesses with Transformative Technologies*. IGI Global. DOI: 10.4018/979-8-3693-0210-1

Nozari, H. (2024). Green supply chain management based on artificial intelligence of everything. *Journal of Economics and Management, 46*, 171–188. DOI: 10.22367/jem.2024.46.07

Nozari, H., & Chobar, A. P. (2024). The Dimensions and Components of Marketing 5.0: Introduction to Marketing 6.0. In Advanced Businesses in Industry 6.0 (pp. 75-86). IGI Global Scientific Publishing.

Nozari, H., & Edalatpanah, S. A. (2023). Smart systems risk management in IoT-based supply chain. In *Advances in reliability, failure and risk analysis* (pp. 251–268). Springer Nature Singapore. DOI: 10.1007/978-981-19-9909-3_11

Nozari, H., Fallah, M., Szmelter-Jarosz, A., & Krzemiński, M. (2021). Analysis of security criteria for IoT-based supply chain: a case study of FMCG industries. Central European Management Journal, 29(4).

Nozari, H., Szmelter-Jarosz, A., & Rahmaty, M. (2024). Smart marketing based on artificial intelligence of things (AIoT) and Blockchain and evaluating critical success factors. In *Smart and Sustainable Interactive Marketing* (pp. 68–82). IGI Global Scientific Publishing. DOI: 10.4018/979-8-3693-1339-8.ch005

Nozari, H., Tavakkoli-Moghaddam, R., & Dolgui, A. (2024, September). Analysis of Critical Success Factors of Sustainable and Resilient Aioe-based Supply Chain in Industry 5.0. In IFIP International Conference on Advances in Production Management Systems (pp. 76-90). Cham: Springer Nature Switzerland. DOI: 10.1007/978-3-031-65894-5_6

Patil, S. (2025). AI-driven personalized learning paths in MOOCS: Optimizing engagement and outcomes in digital education. In *Digital Transformation and Sustainability of Business* (pp. 387–395). CRC Press. DOI: 10.1201/9781003606185-90

Rahmaty, M., & Nozari, H. (2023). Optimization of the hierarchical supply chain in the pharmaceutical industry. *Edelweiss Applied Science and Technology*, *7*(2), 104–123. DOI: 10.55214/25768484.v7i2.376

Reddy, V. K., Said, L., Sengupta, B., Chetlur, M., Costantino, J. P., Gopinath, A., Flynt, S., Balunaini, P., & Vedula, S. (2015). Personalized Learning Pathways: Enabling intervention creation and tracking. *IBM Journal of Research and Development*, *59*(6), 4–1. DOI: 10.1147/JRD.2015.2456711

Stasolla, F., Zullo, A., Maniglio, R., Passaro, A., Di Gioia, M., Curcio, E., & Martini, E. (2025). Deep Learning and Reinforcement Learning for Assessing and Enhancing Academic Performance in University Students: A Scoping Review. *AI*, *6*(2), 40. DOI: 10.3390/ai6020040

Sumathy, V., & Navamani, G. (2024). AI-Driven Personalized Learning: Enhancing Student Success through Adaptive Technologies. Library of Progress-Library Science, Information Technology & Computer, 44(3).

Taylor, R., Fakhimi, M., Ioannou, A., & Spanaki, K. (2024). Personalized learning in education: A machine learning and simulation approach. *Benchmarking*. Advance online publication. DOI: 10.1108/BIJ-06-2023-0380

Ullah, R. S., Hashim, F., Bandcali, M. M., & Akbar, A. (2025). Artificial Intelligence in Curriculum Design a Roadmap for Adaptive and Personalized Learning in Higher Education. *The Critical Review of Social Sciences Studies*, *3*(3), 304–322. DOI: 10.59075/8j71b437

Xia, Y., Shin, S. Y., & Shin, K. S. (2024). Designing personalized learning paths for foreign language acquisition using big data: Theoretical and empirical analysis. *Applied Sciences (Basel, Switzerland)*, *14*(20), 9506. DOI: 10.3390/app14209506

Yekollu, R. K., Bhimraj Ghuge, T., Sunil Biradar, S., Haldikar, S. V., & Farook Mohideen Abdul Kader, O. (2024, February). AI-driven personalized learning paths: Enhancing education through adaptive systems. In International Conference on Smart data intelligence (pp. 507-517). Singapore: Springer Nature Singapore. DOI: 10.1007/978-981-97-3191-6_38

Yuan[1], L., Hou[1], B., Feng, D., & Rahman[1], S. S. A. (2025, June). Predictive Analytics in Education: Leveraging Al for Personalizing Student Learning Trajectories. In Proceedings of the 2nd International Conference on Educational Development and Social Sciences (EDSS 2025) (Vol. 924, p. 309). Springer Nature.

# Chapter 6
# Self-Evolving Neuromorphic Systems for Predictive Learning Interventions

**Hamed Nozari**
http://orcid.org/0000-0002-6500-6708
*Azad University UAE, Dubai, UAE*

## ABSTRACT

*This research presents a novel framework for learning analysis based on self-evolving neuromorphic systems that is capable of real-time prediction and intervention in the learning process. By combining impulse neural networks and evolutionary algorithms, the proposed model was able to significantly increase the accuracy of prediction and personalization of interventions. Simulation results showed that this approach has a more stable performance in detecting cognitive disorders and adjusting intervention compared to static models. This system can be used as a basis for the development of future intelligent educational tools.*

## 1- INTRODUCTION

In the era of digital transformation, educational systems are increasingly faced with big data, complex learner behaviors, and the growing need for personalization. Learning analytics, as an interdisciplinary branch in this field, attempts to extract effective patterns in the learning process by utilizing behavioral, cognitive, and contextual data and transform them into targeted and effective interventions. However, while conventional learning analytics tools are mainly designed based on traditional

DOI: 10.4018/979-8-3373-5117-9.ch006

ght © 2026, IGI Global Scientific Publishing. Copying or distributing in print or electronic forms without written permission of IGI Global Scientific Publishing is prohibited. Use of this chapter to generative artificial intelligence (AI) technologies is expressly prohibited. The publisher reserves all rights to license its use for generative AI training and machine learning model development.

machine learning algorithms and statistical methods, they face challenges such as real-time processing, high consumption of computational resources, and inability to adapt structurally to dynamic data (Herodotou et al., 2020).

In the meantime, approaches based on neuromorphic computing, inspired by the structure of the human brain, provide unique capacities for processing educational data at a deep, fast, and low-energy level. Neuromorphic architectures, especially spiking neural networks (SNNs), unlike conventional artificial networks, are able to operate on temporal events and transient patterns and exploit local learning rules such as STDP (Cogliano et al., 2022). These features not only enable real-time and adaptive analysis, but also make them an attractive option for designing educational intervention systems with real-time performance and high sensitivity to changes in learner behavior.

Given the inherent complexities of learner behavior, including cognitive changes, motivational fluctuations, and multifaceted interactions with content and other users, an effective learning analytics system must be able to dynamically adapt to environmental and individual changes. This requires designing systems that are not only able to predict critical moments in the learning process, but also able to optimize their internal structure in response to new data. The concept of "self-correcting learning" in this context enables the design of such systems; systems that become more effective in predicting and intervening over time by continuously learning from past experiences and continuously modifying their decision-making path (Aliahmadi & Nozari, 2023).

The integration of these two approaches—neuromorphic computing and self-correcting learning—opens a new path in the design of intelligent educational systems. In this path, any interaction-based data from the learner (e.g., response time, level of hesitation, type of error, or interruption patterns) is considered as input to a neuromorphic model that evolves over time. Instead of following static patterns, such a system can continuously and instantaneously align its structure with observed behaviors and provide targeted, personalized, and precise interventions. These interventions can include recommending new content, issuing warnings to the teacher, or suggesting pauses and revisions to the learner; All of them rely on mechanisms inspired by the human brain (Nozari, Ghahremani-Nahr, & Szmelter-Jarosz, 2024).

A key advantage of this approach is the ability to deploy at the edge of the network, where data is processed on local devices such as tablets, wearables, or even augmented reality glasses. This not only helps to increase the speed of analysis and response, but also greatly alleviates privacy concerns. In addition, architectures based on memristors and bio-inspired units significantly reduce the power consumption of these types of systems, which is a critical advantage in long-term applications or resource-constrained environments (Nozari, Szmelter-Jarosz, & Ghahremani-Nahr, 2021).

Furthermore, the self-learning nature of the system allows the model to be individually adjusted over time based on the specific data of each learner. As a result, the level of personalization will be far beyond traditional methods, because this personalization is not only based on initial static characteristics but also on the learner's evolution over time (Aliahmadi et al., 2022). In such an environment, the system can identify potential learning failure behaviors even before performance declines occur and correct the learning path through proactive interventions.

Therefore, research on "self-evolving neuromorphic systems for predictive learning interventions" is not only an attempt to incorporate new technologies in the service of education, but also a fundamental step towards bringing educational systems closer to the natural mechanisms of the human mind. This chapter will begin with the aim of comprehensively reviewing this approach and presenting a conceptual model, and will continue with structural analysis, algorithm design, simulation, and examination of advantages and challenges, providing the reader with a deeper understanding of the future prospects of this field (Smith, Lange, & Huston, 2012).

## 2- THEORETICAL BACKGROUND

As digital learning environments become dynamic, diverse, and complex, traditional static machine learning models face limitations in responding to these developments in real time. Most of these models require manual retraining, initial feature definition by experts, and heavy central processing. Therefore, the need for architectures that can interact naturally with event-driven and distributed data is more than ever felt. This is where neuromorphic computing comes in (Fallah & Nozari, 2021).

Neuromorphic computing is inspired by the structure and dynamics of the human brain and aims to create systems that process information using spikes, similar to the biological nervous system. Rather than being based on continuous times or numerical values, this processing is based on discrete events and therefore only operates when new and meaningful information is received. This reduces energy consumption, increases response speed, and improves fault tolerance (Nozari, Ghahremani-Nahr, & Szmelter-Jarosz, 2023). Models such as spike-timing neural networks (SNNs) use local learning rules such as spike-timing dependent plasticity to adjust their neural connections over time without the need for global retraining.

Another advantage of neuromorphic over conventional deep learning methods is their ability to run on decentralized hardware such as wearables, mobile phones, or educational sensors. This feature paves the way for distributed and privacy-preserving architectures in learning. Furthermore, neuromorphic models are able to interact with real-time data streams, which is a key requirement for designing predictive interventions (Wolff et al., 2014).

Along this path, the concept of self-evolving systems is introduced as a new generation of intelligent systems that have the ability to dynamically adapt their structure to the environment. Unlike static learning models, self-learning systems not only change their weights or coefficients, but also are able to grow, delete, or reconfigure units at the network structure level. This feature provides significant flexibility in the face of noisy, incomplete, or irregular data and leads to increased performance stability in the face of dynamic environments (Nozari, Fallah, Szmelter-Jarosz, & Krzemiński, 2021). In the field of education, this ability means creating a model that continuously learns from past experiences and optimizes its intervention strategy.

*Figure 1. Conceptual framework of a self-evolving neuromorphic system for predictive educational interventions*

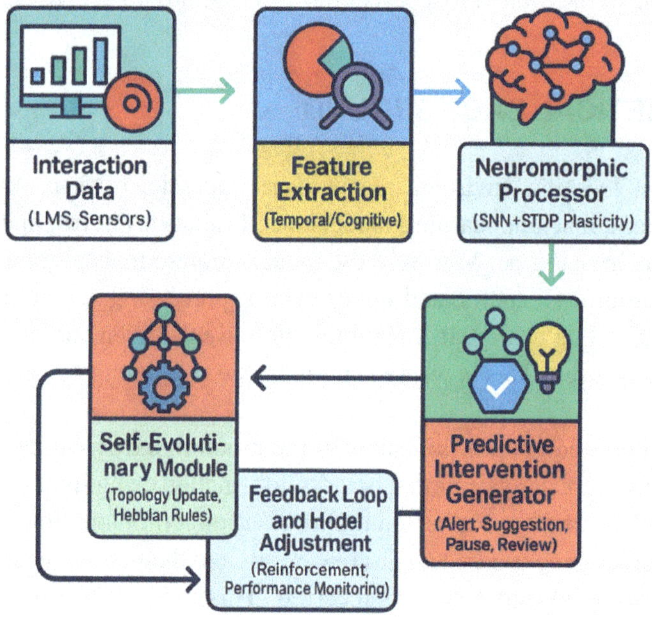


In this model, first, training data is collected through interaction with the system or biosensors (such as EEG or hand pressure). Then, the feature extraction module converts this data into suitable formats for input into the neuromorphic network. Within this network, impulse processing is performed and based on the results, patterns of weakness, decline or need for intervention are identified. Using its evolutionary structure, the system automatically adjusts the predictive rules and selects the appropriate type of intervention. Feedback from this intervention is also included in the model's learning cycle and improves the process (Herodotou et al., 2019).

Such a structure paves the way for systems that can respond to behavioral changes in learners in an automatic, fast, low-power and personalized manner and suggest intelligent interventions to correct the learning path before performance decline occurs.

## 3- CONCEPTUAL FRAMEWORK

The conceptual framework proposed in this chapter is a creative fusion of three previous theoretical foundations: learning analytics, neuromorphic computing, and self-evolving systems. The goal of this framework is to design a system that not only has the ability to identify critical moments in the learning process, but also can automatically rearrange its internal structure based on feedback and new data, and ultimately provide personalized, effective, and real-time interventions. Relying on architectures inspired by the human brain, this model has the ability to provide a live and continuous picture of the cognitive state of the learner by receiving behavioral, cognitive, and environmental signals from the learner and continuously improve its performance (Brooks & Greer, 2014).

In the first step, the user's real-time interactions with the learning system (whether it is test responses, reading speed, level of interaction with multimedia content, or physiological signals such as blink rate, heart rate, or brain waves) are recorded through connected devices such as LMS, wearable sensors, smart cameras, or brain-computer interfaces. These data cannot be analyzed in their raw form; therefore, a feature extraction module is responsible for transforming these data into variables that can be used at the cognitive level by relying on signal processing methods. These features may include reaction time, error sequence, attention dispersion, study pattern, or cognitive load indicators (Nozari, Tavakkoli-Moghaddam, & Gharemani-Nahr, 2022).

The output of the feature extraction module enters the main part of the system, the "neuromorphic processor." This module operates based on impulse neural networks that analyze data in an event-driven manner using biological learning rules such as STDP. The special feature of these networks is their ability to respond to instantaneous changes and sensitivity to the temporal sequence of data. Unlike classical models that require extensive retraining, these models learn and change the connection weights between neurons in real time. As a result, they will have a fast and dynamic response to analyze sudden changes in the learner's behavior (for example, a sudden decrease in concentration or a sudden drop in performance) (Susnjak, 2024).

The next stage in this framework is dedicated to the "self-improvement module". In this section, the system not only modifies its connection weights, but is also able to dynamically rebuild the network structure. This means that when faced with new data or unexpected behaviors, it can add new neurons, remove or replace some paths, and generally optimize the internal connection map. This evolutionary capability is realized by utilizing Hebb's rules and evolutionary algorithms inspired by biology, allowing the system to build its own unique structure over time based on each user's learning patterns (Nozari, Abdi, & Jahangard, 2025).

From these analyses, a module called the "Predictive Intervention Generator" uses these analyses to generate the best possible intervention in real time, given the output of the neuromorphic system and the updated structure of the model. This intervention can take the form of a soft warning to the learner, a content suggestion, a temporary pause, a complementary activity, or a signal to the teacher. The choice of the type of intervention is made based on the severity and type of impairment identified in the learning process, and its goal is to immediately improve the learning conditions before entering a phase of serious performance decline (Dyagilev & Saria, 2016).

Finally, a feedback loop is designed so that the system learns from the results of its interventions. If the intervention leads to improved performance or focus, this reinforcement is fed back to the model and strengthens its structure; And if the intervention is ineffective, corrections are made to the analysis path. This mechanism injects reinforcement learning into the system and allows the model to dynamically improve its performance under different conditions (Movahed, Aliahmadi, Parsanejad, & Nozari, 2023).

To better understand this mechanism, Figure 2 is designed to visually display the data flow and various modules of the system. In this diagram, colored icons and arrow paths clearly show the flow of information from the moment of learner interaction to the final intervention and model correction. Each section is marked with a specific color and its functional relationship with other components is precisely drawn.

*Figure 2. Operational model of a self-evolving neuromorphic system for predictive learning interventions*

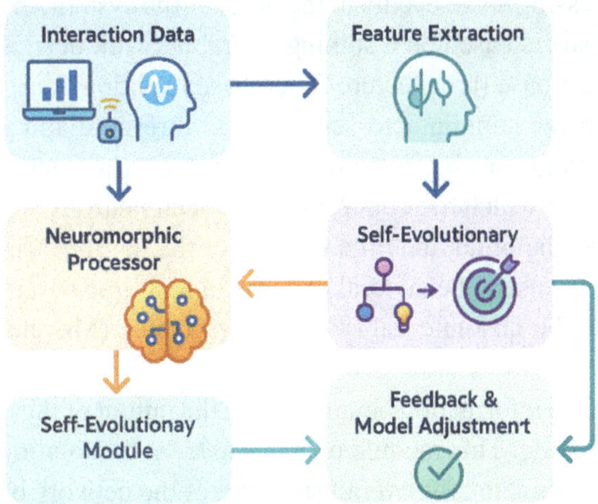


This framework is designed not only to increase the accuracy of educational interventions, but also has the ability to run in distance learning platforms, smart classrooms, and educational wearable devices, by utilizing low-power and adaptable architectures.

## 4- SYSTEM MODELING AND ALGORITHMIC DESIGN

Modeling a self-evolving neuromorphic system for predictive learning interventions is based on the conceptual framework outlined in the previous section and aims to translate the conceptual architecture into an operationally implementable system. This modeling involves designing the internal structure of each module, defining the precise data flow, and specifying the algorithms that manage the learning, adaptation, and decision-making mechanisms in the system. The proposed approach combines impulse neural networks, biological learning logic, and evolutionary algorithms for structural reconfiguration that together create a self-regulating and real-time system (Nozari, 2025).

In the first step, the raw data of the learner interaction consists of a set of temporal, cognitive, and behavioral parameters that are received at a certain rate (e.g., every 3 seconds) from various sources such as a learning management system, wearable sensors, or eye movement recording. This data is fed into the preprocessing module and, after noise removal, normalization, and extraction of key features such as average response time, number of consecutive errors, or sudden drops in interaction speed, is prepared as standard input vectors for the next stage (Zhai et al., 2025).

The main processing stage occurs in the heart of the system, the "neuromorphic processor". This part is based on a spiking neural network designed with neurons operating with a time-based architecture (Time-based Spiking Neurons). Each neuron is activated only if the stimulus crosses a certain threshold and within a specific time pattern. The main learning rule in this network is "time-dependent plasticity" (STDP), according to which the connections between neurons are strengthened or weakened based on the order and time interval of the neurons' firing. In this way, the network analyzes users' behavioral patterns in real time based on the temporal sequence, not just the absolute values of the variables (Movahed, Movahed, & Nozari, 2024).

After this step, the information obtained from the output of the neurons is sent to an evolutionary module. This module operates as a "self-evolutionary model" and is responsible for optimizing the overall structure of the network based on previous feedback. Algorithms such as simplified natural selection, structural mutation, and neuron assimilation are used in this section to adapt the topology of the neuromorphic network to the specific conditions of each learner over time. For example, if a recurring but emerging behavioral pattern is detected in the input data, this module will be able to create a new neuron to understand and process that pattern and combine it with the current paths of the network. The final structure will be an adaptive and living memory that creates a separate learning path for each user (Jin et al., 2024).

The output of the evolutionary module is sent to the decision-making engine for intervention. In this section, the system decides whether an intervention is needed by comparing the learner's current state with predefined optimal patterns (e.g., desired concentration state, natural study rhythm, or balanced interaction distribution). If critical thresholds such as severe attention lapses, severe cognitive fluctuations, or a pattern of consecutive interaction failures are detected, the intervention engine activates one of the pre-designed options. These options can include a warning message, a recommendation to take a break, a suggestion for a side activity, or notification to the teacher (Nozari, 2025).

At the end of the cycle, an intelligent feedback module is designed that monitors the learner's reaction to the intervention. If performance improves after the intervention, this information is fed into the system as positive reinforcement, making the model structure more stable in its current state. However, if the situation worsens or remains unchanged, the model is automatically readjusted to avoid similar interventions in the future. This process is considered a form of adaptive reinforcement learning, integrated into the neuromorphic framework (Baxter et al., 2019).

Figure 3 is designed to graphically represent the information flow in this system. This colorful diagram includes data paths, visual symbols for each module, and the dynamic connectivity between components. A brain symbol for neuromorphic, a target symbol for intervention, a brain diagram for interactive data, and adaptive gears for the evolutionary module are used to make abstract concepts tangible for the reader.

*Figure 3. Algorithmic model of a self-evolving neuromorphic system for real-time educational interventions*

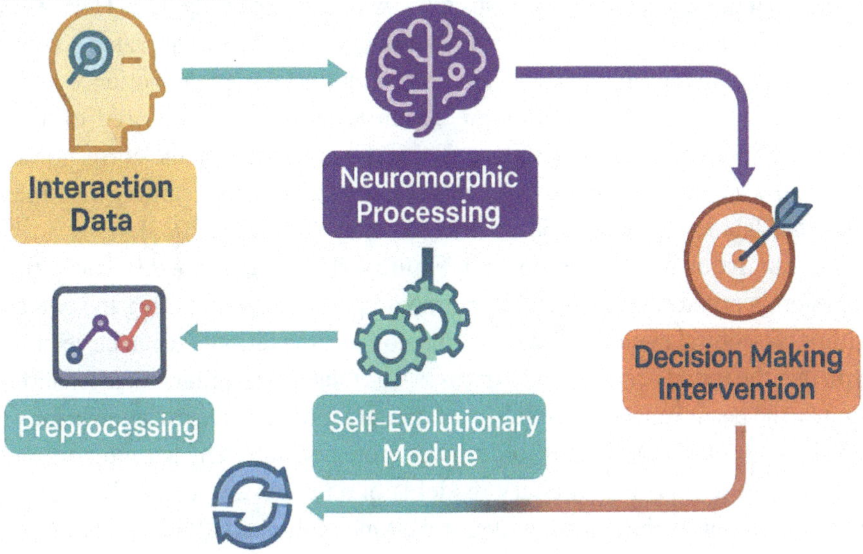


Overall, by linking temporal learning, structural evolution, and predictive decision-making, this model provides a system that is capable of providing accurate, personalized, and effective interventions in dynamic educational contexts with limited resources and the need for rapid analysis.

## 5- SIMULATION AND INITIAL EVALUATION

To practically investigate the performance of the proposed self-evolving neuromorphic system, an initial simulation was designed to evaluate the model's ability to detect critical moments in the learning process and improve the accuracy of predictive interventions over time. This simulation was conducted using a combination of real and semi-synthetic data to test both the dynamics of learner behavior under varying conditions and the system's response to feedback (Nozari & Edalatpanah, 2023).

The data used included interactions of 60 hypothetical learners on an online learning platform, in which indicators such as response time to questions, success rate, level of interaction with content, concentration level (based on eye movement), and motivation level (through hand pressure on the touch device) were recorded in a timed manner. This data was simulated periodically (every 10 seconds) for each learner over a 45-minute period, and patterns of performance decline, decreased concentration, and increased cognitive load were considered as gradual or sudden (Nozari, Abdi, & Rafiei, 2025).

Initially, the neuromorphic model was run without the self-evolutionary module activated. In this case, the network structure was fixed and only the STDP rule was used to adjust the weights. Next, the evolutionary module was activated so that the network could reconfigure its structure based on the learner's experience and past errors. At each step, the system's prediction accuracy was measured to identify appropriate moments for intervention. The main criterion was the correspondence between the system's detection time and the actual time of the learning disturbance, which was labeled by human observers (Rahmaty & Nozari, 2023).

The simulation results are shown in Figure 4. This graph shows the evolution of the system's prediction accuracy over time; in particular, comparing the two cases "without structural evolution" and "with automatic evolution". It can be seen in the graph that the initial accuracy in both cases was relatively similar, but after about 15 minutes, the performance of the self-evolutionary model increased significantly and the ability to detect cognitive disorders was more accurate. The learning process of the system in the self-evolutionary model is of an ascending and stabilizing type; while in the non-evolutionary model, it becomes saturated after a short period of time and no noticeable progress is observed (Mudawi et al., 2023).

*Figure 4. Evolution of the system's accuracy in predicting optimal intervention over time*

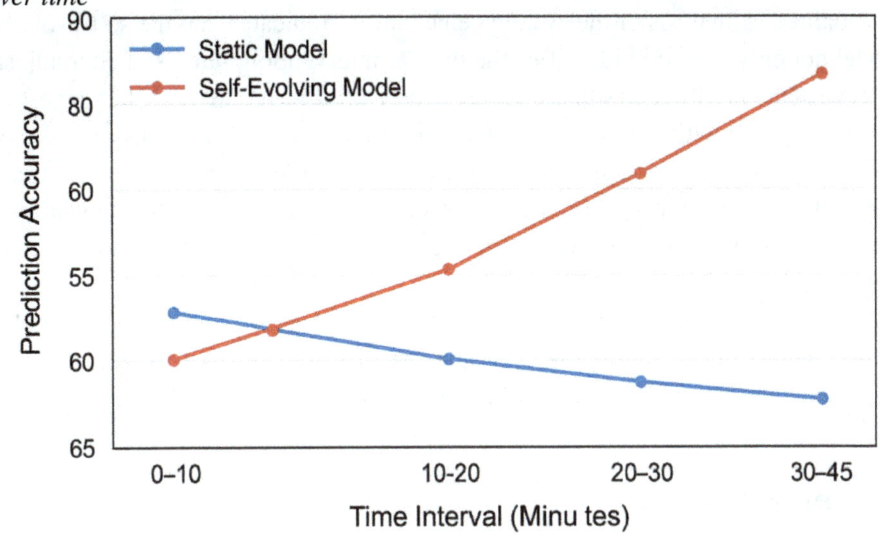


To complete this analysis, Table 1 compares the system's prediction accuracy over different time periods. This table shows that in the early time periods, there is not much difference between the two models; but later on, the evolutionary system has shown much more stable performance. Especially in the 30-45 minute period, when the learner's behavior becomes more complex and fluctuating, the self-evolving model has predicted the appropriate time for intervention more accurately.

*Table 1. Comparison of prediction accuracy in models without evolution and with auto-evolution*

| Time Interval (Minutes) | Prediction Accuracy (Static Model) [%] | Prediction Accuracy (Self-Evolving Model) [%] |
|---|---|---|
| 0–10 | 68.2 | 69.1 |
| 10–20 | 70.6 | 75.4 |
| 20–30 | 69.3 | 81.7 |
| 30–45 | 65.9 | 86.2 |

These results indicate that the proposed self-evolving system is able to gain a deeper understanding of the specific characteristics of each learner over time and, as a result, provide more accurate, timely, and personalized interventions. On the other hand, static models, despite acceptable initial ability, suffer from performance degradation when faced with more complex situations and require manual retraining (Nozari, Abdi, & Szmelter-Jarosz, 2025).

Qualitative analysis of the system behavior also indicates that the self-evolving model not only correctly identifies the time of intervention, but also better adjusts the type of intervention. In situations where motivation has decreased, the suggestion of a variety-generating activity has been more effective, and in cases of attention loss, the provision of concentration exercises has been more efficient. This accuracy in selection has been a direct result of the structural adaptation of the network and the optimization of its internal connections to the individual behavioral pattern (Kumar et al., 2022).

Overall, the findings of this simulation prove that combining neuromorphic computing and self-evolving systems can be an effective step towards transforming learning analysis methods and educational interventions.

## 6- CONCLUSION

The results of this research show that the integration of neuromorphic computing concepts and self-evolving systems in the field of learning analytics can open a new horizon in the field of designing predictive educational intervention systems. By using impulse neural networks and temporal mechanisms in analyzing behavioral and cognitive data of learners, a deeper understanding of the learning process of individuals is provided, and accordingly, decision-making for intervention is transformed from a static and general state to an intelligent, dynamic and individual-centered mechanism. Especially in digital educational environments where learner behavior is highly nonlinear and affected by momentary conditions, the necessity of using a system that has the capability of structural adaptation and real-time analysis is doubled.

In the simulation process, it was also observed that, compared to static models, the proposed system with a self-evolving structure is able to not only increase its prediction accuracy over time, but also adjust the type of intervention more accurately to the learner's actual needs through its internal and dynamic adjustments. This feature plays a vital role, especially in longer time periods when learner behavioral patterns fluctuate and change. The results of the performance evaluation graphs and tables also confirmed that the self-evolving model has a more stable, intelligent, and personalized performance in the final stages of the learning process than the static model. One of the important achievements of this research is to demonstrate the capacity of neuromorphic architectures to run on edge platforms; meaning that with low energy consumption and high processing speed, such systems can be implemented in wearable devices, smart classrooms, and even distance learning platforms. This not only increases the autonomy of the system's operation, but also significantly strengthens the privacy concerns of the learner. Because many analyses can be performed locally, eliminating the need to send sensitive data to a central server.

In addition to the technical achievements, this research provides a basis for rethinking educational intervention models. If interventions are based on real, real-time, and analysis-driven behaviors, not only will their effectiveness increase, but they will also prevent the emergence of a sense of external control or imposition of content on the learner. In effect, the proposed system is upgraded from a mere educational system to an intelligent cognitive companion; a companion that seeks not to judge, but to understand and help more effectively learn.

However, it should be noted that deploying such a system on a real scale also faces challenges. First, the need to collect accurate and multifaceted data from learners requires specific technical and sensor infrastructure that may not be available in all educational settings. Second, the interpretation of the outputs of this system for teachers and instructional designers must be accompanied by a suitable user interface and understandable language so that they can effectively utilize it in educational decisions. Third, the discussion of ethics in real-time educational interventions requires clear guidelines to preserve agency, autonomy, and human dignity in the learning process.

In this regard, it is recommended that future studies examine the human, psychological, and social dimensions of this technology more comprehensively. Also, implementing prototypes in real educational settings and conducting field tests can pave the way for technical improvements, interactive design, and cultural adaptation of these systems. On the other hand, with the development of technologies such as Brain-Computer Interfaces and minimally invasive biological sensors, it will be possible to record more accurate signals of the mental and cognitive state of the learner, which can further increase the accuracy of the system analysis.

Overall, this research showed that the use of self-evolving neuromorphic systems can be considered as an innovative solution to promote the intelligentization of education. Such an approach will play an effective role not only in improving the individual learning process, but also in shaping a new generation of adaptive, flexible, and learner-aware educational environments. In the future, by evolving these systems and combining them with other technologies such as transfer learning, augmented reality, or educational digital twins, it will be possible to design environments that not only teach, but also understand, accompany, and participate in the learning process themselves.

## REFERENCES


Aliahmadi, A., & Nozari, H. (2023, January). Evaluation of security metrics in AIoT and blockchain-based supply chain by Neutrosophic decision-making method. In Supply chain forum: an international journal (Vol. 24, No. 1, pp. 31-42). Taylor & Francis. DOI: 10.1080/16258312.2022.2101898

Aliahmadi, A., Nozari, H., Ghahremani-Nahr, J., & Szmelter-Jarosz, A. (2022). Evaluation of key impression of resilient supply chain based on artificial intelligence of things (AIoT). arXiv preprint arXiv:2207.13174.

Baxter, S. L., Marks, C., Kuo, T. T., Ohno-Machado, L., & Weinreb, R. N. (2019). Machine learning-based predictive modeling of surgical intervention in glaucoma using systemic data from electronic health records. *American Journal of Ophthalmology*, *208*, 30–40. DOI: 10.1016/j.ajo.2019.07.005 PMID: 31323204

Brooks, C., & Greer, J. (2014, March). Explaining predictive models to learning specialists using personas. In *Proceedings of the fourth international conference on learning analytics and knowledge* (pp. 26-30). DOI: 10.1145/2567574.2567612

Cogliano, M., Bernacki, M. L., Hilpert, J. C., & Strong, C. L. (2022). A self-regulated learning analytics prediction-and-intervention design: Detecting and supporting struggling biology students. *Journal of Educational Psychology*, *114*(8), 1801–1816. DOI: 10.1037/edu0000745

Dyagilev, K., & Saria, S. (2016). Learning (predictive) risk scores in the presence of censoring due to interventions. *Machine Learning*, *102*(3), 323–348. DOI: 10.1007/s10994-015-5527-7

Fallah, M., & Nozari, H. (2021). Neutrosophic mathematical programming for optimization of multi-objective sustainable biomass supply chain network design. *Computer Modeling in Engineering & Sciences*, *129*(2), 927–951. DOI: 10.32604/cmes.2021.017511

Herodotou, C., Naydenova, G., Boroowa, A., Gilmour, A., & Rienties, B. (2020). How can predictive learning analytics and motivational interventions increase student retention and enhance administrative support in distance education? *Journal of Learning Analytics*, *7*(2), 72–83. DOI: 10.18608/jla.2020.72.4

Herodotou, C., Rienties, B., Boroowa, A., Zdrahal, Z., & Hlosta, M. (2019). A large-scale implementation of predictive learning analytics in higher education: The teachers' role and perspective. *Educational Technology Research and Development*, *67*(5), 1273–1306. DOI: 10.1007/s11423-019-09685-0

Jin, M., Zhou, Z., Li, M., & Lu, T. (2024). A Deep Learning-based Predictive Analytics Model for Remote Patient Monitoring and Early Intervention in Diabetes Care. Journal of Artificial Intelligence General science (JAIGS) ISSN: 3006-4023, 6(1), 479-491.

Kumar, M., Ang, L. T., Ho, C., Soh, S. E., Tan, K. H., Chan, J. K. Y., Godfrey, K. M., Chan, S.-Y., Chong, Y. S., Eriksson, J. G., Feng, M., & Karnani, N. (2022). Machine learning–derived prenatal predictive risk model to guide intervention and prevent the progression of gestational diabetes mellitus to type 2 diabetes: Prediction model development study. *JMIR Diabetes*, *7*(3), e32366. DOI: 10.2196/32366 PMID: 35788016

Movahed, A. B., Aliahmadi, A., Parsanejad, M., & Nozari, H. (2023). A systematic review of collaboration in supply chain 4.0 with meta-synthesis method. *Supply Chain Analytics*, *4*, 100052. DOI: 10.1016/j.sca.2023.100052

Movahed, A. B., Movahed, A. B., & Nozari, H. (2024). Opportunities and challenges of marketing 5.0. Smart and Sustainable Interactive Marketing, 1-21.

Mudawi, N. A., Pervaiz, M., Alabduallah, B. I., Alazeb, A., Alshahrani, A., Alotaibi, S. S., & Jalal, A. (2023). Predictive Analytics for Sustainable E-Learning: Tracking Student Behaviors. Sustainability (2071-1050), 15(20).

Nozari, H. (Ed.). (2025). *Dynamic and Safe Economy in the Age of Smart Technologies*. IGI Global. DOI: 10.4018/979-8-3693-4369-2

Nozari, H. (2025). Cognitive Targeting and Neuromarketing Applications in AI-Driven Digital Advertising. *Applied Innovations in Industrial Management*, *5*(2), 52–58. DOI: 10.63630/aiim.52.52

Nozari, H., Abdi, H., & Jahangard, S. (2025). Quantum Cognitive Intelligence Network Q-CIN as a Transformative Framework for Industry 6.0. *ALL Bioscience*, *1*(1), 27–37.

Nozari, H., Abdi, H., & Rafiei, K. (2025). Edge Computing and Marketing in the Smart Economy: Processing Consumer Data in Real-Time. In Dynamic and Safe Economy in the Age of Smart Technologies (pp. 191-208). IGI Global Scientific Publishing.

Nozari, H., Abdi, H., & Szmelter-Jarosz, A. (2025). A Neuromorphic and Bio-Inspired Framework for Optimization in Multi-Echelon Supply Networks. *Transformative Science*, *1*(1), 9–17.

Nozari, H., & Edalatpanah, S. A. (2023). Smart systems risk management in IoT-based supply chain. In *Advances in reliability, failure and risk analysis* (pp. 251–268). Springer Nature Singapore. DOI: 10.1007/978-981-19-9909-3_11

Nozari, H., Fallah, M., Szmelter-Jarosz, A., & Krzemiński, M. (2021). Analysis of security criteria for IoT-based supply chain: a case study of FMCG industries. Central European Management Journal, 29(4).

Nozari, H., Ghahremani-Nahr, J., & Szmelter-Jarosz, A. (2023). A multi-stage stochastic inventory management model for transport companies including several different transport modes. *International Journal of Management Science and Engineering Management, 18*(2), 134–144. DOI: 10.1080/17509653.2022.2042747

Nozari, H., Ghahremani-Nahr, J., & Szmelter-Jarosz, A. (2024). AI and machine learning for real-world problems. []. Elsevier.]. *Advances in Computers, 134*, 1–12. DOI: 10.1016/bs.adcom.2023.02.001

Nozari, H., Szmelter-Jarosz, A., & Ghahremani-Nahr, J. (2021). The ideas of sustainable and green marketing based on the internet of everything—The case of the dairy industry. *Future Internet, 13*(10), 266. DOI: 10.3390/fi13100266

Nozari, H., Tavakkoli-Moghaddam, R., & Gharemani-Nahr, J. (2022). A neutrosophic fuzzy programming method to solve a multi-depot vehicle routing model under uncertainty during the covid-19 pandemic. *International Journal of Engineering, 35*(2), 360–371.

Rahmaty, M., & Nozari, H. (2023). Optimization of the hierarchical supply chain in the pharmaceutical industry. *Edelweiss Applied Science and Technology, 7*(2), 104–123. DOI: 10.55214/25768484.v7i2.376

Smith, V. C., Lange, A., & Huston, D. R. (2012). Predictive modeling to forecast student outcomes and drive effective interventions in online community college courses. *Online Learning : the Official Journal of the Online Learning Consortium, 16*(3), 51–61. DOI: 10.24059/olj.v16i3.275

Susnjak, T. (2024). Beyond predictive learning analytics modelling and onto explainable artificial intelligence with prescriptive analytics and ChatGPT. *International Journal of Artificial Intelligence in Education, 34*(2), 452–482. DOI: 10.1007/s40593-023-00336-3

Wolff, A., Zdrahal, Z., Herrmannova, D., Kuzilek, J., & Hlosta, M. (2014). Developing predictive models for early detection of at-risk students on distance learning modules.

Zhai, Y., Zhang, Y., Chu, Z., Geng, B., Almaawali, M., Fulmer, R., Lin, Y.-W. D., Xu, Z., Daniels, A. D., Liu, Y., Chen, Q., & Du, X. (2025). Machine learning predictive models to guide prevention and intervention allocation for anxiety and depressive disorders among college students. *Journal of Counseling and Development, 103*(1), 110–125. DOI: 10.1002/jcad.12543

Chapter 7

# The Holistic Framework for the Integration of Learning Analytics to Decision-Making Process in the Context of Stakeholder Theory

**Atajan Rovshenov**
http://orcid.org/0000-0001-9189-3438
*Izmir Bakircay University, Turkey*

**Erman Coşkun**
*Bahcesehir University, Turkey*

## ABSTRACT

*Success in any process hinges on well-made decisions, but evaluating the effectiveness of these decisions can be challenging. Utilizing evidence-based decision-making enables informed choices based on data and experimental results, particularly in learning environments. Learning analytics—comprising static and dynamic data from learners—enhances decision-making and the overall learning process. All stakeholders, including learners, teachers, instructional designers, researchers, and administrators, should stay updated on trends in learning analytics to make effective decisions. This chapter presents a theoretical framework for using learning analytics in decision-making, framed within Stakeholder Theory. We will explore the intersection of assessment, learning analytics, and stakeholder theory, offering*

DOI: 10.4018/979-8-3373-5117-9.ch007

ght © 2026, IGI Global Scientific Publishing. Copying or distributing in print or electronic forms without written permission of IGI Global Scientific Publishing is prohibited. Use of this chapter to generative artificial intelligence (AI) technologies is expressly prohibited. The publisher reserves all rights to license its use for generative AI training and machine learning model development.

*suggestions for its application in educational settings. This study aims to enrich literature on assessing and applying learning analytics from various stakeholder perspectives.*

## INTRODUCTION

This section will provide a detailed examination of the paradigm shift in higher education and its effects. Additionally, readers will learn about the reasons behind the emergence of concepts such as Big Data, Data Analytics, and Learning Analytics in higher education.

Higher education institutions operate within highly competitive and complex environments, facing pressure to meet both national and international objectives while consistently enhancing their educational and training quality policies in response to the evolving social landscape. The growing complexity of higher education activities and the demand for quality education services necessitate a comprehensive revaluation of these challenges (Hart & Coates, 2011; Williams, 2016). Concurrently, the digital transformation occurring globally in higher education, along with the emergence of new technologies, has significantly influenced the interplay between learning activities and technology. Over the past decade, the advancement of flexible and distance learning environments has transformed the understanding of access to education and training programs. Consequently, higher education institutions are designing environments that foster innovative learning experiences and technologies tailored to the needs of learners, ultimately helping to reduce institutional operating costs. These developments have spurred research into how higher education institutions can adapt efficiently and effectively to these changes. A critical requirement for this adaptation is the ability to make informed decisions based on the meaningful information derived from processing the raw data available within these institutions. This generation of meaningful information can also be utilized to assess how effectively higher education institutions manage their operational processes in relation to their institutional and social goals (Clarke et al., 2013; Daniel, 2015).

In higher education institutions that have expanded in response to the COVID-19 pandemic, digital technologies are capturing the attention of decision-makers, learners, parents, and stakeholders invested in technological development for the sector. The widespread adoption of digital technologies has amplified the significance of digital data, particularly in its collection, analysis, and application. The rising trend of big data in education has garnered considerable interest from researchers and decision-makers alike. Universities have started to leverage learning analytics, using learner data to inform decision-making across institutional and pedagogical dimensions.

Unlike traditional evaluation methods, the evaluation of data derived from learning analytics has prompted the involvement of various stakeholders, including parents, content experts, learning management system specialists, data analysts, and data security professionals, in the decision-making process. This shift underscores the necessity of investigating and examining the role of learning analytics from multiple perspectives to generate meaningful insights from the information gathered through an increasingly digitalized learning environment (Gašević et al., 2022).

This study offers a comprehensive roadmap for decision-makers and practitioners aiming to integrate Learning Analytics into education, informed by Stakeholder Theory, which is grounded in Information Systems theories. The integration of Learning Analytics is frequently cited as a significant challenge in empirical research, and there is a growing concern about establishing a robust theoretical foundation for academics, researchers, distance education specialists, data analysts, data security experts, and learning management system developers who stand to benefit from learning analytics, ultimately paving the way for experimental research. This chapter presents a theoretical framework for applying learning analytics in decision-making throughout the learning process, specifically within the context of Stakeholder Theory, with a primary focus on the following areas:

1. How have educational paradigms and usage of education changed in recent years, and what are their effects?
2. How should the integration of Learning Analytics be done for effective education using different theories from the Information Systems discipline?
3. How to design a theoretical roadmap for the practical use of LA using the Holistic Framework for the Integration of Learning Analytics to Decision-Making Process in the context of Stakeholder Theory?

The chapter is divided into five sections. Section 2 will consider the conceptual intersection of Big Data, Data Analytics, and Pedagogical Decision-Making. The third section provides an overview of Stakeholder Theory and its applications. Section 4 presents the details of the proposed framework, and Section 5 discusses implementations for future research.

## General Overview of Big Data and Usage of Higher Education

Big data analytics can be defined as the process of transforming valuable data into meaningful insights that support the sustainability of institutions in a competitive market (Goes, 2014; McAfee & Brynjolfsson, 2012). Numerous companies and institutions capitalize on the opportunities presented by big data analytics to fulfill their operational and strategic objectives. While the integration of data into the decision-making process has gained prominence in recent years, its roots can be traced back to the advent of data storage and data warehousing, which have existed since the early 1990s. The complexity of data—both in structure and types poses management challenges for organizations, underscoring the necessity of keeping abreast of ongoing developments (Duan et al.,2019).

Research by Basu (2013) indicates that businesses continue to derive benefits from structured data (including both numerical and categorical formats) in their decision-making processes. According to an IBM study, approximately 80% of the data within organizations is unstructured, existing in various formats such as text, video, audio files, visuals, and diagrams. This unstructured data is primarily stored in the organization's data warehouse, which serves as a centralized repository for managing all types of data. Recent advances in database and data warehousing technologies have facilitated the collection and management of complex data from multiple sources, including unstructured data. Analytical tools have been developed to convert this complex, multi-source data into actionable insights, playing a crucial role in the realm of big data analytics. Furthermore, big data analytics contributes significantly to the development of innovative and contemporary methods for collecting, storing, distributing, managing, and analyzing data.

Big data is built upon several fundamental concepts that, while varying in interpretation among researchers, collectively aim to explain how meaningful information is generated from large datasets. The key concepts are outlined below (Wang et al.,2016):

*Figure 1. Concepts of Big Data*

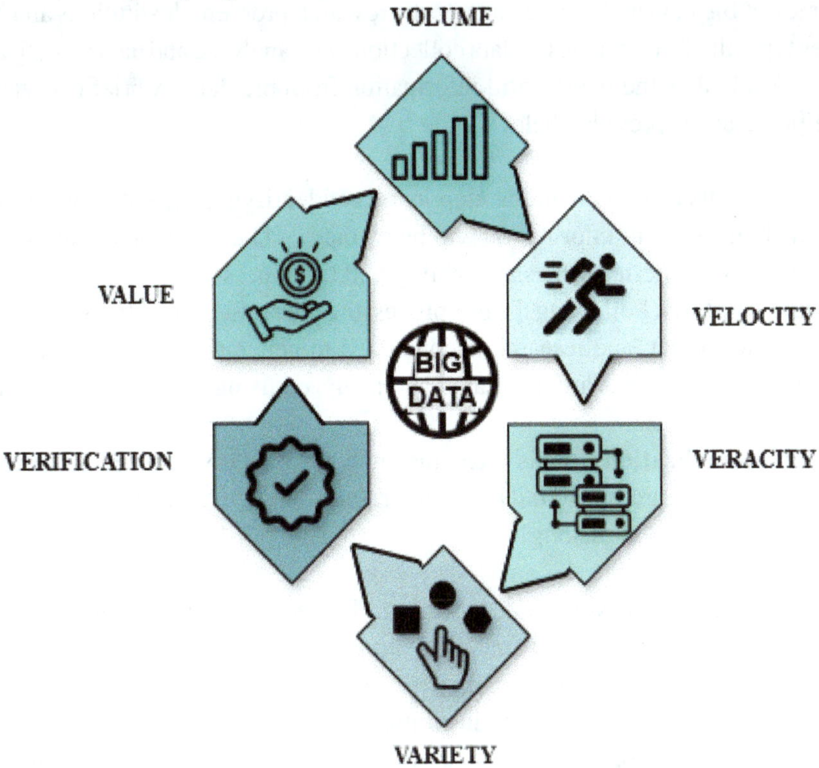


*Note. Adapted from Wang, H., Xu, Z., Fujita, H., & Liu, S. (2016). Towards felicitous decision making: An overview on challenges and trends of Big Data. Information Sciences, 367, 747-765.*

- **Volume:** Refers to the vast amounts of information that can pose challenges in terms of storage, processing, transfer, analysis, and presentation.
- **Velocity:** Relates to the increasing speed at which information flows within an organization.
- **Veracity:** Concerns the biases, noise, and anomalies present in the data. It also assesses how data is stored and analyzed meaningfully in relation to the problem being investigated, addressing questions of trust and uncertainty.
- **Variety:** Involves the diverse formats of data, both structured and unstructured.
- **Verification:** Pertains to the processes of data validation and security.
- **Value:** Most importantly, this concept examines whether the data has been utilized to generate insights, benefits, and improvements in business processes for the organization.

In addition to these concepts, the notion of validity is crucial for evaluating the accuracy of big data and its relevance to the research problem. Institutions and businesses typically follow stages of data collection, data analysis, and data visualization to derive valuable and meaningful information from big data. A brief overview of these processes is provided below:

1. **Data Collection:** This initial step involves identifying the data sources from which meaningful information will be extracted. The selection of data sources is based on criteria such as availability and timeliness.
2. **Data Analysis:** Following the pre-processing phase, the data is transformed into a usable format, and research is conducted to generate insights. Various data formats and sources are integrated and analyzed using appropriate techniques during this phase.
3. **Data Visualization:** In this stage, the analyzed data is visualized in a way that allows all user groups to interpret the produced information and leverage it for informed decision-making.

Overall, these processes work together to harness the potential of big data effectively. There is a substantial amount of stored data within the databases and data warehouses of various institutions. In recent years, there has been a notable increase in the number of higher education institutions conducting their teaching activities online (Adedoyin & Soykan, 2023; Kew & Tasir, 2022). All data pertaining to students' academic and social lives is retained within the university's information system. As mentioned earlier, the nature of big data means it can exist in various formats, leading to a growing demand for current analytical approaches and techniques to effectively analyze this information. Mayer (2009) attributes the expansion of the market for advanced analytical methods to advancements in information and communication technologies, as well as the rising mobility of devices capable of accessing information. Tools such as Apache Hadoop, MapReduce, IBM SPSS, Weka, and HortonWorks are widely utilized for performing analytical operations on big data, and they do not necessitate extensive technical expertise (Analytic Steps, 2021).

Big data is an information system designed to extract meaningful insights from various types of data it encompasses. When employed effectively, it can significantly accelerate the decision-making process across all sectors and offer positive contributions (Boyd & Crawford, 2012). In higher education institutions, big data is utilized to assess institutional and academic objectives, evaluate performance, and forecast future educational endeavors (Hrabowski et al., 2011; Picciano, 2012). The OECD study (2013) underscores the potential for higher education institutions to enhance their research on big data, enabling universities to make informed decisions that foster academic success by aligning operational management processes with educational goals. The digital interactions and virtual connections between learners and educators generate the content that constitutes big data within the realm of higher education.

The landscape of big data in higher education is comprised entirely of digital information related to the learning process. Literature suggests that key concepts from fields such as Educational Technology, Statistics, Computer Science, and Information Systems can benefit from interdisciplinary approaches to derive meaningful insights from this data. One notable approach that explores big data in higher education, focusing on the core principles at the intersection of these disciplines, is learning analytics.

## General Overview of Learning Analytics

Examining the definitions and concepts in theoretical studies on learning analytics is crucial. The 1st International Conference on Learning Analytics (LAK'11), where this concept was first introduced, along with the Society for Learning Analytics Research (SoLAR), which provided the definition, are key sources cited in the literature. According to SoLAR (2011), learning analytics is defined as the collection, analysis, and reporting of data about learners to enhance the learning process. In one of the early theoretical studies on the topic, George Siemens (2010) defined learning analytics as the creation of information about learners derived from the data collected from them, which is then utilized to make predictions and support the learning process. Elias (2011) approached learning analytics from a technical viewpoint, describing it as a research area that includes analytical tools to support learning and education.

Learning analytics is driven by data and continues to evolve as a field, yet it remains loosely connected to theoretical frameworks. It has struggled to establish itself as an academic discipline due to its relatively nascent nature. One reason for this is the rapid application of techniques such as web analytics, social network analysis, natural language processing, and predictive estimation in analyzing the collected data (Cowl, 2012). These techniques often produce general information about learners, making it challenging to conduct an in-depth analysis of the learning process within a virtual environment.

*Figure 2. Process of Learning Analytics*

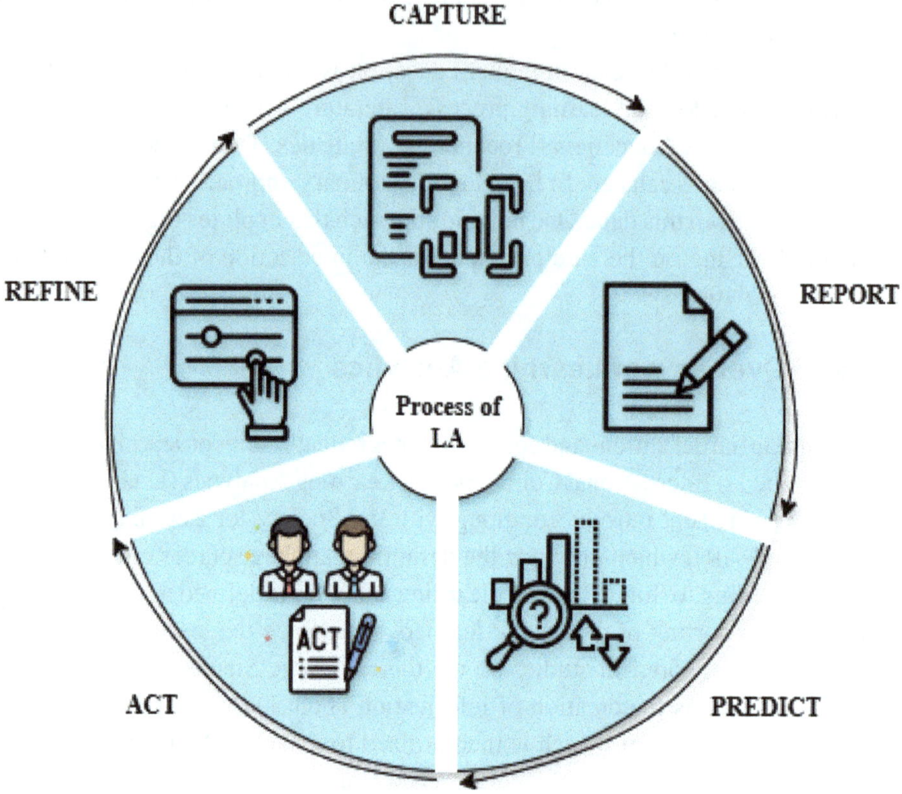


*Note. Adapted from Pardo, A. (2014). Designing Learning Analytics Experiences. In: Larusson, J., White, B. (eds) Learning Analytics. Springer, New York, NY. https://doi.org/10.1007/978-1-4614-3305-7_2*

Clow (2013) identified five primary uses of learning analytics. The first is predictive modeling, wherein a mathematical framework is developed using collected data to anticipate possible outcomes, enabling informed decision-making based on these forecasts. The second application pertains to social network analysis, which investigates the connections formed in social networks and their interrelations. The third application is usage/user tracking, wherein data extracted from Learning Management Systems (LMS) is used to monitor engagement through the creation of learning dashboards. The fourth application involves content and semantic analysis, which consists of collecting and examining qualitative data through natural language processing and semantic analysis methods. Lastly, the fifth application is the recommendation engine, which analyzes similar user behaviors within the system to build an engine that proposes topics of interest to users. A detailed analysis of the aims of learning analytics can lead to new research opportunities in this domain. Additionally, contemporary literature emphasizes the dynamic character of learning analytics, highlighting the need for theoretical research and systematic literature reviews to act as a guide for upcoming studies.

*Figure 3. Usage of Learning Analytics*

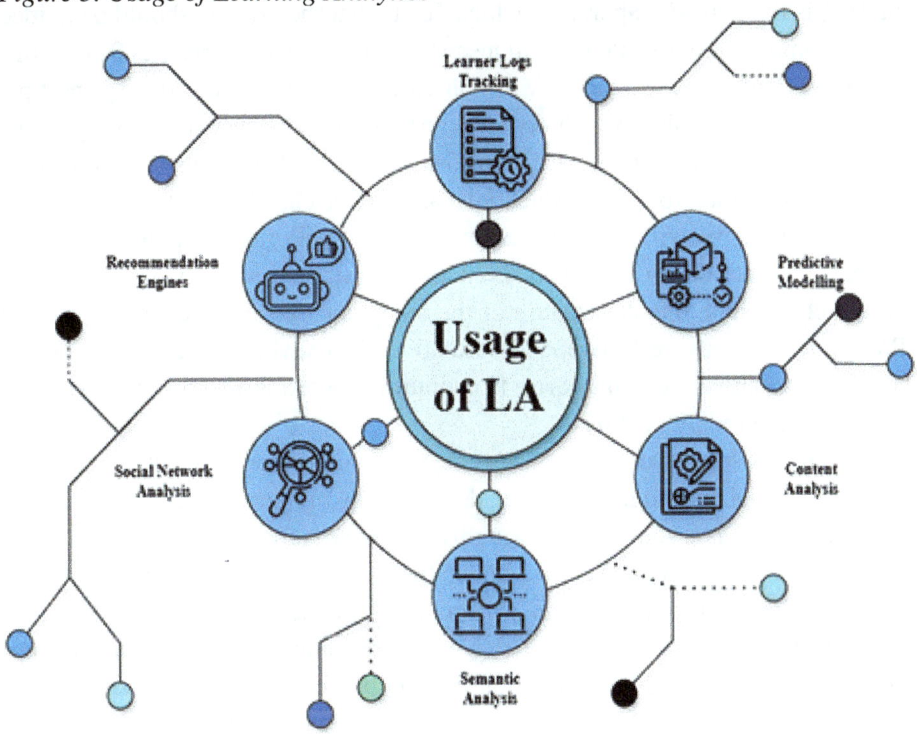


*Note. Adapted from Clow, D. (2013). An overview of learning analytics. Teaching in Higher Education, 18(6), 683-695.*

To effectively utilize learning analytics, it is essential to adopt both a technical and a socio-technical perspective. This dual approach allows for a more comprehensive understanding of learners and the contexts in which their learning occurs. Considering the pedagogical decision-making process that follows the application of learning analytics, engaging relevant stakeholders to incorporate the social dimension into these systems, and designing methods to effectively include these stakeholders based on academic literature will significantly strengthen the theoretical foundation of learning analytics.

## Pedagogical Decision- Making

This section discusses the pedagogical decision-making process. It first examines decision-making approaches, then highlights the similarities between the pedagogical decision-making process and current methods used in the field. While there are various mechanisms and definitions pertaining to decision-making, the core nature of the decision-making process remains consistent (Evans, 2008). The literature typically identifies two primary categories related to decision-making. The first is the heuristic approach, which posits that the process should be guided by autonomous or automated techniques (Kahneman & Frederick, 2002). In this framework, decisions are made with conscious awareness, considering multiple sources simultaneously (Betsch & Glöckner, 2010). The second category is the analytical approach, where the decision-making process is meticulously controlled and executed in a step-by-step, sequential manner (Betsch, 2008). Although intuitive decision-making is swift and requires minimal effort, it often struggles to produce optimal outcomes due to its intrinsic limitations, which can result in poor decisions. Conversely, despite the slow nature of the analytical decision-making process, it allows for conscious, reflective, and normative results while safeguarding against the erroneous choices that may arise from intuitive decision-making (Evans, 2003; Kahneman & Frederick, 2002).

Upon reviewing the aforementioned categories, it becomes evident that the most significant variables and factors in the decision-making process need to be clearly defined, and the data should be thoroughly and accurately modeled (Khajah et al., 2016). A comprehensive and correct understanding of the decision-making process can provide valuable opportunities, particularly for educators, in making informed decisions that benefit students. One area where decision-making is crucial and has been extensively studied is the decision-making process in learning environments. Pedagogical decision-making is the process through which effective education and training plans are designed to help students achieve their career goals, allowing them to discover their potential through the use of information and communication technologies (Ender et. al.,1982; Okewu & Daramola, 2017). This process typically involves face-to-face meetings between the teacher, who facilitates the decision-making process, and the student, who ultimately implements the decisions made. During these meetings, the teacher asks the student questions about their interests and aspirations and suggests relevant academic or social content based on the student's responses. The history of pedagogical decision-making processes in formal learning environments traces back to the foundations established in American universities during the 1800s, and universities worldwide are currently building their decision-making policies on these foundations (Gordon et al., 2011). Research has shown that academic counseling activities conducted after a robust pedagogical decision-making process positively impact learners' academic success and attendance (Bahr, 2008; Drake, 2011; Sharkin, 2004; Young-Jones et al., 2013). Despite the positive contributions of academic counseling to the pedagogical decision-making process, these activities have often been overshadowed by technological advancements. It is well-known that pedagogical decision-making and academic counseling are still carried out through traditional methods (Barron & Powell, 2014). With the rise of distance education, academic counseling is increasingly performed through interviews and emails in virtual environments (Steele, 2018).

A key advantage of offering pedagogical and educational counseling in virtual settings, along with various resources and activities related to students' career goals, is the opportunity to gather diverse digital data that can enhance the decision-making process. Additionally, studies have indicated that integrating different information sources positively impacts the decision-making process (Ratcliff et al., 2016).

The systems and techniques used in technology-supported pedagogical decision-making in learning environments today include the following (Klašnja-Milićević et al., 2017; Kotsiantis, 2012):

1. **Decision Support Systems:** Developed for systematic decision-making and implementation across various fields.
2. **Educational Decision Support Systems:** Created to aid education and training activities with a data-oriented approach.
3. **Data Mining (DM):** These systems utilize statistical models like artificial neural networks, decision trees, and linear regression to produce meaningful information and visualize data in databases and data warehouses, drawing on concepts from Computer Science and Statistics.
4. **Educational Data Mining (EDM):** This application focuses on using data mining primarily to enhance and strengthen educational and training activities.
5. **Learning Analytics (LA):** These systems convert data related to the learning process into meaningful information by applying concepts from Cognitive Science and Computer Science.
6. **Machine Learning (ML):** This field employs algorithms to extract valuable information from data, contributing to research aimed at understanding the learning process by addressing issues relevant to the research problem, grounded in the raw data obtained from educational experiments.

In contemporary higher education institutions, decision-making processes often stem from frameworks developed internally or arise from intuitive choices that align closely with their strategic objectives in academics and pedagogy. Given the complexity of these decisions, it is reasonable to assert that these strategic plans may have limitations and a minimal impact on teaching activities. The selection of courses students will take, the monitoring of their academic performance, and the timely identification of students requiring more frequent interaction by instructors are all critical components of this process (Gutiérrez et al., 2020).

## Stakeholder Theory and Stakeholder Management

Research indicates that universities often struggle to meet the needs of their stakeholders due to their management approaches (Pew Research Centre, 2016). These findings highlight the necessity of considering stakeholder opinions and making decisions based on their needs in all managerial actions taken by universities.

Stakeholder management is essential for both public and private institutions. Nutt & Backoff (1992) define stakeholders as entities that are affected by, or can affect, the strategic management of organizations. To achieve strategic success, institutions should prioritize their interactions and communications with stakeholders (Gomes & Liddle, 2009). Therefore, identifying stakeholders, understanding their needs, and managing those needs is a fundamental management concept.

Various approaches in the literature are used to identify and manage stakeholders. Common methods include categorizing stakeholders as voluntary or involuntary (Clarkson, 1995), assessing their power, legitimacy, and urgency (Mitchell et al., 1997), evaluating their level of control and degree of interest (Johnson & Scholes, 2002), and considering participation (Reed, 2008). Despite the existence of diverse approaches and frameworks for stakeholder identification, decisions are often made within limited dimensions in educational institutions, particularly in higher education, where stakeholder engagement is frequently overlooked. Although stakeholder identification is not a widely studied topic in the context of private institutions, it has been largely neglected in universities. This indicates a need for researchers to focus on and encourage further study in this area (Christopher et al., 2002; Rutterford et al., 2016; Bryson, 2004).

Stakeholder identification typically occurs in groups, and managing stakeholders can be complex. Thus, educational and training activities should be designed based on stakeholder perspectives to achieve the desired outcomes. The first stage of effective stakeholder management involves identifying relevant stakeholders. Once stakeholders are identified, the next step is to make informed decisions to develop appropriate strategies (Mitchell et al., 1997; Bryson, 2004). The process of stakeholder identification may vary depending on the specific area in which stakeholder management is applied (Mitchell et al., 1997).

## Components of Learning Analytics Information Systems

Information systems consist of various components. From a conceptual perspective, these systems can be viewed as artefacts (Beckman, 2002). Artefacts encompass more than just technology; they represent a "complex and evolving combination of people and technology" (Dahlbom, 1996, p. 43). While technology embodies these artefacts, information technology ultimately serves human purposes by supporting a variety of tasks (March & Smith, 1995). In this section, we will explore the potential components of Learning Analytics systems identified in the literature and outline our proposed framework.

### Analyzing and Defining Potential Stakeholders

Stakeholder analysis involves identifying both internal and external groups or individuals that can have a direct or indirect impact on an organization (Freeman, 2010; Stoner et al., 1995). As previously noted, stakeholder theory is applicable in fields beyond management (Phillips et al., 2003). In Information Systems (IS) studies, stakeholder analysis has been employed to identify users of systems and their interactions, both direct and indirect (Papazafeiropoulou et al., 2001). We will advance the development of our proposed theoretical framework by conducting a literature review to identify potential stakeholders. The following section summarizes current research on learning analytics and identifies these stakeholders using key concepts derived from that research.

## LITERATURE REVIEW

One of the main goals of learning analytics is to facilitate teachers using technological solutions and pedagogical concepts while designing the learning process and to help them make more effective and faster learner decisions. However, because learning analytics is a relatively new research area, there is a lack of research on its theoretical and practical dimensions, and the fact that the people who will use it do not possess the necessary technical skills limits the potential contributions of learning analytics to the learning process. These limitations highlight the need for theoretical studies to advance the development of learning analytics as a research area. The objectives, strengths, and weaknesses of learning analytics, its contribution to learning design, and the increasing compulsory and optional needs for distance education systems in recent years have led to the initiation of theoretical research to examine these fields from a holistic perspective. This section will identify the stakeholders involved in learning analytics based on literature. A theoretical framework will then be developed using a recognized system design approach, based on the themes found in the literature review.

Gray et al. (2022) explored the perspectives of key stakeholders, including staff and students, regarding their expectations of learning analytics. The study focused on their priorities for utilizing student data and identified how they should be supported in acting on that data to aid institutions in implementing learning analytics effectively. The findings revealed a significant need for additional training and ongoing support to enhance stakeholder understanding and achieve their goals related to learning analytics. The study emphasized the importance of transparency and the need for students to be informed about their rights in a clear, student-friendly manner. This includes details about the types of data collected, its uses, and how it is governed. Both students and staff expressed that training aimed at increasing awareness of their rights concerning learner data, the legitimate interests of higher education institutions (HEIs) policies, and the potential of learning analytics would be beneficial for both students and HEIs in operationalizing learning analytics and managing expectations. Surveys and focus groups indicated that while students generally maintained a high level of trust in their HEI's use of data, there were concerns regarding the potential misuse of their information by individual staff members.

Raj and Genumol (2022) explored how learning duration and expected scores can be predicted within the scope of recommending learning paths. The study focused on modifying the difficulty level of educational materials based on the immediate performance analysis of 96 subjects. Learning resource suggestions were customized to fit personal learning styles and the learner's capability to interact with particular resources. Results showed that utilizing real-time learning analytics through implicit learner log data improves the recommendation process.

Huang et al. (2021) examined the development of feelings among 38 postgraduate students participating in a blended Fundamental Educational Technology Theory Course at a university in China. Utilizing text mining and Epistemic Network Analysis (ENA), the research showed that negative emotions were moderately connected to other feelings such as humor, confusion, and neutrality. The students' emotions commonly shifted from negative to insightful, especially during in-depth interactions. Conversely, the sentiment network created from social-emotional exchanges revealed stronger links between joking-positive and joking-negative sentiments in comparison to the other two interaction levels. Importantly, the investigation of co-occurring feelings uncovered three unique phases in the blended learning experience: initial, collision (or sublimation), and stable periods. The results indicated that students' emotions progressed from positive to confused or hostile, ultimately culminating in more insightful reflections.

Silvola et al. (2021) conducted a study on the needs and expectations of pre-service teachers regarding Learning Analytics (LA) to enhance student engagement throughout their academic journey, which involves monitoring various study periods and academic years. Students expressed that LA tools could enhance their engagement by facilitating the flow of information between themselves and the institution, aiding effective study habits, fostering self-awareness as learners, offering assistance during challenging times, and serving as a feedback mechanism to tailor learning environments to their individual preferences. The findings of this research highlight that students' needs can often be contradictory, such as when they desire more opportunities for autonomous decisions in their studies while also requesting increased institutional oversight of their academic progress.

Tzimas and Demetriadis (2021) analyzed the data used in learning analytics studies in the context of ethical values. As a result of the research, it has been revealed that there is a need for guidelines and standards that can be applied by teachers and researchers about the data to be used and evaluated in experimental research on learning analytics.

Kollom et al. (2021) aim to investigate the expectations of academic staff regarding learning analytics in higher education in Spain, Estonia, and the Netherlands. They researched a working group of academics based in the UK. In his research, learning analytics creates opportunities for academicians to constantly monitor the academic development of their students and determine their learning outcomes, increase the quality of teaching activities, and provide suggestions to improve their learning and professional skills. There are sections in the developed systems where opinions about learning experiences can be taken and analyzed. They stated that they expect to have features that can quickly produce information from the obtained data and accelerate decision-making, as well as functions that can measure student interaction with the course content and incorporate learner characteristics into the course content. However, they have difficulties controlling and understanding the accuracy of the data and accessing it (due to ethical and confidentiality concerns); they stated that they expect universities to prepare guidelines on how to use the system and adopt learning analytics as a cultural practice at the administrative level.

Munguia et al. (2020) stated that universities should adopt learning analytics at the institutional level, the lack of a data strategy in front of the application of learning analytics in higher education institutions, the lack of virtual communities where academic staff can develop their practical skills about learning analytics and Information Technologies explained that their departments had little support for the process.

Tsai et al. (2020) examined the application of learning analytics in higher education in Europe, considering trends and barriers. As a result of the research, it was seen that learning analytics improved and facilitated the learning process, and the interaction between students was low. New research on the subject suggests that addressing student-teacher mismatches and including students as stakeholders is necessary.

Gaftandzhieva et al. (2021) examined the application of Learning Analytics in the context of Secondary Education from the viewpoints of various stakeholders. Their findings indicated that school administrators can leverage Learning Analytics tools to gather data that supports informed decision-making at every level within the institution. Additionally, school managers are a key stakeholder group that benefits from these tools, while external stakeholders also show interest in the outcomes generated by Learning Analytics. Teachers find it valuable for monitoring student engagement and progress in learning activities, as well as tracking academic absences. With the aid of specific data, teachers can make data-driven decisions and collaborate with class teachers, parents, or other educational specialists to enhance the motivation and engagement of individual students or groups. Furthermore, teachers noted that insights into students' course activity can serve as a feedback mechanism, prompting them to present learning materials in a more modern and engaging manner, ultimately improving the quality of the educational content provided.

Galaige et al. (2022) developed and assessed a learning analytics framework aimed at students that seeks to enhance self-regulated learning. The findings reveal that three interrelated contexts must be considered in designing a student-facing learning analytics tool that fosters the development of self-regulated learning, based on insights from a survey of learning analytics experts and issues highlighted in the existing literature: the student context, the theoretical context, and the designer context. The optimal design for the student-facing learning analytics tool occurs when it draws from knowledge at the intersection of these three contexts. It is important to analyze students' differences to cater to individual user needs instead of applying a uniform approach. The results underscore the necessity of understanding the student's perspective on the learning analytics framework to address any concerns, usability issues, and adoption challenges that may emerge. Engaging with experts who have theoretical insights can enhance the design and evaluation of learning analytics tools.

Wong and Li (2020) reviewed the intervention of learning analytics in higher education. In their study, the authors stated that the studies generally examined the relationship between learning analytics and student performance and only examined the online behaviours of learners as data. The research suggested that studies should be conducted to enhance the long-term effectiveness, sustainability, and quality of human resources and infrastructure, integrating them into the system.

Hilliger et al. (2020) examined the needs of learning analytics stakeholders in their research. As a result of the study, it has been observed that students require quality feedback and prompt support, faculty members need performance evaluations, and administrators require high-quality information to conduct research. Additionally, it has been suggested that individuals interested in ethical values and data confidentiality should be included as stakeholders in the study.

Laet et al. (2020) conducted a case study to explore the adoption and impact of new modules in a learning analytics dashboard designed to facilitate dialogue between student advisors and students regarding study plans for the upcoming academic semester. The results of the case study demonstrate that an institution-wide implementation of dashboard modules tailored to the advisors' needs can enhance the level of support perceived by advisors and significantly reduce the discrepancy between the suggested study plans in advising discussions and the actual study plans that students register for. Interviews revealed that while advisors expressed a positive outlook towards the new modules, they still expect additional support from the higher education institution beyond the dashboard.

Whitelock-Wainwright (2020) conducted a latent analysis clustering study to segment students' expectations regarding learning analytics services. The clustering results indicate that while expectations concerning ethical and privacy aspects of these services remain consistent across all participant groups, they do exhibit significant variability. Most respondents anticipated that the university would handle student data ethically, which is fundamental to any service provided.

Cerro Martinez et al. (2020) explored how teachers utilize learning analytics for monitoring and assessment to impact student and classroom performance within the context of online higher education. The data revealed two key trends: first, the implementation of learning analytics led to a 5.67% reduction in student dropout rates, and second, the feedback provided to students based on learning analytics data significantly improved their performance. Additionally, the study highlighted how teachers access, process, and interpret information related to online educational practices. Educators face the challenge of comprehending complex phenomena linked to learning in educational environments, especially when numerous variables and contexts are involved. The focus is less on how to gather the necessary information and more on how to analyze it to form value judgments that support effective decision-making. In this context, teachers play a crucial and indispensable role, making decisions based on their interpretation of the data, regardless of how well that data is represented.

Clark et al. (2020) introduced a framework designed to identify and examine the critical success factors (CSFs) for implementing learning analytics (LA) within the higher education sector, focusing on the perspectives of higher education professionals. To gain a comprehensive understanding of stakeholders' perceptions, the researchers employed a mixed-methods approach that included factor analysis, profile analysis, and thematic analysis of both quantitative and qualitative data from a diverse sample. The findings emphasized the significance of data quality and the skills and expertise of the personnel involved, highlighting concerns about these crucial elements of implementation. The results underscored the vital role of data scientists in determining appropriate measures to ensure data quality. Participants stressed the importance of organizational-level strategies and policies, pointing to the necessity for managerial support in both financial and strategic capacities. The study's findings advocate for a multilayered and multidisciplinary approach to implementation, guided by five interconnected factors: organizational strategy and policy, technological readiness, performance and impact evaluation, personnel skills and expertise, and data quality.

Shibani et al. (2020) explored the motivations, implementation strategies, outcomes, and challenges faced by educators when using Learning Analytics (LA) in authentic practice. They found that effective implementation strategies are crucial for successfully adopting LA in the classroom. A key factor in their success was the educators' readiness to collaborate with the analytics team, aligning their teaching and assessment with the innovative capabilities of the analytics tool. Educators expressed a strong appreciation for the level of agency they were provided in designing and implementing the learning analytics application within their classrooms. This sense of agency was identified as vital, as a lack of it can lead to distrust in the LA application, ultimately hindering its adoption.

Mangaroska and Giannakos (2018) examined the effect of learning analytics on accelerating the learning process in their study. As a result of the research, learning analytics has a positive contribution to accelerating the learning process and a positive effect on teachers' decision-making processes. As a result of the research, it is recommended that theoretical studies be carried out to strengthen and redesign learning activities using learning analytics.

Akcapınar and Bayazıt (2018) performed a study on the video viewing habits of students, focusing on those who utilized deep and surface learning strategies through video analytics methods. In their research, 31 participants watched ten 10-minute videos related to the Computer Hardware course. Data was gathered using the Learning Approach Scale. The results showed that students employing a surface learning approach were significantly more likely to watch the videos in a linear manner compared to those who adopted a deep learning approach. Additionally, students with a deep learning strategy were more likely to engage with the video by frequently using the pause and "play" buttons, with their interactions surging at certain points in the videos. The time series graphs for both groups illustrated that surface learners had overall fewer interactions.

Ifenthaler (2017) explored the current capabilities of Learning Analytics (LA) within higher education institutions and highlighted the significance of various data sources for establishing a valid LA framework. The results indicate that many institutions lack the necessary technology to implement effective LA frameworks and do not utilize data warehouses systematically. The study underscores the importance of relevant data sources for a valid LA framework, suggesting that information from students and their learning environments is regarded as equally crucial.

Li et al. (2015) conducted a systematic literature review on the use of learning analytics in educational sciences. In their study, the distribution of stakeholders was found to be teachers (29.2%), academic institutions (26.4%), and students (23.6%). They stated that very few studies included researchers (16.7%) and system designers (4.2%) as stakeholders.

From literature review we can see that, it's clear that designing information systems for learning analytics requires input from a diverse group of stakeholders, including academicians, students, career counselors, data analysts, data security experts, software developers, and human resources personnel. Research indicates that various tools can help academicians enhance their skills in designing systems that facilitate pedagogical decision-making through learning analytics. These systems can collect and analyze feedback on learning experiences, provide quick data insights, and measure student engagement with course content. To improve these systems, academics and researchers need capabilities such as data analysis, security, infrastructure, and strong connections between learners and instructors. Generally, both learners and teachers are viewed as key stakeholders in this process. This study seeks to explore how engaging a diverse range of stakeholders can lead to more effective pedagogical decisions when using learning analytics. Additionally, it's important to focus on the strategic management aspects when developing systems for implementing learning analytics in research.

## STAKEHOLDERS OF LEARNING ANALYTICS INFORMATION SYSTEMS

In this paper, we do not put forth a new theory; rather, we design a framework that integrates the concepts of Stakeholder Theory and Learning Analytics. As discussed in previous sections, stakeholder analysis involves identifying both internal and external groups or individuals that can influence an organization, either directly or indirectly. We will summarize the stakeholders involved in learning analytics systems according to their job group and participation status during the system's development in Table 1.

*Table 1. Stakeholders of Learning Analytics Information Systems*

| Potential Stakeholder | Direct Action | Internal | External |
|---|---|---|---|
| Learners/ Students | ✓ | | ✓ |
| Instructors/ Teachers | ✓ | ✓ | |
| Parents | ✓ | | ✓ |
| Distance Education, LMS Experts | ✓ | ✓ | |
| System Developers/ Technical Board | ✓ | ✓ | |
| Data Engineers | ✓ | ✓ | |
| Measurement and Evaluation Experts | ✓ | ✓ | |

continued on following page

*Table 1. Continued*

| Potential Stakeholder | Direct Action | Internal | External |
|---|---|---|---|
| UX/UI and Instructional Designers | ✓ | ✓ | |
| Educational Institutions | ✓ | ✓ | |
| Accreditation Committee | ✓ | | ✓ |
| Content Suppliers | ✓ | ✓ | |
| Technology Suppliers | ✓ | | ✓ |

## PROPOSED THEORITICAL FRAMEWORK

A framework "classifies the important factors in information systems development can imply that these factors are causally connected with successful systems development" (Gregor et al., 2006, p. 619). In Figure 4, we will combine the main information systems dimensions and stakeholders of learning analytics. This framework is a theoretical generalization (Carroll & Swatman, 2000; Lee & Baskerville, 2003) resulting from the literature review on stakeholder analysis that we mentioned in the literature review. Figure 4 provides the Holistic Framework for the Integration of Learning Analytics to Decision-Making Process in the context of Stakeholder Theory.

*Figure 4. Holistic Framework for the Integration of Learning Analytics to Decision-Making Process in the context of Stakeholder Theory*

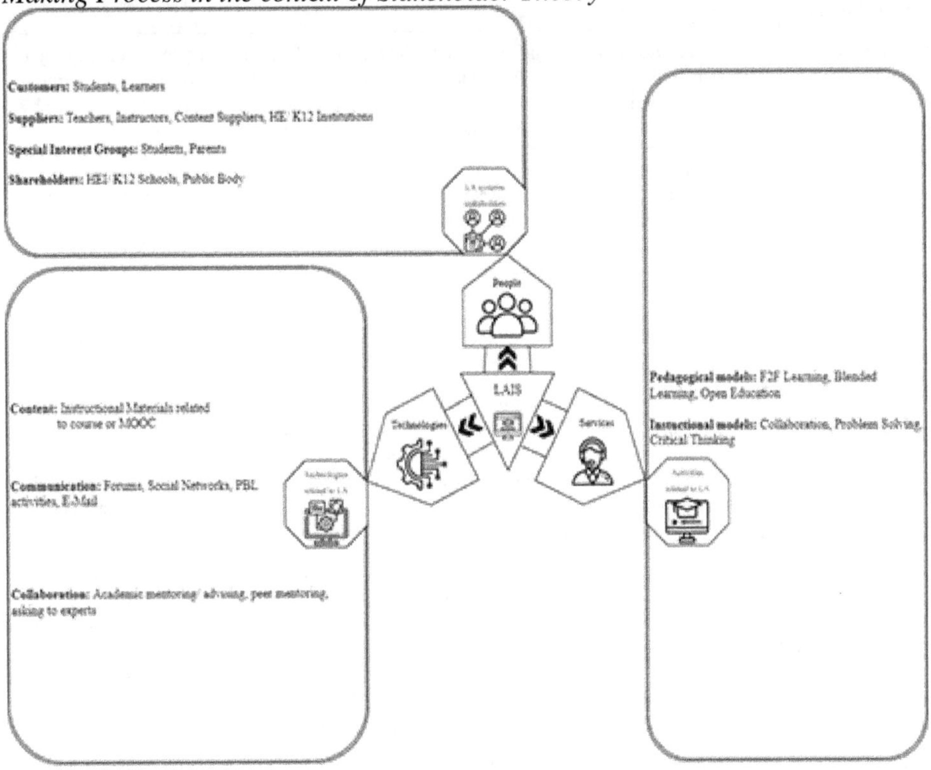


The flowchart illustrates that our framework facilitates the development and adaptation of Learning Analytics (LA) solutions by educational institutions, allowing them to utilize their own LA policies or service-oriented approaches. Rather than striving to create a standardized LA Information System, the framework encourages the design of inclusive Learning Analytics Information Systems (LAIS). As a theoretical framework, it serves as a roadmap for developing LAIS and alleviating the workload of teachers and instructors, ultimately supporting data-driven decision-making. While the definition of stakeholders for LAIS is essential, it alone is insufficient for establishing a successful theoretical roadmap. Clearly outlining the roles of stakeholders ensures a proper team structure, defines success factors and key performance indicators, and promotes improvements in the design of the proposed system based on our framework. Table 2 will provide a summary of the job descriptions for potential stakeholders.

*Table 2. Job Descriptions and Roles Stakeholders of LA Information Systems*

| Potential Stakeholder | Job/ Role Description |
|---|---|
| Learners/ Students | The stakeholder is responsible for participating in all learning activities and is expected to gain skills such as self-directed learning, competency, collaboration, and peer learning. In this system, learners have a more independent and self-regulated role that is driven by technology, in contrast to traditional learning environments. |
| Instructors/ Teachers | The stakeholder is responsible for course design and academic advising using Learning Analytics and Information Systems (LAIS). They utilize data literacy skills to model student behavior, manage team coordination, facilitate collaborative learning activities, and assess and evaluate student performance. Additionally, they provide emotional presence and adhere to other essential principles of distance and blended learning theories. |
| Parents | The stakeholder is responsible for assisting learners' activities, fostering students' self-regulation skills, and enhancing their technology competence skills. |
| Distance Education and LMS Experts | The stakeholder is responsible for the successful technical and pedagogical operation of LAIS. This stakeholder actively engages in functionality assessment and system enhancement, evaluates the system to identify gaps from other stakeholders, ensures data privacy and accessibility, provides technical assistance, and addresses access and performance issues. They work to guarantee seamless use by both staff and students, oversee system upgrades, implement user feedback, and maintain overall quality, stability, and innovation within the system. |
| System Developers/ Technical Board | The stakeholder is responsible for overseeing the System Developers tasked with building, maintaining, and evolving the technological infrastructure for LAIS. This team collaborates with instructors, instructional designers, and LMS experts to assess both pedagogical and technical requirements for LAIS. They design and integrate learning analytics services into educational institutions' systems, while also providing testing, maintenance, and training support. |
| Data Engineers | This stakeholder is tasked with the design, construction, and maintenance of pipelines and storage systems that collect raw data from learner logs. Their role ensures that this data is cleaned, structured, reliable, and easily accessible for the application of learning analytics techniques. Additionally, they are responsible for developing ETL (Extract-Transform-Load) pipelines that automate the process of collecting, sanitizing, and loading student interaction data—such as quiz scores, logins, and forum activity—into centralized data repositories or data lakes. They also design algorithms aimed at facilitating personalized learning and identifying at-risk students. |
| Measurement and Evaluation Experts | This stakeholder is responsible for defining metrics to evaluate learning outcomes. This group designs novel frameworks for assessing learning goals and aligning them with measurable indicators—academic achievement, learner engagement, and satisfaction. It also provides feedback to teachers and students. |
| UX/UI and Instructional Designers | This stakeholder is responsible for designing human-centered dashboards that align with multimedia learning principles and visual design standards. This group actively collaborates with instructional designers, developers, and instructors to create designs that enhance learning outcomes, incorporating elements of gamification and teamwork activities. |
| Educational Institutions | This stakeholder is responsible for adopting Learning Analytics (LA) as an organizational policy and centralizing it as the institution's Mission and Strategic Direction. They will also support the accreditation process by advocating for LA policies. Additionally, this stakeholder will conduct training activities for teachers and instructors. |

## CONCLUSIONS AND FUTURE WORK

Success in any process hinges on making well-informed decisions. However, assessing the effectiveness of these decisions throughout the decision-making journey can pose challenges. An evidence-based approach, rooted in data and empirical outcomes, fosters sound decision-making. A crucial resource for evidence-based decision-making in educational contexts is, quite simply, data itself. Learning Analytics, which includes both static and dynamic data collected from learners, plays a vital role in academic settings by enhancing decision-making and improving the overall learning experience. To make effective and well-structured decisions, all stakeholders involved in the educational process—such as learners, teachers, instructional designers, researchers, and administrators—must stay informed about current trends in Learning Analytics. Learning Analytics employs data mining techniques in education to provide insights that empower educators to make informed decisions. This field is increasingly recognized as a significant area of research, particularly regarding its practical application in learning environments. The growing importance of Learning Analytics highlights the necessity for theoretical research to advance discipline and calls for an increase in empirical studies in this domain.

In this study, we aimed to construct a Holistic Framework for Integrating Learning Analytics into the Decision-Making Process, framed within the context of Stakeholder Theory. The objective of our framework is to identify the various stakeholders involved in the design process of Learning Analytics Information Systems. Prior to proposing our framework, we conducted a comprehensive literature review focusing on learning analytics, pedagogical decision-making, and stakeholder theory. After defining the stakeholders, we developed our framework based on the three primary components of an information system: people, technology, and the services provided by that technology. Additionally, we outlined the job descriptions of stakeholders to clarify how each party can collaborate throughout the process.

We believe that this study, which delineates all aspects involved in the system's development through an extensive literature review, will serve as a valuable guide for researchers, software developers, and system experts. The stakeholders included in the process of our proposed system were determined based on existing literature, highlighting the importance of incorporating their perspectives during the development stage of the framework.

Future research could explore user opinions regarding the system designed according to this theoretical framework, as well as user satisfaction, its impact on the learning process, and the management of learning services through experimental studies. We intend to use this framework as a foundational tool to guide the design of learning analytics systems in future work.

## REFERENCES


Adedoyin, O. B., & Soykan, E. (2023). Covid-19 pandemic and online learning: The challenges and opportunities. *Interactive Learning Environments, 31*(2), 863–875. DOI: 10.1080/10494820.2020.1813180

Akcapınar, G., & Bayazıt, A. (2018). Investigating Video Viewing Behaviors of Students with Different Learning Approaches Using Video Analytics. *Turkish Online Journal of Distance Education, 19*(4), 116–125. DOI: 10.17718/tojde.471907

Analytic Steps. (2021). Top 10 Big Data Analytics Tools. https://www.analyticssteps.com/blogs/top-10-big-data-analytics-tools

Barron, K. E., & Powell, D. N. (2014). Options on how to organize and structure advising. *Academic advising: A handbook for advisors and students, 1*, 14-23.

Basu, T. (2013). Five pillars of prescriptive analytics success. *Analytics magazine, 8*,8-12.

Beckman, S. (2002). The Nature of artifacts. In Dahlbom, B., Beckman, S., & Nilsson, G. B. (Eds.), *Artifacts and Artificial Science* (pp. 45–92). Almqvist & Wiksell International.

Betsch, T. (2008). The nature of intuition and its neglect in research on judgment and decision making. *Intuition in judgment and decision making*, 3-22.

Betsch, T., & Glöckner, A. (2010). Intuition in judgment and decision making: Extensive thinking without effort. *Psychological Inquiry, 21*(4), 279–294. DOI: 10.1080/1047840X.2010.517737

Boyd, D., & Crawford, K. (2012). Critical questions for big data: Provocations for a cultural, technological, and scholarly phenomenon. *Information Communication and Society, 15*(5), 662–679. DOI: 10.1080/1369118X.2012.678878

Bryson, J. (2004). What to do when stakeholders matter. *Public Management Review, 6*(1), 21–53. DOI: 10.1080/14719030410001675722

Carroll, J. M., & Swatman, P. A. (2000). Structured-case: A methodological framework for building theory in information systems research. *European Journal of Information Systems, 9*(4), 235–242. DOI: 10.1057/palgrave.ejis.3000374

Cerro Martinez, J. P., Guitert Catasus, M., & Romeu Fontanillas, T. (2020). Impact of using learning analytics in asynchronous online discussions in higher education. *International Journal of Educational Technology in Higher Education, 17*(1), 1–19. DOI: 10.1186/s41239-020-00217-y

Christopher, M., Payne, A., & Ballantyne, B. (2002). *Relationship Marketing: Creating Stakeholder Value* (2nd revised edition). Butterworth-Heinemann.

Clark, J. A., Liu, Y., & Isaias, P. (2020). Critical success factors for implementing learning analytics in higher education: A mixed-method inquiry. *Australasian Journal of Educational Technology*, *36*(6), 89–106. DOI: 10.14742/ajet.6164

Clarke, J., Nelson, K., & Stoodley, I. (2013, January). The place of higher education institutions in assessing student engagement, success and retention: A maturity model to guide practice. In *Proceedings of the 36th Higher Education Research and Development Society of Australasia Conference (HERDSA 2013)*. University of Southern Queensland.

Clarkson, M. E. (1995). A stakeholder framework for analyzing and evaluating corporate social performance. *Academy of Management Review*, *20*(1), 92–117. DOI: 10.2307/258888

Clow, D. (2013). An overview of learning analytics. *Teaching in Higher Education*, *18*(6), 683–695. DOI: 10.1080/13562517.2013.827653

Dahlbom, B. (1996). The New informatics. *Scandinavian Journal of Information Systems*, *8*, 29–48.

Daniel, B. (2015). Big Data and analytics in higher education: Opportunities and challenges. *British Journal of Educational Technology*, *46*(5), 904–920. DOI: 10.1111/bjet.12230

De Laet, T., Millecamp, M., Ortiz-Rojas, M., Jimenez, A., Maya, R., & Verbert, K. (2020). Adoption and impact of a learning analytics dashboard supporting the advisor—Student dialogue in a higher education institute in Latin America. *British Journal of Educational Technology*, *51*(4), 1002–1018. DOI: 10.1111/bjet.12962

Duan, Y., Edwards, J. S., & Dwivedi, Y. K. (2019). Artificial intelligence for decision making in the era of Big Data–evolution, challenges and research agenda. *International Journal of Information Management*, *48*, 63–71. DOI: 10.1016/j.ijinfomgt.2019.01.021

Elias, T. (2011). Learning analytics. *Learning*, 1-22.Retrieved June 16, 2025, from https://citeseerx.ist.psu.edu/document?repid=rep1&type=pdf&doi=732e452659685fe3950b0e515a28ce89d9c5592a

Ender, S. C., Winston, R. B.Jr, & Miller, T. K. (1982). Academic advising as student development. *New Directions for Student Services*, *1982*(17), 3–18. DOI: 10.1002/ss.37119821703

Evans, J. (2003). In two minds: Dual-process accounts of reasoning. *Trends in Cognitive Sciences, 7*(10), 454–459. DOI: 10.1016/j.tics.2003.08.012 PMID: 14550493

Freeman, R. E. (2010). *Strategic management: A Stakeholder approach.* Cambridge University Press. DOI: 10.1017/CBO9781139192675

Gaftandzhieva, S., Docheva, M., & Doneva, R. (2021). A comprehensive approach to learning analytics in Bulgarian school education. *Education and Information Technologies, 26*(1), 145–163. DOI: 10.1007/s10639-020-10261-w

Galaige, J., Steele, G. T., Binnewies, S., & Wang, K. (2022). A framework for designing student-facing learning analytics to support self-regulated learning. *IEEE Transactions on Learning Technologies, 15*(3), 376–391. DOI: 10.1109/TLT.2022.3176968

Gašević, D., Tsai, Y. S., & Drachsler, H. (2022). Learning analytics in higher education–Stakeholders, strategy and scale. *The Internet and Higher Education, 52*, 1–5. DOI: 10.1016/j.iheduc.2021.100833

Goes, P. B. (2014). Editor's comments: Big data and IS research. *Management Information Systems Quarterly, 38*(3), 3–8.

Gomes, R. C., & Liddle, J. (2009). The balanced scorecard as a performance management tool for third sector organizations: The case of the Arthur Bernardes Foundation, Brazil. *BAR - Brazilian Administration Review, 6*(4), 354–366. DOI: 10.1590/S1807-76922009000400006

Gordon, V. N., Habley, W. R., & Grites, T. J. (Eds.). (2011). *Academic advising: A comprehensive handbook.* John Wiley & Sons.

Gray, G., Schalk, A. E., Cooke, G., Murnion, P., Rooney, P., & O'Rourke, K. C. (2022). Stakeholders' insights on learning analytics: Perspectives of students and staff. *Computers & Education, 187*, 1–16. DOI: 10.1016/j.compedu.2022.104550

Gregor, S., Martin, M., Fernandez, W., Stern, S., & Vitale, M. (2006). The Transformational dimension in the realization of business value from information technology. *The Journal of Strategic Information Systems, 15*(3), 249–270. DOI: 10.1016/j.jsis.2006.04.001

Gutiérrez, F., Seipp, K., Ochoa, X., Chiluiza, K., De Laet, T., & Verbert, K. (2020). LADA: A learning analytics dashboard for academic advising. *Computers in Human Behavior, 107*, 105826. DOI: 10.1016/j.chb.2018.12.004

Hart, D., & Coates, N. (2011). International student complaint behaviour: Understanding how East-Asian business and management students respond to dissatisfaction during their university experience. *International Journal of Management Education, 9*(4), 57–66. DOI: 10.3794/ijme.94.380

Hilliger, I., Ortiz-Rojas, M., Pesántez-Cabrera, P., Scheihing, E., Tsai, Y. S., Muñoz-Merino, P. J., Broos, T., Whitelock-Wainwright, A., & Pérez-Sanagustín, M. (2020). Identifying needs for learning analytics adoption in Latin American universities: A mixed-methods approach. *The Internet and Higher Education, 45*, 100726. DOI: 10.1016/j.iheduc.2020.100726

Hrabowski, F., Suess, J., & Fritz, J. (2011). *Assessment and analytics in institutional transformation*. UMBC Office of the Vice President of Information Technology.

Huang, C., Han, Z., Li, M., Wang, X., & Zhao, W. (2021). Sentiment evolution with interaction levels in blended learning environments: Using learning analytics and epistemic network analysis. *Australasian Journal of Educational Technology, 37*(2), 81–95. DOI: 10.14742/ajet.6749

Ifenthaler, D. (2017). Are higher education institutions prepared for learning analytics? *TechTrends, 61*(4), 366–371. DOI: 10.1007/s11528-016-0154-0

Kahneman, D., & Frederick, S. (2002). Representativeness revisited: Attribute substitution in intuitive judgment. *Heuristics and biases: The psychology of intuitive judgment, 49*(49-81), 74.

Kew, S. N., & Tasir, Z. (2022). Learning analytics in online learning environment: A systematic review on the focuses and the types of student-related analytics data. *Technology, Knowledge and Learning*, 1-23. https://doi.org/DOI: 10.1007/s10758-021-09541-2

Khajah, M., Lindsey, R. V., & Mozer, M. C. (2016). How deep is knowledge tracing? *arXiv preprint arXiv:1604.02416*. https://doi.org//arXiv.1604.02416DOI: 10.48550

Klašnja-Milićević, A., Ivanović, M., & Budimac, Z. (2017). Data science in education: Big data and learning analytics. *Computer Applications in Engineering Education, 25*(6), 1066–1078. DOI: 10.1002/cae.21844

Kollom, K., Tammets, K., Scheffel, M., Tsai, Y. S., Jivet, I., Muñoz-Merino, P. J., Moreno-Marcos, P. M., Whitelock-Wainwright, A., Calleja, A. R., Gasevic, D., Kloos, C. D., Drachsler, H., & Ley, T. (2021). A four-country cross-case analysis of academic staff expectations about learning analytics in higher education. *The Internet and Higher Education, 49*, 100788. DOI: 10.1016/j.iheduc.2020.100788

Kotsiantis, S. B. (2012). Use of machine learning techniques for educational proposes: A decision support system for forecasting students' grades. *Artificial Intelligence Review, 37*(4), 331–344. DOI: 10.1007/s10462-011-9234-x

Lee, A. S., & Baskerville, R. L. (2003). Generalizing generalizability in information systems research. *Information Systems Research, 14*(3), 221–243. DOI: 10.1287/isre.14.3.221.16560

Li, K. C., Lam, H. K., & Lam, S. S. (2015). A review of learning analytics in educational research. In *Technology in Education. Technology-Mediated Proactive Learning: Second International Conference, ICTE 2015, Hong Kong, China, July 2-4, 2015, Revised Selected Papers 2* (pp. 173-184). Springer Berlin Heidelberg. DOI: 10.1007/978-3-662-48978-9_17

Mangaroska, K., & Giannakos, M. (2018). Learning analytics for learning design: A systematic literature review of analytics-driven design to enhance learning. *IEEE Transactions on Learning Technologies, 12*(4), 516–534. DOI: 10.1109/TLT.2018.2868673

March, S. T., & Smith, G. F. (1995). Design and natural science research on information technology. *Decision Support Systems, 15*(4), 251–266. DOI: 10.1016/0167-9236(94)00041-2

Mayer, M. (2009). *Innovation at Google: The physics of data [PARC forum].* Retrieved 11 August, 2009, from https://www.slideshare.net/PARCInc/innovation-at-google-the-physics-of-data

McAfee, A., Brynjolfsson, E., Davenport, T. H., Patil, D. J., & Barton, D. (2012). Big data: The management revolution. *Harvard Business Review, 90*(10), 60–68. PMID: 23074865

Mitchell, R. K., Agle, B. R., & Wood, D. J. (1997). Toward a theory of stakeholder identification and salience: Defining the principle of who and what really counts. *Academy of Management Review, 22*(4), 853–886. DOI: 10.2307/259247

Munguia, P., Brennan, A., Taylor, S., & Lee, D. (2020). A learning analytics journey: Bridging the gap between technology services and the academic need. *The Internet and Higher Education, 46*, 100744. DOI: 10.1016/j.iheduc.2020.100744

Nutt, P. C., & Robert, W. (1992). *Backoff. 1992. Strategic management of public and third sector organizations: A handbook for leaders*. JosseyBass.

OECD. (2013). *OECD Report: The State of Higher Education 2013*. Retrieved March 24, 2025, from http:// www.oecd.org/edu/imhe/thestateofhighereducation2013.htm

Okewu, E., & Daramola, O. (2017, October). Design of a learning analytics system for academic advising in Nigerian universities. In *2017 International Conference on Computing Networking and Informatics (ICCNI)* (pp. 1-8). IEEE. https://doi.org/ DOI: 10.1109/ICCNI.2017.8123785

Papazafeiropoulou, A., Pouloudi, A., & Currie, W. L. (2001). Applying the stakeholder concept to electronic commerce: Extending previous research to guide government policy makers. In *Proceedings of the 34th Annual Hawaii International Conference on System Sciences* (pp. 1–10). https://doi.org/DOI: 10.1109/HICSS.2001.926521

Pew Research Center. (2016), From universities to churches, Republicans and Democrats differ in views of major institutions. Retrieved from https://www.pewresearch.org/fact-tank/2016/09/26/from-universities-to-churches-republicans-and-democrats-differ-in-views-of-major-institutions/

Phillips, R., Freeman, R. E., & Wicks, A. C. (2003). What stakeholder theory is not. *Business Ethics Quarterly*, *13*(4), 479–502. DOI: 10.5840/beq200313434

Picciano, A. G. (2012). The evolution of big data and learning analytics in American higher education. *Online Learning : the Official Journal of the Online Learning Consortium*, *16*(3), 3, 9–20. DOI: 10.24059/olj.v16i3.267

Raj, N. S., & v G, R. (2022). Early prediction of student engagement in virtual learning environments using machine learning techniques. *E-Learning and Digital Media*, *19*(6), 537–554. DOI: 10.1177/20427530221108027

Ratcliff, R., Smith, P. L., Brown, S. D., & McKoon, G. (2016). Diffusion decision model: Current issues and history. *Trends in Cognitive Sciences*, *20*(4), 260–281. DOI: 10.1016/j.tics.2016.01.007 PMID: 26952739

Reed, M. S. (2008). Stakeholder participation for environmental management: A literature review. *Biological Conservation*, *141*(10), 2417–2431. DOI: 10.1016/j.biocon.2008.07.014

Rutterford, J., Upton, M., & Kodwani, D. (2006). *Financial Strategy: Adding Stakeholder Value* (2nd ed.). John Wiley & Sons.

Saqr, M., & Alamro, A. (2019). The role of social network analysis as a learning analytics tool in online problem based learning. *BMC Medical Education*, *19*(160), 1–11. DOI: 10.1186/s12909-019-1599-6 PMID: 31113441

Sharkin, B. S. (2004). College counseling and student retention: Research findings and implications for counseling centers. *Journal of College Counseling*, *7*(2), 99–108. DOI: 10.1002/j.2161-1882.2004.tb00241.x

Shibani, A., Knight, S., & Shum, S. B. (2020). Educator perspectives on learning analytics in classroom practice. *The Internet and Higher Education*, *46*, 100730. DOI: 10.1016/j.iheduc.2020.100730

Silvola, A., Näykki, P., Kaveri, A., & Muukkonen, H. (2021). Expectations for supporting student engagement with learning analytics: An academic path perspective. *Computers & Education*, *168*, 1–12. DOI: 10.1016/j.compedu.2021.104192

Steele, G. E. (2018). Student success: Academic advising, student learning data, and technology. *New Directions for Higher Education*, *2018*(184), 59–68. DOI: 10.1002/he.20303

The Society for Learning Analytics Research (SoLAR). 2023. SoLAR Publications (https://www.solaresearch.org/)

Tsai, Y. S., Rates, D., Moreno-Marcos, P. M., Muñoz-Merino, P. J., Jivet, I., Scheffel, M., Drachsler, H., Delgado Kloos, C., & Gašević, D. (2020). Learning analytics in European higher education—Trends and barriers. *Computers & Education*, *155*, 103933. DOI: 10.1016/j.compedu.2020.103933

Tzimas, D., & Demetriadis, S. (2021). Ethical issues in learning analytics: A review of the field. *Educational Technology Research and Development*, *69*(2), 1101–1133. DOI: 10.1007/s11423-021-09977-4

Wang, H., Xu, Z., Fujita, H., & Liu, S. (2016). Towards felicitous decision making: An overview on challenges and trends of Big Data. *Information Sciences*, *367*, 747–765. DOI: 10.1016/j.ins.2016.07.007

Whitelock-Wainwright, A., Tsai, Y. S., Drachsler, H., Scheffel, M., & Gašević, D. (2021). An exploratory latent class analysis of student expectations towards learning analytics services. *The Internet and Higher Education*, *51*, 1–12. DOI: 10.1016/j.iheduc.2021.100818

Williams, J. (2016). Quality assurance and quality enhancement: Is there a relationship? *Quality in Higher Education*, *22*(2), 97–102. DOI: 10.1080/13538322.2016.1227207

Wong, B. T. M., & Li, K. C. (2020). A review of learning analytics intervention in higher education (2011–2018). *Journal of Computers in Education*, *7*(1), 7–28. DOI: 10.1007/s40692-019-00143-7

Young-Jones, A. D., Burt, T. D., Dixon, S., & Hawthorne, M. J. (2013). Academic advising: Does it really impact student success? *Quality Assurance in Education*, *21*(1), 7–19. DOI: 10.1108/09684881311293034

## ADDITIONAL READING

Ahmad, K., Iqbal, W., El-Hassan, A., Qadir, J., Benhaddou, D., Ayyash, M., & Al-Fuqaha, A. (2023). Data-driven artificial intelligence in education: A comprehensive review. *IEEE Transactions on Learning Technologies*, *17*, 12–31. DOI: 10.1109/TLT.2023.3314610

Aljohani, N. R., Daud, A., Abbasi, R. A., Alowibdi, J. S., Basheri, M., & Aslam, M. A. (2019). An integrated framework for course adapted student learning analytics dashboard. *Computers in Human Behavior*, *92*, 679–690. DOI: 10.1016/j.chb.2018.03.035

Alzahrani, A. S., Tsai, Y. S., Aljohani, N., Whitelock-Wainwright, E., & Gasevic, D. (2023). Do teaching staff trust stakeholders and tools in learning analytics? A mixed methods study. *Educational Technology Research and Development*, *71*(4), 1471–1501. DOI: 10.1007/s11423-023-10229-w PMID: 37359481

Banihashem, S. K., Noroozi, O., Van Ginkel, S., Macfadyen, L. P., & Biemans, H. J. (2022). A systematic review of the role of learning analytics in enhancing feedback practices in higher education. *Educational Research Review*, *37*, 1–21. DOI: 10.1016/j.edurev.2022.100489

Cerezo, R., Lara, J. A., Azevedo, R., & Romero, C. (2024). Reviewing the differences between learning analytics and educational data mining: Towards educational data science. *Computers in Human Behavior*, *154*, 1–10. DOI: 10.1016/j.chb.2024.108155

Chen, X., Zou, D., & Xie, H. (2022). A decade of learning analytics: Structural topic modeling based bibliometric analysis. *Education and Information Technologies*, *27*(8), 10517–10561. DOI: 10.1007/s10639-022-11046-z

Du, X., Yang, J., Shelton, B. E., Hung, J. L., & Zhang, M. (2021). A systematic meta-review and analysis of learning analytics research. *Behaviour & Information Technology*, *40*(1), 49–62. DOI: 10.1080/0144929X.2019.1669712

Liñán, L. C., & Pérez, Á. A. J. (2015). Educational Data Mining and Learning Analytics: Differences, similarities, and time evolution. *RUSC. Universities and Knowledge Society Journal*, *12*(3), 98–112. DOI: 10.7238/rusc.v12i3.2515

Munguia, P., Brennan, A., Taylor, S., & Lee, D. (2020). A learning analytics journey: Bridging the gap between technology services and the academic need. *The Internet and Higher Education*, *46*, 1–9. DOI: 10.1016/j.iheduc.2020.100744

Nguyen, A., Tuunanen, T., Gardner, L., & Sheridan, D. (2021). Design principles for learning analytics information systems in higher education. *European Journal of Information Systems*, *30*(5), 541–568. DOI: 10.1080/0960085X.2020.1816144

Nistor, N., & Hernández-García, Á. (2018). What types of data are used in learning analytics? An overview of six cases. *Computers in Human Behavior*, *89*, 335–338. DOI: 10.1016/j.chb.2018.07.038

# Chapter 8
# Trusted Credentialing Systems Using Blockchain Technology for Learning Analytics Dashboards

**Naser Heidari**
*Bio10, Australia*

## ABSTRACT

*This chapter introduces a new framework for issuing and analyzing educational credentials using blockchain technology and learning analytics. The goal is to create a system where credentials are issued dynamically, transparently, and data-driven, and that guides the learning path in real time through self-adaptive dashboards. This model not only increases the validity of credentials, but also elevates the role of the learner from a passive recipient to an active owner of the learning path. The nexus of blockchain, smart contracts, and analytics opens up new horizons for assessment, digital trust, and personalized learning.*

## 1. INTRODUCTION

In this era where digital learning has become a key pillar of education on a global scale, the issue of trust in issued certificates and analytical data related to the learning path of learners has become one of the fundamental challenges for educational institutions, assessment organizations, and end users. In environments where education is provided virtually, blended, or based on open learning platforms (such as massive online courses), the validity and authenticity of certificates is no longer limited to the seal of an institution, but depends on technological infra-

DOI: 10.4018/979-8-3373-5117-9.ch008

ght © 2026, IGI Global Scientific Publishing. Copying or distributing in print or electronic forms without written permission of IGI Global Scientific Publishing is prohibited. Use of this chapter to generative artificial intelligence (AI) technologies is expressly prohibited. The publisher reserves all rights to license its use for generative AI training and machine learning model development.

structures and transparent systems that can guarantee validity in a data-driven and forgery-resistant manner. In such a context, the concept of "learning analytics" as a tool for understanding, predicting, and optimizing the learning process becomes doubly important, but at the same time, without a reliable infrastructure, its data-driven nature can lead to skepticism, manipulation, or doubt in the results (Movahed, Movahed, & Nozari, 2024).

Learning analytics refers to the process of collecting, processing, and interpreting educational data to improve teaching and learning processes. These include data such as learner engagement, course progress, content engagement, tests, feedback, and learning paths. However, one of the most important challenges for learning analytics in the digital age is the issue of data trust, the authenticity of learning records, and the lack of a transparent and immutable infrastructure for recording educational credentials (Nozari & Aliahmadi, 2023). Certificates issued manually or even digitally without traceable systems can be easily forged, creating severe vulnerabilities in the learning analytics ecosystem, especially when this data is involved in macro-decision making, recruitment, or organizational analytics.

In response to this growing need, blockchain technology has emerged as a new solution to create trust, transparency, and immutability in data-driven educational systems. By creating a distributed, untampered chain of data, blockchain enables certificates to be recorded in an encrypted, verified, and traceable form on a secure network (Rahmaty & Nozari, 2023). In addition, through smart contracts, the process of issuing, evaluating, expiring, or updating educational certificates can be managed automatically and without the need for human intervention. This transformation can upgrade the structure of issuing certificates from a centralized and static model to a dynamic and distributed model in which each certificate is a unique and verifiable digital asset (Nozari, Szmelter-Jarosz, & Ghahremani-Nahr, 2022).

One of the most important consequences of this transformation is the possibility of directly connecting these blockchain certificates to learning analytics dashboards. Such dashboards, which typically provide data on learning progress, successes, weaknesses, and behavioral patterns, can become a valid decision-making reference for users, educational institutions, employers, and assessment organizations when connected to valid and immutable certificates (Movahed, Movahed, & Nozari, 2024). In this structure, not only is the accuracy of the analyzed data guaranteed, but it also allows for a more comprehensive and personalized assessment of the learner's capabilities, as the certificates issued will be based on real-time and accurate analysis of his/her performance.

In addition, the ability to combine blockchain with other emerging technologies such as decentralized digital identity, educational NFTs, tokenized economy, and AI-based learning analytics, outlines new perspectives for the future of education and learning (Nozari, Fallah, Kazemipoor, & Najafi, 2021). In such a system, the learner is not only a recipient of data and certificates, but also becomes an active owner of his/her educational assets and can, with his/her consent, share information with others, develop his/her learning path, or use them for career and academic opportunities. This conceptual shift creates a kind of democratization of the digital education system, where the learner will be the main focus of analysis and validation, not just the recipient of a certificate from a centralized entity (Ghahremani-Nahr, Nozari, Rahmaty, Zeraati Foukolaei, & Sherejsharifi, 2023).

Ultimately, the integration of blockchain certificates with learning analytics dashboards is not just about adding a new technology to the existing structure, but also a fundamental change in the logic of designing educational and assessment systems. This integration allows for observation, analysis, and decision-making based on authentic, immutable, and digitally owned data. In other words, blockchain can become the backbone of future learning analytics systems; a system where trust, transparency, and data authority, along with advanced analytics, will make the learning journey not only smarter, but also fairer and more humane (Nozari, Szmelter-Jarosz, & Ghahremani-Nahr, 2021).

## 2. FROM LEARNING ANALYTICS TO DIGITAL CREDENTIALS

Before we can address the applications of blockchain in issuing educational certificates and connecting it to learning analytics systems, it is essential to properly understand the conceptual and technological evolution in the two areas of "learning analytics" and "digital accreditation." These two areas appear independent of each other on the surface, but at their core, they are rooted in a common evolution: the digitization of education and the data-driven decision-making in teaching-learning systems. This section first examines the evolution of learning analytics as a tool for interpreting educational data, and then refers to the formation of digital certificates and the challenges of trust in traditional structures to provide a theoretical basis for integrating the two in the blockchain context.

Learning analytics, in its simplest definition, refers to the use of educational data to understand learner behavior, performance, and needs and to provide intelligent educational decisions. Over time, the concept has evolved from a purely statistical approach to describing learning progress to an analytical and predictive tool in the field of education. With the advent of digital learning environments, a variety of data, including study time, interaction with resources, test responses, content return rates, and even emotional patterns, became available. These data were used as key resources for designing personalized learning paths, timely educational interventions, and evaluating content effectiveness (Tavakkoli-Moghaddam, Nozari, Bakhshi-Movahed, & Bakhshi-Movahed, 2024).

However, as learning analytics grew, challenges arose in the areas of transparency of analytics, quality of raw data, and the role of the learner in the decision-making cycle. Many learning analytics systems in universities or commercial platforms collected data in a one-way manner, with outputs primarily available to teachers or administrators. Not only did the learner have no control over his or her data, but he or she was often unaware of the analysis that was being conducted on his or her performance (Nozari, Najafi, Fallah, & Hosseinzadeh Lotfi, 2019). This led to criticism that learning analytics, despite its extensive technical capabilities, was sometimes accompanied by a lack of participation, transparency, and accountability.

Alongside this trend, the issue of accreditation and the issuance of educational certificates also underwent fundamental changes. In traditional systems, educational certificates were often issued by centralized institutions, and their validity depended on the name and status of the issuing institution. With the growth of informal learning, online courses, project-based learning, and skills-based training, the demand for certificates that reflected an individual's actual competence in specific areas increased. This need led to the growth of digital certificates and skill badges that were awarded to individuals based on specific and measurable evidence (Movahed, Movahed, Aliahmadi, & Nozari, 2024).

Digital certificates, as an advanced version of educational documents, are provided as encrypted files or verifiable links on the Internet. These certificates can include information about the issuer, the holder, the skills demonstrated, the date of issuance, and the assessment standards. However, the current structure also faces challenges such as the possibility of forgery, the lack of a unified validation infrastructure, and inconsistency between certificates from different platforms. These problems can prevent the effective use of these documents, especially when transferred between institutions or used in employment (Nozari, Ghahremani-Nahr, & Szmelter-Jarosz, 2024).

Furthermore, digital certificates, in many cases, operate in a static and isolated manner from other learning data. This means that, for example, an individual may have received multiple online certificates from different platforms, but cannot view them in an analytical and combined view. This gap in cross-certificate analysis and the lack of the ability to assess the learning path in an integrated manner have resulted in many digital documents having limited analytical and decision-making value, despite their apparent validity (Ghahremani-Nahr, Nozari, & Aliahmadi, 2023).

In this context, the link between learning analytics and digital certificates, particularly in the form of dashboards that provide a combined view of data, progress, and earned credentials, is a new step towards increasing the transparency and meaning of education. Rather than focusing solely on grades or course completion, such dashboards can provide a deeper picture of a learner's skill and cognitive growth. In this structure, each certificate is not just a document of completion of a course, but also represents a process of data, feedback, and analysis that led to its issuance (Nozari, Ghahremani-Nahr, & Szmelter-Jarosz, 2023).

But creating such systems requires an infrastructure that allows for the immutable recording of learning records, the ability to link data to credentials, and the ability for users to control the ownership and sharing of their data. This is where blockchain technology comes into play. Blockchain can store certificates in a distributed, encrypted, and tamper-proof manner, while enabling direct connections between learning analytics data and automated issuance of certificates through smart contracts (Ayub Khan et al., 2021).

This approach not only helps to address challenges related to certificate forgery, institutional trust, and data ownership, but also creates a conceptual shift in learning analytics. In traditional models, data was a tool for predicting or interpreting behavior; however, in models combined with blockchain, data becomes part of a formal validation structure. In other words, each individual's learning trajectory is transformed from a hidden process into an encrypted and verifiable document that can play a role in educational, career, and even economic decision-making (Szmelter-Jarosz, Ghahremani-Nahr, & Nozari, 2021).

On the other hand, the connection between these two areas can pave the way for concepts such as "smart certificates"; That is, documents that are updated in real time, connected to live learning data, and can remain adaptable as learners change direction or enter new domains. This requires redefining the role of the certificate from a final document to a living, dynamic entity that grows and remains analyzable as learners grow (Nozari, Tavakkoli-Moghaddam, Ghahremani-Nahr, & Najafi, 2023).

In sum, the evolution of learning analytics and digital accreditation began on two relatively independent paths, but has now converged at a point where there is a shared need for transparency, trust, and analyzability. Technologies such as blockchain can bridge this gap and pave the way for a new generation of learning systems in which educational documents not only verify learning, but also provide an analytical, transparent, and personalized reflection of it (Aliahmadi & Nozari, 2023).

## 3. BLOCKCHAIN FOUNDATIONS FOR CREDENTIALING SYSTEMS

Blockchain technology has emerged as one of the most influential digital trust infrastructures in various fields over the past decade. While its early applications were mostly seen in the field of cryptocurrencies and financial value transfer, the fundamental capabilities of this technology have quickly gained attention in other fields, including digital education and learning. In the field of educational certificates and learning analytics systems, blockchain plays a role not only as a technical tool, but also as a framework for trust and immutability. This section explains the main concepts of blockchain, its application in educational systems, and how it can be used to validate learning analytics dashboards.

In its basic definition, blockchain is a distributed database and a chain of blocks, each block containing a set of transactions or data and connected to the previous block using cryptographic algorithms. This encrypted connection prevents tampering or deletion of previous information, which is why blockchain is known as an "immutable" technology (Nozari, Szmelter-Jarosz, & Rahmaty, 2024). In conventional architectures, blockchains can be public or private, and permissioned or permissionless. In the field of education, most operational applications tend to use private or semi-private chains to both maintain data security and ensure system performance at scale (Najafi, Nozari, & Edalatpanah, 2022).

A prominent feature of blockchain in the educational context is the ability to create and store "verified digital certificates." In this model, each certificate or skill badge is recorded as a transaction on the blockchain. This record includes information such as the individual's ID, the skill or course specification, the issuing authority, and the time of issuance. Since the data is recorded on the chain and verified by multiple nodes, no single entity can alter or forge it on its own. On the other hand, it is possible to verify the authenticity of a certificate without having to contact the issuing authority, just by observing the blockchain (Nozari & Ghahremani-Nahr, 2023).

But the real power of blockchain in the field of learning analytics is revealed when it is combined with the concept of smart contracts. A smart contract is code that runs on the blockchain and automatically performs an action when predefined conditions are met. In the context of education, these contracts can act as an automated certificate issuance engine. For example, when a learner consistently participates in a specific course, successfully passes the exam, and completes all required activities, the smart contract will automatically issue a digital certificate and record it on the blockchain (Bathaee, Nozari, & Szmelter-Jarosz, 2023).

This automated certificate issuance structure, when combined with learning analytics dashboards, can create a fully intelligent, transparent, and responsive environment. In other words, in an integrated system, learner behavioral and analytical data are used not only to display the learning process but also to enable the issuance of educational certificates. In this situation, learning analytics is transformed from a purely observational tool to an active driver; that is, the data directly leads to official and credentialed certificates (Nozari, Ghahremani-Nahr, & Najafi, 2023).

Figure 1 shows the conceptual architecture of a blockchain-based certification and learning analytics system. In this architecture, behavioral data is collected from the learning management system (LMS) and transferred to the data analytics engine. After analyzing behavior, performance, and results, if the necessary criteria are met, the smart contract is activated and a certificate is issued and recorded on the blockchain. This certificate is immediately displayed on the learner's dashboard and can be shared or used in other systems.

*Figure 1. Blockchain-based educational certification and learning analytics architecture*

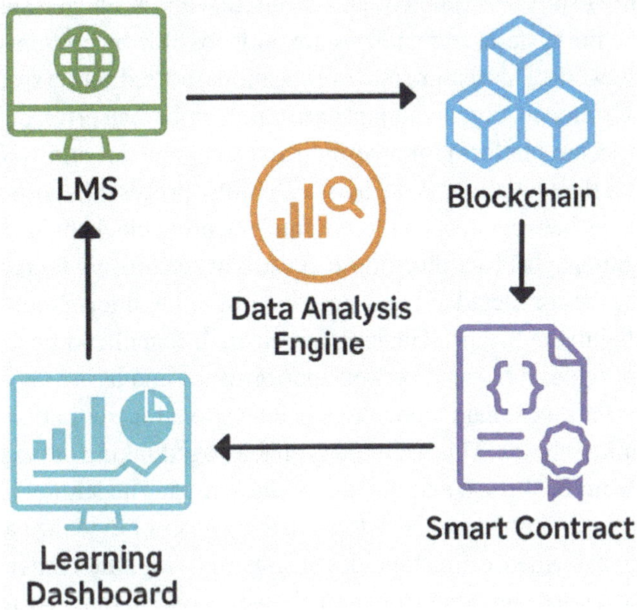


This model not only increases trust between the learner and the educational institution, but also enables hybrid analysis between learning data and official documents. Also, since certificates are recorded on the chain, they can be easily transferred and verified in other environments such as job platforms, other universities, or professional networks (Aliahmadi, Ghahremani-Nahr, & Nozari, 2023).

Another important issue that arises in this context is the discussion of digital identity and its role in issuing blockchain-based certificates. In traditional structures, individuals' identities are usually defined in the form of usernames and passwords. However, in decentralized structures, identity is managed through cryptographic keys. Each learner has a private key that proves his ownership of the certificates. As a result, not only is it possible to issue and verify documents without the need for an intermediary entity, but also the learner remains in full control of the data (Nozari, Rahmaty, & Szmelter-Jarosz, 2024).

In addition, blockchain can be integrated with international standards such as Verifiable Credentials and Decentralized Identifiers, which provide an interoperable infrastructure for issuing and using certificates on a global scale. These standards allow documents issued in one country or platform to be easily read, analyzed, and verified in other countries or platforms (Najafi, Nozari, & Edalatpanah, 2022). This is especially important in situations where learning is pursued cross-border, blended, and lifelong.

From a technical perspective, one of the important advantages of blockchain in this area is its ability to be decentralized. This means that no centralized authority is able to fully control the system, and changes are only possible by consensus among the nodes of the network. This feature makes educational accreditation systems resistant to political interference, organizational corruption, or human error, and provides an impartial and secure platform for recording and analyzing learning (Nozari, 2023).

At the same time, challenges such as scalability, processing costs, and compliance with privacy laws cannot be ignored. Implementing blockchain on a large scale requires designing hybrid architectures that use blockchain only for parts of the data (e.g., record hashes or metadata) and store the rest of the information in traditional databases (Aliahmadi, Nozari, Ghahremani-Nahr, & Szmelter-Jarosz, 2022). Such an approach provides a balance between performance and trust.

Ultimately, the blockchain foundation for educational accreditation systems goes beyond a technical choice. This technology enables a rethinking of the philosophy of education, institutional trust, and the role of the learner. The learner is transformed from a passive recipient of evidence to an active owner of evidence and data. Certificates are transformed from static documents to living, interactive entities, and learning analytics are upgraded from descriptive reports to tools for issuing formal decisions. This path, relying on blockchain, will pave the way towards transparent, accountable, and universal education (Nozari, Tavakkoli-Moghaddam, Rohaninejad, & Hanzalek, 2023).

## 4. ARCHITECTURE OF A BLOCKCHAIN-BACKED LEARNING ANALYTICS DASHBOARD

Designing a learning analytics dashboard that fully leverages blockchain infrastructure to issue, display, and manage educational credentials requires a coherent, multi-layered architecture. This architecture must be able to not only collect and process analytics data from multiple sources, but also manage it in a way that automates and transparently authenticates the issuance and authentication of digital certificates through smart contracts. In this structure, all system components must communicate with each other in a seamless, interactive manner that is both understandable to the end user and technically responsive to the needs of trust, scalability, and inter-organizational interoperability.

At the core of this architecture is a powerful analytics engine that receives learner behavioral and performance data from learning management systems or virtual learning platforms. This data includes information such as attendance, duration of interaction with educational content, test results, progress, participation in interactive activities, and other learning indicators. Once collected, this data is transmitted to the learning analytics system in real time or in a turn. Here, statistical models, machine learning algorithms, or logical rules are used to obtain an analytical picture of each learner's performance (Fallah & Nozari, 2021).

The results of the analysis will trigger smart contracts if they reach specified thresholds. These contracts are defined in such a way that they check criteria such as minimum score, level of activity, completion of modules, or other performance indicators, and if they are met, a certificate will be automatically issued and stored on the blockchain. These certificates will be in the form of encrypted data including the learner's profile, the course or skill completed, the time of issuance, and the issuing entity. The presence of this information on the blockchain allows for its immutable and unmediated verification (Ghahremani-Nahr, Najafi, & Nozari, 2022).

Since the ultimate goal of this architecture is to present data to users in an intelligent, meaningful, and useful way, all analyzed information, along with the certificates issued, are displayed in an interactive environment called a learning dashboard. This dashboard can display a graphical representation of the learner's progress, certificates earned, skill paths taken, new learning opportunities, and suggestions for further development. The dashboard also allows for the status of certificates (approved, pending, rejected) to be viewed and shared with other systems (Nozari, Fallah, Szmelter-Jarosz, & Krzemiński, 2021).

A key element in the design of such an architecture is the existence of a decentralized authentication portal for the learner. In this model, each user has an encrypted identifier that is managed as a public-private key. This identifier both guarantees their ownership of the data and allows only them to manage access to their information and certificates. This identity model, unlike traditional centralized structures, gives the individual complete control over the data and is in line with the principles of personal data governance (Alsobhi, Alakhtar, Ubaid, Hussain, & Hussain, 2023).

In Figure 2, the conceptual structure of this architecture is visually depicted. In this image, there are four main layers: the data collection layer from the LMS, the data analysis and smart contract activation layer, the blockchain layer for registering certificates, and finally the dashboard layer for displaying information. Each of these layers is distinguished by colored icons, and the arrows between them indicate the data flow and operations within the system. This image, in a simple but accurate way, shows the interaction mechanism of components for issuing and analyzing blockchain certificates.

*Figure 2. Learning analytics dashboard architecture with support for blockchain and smart contracts*

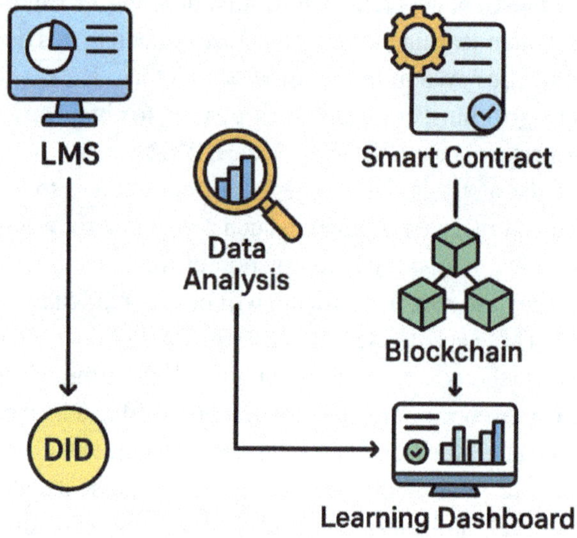


In addition to these components, there is a need for additional infrastructure to make this architecture practical. For example, complementary databases, local caches for temporary storage, and API services for connecting to external systems such as job search or skills validation platforms can play a role in this architecture. Also, security layers to prevent unauthorized access to data should be considered at all points of exchange (Lotfi, Najafi, & Nozari, 2016).

The advantage of this type of design is that the process of analyzing, issuing certificates, and presenting them to the user is placed in a completely integrated and automated path. This allows learning data to not only remain as a training record, but also to become a decision-making tool and guide the learner's future path. This structure can also allow certification bodies to implement the accreditation process in a stable and transparent manner without direct intervention and without the need for manual verification (Aliahmadi, Movahed, & Nozari, 2024).

Furthermore, the analytics dashboard in this model can be updated in real time. This means that after each learning activity, new data is sent to the analytics engine, checked, and if the status changes, the new information appears in the dashboard. Also, if a user receives a new certificate, it is immediately recorded in the blockchain and displayed in his profile. This feature increases the level of interactivity and responsiveness of the system and changes the learning experience from a passive to a participatory one (Nozari, Tavakkoli-Moghaddam, & Gharemani-Nahr, 2022).

Finally, such architectures should be designed with interoperability in mind. Standards such as Open Badges, Verifiable Credentials, and W3C DID can provide frameworks for secure and readable exchange between learning dashboards, recruitment systems, professional social networks, and educational institutions. If this interoperability is designed properly, certificates registered on one platform will be usable in a variety of other spaces, and the value of analytical data will be multiplied (Li, Wang, Gasevic, Yu, & Liu, 2023).

In this description, the architecture of a blockchain-based learning dashboard is not just a set of technical components, but a model for forward-looking, trust-building, and data-driven education. A model in which the learner is not just an observer of analytics and certificates, but a key player in owning, managing, and exploiting his or her own learning path. This path, relying on blockchain transparency, data analytics intelligence, and interactive design, could become one of the most important developments in digital education.

## 5. DYNAMIC CREDENTIAL PATHWAYS AND SELF-ADAPTIVE LEARNING DASHBOARDS

In the era of digital learning, where learning paths are increasingly diverse, distributed, and non-linear, there is a growing need for systems that can generate and manage certificates based on real-time learner performance and analytics. Traditional certificates are often a static reflection of success at the end of a course of study and do not typically reflect incremental growth, ongoing interventions, or changing learning paths. In this context, the concepts of "dynamic paths to certification" and "self-adaptive learning dashboards" are emerging; concepts that leverage learning analytics, blockchain technology, and personalized mechanisms to offer a new approach to designing, issuing, and interpreting educational certificates.

In traditional educational paths, certificates are typically issued upon successful completion of a specific course or program. This static process is inefficient in systems where learning is continuous, project-based, or skill-based. In these systems, the learner's progress may be non-linear, with a variety of paths chosen based on their interests or job status. To meet this challenge, accreditation systems need to be able to monitor learning paths in real time and generate dynamic and adaptive certificates in response to data analysis (Nozari, Najafi, Jafari-Eskandari, & Aliahmadi, 2016).

In the meantime, blockchain technology, especially with the help of smart contracts, provides an infrastructure in which certificates can be defined not as final results, but as intermediate and living points in the learning path. For example, if a learner reaches a certain threshold of performance in the middle of a specific skill path, the system can issue a temporary, scalable microcredential that can later be upgraded or converted into a formal certificate upon completion of other elements of the path. Such certificates can also be recorded in the form of educational NFTs, ensuring their ownership, portability, and validity (Awaji & Solaiman, 2022).

In this architecture, the analytics dashboard plays a key role. A self-adaptive dashboard is a tool that not only displays learning data, but also changes the proposed learning path in real time, suggests new opportunities, and even sets future prerequisites for issuing subsequent certificates. Using AI or decision-making algorithms, the dashboard can understand which pathways are working best for the learner, where intervention is needed, and how to issue credentials that best align with the learner's capabilities and needs (Movahed, Aliahmadi, Parsanejad, & Nozari, 2023).

For example, if a learner is performing well in the data analytics skills track in the areas related to data visualization but is weak in machine learning algorithms, the dashboard can provide suggestions for additional study, participation in customized exercises, or access to specific resources. Meanwhile, if the learner's performance in visualization reaches a threshold level, a smart contract is activated and a micro-credential is automatically issued and recorded on the blockchain (Nozari, 2024).

Figure 3 illustrates the conceptual structure of this cycle. In this figure, the learning path is represented as a dynamic loop that includes behavioral data collection, performance analysis, adaptive decision-making, smart contract activation, certification, and feedback to the learner dashboard. Each step in this cycle is distinguished by colored icons and interactively linked to other components. This cycle represents the non-static, living logic in certification-based paths that can change based on both actual performance and learner needs.

*Figure 3. Dynamic certification cycle in blockchain-based adaptive learning analytics systems*

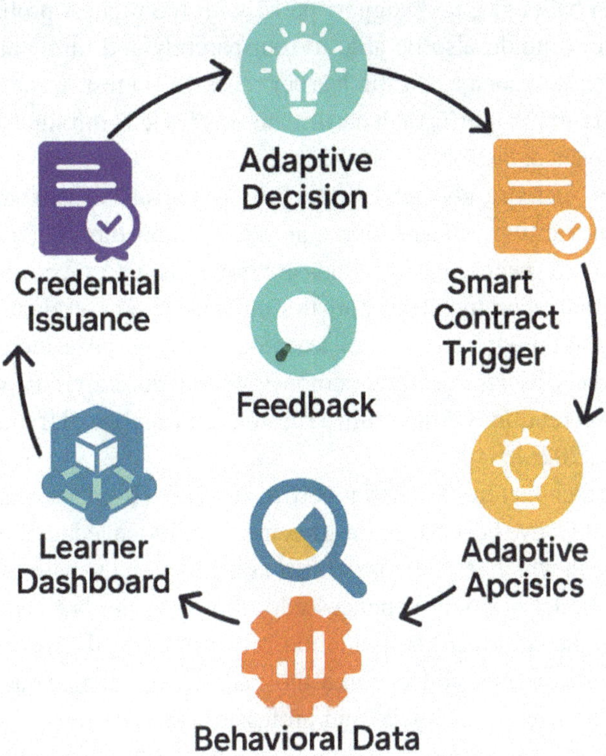


One of the important features of this model is the possibility of designing hybrid and interdisciplinary paths. The learner can collect paths from different platforms through a dashboard, and the system, by comparative analysis of his performance in these paths, issues interdisciplinary or customized certificates. For example, combining coding skills with design thinking can lead to a certificate in "human-centered software design" that is jointly issued by several institutions and also registered on the blockchain in a multi-signature manner (Mohammadi, Ghazanfari, Nozari, & Shafiezad, 2015).

In such a situation, the certificate is no longer a static document, but becomes a profile of a "learning journey"; a journey in which data, analysis, comparative decisions and formal results are recorded in a secure chain. At each stage, the learner can review, modify, or expand their path, while benefiting from the added value of intermediate certificates. These certificates are not only verifiable, but also recombinable, re-evaluated, and updated (Nozari & Szmelter-Jarosz, 2024).

From a technical perspective, this process requires the design of dynamic matching algorithms that can learn from the learner's past data, predict potential successes and challenges, and suggest paths with the highest probability of success. The system should also be able to transparently and immutably implement multi-step processes, such as "if the learner scores Y on test X and has at least 40 hours of activity in module Z, then certificate A is issued" through smart contracts (Movahed, Movahed, & Nozari, 2024).

Furthermore, in more advanced models, the system can use machine learning to identify hidden learning patterns. For example, an algorithm might recognize that some learners with specific backgrounds are more likely to succeed in a particular path, and therefore recommend that path to similar users. These adaptive capabilities not only increase the effectiveness of learning paths, but also increase the credibility of issued certificates, as they demonstrate that an individual has achieved a specific skill, not randomly, but within a rigorous and analytical framework (Nozari & Edalatpanah, 2023).

Overall, the architecture of dynamic certificates and self-adaptive analytical dashboards is a way to move beyond the limitations of traditional educational credentials and enter an era in which learning is defined as a living, multi-path, and data-driven process. This model not only enhances educational value, but also increases the level of trust in the labor market, academia, and professional networks. In the near future, such certificates could become the mainstay of competency assessment, career progression, and even social and professional evaluations.

## 6. CONCLUSION

At the end of this chapter, what emerges most is the urgent need to redefine traditional concepts of certification, assessment, and learning analytics in the context of digital education. With the acceleration of informal, blended, and lifelong learning, it is no longer possible to settle for models in which a certificate is simply a final piece of paper proving the completion of a course. Technological developments, especially in the areas of blockchain, learning analytics, and smart contracts, have made it possible to transform educational documents into dynamic, transparent, and data-driven mechanisms. In such a model, validity does not come solely from the issuing authority, but from data that has continuously, accurately, and analyzed, recorded and interpreted the behavior and progress of the learner.

This chapter has attempted to show that digital certificates can be designed in such a way that they are not only verifiable but also interpretable. This interpretation is based on data collected throughout the learning process through learning management systems, tests, interactions, and behavioral analytics. Blockchain, as the main infrastructure of this model, enables immutable, distributed, and encrypted storage of certificates. This feature, while increasing security and credibility, creates a kind of digital trust that goes beyond traditional, hierarchical educational frameworks.

On the other hand, the link between learning analytics and educational accreditation makes certificates an accurate reflection of the learner's actual performance. The final score or assessment is no longer the only factor in issuing a certificate, but behavioral trends, inter-course interactions, the learner's level of engagement, and even the type of participation in group learning also play a role in accreditation. This can be taken to a deeper and more precise level with the introduction of artificial intelligence and machine learning algorithms into data analysis. Such certificates not only validate knowledge, but also recognize the path of learning, effort, and repetition.

Another point addressed in this chapter is the concept of "dynamic paths" for certification. In this model, the learning path is not a fixed and predetermined path, but an open, flexible structure that can be reshaped based on analytical feedback. This path can be interdisciplinary, hybrid, or personalized, and can be adjusted based on the learner's current performance and personal or professional goals. Such flexibility gives the learner a sense of ownership over his or her educational path and can better plan for the continuation of the path with a better understanding of the situation.

Self-adaptive dashboards also play a very important role in realizing this approach. These dashboards are not just tools for displaying information, but are the engine for decision-making, recommendations, and guidance of the learner based on real-world data analysis. They can display existing credentials, introduce upcoming opportunities, suggest alternative pathways, and even explain what prevented them from earning a specific certification. These dashboards can also connect with tools outside the education system, such as job boards or professional networks, and present certifications in a seamless manner.

Contrary to the common perception that certification is the end point of a process, such a model turns it into a starting point for a conversation and a continuation of learning. With a digital profile of their credentials, all stored encrypted on the blockchain, the learner can use them anytime, anywhere for assessment, employment, further education, or even self-directed learning. This profile not only shapes their academic identity, but also represents a continuous investment in their personal learning path.

From the perspective of educational institutions and policymakers, this transformation means creating a new kind of infrastructure for transparency, accountability, and educational equity. In traditional structures, access to official certificates was often difficult, time-consuming, or limited to certain groups. But using blockchain and learning analytics, it is possible to issue certificates in real time, without intermediaries, and based on data. This model can also provide solutions to problems such as document forgery, delays in issuance, or the inability to obtain international validation.

There are challenges along the way. These include issues related to data privacy, the costs of implementing blockchain infrastructure, the need to adapt to global standards, and the training of users and institutions. In addition, for these certificates to be accepted internationally, their interoperability with other systems, compatibility with legal frameworks, and compliance with open standards must be ensured. But the reality is that the benefits of these systems, especially in the long term, far outweigh the implementation challenges.

Ultimately, learning analytics and blockchain-based certificates represent a new era of education and assessment; one in which trust is built not on authority, but on data, transparency, and interaction. The learner is no longer a passive entity in the system, but an active actor, a decision-maker, and the owner of his or her own information and certificates. Educational systems are also moving away from static and linear structures and becoming living, intelligent, and responsive structures that can continuously adapt to individual and societal needs.

Such horizons will not only enable the realization of lifelong learning, but will also establish a new paradigm for educational equity, digital meritocracy, and sustainability in learning. In this way, smart certificates can become the connecting link between data, analytics, learning, and identity; a link that will shape the future of global education.

## REFERENCES


Aliahmadi, A., Ghahremani-Nahr, J., & Nozari, H. (2023). Pricing decisions in the closed-loop supply chain network, taking into account the queuing system in production centers. *Expert Systems with Applications*, *212*, 118741. DOI: 10.1016/j.eswa.2022.118741

Aliahmadi, A., Movahed, A. B., & Nozari, H. (2024). Collaboration analysis in supply chain 4.0 for smart businesses. In *Building Smart and Sustainable Businesses With Transformative Technologies* (pp. 103–122). IGI Global Scientific Publishing.

Aliahmadi, A., & Nozari, H. (2023, January). Evaluation of security metrics in AIoT and blockchain-based supply chain by Neutrosophic decision-making method. In Supply chain forum: an international journal (Vol. 24, No. 1, pp. 31-42). Taylor & Francis. DOI: 10.1080/16258312.2022.2101898

Aliahmadi, A., Nozari, H., Ghahremani-Nahr, J., & Szmelter-Jarosz, A. (2022). Evaluation of key impression of resilient supply chain based on artificial intelligence of things (AIoT). arXiv preprint arXiv:2207.13174.

Alsobhi, H. A., Alakhtar, R. A., Ubaid, A., Hussain, O. K., & Hussain, F. K. (2023). Blockchain-based micro-credentialing system in higher education institutions: Systematic literature review. *Knowledge-Based Systems*, *265*, 110238. DOI: 10.1016/j.knosys.2022.110238

Awaji, B., & Solaiman, E. (2022). Design, implementation, and evaluation of blockchain-based trusted achievement record system for students in higher education. arXiv preprint arXiv:2204.12547. DOI: 10.5220/0011044200003182

Ayub Khan, A., Laghari, A. A., Shaikh, A. A., Bourouis, S., Mamlouk, A. M., & Alshazly, H. (2021). Educational blockchain: A secure degree attestation and verification traceability architecture for higher education commission. *Applied Sciences (Basel, Switzerland)*, *11*(22), 10917. DOI: 10.3390/app112210917

Bathaee, M., Nozari, H., & Szmelter-Jarosz, A. (2023). Designing a new location-allocation and routing model with simultaneous pick-up and delivery in a closed-loop supply chain network under uncertainty. *Logistics (Basel)*, *7*(1), 3. DOI: 10.3390/logistics7010003

Fallah, M., & Nozari, H. (2021). Neutrosophic mathematical programming for optimization of multi-objective sustainable biomass supply chain network design. *Computer Modeling in Engineering & Sciences*, *129*(2), 927–951. DOI: 10.32604/cmes.2021.017511

Ghahremani-Nahr, J., Najafi, S. E., & Nozari, H. (2022). A combined transportation model for the fruit and vegetable supply chain network. *Journal of Optimization in Industrial Engineering*, *15*(2), 131–145.

Ghahremani-Nahr, J., Nozari, H., & Aliahmadi, A. (2023). Contract Design for Return Products in a Cooperative Closed-Loop Supply Chain. *Global Business Review*, •••, 09721509221148892. DOI: 10.1177/09721509221148892

Ghahremani-Nahr, J., Nozari, H., Rahmaty, M., Zeraati Foukolaei, P., & Sherejsharifi, A. (2023). Development of a novel fuzzy hierarchical location-routing optimization model considering reliability. *Logistics (Basel)*, *7*(3), 64. DOI: 10.3390/logistics7030064

Li, Z. Z., Wang, H., Gasevic, D., Yu, J., & Liu, J. K. (2023). Enhancing blockchain adoption through tailored software engineering: An industrial-grounded study in education credentialing. *Distributed Ledger Technologies: Research and Practice*, *2*(4), 1–24. DOI: 10.1145/3632532

Lotfi, F. H. Z., Najafi, S. E., & Nozari, H. (Eds.). (2016). *Data envelopment analysis and effective performance assessment*. IGI Global.

Mohammadi, H., Ghazanfari, M., Nozari, H., & Shafiezad, O. (2015). Combining the theory of constraints with system dynamics: A general model (case study of the subsidized milk industry). International journal of management science and engineering management, 10(2), 102-108.

Movahed, A. B., Aliahmadi, A., Parsanejad, M., & Nozari, H. (2023). A systematic review of collaboration in supply chain 4.0 with meta-synthesis method. *Supply Chain Analytics*, *4*, 100052. DOI: 10.1016/j.sca.2023.100052

Movahed, A. B., Movahed, A. B., Aliahmadi, B., & Nozari, H. (2024). Green and sustainable supply chain in Agriculture 6.0. In *Advanced Businesses in Industry 6.0* (pp. 32–45). IGI Global. DOI: 10.4018/979-8-3693-3108-8.ch003

Movahed, A. B., Movahed, A. B., & Nozari, H. (2024). Opportunities and challenges of smart supply chain in Industry 5.0. Information Logistics for Organizational Empowerment and Effective Supply Chain Management, 108-138.

Movahed, A. B., Movahed, A. B., & Nozari, H. (2024). Marketing 6.0 Conceptualization. In Advanced Businesses in Industry 6.0 (pp. 15-31). IGI Global.

Movahed, A. B., Movahed, A. B., & Nozari, H. (2024). Opportunities and challenges of marketing 5.0. Smart and Sustainable Interactive Marketing, 1-21.

Najafi, S. E., Nozari, H., & Edalatpanah, S. A. (2022). Investigating the key parameters affecting sustainable IoT-based marketing. In *Computational Intelligence Methodologies Applied to Sustainable Development Goals* (pp. 51–61). Springer International Publishing. DOI: 10.1007/978-3-030-97344-5_4

Najafi, S. E., Nozari, H., & Edalatpanah, S. A. (2022). Artificial Intelligence of Things (AIoT) and Industry 4.0–Based Supply Chain (FMCG Industry). A roadmap for enabling industry 4.0 by artificial intelligence, 31-41.

Nozari, H. (Ed.). (2023). *Building Smart and Sustainable Businesses with Transformative Technologies*. IGI Global. DOI: 10.4018/979-8-3693-0210-1

Nozari, H. (2024). Green Supply Chain Management based on Artificial Intelligence of Everything. *Journal of Economics and Management*, *46*, 171–188. DOI: 10.22367/jem.2024.46.07

Nozari, H., & Aliahmadi, A. (2023). Analysis of critical success factors in a food agile supply chain by a fuzzy hybrid decision-making method. [Formerly known as Iranian Journal of Management Studies]. *Interdisciplinary Journal of Management Studies*, *16*(4), 905–926.

Nozari, H., & Edalatpanah, S. A. (2023). Smart systems risk management in IoT-based supply chain. In *Advances in reliability, failure and risk analysis* (pp. 251–268). Springer Nature Singapore. DOI: 10.1007/978-981-19-9909-3_11

Nozari, H., Fallah, M., Kazemipoor, H., & Najafi, S. E. (2021). Big data analysis of IoT-based supply chain management considering FMCG industries. *Бизнес-информатика*, *15*(1, 1 (eng)), 78–96. DOI: 10.17323/2587-814X.2021.1.78.96

Nozari, H., Fallah, M., Szmelter-Jarosz, A., & Krzemiński, M. (2021). Analysis of security criteria for IoT-based supply chain: a case study of FMCG industries. Central European Management Journal, 29(4).

Nozari, H., & Ghahremani-Nahr, J. (2023). A comprehensive strategic-tactical multi-objective sustainable supply chain model with human resources considerations. *Supply Chain Analytics*, *4*, 100044. DOI: 10.1016/j.sca.2023.100044

Nozari, H., Ghahremani-Nahr, J., & Najafi, E. (2023). The role of Internet of things and Blockchain in the development of agile and sustainable supply chains. In Digital Supply Chain, Disruptive Environments, and the Impact on Retailers (pp. 271-282). IGI Global. DOI: 10.4018/978-1-6684-7298-9.ch015

Nozari, H., Ghahremani-Nahr, J., & Szmelter-Jarosz, A. (2023). A multi-stage stochastic inventory management model for transport companies including several different transport modes. *International Journal of Management Science and Engineering Management, 18*(2), 134–144. DOI: 10.1080/17509653.2022.2042747

Nozari, H., Ghahremani-Nahr, J., & Szmelter-Jarosz, A. (2024). AI and machine learning for real-world problems. [). Elsevier.]. *Advances in Computers, 134*, 1–12. DOI: 10.1016/bs.adcom.2023.02.001

Nozari, H., Najafi, E., Fallah, M., & Hosseinzadeh Lotfi, F. (2019). Quantitative analysis of key performance indicators of green supply chain in FMCG industries using non-linear fuzzy method. *Mathematics, 7*(11), 1020. DOI: 10.3390/math7111020

Nozari, H., Najafi, S. E., Jafari-Eskandari, M., & Aliahmadi, A. (2016). Providing a model for virtual project management with an emphasis on IT projects. In *Strategic Management and Leadership for Systems Development in Virtual Spaces* (pp. 43–63). IGI Global Scientific Publishing. DOI: 10.4018/978-1-4666-9688-4.ch003

Nozari, H., Rahmaty, M., & Szmelter-Jarosz, A. (2024). A framework for AIoT-based smart sustainable marketing system. In *Artificial Intelligence of Things for Achieving Sustainable Development Goals* (pp. 255–271). Springer Nature Switzerland. DOI: 10.1007/978-3-031-53433-1_13

Nozari, H., & Szmelter-Jarosz, A. (2024). An analytical framework for smart supply chains 5.0. In *Building Smart and Sustainable Businesses With Transformative Technologies* (pp. 1–15). IGI Global Scientific Publishing.

Nozari, H., Szmelter-Jarosz, A., & Ghahremani-Nahr, J. (2021). The ideas of sustainable and green marketing based on the internet of everything—The case of the dairy industry. *Future Internet, 13*(10), 266. DOI: 10.3390/fi13100266

Nozari, H., Szmelter-Jarosz, A., & Ghahremani-Nahr, J. (2022). Analysis of the challenges of artificial intelligence of things (AIoT) for the smart supply chain (case study: FMCG industries). *Sensors (Basel), 22*(8), 2931. DOI: 10.3390/s22082931 PMID: 35458916

Nozari, H., Szmelter-Jarosz, A., & Rahmaty, M. (2024). Smart marketing based on artificial intelligence of things (AIoT) and Blockchain and evaluating critical success factors. In *Smart and Sustainable Interactive Marketing* (pp. 68–82). IGI Global Scientific Publishing. DOI: 10.4018/979-8-3693-1339-8.ch005

Nozari, H., Tavakkoli-Moghaddam, R., Ghahremani-Nahr, J., & Najafi, E. (2023). A conceptual framework for Artificial Intelligence of Medical Things (AIoMT). In Computational Intelligence for Medical Internet of Things (MIoT) Applications (pp. 175-189). Academic Press.

Nozari, H., Tavakkoli-Moghaddam, R., & Gharemani-Nahr, J. (2022). A neutrosophic fuzzy programming method to solve a multi-depot vehicle routing model under uncertainty during the covid-19 pandemic. *International Journal of Engineering*, *35*(2), 360–371.

Nozari, H., Tavakkoli-Moghaddam, R., Rohaninejad, M., & Hanzalek, Z. (2023, September). Artificial intelligence of things (AIoT) strategies for a smart sustainable-resilient supply chain. In IFIP International Conference on Advances in Production Management Systems (pp. 805-816). Cham: Springer Nature Switzerland. DOI: 10.1007/978-3-031-43670-3_56

Rahmaty, M., & Nozari, H. (2023). Optimization of the hierarchical supply chain in the pharmaceutical industry. *Edelweiss Applied Science and Technology*, *7*(2), 104–123. DOI: 10.55214/25768484.v7i2.376

Szmelter-Jarosz, A., Ghahremani-Nahr, J., & Nozari, H. (2021). A neutrosophic fuzzy optimisation model for optimal sustainable closed-loop supply chain network during COVID-19. *Journal of Risk and Financial Management*, *14*(11), 519. DOI: 10.3390/jrfm14110519

Tavakkoli-Moghaddam, R., Nozari, H., Bakhshi-Movahed, A., & Bakhshi-Movahed, A. (2024). A Conceptual framework for the Smart Factory 6.0. In *Advanced Businesses in Industry 6.0* (pp. 1–14). IGI Global. DOI: 10.4018/979-8-3693-3108-8.ch001

# Chapter 9
# The Future of Brand Experience:
## AI-Powered AR/VR and the Rise of Immersive Interactions

**Abdul Basith**
http://orcid.org/0009-0001-8858-2636
*Woxsen University, India*

**Nida Bashiruddin Shaikh**
http://orcid.org/0009-0006-0630-4832
*Woxsen University, India*

**Anikha Ahmed**
http://orcid.org/0009-0003-3525-3913
*Woxsen University, India*

**Mohd Azhar**
http://orcid.org/0000-0003-3222-5565
*New Delhi Institute of Management, India*

## ABSTRACT

*With a generation of technological advancements, AI, AR and VR are the hotspots of a paradigm shift in the interactions between the brands and the consumer. In this chapter, the technology of engaging the consumers in some new forms and ways using these emerging technologies is discussed, where the traditional experiences of a brand are turning to innovative immersive experiences. The key driver in the process, AI fits perfectly into these strategies, boosting data-driven personalization, predictive storytelling, and emotional connection with avatars, chatbots, and recommendation engines. At the same time, the immersive worlds which are fuelled*

DOI: 10.4018/979-8-3373-5117-9.ch009

ght © 2026, IGI Global Scientific Publishing. Copying or distributing in print or electronic forms without written permission of IGI Global Scientific Publishing is prohibited. Use of this chapter to generative artificial intelligence (AI) technologies is expressly prohibited. The publisher reserves all rights to license its use for generative AI training and machine learning model development.

*by the technologies of AR and VR are redefining consumer behaviour. This chapter discusses important ethical dilemmas that include data privacy, algorithm bias, and digital fatigue that provide future outlook on metaverse, spatial computing, and digital twins. Overall, the study offers comprehensive road guide the brands can use in walking with the immersive brand experiences in the future.*

## INTRODUCTION

The rapid progress of artificial intelligence (AI) is causing an unusual disruption in the global economy, fundamentally changing the retail industry and the nature of the consumer shopping experience (Annapareddy et al., 2025). AI-enabled real-time interaction systems are resulting in "major behavioural shifts" in the retail industry, changing how consumers interact with brands and how they purchase. What was once simply science fiction is now part of everyday interactions, often without consumers even being aware of these technologies, thus changing the way companies engage with brands and the way consumers make purchasing decisions (Ahmad et al., 2025; Sagio et al., 2025). This technology disruption is not only a mere enhancement of business processes; it is inadequate to say it will transform market dynamics in rewarding ways. It is incumbent upon organizations to innovate responsibly and opportune change in accordance with ethical guidelines, social parity, environmental practices and long term-value.

As we transition toward a digital economy, the traditional retail models can no longer do because they are static recommendations based on past purchasing histories, and cannot support collaborative exchanges in the present dynamic space of consumer preferences and usage complexity (Anderson, 2025; Ahmad et al., 2025) The modern consumer is no longer described as a passive recipient of marketing messages, but now is an active participant, a co-creator and critic of brand stories, demanding relevance, speed, personalization, trust, and immersive experiences for every contact point (Gokhan Nalbant & Aydin, 2025).

This chapter, The Future of Brand Experience: AI-Driven AR/VR and the Future of Immersive Interactions, discusses the integration of innovation in AI-assisted technology, and immersive technology, and how these can envision new ways to create brand consumer linkages. It aims to offer a coherent summary of the ways in which AI is reconceptualizing not simply the products people buy, but the motives and behaviours motivating those purchases. There is a special focus on the rising field of AI-assisted augmented reality (AR) and virtual reality (VR), as the discussion provides an explanation for why businesses in this sector will dominate the future of enhanced brand experiences. By outlining the considerations, it addresses the research gap in synthesizing a customer's personalized information and the augmented realities behind retail shopping journeys, which will provide the researchers with the ability to validate, in the real-world case of the experimental scenario, what might have previously required a high degree of simulation modelling, or generalized, in a more common research comparison with sources of AI (Annapareddy et al., 2025).

The scope and significance of this chapter, covering the fundamental processes and methods by which AI and immersive technologies are addressing modern consumer expectations and influencing brand experiences:

- Hyper-Personalization and Predictive Analytics
- Immersive Technologies (AR/VR/Metaverse)
- AI-Powered Chatbots and Virtual Assistants
- Emotional AI

Although AI has significant advantages in the way it significantly improves customer engagement, increases conversion rates, and generates consumer trust, very serious challenges and ethical implications arise from its widespread implementation . These challenges include considerations of privacy, issue of algorithmic biases and even, over-personalization which could violate consumer autonomy or create an unwanted sense of intrusion (Azmir, 2025; Gomes et al., 2025). The dependence on AI technologies also risks losing the humanness of customer interactions in favour of reliance on systems, risk developing a kind of dependency, as well as cognitive loss. The implementation of digital AI solutions can also entail excessive initial costs and skills of expertise (Sagio et al., 2025).

Tackling these issues is essential to building long-term trust and sustainability into the AI-driven retail ecosystem. The customer-centric ideology should be first and foremost for companies; AI can create value for businesses but also must enhance the overall shopping experience.

This chapter will unpack these constructs, in conjunction with academic theory, technology development, and practice. The aim of the chapter is to address the ensuing gaps in research by addressing the association of personalized consumer insight in conjunction with one's real-augmented retail shopping journeys, such as the steps undertaken by retailers to test AI-generated initiatives through practical applications and case studies (Gokhan Nalbant & Aydin, 2025). The exploration of these complex connections offers retailers, AI designers and developer teams, and policy-makers with insights into developing scalable, consumer-centred, and ethics-first AI applications in the retail space (Annapareddy et al., 2025).

## UNDERSTANDING BRAND EXPERIENCE IN THE DIGITAL AGE

Brand experience fundamentally refers to the holistic perception and interaction consumers have with a brand across various touchpoints. It is a multifaceted construct that encompasses several key components, influencing how consumers feel, think, and behave towards a brand. In modern branding, understanding and shaping these dimensions are paramount for fostering strong, lasting relationships with customers.

As an essential item in the process to understand the future directions of brand experience, there must be the establishment of a basic appreciation of what brand experience is all about in the current digitalised environment, and how this scenario has developed, and why the emotional involvement and personalisation have become so important.

### Timeline of Brand Evolution: Traditional → Digital → Immersive

The brand experience terrain has been deeply changed, shifting from traditional static models to extremely dynamic, immersive experiences. This change represents consumer behaviour shifts, technological advancements, and marketing strategy moves (Annapareddy et al., 2025).

In past times, conventional retail models had very much depended on static product suggestion and past buying data, whose limitation was that they could not react instantly to changing customer tastes (Annapareddy et al., 2025). Brand communication tended to be a one-way flow of messages from the brand to the consumer with minimal direct interaction or customisation (Hussain et al., 2025).

*Figure 1. Evolution of Brand Communication*

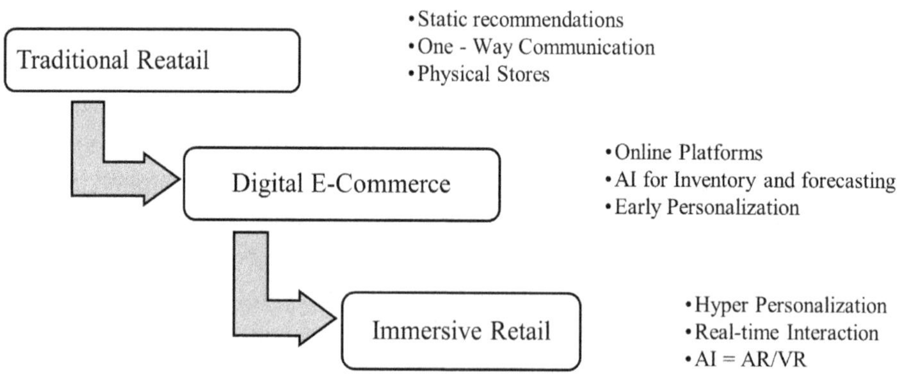


*Source: Author's own elaboration*

This framework outlines the evolution of retail experiences as the industry moves from Traditional Retail to Digital E-commerce to Immersive Retail, and the central role of technology especially AI in redefining business and consumer interaction.

Traditional Retail model exhibits low level of interactivity, static consumer experiences, and low level of personalization. Communication in this stage was unidirectional, that is, brands shared information and received no or little input from consumers. Most of consumer's transactions were in-store type retail environment and with product recommendations being generic and largely uninformed by individual preferences or behaviours.

The advent of the Digital E-commerce era changed the way retail operates. The greater availability and ease of online buying created greater accessibility and convenience. The emergence of Artificial Intelligence allowed the integration (in many cases) with some of the core functions of retail such as inventory management, forecasting of demand, and basic personalization. AI technologies empowered systems to provide tailored product recommendations based on user data such as; browsing history, purchase history and other variations of consumer behaviour. While advances were made in the adoption of AI in retail, a clear distinction remained between digital and physical channels with a fully cohesive customer experience elapsed.

The launch of Immersive Retail is the most sophisticated evolutionary step in this paradigm shift. It is defined by the intersection of AI and immersive technology (AR, VR) to introduce hyper-personalized and real-time consumer engagement, as well as, create a unified omnichannel environment that completely joined the digital and physical interface with synchronizing tech. In addition, organizations began to adopt ethical AI practices that could help to develop confidence in their customers that they are using (AI) responsibly, transparently and accountably, while avoiding issues around data privacy or compliance.

Conventional marketing activities were centred on

a) Recommendation systems
b) Demand forecasting
c) Inventory management
d) Dynamic pricing mechanisms, mainly in physical stores (Annapareddy et al., 2025).

The introduction of the internet brought about a tremendous transformation from physical markets to the virtual world, with the emergence of e-commerce (Hussain et al., 2025; Zaheer, 2025a). This phase witnessed the growing use of AI for the improvement of efficiency in such areas as inventory management, demand forecasts, and recommendation systems (Annapareddy et al., 2025). AI solutions came in to provide highly personalised shopping experiences based on data analysis, above and beyond simple automation. This phase was also mostly limited to either online or offline models without truly real-time AI-powered personalisation systems that brought together the two worlds of retail seamlessly. It was mostly a case of consumers having to scroll through websites for hours and read reviews, which were tedious (Hu et al., 2025).

The era today is characterised by the joining of the physical and virtual shopping worlds into effortless, immersive environments (Zaheer, 2025; Vuyyuru, 2025). The Metaverse has risen to be a revolutionary platform, transforming the way businesses engage with customers by providing immersive experiences that go beyond conventional marketing channels (Hussain et al., 2025). Physical digital ecosystem that combines VR, AR, blockchain, and other converging technologies (Hussain et al., 2025).

This paradigm change enables hyper-personalised shopping experiences, customer insights in real time, and augmented shopping experiences in immersive augmented reality that increase both online and offline interactions (Annapareddy et al., 2025; Hu et al., 2025). The driving force behind this change lies in the convergence of deep learning, reinforcement learning, augmented reality (AR)/virtual reality (VR), and privacy-preserving AI models into a potent weapons cache for retail transformation.

This period centres on

- Hyper-personalised and dynamic interaction with the consumer,
- Giving ethical deployment of AI topmost priority
- Privacy protection

In connection with innovative technologies, it is observed that three significant dimensions have a major influence on what a customer buys, i.e., channel selection, value dimensions which relate to ease and enjoyment, and also social interaction (Ylilehto et al., 2021). These three are strongly interdependent in how they feed on one another to cause the aggregate effect (Ylilehto et al., 2021). The value dimensions, specifically, emerge based on the utilitarian studies and hedonic value studies of shopping, emphasizing the fact that the customers can derive value not only at the level of the usefulness of a purchase but also at the level of the enjoyment and fun of a purchase (Ylilehto et al., 2021).

Initially, most of the trade was done face-to-face, but with online trading came the birth of e-commerce, where customers can make purchases wherever they are (Ylilehto et al., 2021).

> *The advent of the multi-channel strategies further pushed marketers to connect their brick-and-mortar stores with other forms of alternatives, including catalogues, call centres, e-commerce, and mobile apps, and they realised that customers were pursuing different channel-based experiences. (Ylilehto et al., 2021)*

## The Metaverse and the Next Digital Frontier

The latest example of this evolution is the explosion of effectiveness and the spread of innovative technologies with additional expansion of boundaries (Ylilehto et al., 2021). The Metaverse, e.g., is considered a new step and a far-reaching vision of the digital transformation that is significantly going to change the way we work, divert ourselves, and interact with each other (Xu et al., 2022). It is characterised as an avatar representation of the Internet that merges with interoperable, immersive, and shared virtual worlds, which can be navigated by the user avatars (Xu et al., 2022). The digital space erases the boundaries between the physical and the virtual, enabling the user to interact with VR worlds to a certain extent physically by providing a sense of interaction that people can touch, hear, feel, and even sense through haptics (Xu et al., 2022). It can even give a chance to extend the virtual spin on a real one by such means as the Augmented Reality (Xu et al., 2022).

Initial versions, or "lite" versions, of the Metaverse have been rendered by Massive Multiplayer Online (MMO) games, as well, with virtual concerts on platforms such as Roblox and Fortnite screened by millions of viewers (Xu et al., 2022). The idea renders a digitalized illusionary experience that was tolerated as a virtual reality, through which the so-called prosumers (the producers and individuals consuming their relevant goods) communicate using their digital avatars, which are duly empowered in the virtual space (Reddy Gadekallu et al., 2022). Metaverse is simply a combination of diverse state-of-the-art technologies, such as 6G, Artificial Intelligence, Virtual Reality, and digital twin, which are collaboratively used to provide a ubiquitous digital medium where people engage in interaction (Reddy Gadekallu et al., 2022). The future of e-commerce, most specifically, is projected to be a smooth complement of AI, AR, VR, and the Metaverse that will bring greater efficiencies in operations and offer more commendable, relational, and sustainable customer experiences (Kasap, 2025).

## Emotional Involvement and Personalisation as Differentiators

In the contemporary branding landscape, emotional engagement and hyper-personalisation have become cornerstones for fostering deep customer connections, driving loyalty, and influencing purchasing decisions. Consumers are no longer passive recipients of marketing messages; they actively seek interactive, co-created experiences that resonate with their individual preferences and allow for self-expression (Hussain et al., 2025).

1) **Drives Customer Satisfaction and Loyalty:**

- Consumers perceive personalised interactions as more relevant, intuitive, and value-adding. This AI tailoring of content, timing, and tone, based on historical behaviour and predictive modelling, enables brands to engage with consumers on a deeper level.
- Results from research indicate that AI-Infused Real-Time Interaction Systems dramatically impact consumer engagement and purchase intention (Annapareddy et al., 2025). Optimise advertising and interface design, enhancing the emotional connection between consumers and brands for the long term.

2) **Influencing Purchasing Decisions and Conversion Rates:**
   - AI facilitates a shift from reactive to proactive marketing, resulting in higher engagement and conversion rates. Personalised product recommendations, powered by AI, have been shown to beat traditional recommendations in enhancing customer satisfaction and profitability, leading to increased income and ongoing development (Hussain et al., 2025).
   - With AR/VR integration for immersive shopping experiences, the uncertainties in purchase decisions are reduced significantly, and product return rates are decreased, while interaction time is increased (Annapareddy et al., 2025).
   - A study on AI-driven marketing activities found that AI-driven customisation had the strongest effect on brand experience ($\beta = 0.364$, $p < 0.001$), indicating its crucial role in enhancing consumer perceptions (Ahmad et al., 2025). This suggests that personalisation plays a defining role in shaping positive brand experiences, which, in turn, directly impact brand preference and loyalty.

## Towards a Fully Immersive, User-Centric Future

Personalisation opportunities that are made possible with AI are capable of enriching the shopping experience in tangible ways.

E.g., one can think of how an AI system can merely take cognisance that a specific user has spent significant time on a specific product page and will automatically offer a special discount on the same item (Kasap, 2025). This also maximises customer satisfaction, as well as increases the conversion rates (Kasap, 2025).

In addition, sentiment analysis using AI allows organisations to find out what consumers feel and whether they like or dislike something in real-time by monitoring their comments on social media, reviews, and call centre interactions. This component helps the brands modify their advertising suits to suit the requirements of the customers, and hence, better engagement and long-term attachment are attained (Kasap, 2025). AI supports by enabling personalised AR/VR suggestions to an end user based on their historical and situational data, leading to improved Quality of Experience (QOE) (Xu et al., 2022). Metaverse will take this even a step ahead by enabling the creation of individualised systems attuned to the requirements of users, with assistance from AR/VR, IoT devices (Reddy Gadekallu et al., 2022). The emphasis of user-focused computing in the Metaverse is to secure sensitive personal information, such as GPS location, voice, and eye movement tracked by an AR/VR device, and provide AI algorithms that require resources to increase the immersive aspect of reality (Xu et al., 2022).

## THE RISE OF IMMERSIVE TECHNOLOGIES: AR, VR, AND MR

Immersive technologies are reshaping human-computer interaction and consumer experiences by blurring the lines between the digital and physical worlds (Hussain et al., 2025; Zaheer, 2025b). These technologies—Augmented Reality (AR), Virtual Reality (VR), and Mixed Reality (MR)—are central to the evolution of the metaverse and are rapidly gaining prominence across various industries (Hussain et al., 2025).

Extended Reality (XR) is a broad definition, and it refers to all the immersive technologies in the current supply, and they are virtual reality (VR), mixed reality (MR), and augmented reality (AR) (Vincs et al., 2022) It depicts the entire realm of experiences, crossing the borders between the real and the simulated world, and is created with the help of computer technology and wearable devices to exploit human-machine interactions (Vincs et al., 2022). The major aim of XR is to place the user in the immersive experience due to various types of stimuli such as visual, auditory, and even olfactory and haptic senses (Vincs et al., 2022).

### What Is Virtual Reality?

It has been described as a synthetic environment created with the help of the computer that allows an individual to manipulate an artificial three-dimensional (3D) world through electronic gadgets (Vincs et al., 2022). It is a fully artificially created digital world and one that has absolutely nothing to do with the real world (Vincs et al., 2022). These virtual worlds are constructed by the sensory images that are generated by VR systems (Xu et al., 2022). The practical uses include allowing users to experience virtual museum tours remotely, space simulations such as a spacewalk (Vincs et al., 2022).

VR Experiences can be divided into Immersive and Flat/Low Immersive:

1) *Non-immersive VR:* In which only part of the senses of the user are activated and the user still perceives the real world (e.g., working through a desktop, laptop, smartphone, or projections) (Vincs et al., 2022).
2) *Semi-immersive VR:* In the case where the user is under the virtual reality partially (e.g., a flight simulator) (Vincs et al., 2022).
3) *Full-immersion VR:* In this one, a head-mounted viewer is worn so that a person can see the virtual world, and motion-sensor devices are used to engage the senses, and the experience is as real as it can get, entirely immersive (Vincs et al., 2022).

## What Is Augmented Reality?

Augmented Reality (AR) is a more enhanced reality of the actual physical world through the overlaying of digital visual aspects, audio, or even other sensations in the vision of the user of reality through the use of technology (Vincs et al., 2022). The concept postulates that AR superimposes the computer augmentations on top of an actual existing reality (Ylilehto et al., 2021). This technology is expanding the visual field of the person by means of insertion of virtual information like text, three-dimensional models, sounds, and particles, and contributing to their seeing the real world with superimposed digital information (Vincs et al., 2022).

AR may be distinguished into a few kinds depending on the way it operates:

1) *Markers AR:* requires a camera and the presence of a particular, visible anchor (an example would be a QR code or picture) to enter the overlaying virtual material (Vincs et al., 2022).
2) *Marker less AR:* It does not use any particular markers, and it can be able to identify real-world objects or surfaces to place content (Vincs et al., 2022).
3) *Projection-basedAR:* overlays the surface of physical objects with digital images.
4) *Superimposition-based AR:* Overlays a part of the view of the real world with augmented views.

## What Is Mixed Reality?

*Mixed Reality (MR)* is described as the most developed type of a blend between the real and virtual worlds, which creates new spaces where physical and digital items exist and interact in real-time (Vincs et al., 2022). Unlike AR, which is simply done by overlaying it with virtual objects, MR visually fixes the virtual materials to the real world and lets the user interact with the virtual objects (Vincs et al., 2022). It does this by employing real-world data, e.g., spatial data of a room layout, to locate and manipulate the virtual data in the real room precisely (Vincs et al., 2022). MR naturally merges computer processing, human input, and environmental input CR to produce genuinely integrated experiences (Vincs et al., 2022).

## IMPORTANCE OF AR, VR, AND AI TECHNOLOGY

The essential differences in these two technologies are regarding their rate of immersion and connection with the real world. VR fully engulfs participants in a Virtual world and almost eliminates the physical world (Kasap, 2025). AR does not create a new environment; instead, it adds more to what is there (Vincs et al., 2022). MR, in its turn, takes the initiative to combine the two, so the interplay between the actual physical objects and virtual ones is possible in real-time, and within this context, making the layer of an overlay is not enough (Vincs et al., 2022). Hwang and Chien (2022) also contrast Metaverse with AR and VR by describing it as shared, persistent, and decentralized, with AR and VR thus being a subset of the larger Model verse ecosystem, which may be coupled with AI (Tlili et al., 2022).

I) AR Capabilities:
   a) *Improved Shopping:* Almost all retailers believe that AR can dramatically improve the subjective perceptions of informativeness and fun associated with shopping (Ylilehto et al., 2021). It allows giving the consumers the experience of trying on the product (e.g., clothes, make-up) or seeing an item (e.g., furniture) in their real-life settings before purchasing it (Kasap, 2025). This ability minimises uncertainty, increases consumer confidence, and hence results in increased sales and a decrease in the rate of returns (Miller, 2021). They may include the AR shoe-fitting apps by Nike and Adidas and the IKEA furniture visualization app, known as the IKEA Place app, by the IKEA company (Kasap, 2025).
   c) *Customer Engagement:* AR makes the customer experience stimulating in fashion and beauty, enhancing the feeling of brand loyalty and buying intent (Kasap, 2025). In the case of electronics, buyers have an opportunity to preview the device in real-world environments, which enhances the level of confidence in buying (Kasap, 2025).
   d) *Technical Frameworks:* The principal AR development frameworks, such as ARKit (Apple), have advanced capabilities which include markerless AR, light estimation, environment understanding, face tracking, 3D tracking, and image recognition (Vincs et al., 2022). Google ARCore offers the same functionality, with motion tracking, environmental perception, and light estimation being among such options (Vincs

et al., 2022). Vuforia is recognised to be able to track robust objects, intelligent terrain mapping, and cloud recognition (Vincs et al., 2022).

II) Virtual Reality (VR) Capabilities:

a) *Virtual Stores and Showrooms:* Using a 3D Store and Showroom, the retailer can now have an entire simulated virtual store or showroom where users can navigate, browse, and explore products in a way quite similar to actual shopping (Kasap, 2025). It closes the gap between online and physical retailing and provides interactive and personal experiences that help increase conversion rates, brand loyalty (Kasap, 2025).

b) *Training and Education:* It is a widely utilized VR that makes a learning experience immersive and allows developing various skills within a simulated scenario, especially in a high-risk or high-cost situation, such as aircraft maintenance or medical procedure (Tlili et al., 2022)

c) *Hardware:* The most popular VR headsets are HTC Vive Pro, the HTC Vive, Oculus Quest, Oculus Quest 2, and Valve Index (Vincs et al., 2022). Such a distinguishing feature of the Oculus Quest 2 is its standalone, portability, and clear graphics, as well as powerful motion tracking without the help of additional sensors (Vincs et al., 2022).

III) Artificial Intelligence (AI) Capabilities:

a) *Personalization and suggestions:* AI-based algorithms, with the help of analysing consumer data on a large scale, provide unprecedented liberty in shopping and product suggestions, making the experience highly personalized, which also increases customer satisfaction and sales by large margins (Miller, 2021). Such enterprises as Amazon and Netflix are prominently using AI in recommendation (Vincs et al., 2022).

b) *Operational Efficiency:* Spurred by AI, businesses can rise to the reliability level of e-commerce platforms, further able to meet operational efficiency requirements via dynamic pricing strategy, demand forecasts, and fraud detection (Kasap, 2025).

c) *Customer care:* Chatbots and virtual assistants guarantee efficient, quick, and round-the-clock customer service, lowering operational costs and improving interaction (Ylilehto et al., 2021) (Kasap, 2025). Conversational AI based on machine learning and natural language processing (NLP) facilitates human-like communication (Tlili et al., 2022)

d) *Avatars and Content Creation:* AI can de-clutter the content that comes with it, including GANverse3D created by NVIDIA to turn real-life photos into virtual replicas (Tlili et al., 2022). The Metahuman initiative of Epic Games includes the creation of digital characters using AI (Xu et al., 2022). AI can also be used in enabling cognitive avatars and non-player characters (NPCs) in virtual worlds to perform intelligent action and personalise interactions (Xu et al., 2022; Tlili et al., 2022).

e) *Combining with neuromarketing:* AI methods in combination with neuromarketing help understand consumers on a subconscious level and create more productive marketing strategies (Kasap, 2025).

f) *Infrastructure Support:* AI plays a vital role in ensuring that the infrastructure of Metaverse remains sound, tuning 5G and the prospects of 6G towards complex operations such as spectrum control, resource allocation, detection of errors, and others (Tlili et al., 2022). AI models may also be distributed and pushed to miniaturised gadgets with restricted resources in resource-constrained edges (Xu et al., 2022).

## ADOPTION RATES, USAGE BY INDUSTRIES, AND MARKET SIZE FORECASTS

Immersive technologies and the growth of the metaverse are not abstract ideas but are witnessing serious market expansion and extensive use in various industries. The international metaverse market is expected to see explosive growth, from a current estimated level of $40 billion in 2021 to more than $1,607 billion by the year 2030, demonstrating a staggering Compound Annual Growth Rate (CAGR) of 37.73%. Such growth is primarily driven by the emergence of virtual currencies, blockchain, and decentralised technologies. Previous estimates also showed the metaverse market reaching $1 trillion in yearly revenue, which highlights its potential as a business platform. The wider augmented and virtual reality sector was set to reach $200 billion by 2022, and the metaverse market alone was set to $280 billion by 2025 (Hussain et al., 2025).

AR technology itself is witnessing immense growth, with its market development anticipated to surpass $90 billion by 2029 (Rahimi & Hosseini, 2025). This reflects growing integration and demand for AR-fuelled solutions across multiple sectors.

## SECTOR-WISE USAGE OF EMERGING TECHNOLOGY

### A) Retail and E-Commerce

AI technology has already significantly impacted the retail landscape and shopping experience (Annapareddy et al., 2025). AR is transforming online shopping by creating immersive experiences that enable customers to try on products virtually, interact with 3D models, and see products in their surroundings (Zaheer, 2025a).

Immersive technologies are viewed as central to retailers' efforts to stay competitive (Vuyyuru, 2025). A report by Deloitte in 2022 said that 56% of customers would be more inclined to buy from a brand that provides immersive experiences. Additionally, AR alone has been proven to enhance dwell time by 30-40% and conversion rates by as much as 25% in industries that are well-suited.

*Example*: Firms such as Sephora through its Virtual Artist and IKEA through its Place app are named as the best practice models for the integration of utility, interactivity, and sensory involvement in online retailing. The metaverse is revolutionising shopping by enabling customers to navigate virtual spaces via digital avatars and engage with other digital identities (Hu et al., 2025).

## B) Fashion

The fashion sector is one of the major beneficiaries, with AR and VR methods expected to account for part of the $1.5 trillion in revenue by 2030 realised through immersive technologies (Hussain et al., 2025). Online sales can increase up to 30% using virtual try-on technology, with 75% of consumers indicating they are more likely to buy products if they can virtually try them on. Luxury fashion brands are increasingly integrating Non-Fungible Tokens (NFTs) in their offerings, giving rise to a new "virtual luxury" category (Hu et al., 2025).

*Example*: Fly London's case study illustrates the way the metaverse is changing fashion branding. Louis Vuitton, in partnership with the video game League of Legends, boasting more than 115 million players, introduced a virtual showroom in the game where customers can shop and buy products, as well as outfit their avatars with brand-themed skins, essentially bridging physical and digital selling.

## C) Real Estate and Gaming

VR found direct application in real estate with virtual previewing of properties. The gaming industry is a major target for immersive technologies, with consumers playing or interacting in immersive environments for hours on end compared to normal websites (Hussain et al., 2025).

*Example*: Matterport provides 3D virtual tours and digital twins of properties, enabling remote property viewing and exploration

## D) Tourism and Hospitality

The metaverse possesses revolutionary potential in the tourism and hospitality sectors, especially in promoting sustainability through offering virtual substitutes that can minimise carbon prints. Virtual immersive experiences can impact physical travel plans, serving as efficacious advertising media. Hotel operations are being transformed through robotics and AI, such as robot receptionists, automated kiosks, robot cooks, and robot food delivery systems. Voice-enabled smart rooms based on AI are also on the rise.

*Example*: Chatbots, for instance, those utilised by Marriott International on Facebook Messenger for reservations, and facial recognition software in the travel sector are some good examples of it (Vuyyuru, 2025).

### E) Financial Management

The metaverse is becoming a disruptive financial management platform, particularly for SMEs, by combining mobile-based access, virtual currency infrastructure, and NFTs. It provides cost savings through automated smart contracts and AI-based advisory systems, and personalised financial services through AI-based avatars and VR interfaces (Hussain et al., 2025).

*Example*: AR/VR tech is being used by Fidelity, Citi, Mastercard, and Axis Bank for trading, virtual payments, immersive data views, and secure authentication

### F) Small and Medium-Sized Enterprises (SMEs)

The metaverse provides SMEs with an unprecedented opportunity for sustainable growth. The metaverse can transform various core areas of SME business, such as marketing, customer interaction, employee training, and collaboration. Some of the benefits include better communication between remote teams, simulation-based, immersive learning for employee training, geographic barriers between SMEs and global markets, and economical virtual advertisement. Gamification factors within virtual shopping setups work effectively in inducing SME customer loyalty.

These adoption levels and industry-specific applications reflect a widespread and accelerating movement toward immersive technologies as a core component of business and consumer engagement in the future

## AI AS THE ENABLER OF IMMERSIVE BRAND EXPERIENCES

AI-powered immersive brand experience includes hyper-personalisation, complex behavioural data mining, and highly interactive functionalities on a multitude of platforms (Annapareddy et al., 2025). The potential of AI stretches further than automation; its features alter the consumer-brand interactions, predictive buying patterns, and virtual engagement levels in such a way as to generate more adaptable and versatile marketing systems (Ahmad et al., 2025; Pattnaik & Mohanty, 2025).

Personalisation being focused on accuracy, personalisation, and efficiency, AI-driven marketing is all about personalising the entire experience of customers (Kumar Gubbala et al., 2025). Marketers are surrounded by superior AI tools that make it possible to understand the needs and preferences of consumers in extraordinary detail and create truly personalized shopping conditions (Kumar Gubbala et al., 2025). This can be achieved through using large quantities of consumer data in terms of structured and unstructured data to analyse the complex patterns, and predict the future actions and demands (Pattnaik & Mohanty, 2025).

The intelligence of the AI system is based on its capability to learn and progress continuously and analyse complex information to find behavioural tendencies and knowledge that will lead to the formulation of smart judgement. It transforms the marketing process that was being reactive to a proactive one, changing consumer choice, preference, and lifetime loyalty through hyper-personalization and predictive analytics (Pattnaik & Mohanty, 2025).

## Importance and Usage

- Automated predictive analytics is essential in lead scoring, churn prediction, and campaign optimisation (Kumar Gubbala et al., 2025).
- Customer Relationship Management (CRM) programs that are powered through AI will be capable of analysing past purchasing details to create future client buying habits so that companies can create very specific advertising campaigns that will result in improved customer devotion and income.
- IBM's Watson AI platform, used in CRM systems, identifies correlations between various factors like seasonal changes, promotional activities, and shifts in customer preferences to provide precise sales projections, optimizing inventory and marketing strategies.
- AI solutions enable the dynamic market segmentation that is extended beyond demographics to psychological and behavioural dimensions.
- With incoming data, AI systems are very flexible and can continuously modify and optimize their segmentation strategies on the fly to make marketing efforts up-to-date and relevant (Kumar Gubbala et al., 2025).
- In the context of risk mitigation as risk assessment data can be analysed by AI-enabled reporting engines to identify immediate risks, such as fraud, and mitigation actions can be implemented to reduce losses.

## Forms in Which AI Can Be Accessed

### 1) AI-Powered Element in AR/VR Platforms

While known to perform a variety of roles on its own, the true potential of Artificial Intelligence to make immersive experiences becomes unlocked once incorporated into Extended Realities (XR), including AR and VR (Kumar Gubbala et al., 2025). The combination enables brands to get past the simple interactions and build highly immersive and interactive spaces.

### 2) Avatars

Within social VR spaces, deep learning-based avatars take advantage of Natural Language Processing (NLP) and emotion detection tools to emulate the human experience of interaction and improve a sense of connection and presence among users of the system (Kumar Gubbala et al., 2025).

### 3) Chatbots and Virtual Assistants

Specialized chatbots and virtual assistants that will reduce the time spent on improving customer experience will rely on AI (Kumar Gubbala et al., 2025). Such tools offer users personalised help and answers to questions and assist consumers through the shopping process (Gokhan Nalbant & Aydin, 2025). With the help of NLP and GPT-generated architectures, AI assistants provide human-like experience, providing recommendations in real-time, answering questions about products, personalizing the shopping process through the dialogue, which can be held both in the text and by voice., and visual analysis (Annapareddy et al., 2025) This instantaneity and seamlessness meet the growing consumer demand for immediate experiences (Kumar Gubbala et al., 2025).

### 4) Recommendation Engines

Machine learning and deep learning algorithms, as a part of AI-enabled recommendation systems, play a crucial role in predicting the interests of consumers and consumer behaviour (Ahmad et al., 2025; Annapareddy et al., 2025). Such systems extend previous approaches to collaborative filtering and content-based approaches to include a sentiment-aware AI model to deliver hyper-personalised shopping experiences (Annapareddy et al., 2025). Such companies as Netflix and Spotify illustrate this trend, as they apply AI to provide consistently dynamic and extremely relevant customer experiences to build brand-consumer bonds based on a kind of data-driven intimacy (Pattnaik & Mohanty, 2025). In retail, fashion recommendations using AI study the behaviour of consumers to determine future trends.

### 5) Dynamic and Real-Time Brand Storytelling

Predictive analytics, combined with AI's ability to process real-time feedback, helps shape dynamic and adaptive brand storytelling. Through AI, brands can dynamically adjust pricing plans, anticipate consumer trends, and identify the most efficient ways of organising retail outlets to enjoy an immersive shopping experience (Annapareddy et al., 2025). This implies that marketing content and strategies may be able to shift in a moment to consumer behaviour and response. As an example, NLP and machine learning are used in AI-driven content creation platforms, where the technology is used to create large amounts of personalised content, such as blog posts and product descriptions, and even email subject lines, and variants of tone and relevance of the message are tailored to different audiences (Ejjami, n.d.). The tools are fast and automated to write content and augment the copywriting process by incorporating features to attract the target audience (Kumar Gubbala et al., 2025).

With the addition of AI, AR, and VR technologies, open up attractive new directions in digital storytelling. AR mobile applications based on AI enable the consumer to virtually dress in products, see the furniture in their rooms, or walk in-store activation with high fidelity and interactive visualisations powered by 3D Convolutional Neural Networks (3D-CNNs) and Generative Adversarial Networks (GANs) (Annapareddy et al., 2025). AI also allows brands to create marketing content that may better relate to more people, and keep optimizing on this approach, through observing the interactions on their systems (Kumar Gubbala et al., 2025; Ejjami, n.d.). This dynamic adaptation ensures that brand messaging is not only timely and relevant but also deeply engaging, fostering stronger consumer connections and driving conversions (Kumar Gubbala et al., 2025).

## Frameworks Enabling AI-Powered Immersion

AI-enabled immersive experiences are based on different technical and theoretical frameworks.

I) **Technical Framework**: The AI-Infused Real-Time Interaction System integrates:

- Deep Learning
- Reinforcement Learning (RL)
- Natural Language Processing (NLP)
- Computer Vision
- AR/VR

II) **Theoretical Frameworks:**

a. Dynamic Capability Theory: Explains how businesses can adapt and thrive using AI to transform marketing strategies and business processes. *(Kumar Gubbala et al., 2025)*

b. Stimulus-Organism-Response (S-O-R) Framework:

*Figure 2. Stimulus-Organism-Response (S-O-R) Model in an AI-Driven Context*

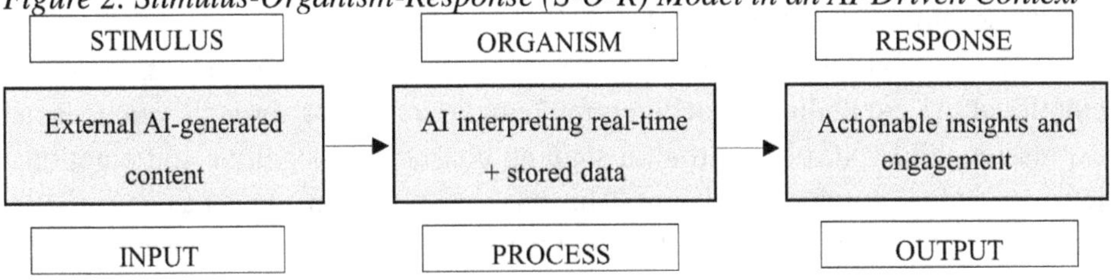


*Source: Author's own elaboration*

Starts with the stimulus, where outside AI-created material is the input, causing a psychological or technological response. The content is subsequently filtered at the organism phase, where AI systems decipher it from real-time and existing information to determine the meaning and context. Lastly, in the output stage, this interpretation generates actionable insights and user interaction, fulfilling the cycle of input, processing, and output in a dynamic AI environment.

c. Technology Acceptance Model (TAM): Evaluates how users interact with and accept AI-generated content.

## CONSUMER BEHAVIOUR IN IMMERSIVE ENVIRONMENTS

The combination of AI with other immersion technologies such as AR and VR is significantly affecting consumer behaviour, altering perceptions, inspiring a feeling of emotional connection, creating trust and brand loyalty in a fashion impossible before (Annapareddy et al., 2025). These technologies pave the way to a dynamic, multi-sensory world, which changes the customer experience.

Customers will have a new definition of customer experience due to the ability to influence, guide, provoke cognitive, emotional, and behavioural, sensory, and social reactions (Pattnaik & Mohanty, 2025). The presence of AR/VR substantially decreases pre-purchase uncertainties, minimises the rate of product returns, and augments the general amounts of time that individuals spend with brands (Annapareddy et al., 2025).

It is demonstrated that the use of AR-driven tools can boost sales and decrease returns. The "enjoyment factor," linked to the perceived coolness and immersive qualities of AR/VR, and the "closeness factor," reflecting perceived proximity to products, notably enhance consumer engagement and purchase intent. Customers who appreciate AI-based marketing campaigns express more loyalty to a brand and evaluate the AI application in marketing practice as the highest value of brand loyalty development (Ahmad et al., 2025).

This effect on the emotional engagement is high. AI in marketing, including emotional AI capabilities that interpret human sentiment through voice, facial expression, and text, plays a role in shaping consumers' cognitive and emotional journeys before purchase decisions. This enables AI systems to act as empathetic, which serves to increase satisfaction and trust levels, especially in a sensitised industry such as beauty, healthcare, and luxury retailing, hence strengthening brand attachment and the tendency to interact again.

The experiential marketing with the help of immersive technologies incurs memorable experiences, which result in increased satisfaction and brand differentiation. The evidence supports the view that having a positive brand experience, frequently created through the AI-driven personalisation, means that the customers are more willing to choose the brand among its competitors and will be more inclined to buy it again (Ahmad et al., 2025). This leads to an emotional and cognitive connection created out of the history of the behaviour-based personalization of content, timing, and tone of the AI-created content, contributing to a stronger consumer connection to brands.

It is essential to create trust in such immersion environments. There is a correlation with high scores on trust and satisfaction indices of brands presenting the information on how their artificial intelligence applications work or permitting users to banish the settings of recommendations. In its turn, explainable AI (XAI) and privacy-preserving AI models are vital towards guaranteeing that consumers show confidence in the AI-powered recommendation systems and contend with their information security (Annapareddy et al., 2025). Still, such issues as data privacy vulnerability, algorithmic biases, and a lack of human interaction may negate the overall performance of becoming more effective in driving consumer trust and brand loyalty (Ahmad et al., 2025)

## Generation Z and Millennials: The Key Adopters

They are becoming more interested in convenience and efficiency in shopping, as well as they are willing to interact with novel digital experiences. Another factor is that this demographic also demonstrates an increase in matching the consumption behaviour to the sustainability aims under the nudging towards the more environmentally-friendly choices provided by AI (Pattnaik & Mohanty, 2025). AR/VR is still at the stage of early adopters, though it is more attractive to these younger generations.

## Consideration of Psychological Dimensions

Presence, Cognitive Immersion, Attention Span, and Memory Retention. Immersive technologies go directly to the area of the psychological dimension that plays an important role in the consumer experience. Presence refers to the feeling of "being there" in a virtual environment, a key feature shared by VR along with immersion and interaction. Cognitive immersion is attained because AR/VR appeals to different senses, which promotes interaction and reality in virtual environments. The multi-channel communication facilitates the capacity of students to store the information in their long-term memory, creating an episodic memory resembling that in real life. To take a specific example, VR simulations may also enhance memory retention, simplifying the task of memorizing historical facts (Thangavel et al., 2025).

Immersive environments are also characterized by fewer distractions and higher levels of attention and concentration, which is good news to those placed in the learning-challenged category (Thangavel et al., 2025). Studies suggest that the impact of immersive advertising solutions on brand memory and intent to purchase is better than that of conventional processes. VR experiences, due to their sensory-enhanced quality, make a great difference in brand immersion and consumer involvement. Furthermore, AI-powered virtual tutors within these environments can analyse facial expressions to assess students' emotional states, adjusting teaching methods to sustain engagement (Thangavel et al., 2025). Advancements in haptic feedback and multi-sensory AR/VR, including haptic gloves and gesture recognition, are expected to enhance tactile sensations and interactivity, making virtual learning more dynamic. The brain-computer interfaces (BCIs) may also be applied in the future to enable the user to feel their touch or temperature without physical contact, making the experience even more immersive (Thangavel et al., 2025).

## Meeting the Consumer Demands

The consumer no longer plays the role of passive recipient of the marketing messages but the curious user of clever, interactive platforms that continuously learn and respond to the consumer and their demands at each moment (Pattnaik & Mohanty, 2025). This has created changing consumer expectations where there is high demand in personalised experiences, such that brands need to recognise their unique needs and make the interaction personalised (Ahmad et al., 2025). The effectiveness of dynamic personalisation (associated with AI) and sentiment-driven recommendations and sensor-mixed sense of presence are critical in improving consumer involvement, purchase desire, and the performance of retailers, highlighting its extreme influence (Annapareddy et al., 2025).

The integration of AR/VR with AI addresses the growing necessity for "experiential commerce," where brands differentiate themselves and build long-term customer relationships through unique and immersive encounters (Zaheer, 2025a). This involves a change of the visual merchandising strategies of physical and online shops (Anderson, 2025). Although AI-induced customisation or personalising a product through its features, as the IKEA Place app succeeds in creating brand love, it is also found in the case study that such technologies must match the consumer convenience requirements, indicating an urgent balance between technology and consumer needs. All in all, 56 per cent of consumers tend to buy a product from a brand that allows them to have an immersive experience, which clearly shows the obvious tendency of the consumer choice to gravitate towards interactive touchpoints to this superior level.

The depth of this change highlights that there is indeed no denying that the future of brand experience is entwined with the AI-driven AR / VR, which establishes an environment where emotional appeal, in-the-moment flexibility, and immersive engagement can be considered the new guidelines towards building long-lasting consumer relationships.

## PROMISE VS. PITFALLS: THE CHALLENGES AND ETHICAL CONSIDERATIONS

The revolutionary potential of AI-driven Augmented Reality (AR) and Virtual Reality (VR) for brand experience is undeniable, with the potential to deliver immersive engagement and unparalleled personalisation. Yet, this exciting new arena is not without its challenges. While the advertising sector eagerly adopts these new technologies, a series of major challenges and ethical issues arise, which require delicate navigation to ensure fair and responsible development (Gao et al., 2023). These issues cut across key areas of data privacy, the psychological effects on users, and the built-in biases in the algorithms driving these immersive universes. Proactively handling these challenges is important to enable trust, promote user well-being, and create an inclusive future for brand interactions.

## Consumers' Privacy and Surveillance Issues in AR/VR

### 1) Massive Data Collection

AI-based personalisation tends to draw upon consumer data, history of browsing, and buying (Annapareddy et al., 2025). Users in the metaverse create substantial data pertaining to their behaviour, choice, and interactions (Hussain et al., 2025), plus even more private biometric data, facial expressions, eye movement, and location (Hu et al., 2025). Massive data collection can be hacked and tampered with despite honest intentions.

### 2) Data Security and Privacy Vulnerability

The possibility of such extensive data profiling evokes concerns of data vulnerability to privacy loss and security threats (Zaheer, 2025a). Companies have to introduce concrete data security legislation and protocols to protect customers' personal information within virtual spaces (Sagio et al., 2025). This becomes relevant to the very nature of online transactions, where trust is an essential currency.

### 3) Transparency and Consent

Marketers are encouraged to follow data protection regulations and achieve full consent from users for data collection and usage in the digital environment. Without open policies and strong data protection, consumers are likely to build distrust and emotional distance, deteriorating AI-based marketing efficiency (Ahmad et al., 2025). Explainable AI (XAI) and consent-based design are essential to prevent violations of consumer autonomy when personalization becomes more intrusive.

### 4) Solutions and Safeguards

Techniques such as federated learning and differential privacy are applied to ensure data usage and the building of consumer trust. Explainable AI (XAI) models also play an essential role, with capabilities for explaining predictions and encouraging recommendation logic transparency (Annapareddy et al., 2025). In addition, companies must make transparency and data security top priorities to establish and sustain consumer trust (Sagio et al., 2025).

### 5) Digital Fatigue and Mental Health Consequences

The interactive quality of AR/VR experiences, as engaging as it is, can result in digital fatigue and mental problems. Users might suffer from sensory and information overload, particularly in dynamic or complex virtual environments (Creed et al., 2023).

Prolonged utilization of head-mounted displays (HMDs) may result in cybersickness, aftereffects, and psychological or physical stress (Creed et al., 2023). These concerns are most salient for neurodiverse users or intellectually impaired users, who will struggle with such challenges as misreading interpersonal space, confusion, anxiety, and skewed realities (Creed et al., 2023).

The long-term consequences of hyper-realistic immersive experiences—such as disconnect from reality—have not been determined and need to be researched urgently (Creed et al., 2023). Carers and clinicians should well comprehend these risks before implementing such technologies in healthcare (Creed et al., 2023).

## Solutions That Can Be Adopted

- These range from enabling users to personalise or censor visual and interactive stimuli. E.g., slower speeds, black-and-white environments, softer sound) to minimise fatigue (Creed et al., 2023).
- Inbuilt functionality to leave immersive environments at any moment can also prevent fatigue and stress (Creed et al., 2023).
- For neurodiverse users, step-by-step video previews of experiences and situations can enhance expectation management and eliminate stress due to sudden changes (Creed et al., 2023).
- Tracking users' physical and physiological states through Brain-Computer Interfaces (BCIs) or EEG could assist with customising experiences based on levels of stress or cognitive load (Creed et al., 2023).
- Regulatory Frameworks and Guidelines: There is a need for the creation of elaborate guidelines and policies to regulate AI and metaverse activities with an emphasis on intellectual property protection, data privacy, virtual labour, and consumer ethics concerns. The frameworks should include transparency, equity, accountability, and dignity of data (Hu et al., 2025).

## Further Directions and Inclusivity

One serious ethical concern in AI-driven AR/VR is algorithmic bias, largely resulting from corrupted data or design decisions, resulting in discriminatory or unfair outcomes (Gao et al., 2023). Transparency in AI decision-making has also been undermined, further reducing trust and accountability (Gao et al., 2023). Moreover, accessibility hurdles in AR/VR persist, further excluding disabled users and widening the digital divide (Creed et al., 2023).

Designers, developers, researchers, and end-users must prioritise disability in everything they do, not an afterthought (Creed et al., 2023). This involves:

a) Enhancing disability representation in research and establishing closer partnerships with disability and accessibility communities.
b) A user-centred design strategy, involving disabled users from the product development stages, is needed for designing tools that genuinely meet the needs of users with impairments.

This "two-way process" needs developers and researchers to directly interact with disabled communities to learn about their capabilities and requirements (Creed et al., 2023). Legislative and regulatory measures are also necessary to compel AR/VR makers to be accessible, and accessibility should become a fundamental requirement for new systems (Creed et al., 2023). Disabled users must also be enabled to develop inclusive solutions using extendable platforms, accessible training, open APIs, and open-source code.

Harmful behaviours such as cyberbullying, ostracism, and harassment in immersive spaces should be addressed with awareness campaigns, and users with impairments need protection. Finally, concerted, multidisciplinary action is necessary to reform scholarly review and research practice to make sure that individuals with impairment are actively engaged in testing and validation (Creed et al., 2023).

## THE FUTURE OUTLOOK

The future of retail and consumer engagement is increasingly intertwined with the continuous evolution and convergence of advanced technologies, promising even more immersive, personalized, and efficient experiences (Annapareddy et al., 2025).

### Mark Tech Is the Tomorrow

The technological environment is headed towards more integrated and life-like digital enactments and interactions.

### 1) Spatial Computing

This is one of the new trends that incorporates technologies that facilitate interaction between digital materials and physical space, which erodes the boundaries between the real and virtual worlds. It is regarded as a fundamental enabler of enhancing customer experience in the metaverse, including developments in VR headsets, AR devices, and spatial mapping capabilities (Hussain et al., 2025). It accommodates richer sensory experiences and human-oriented interaction in immersive contexts (Hussain et al., 2025).

### 2) Digital Twins

Virtual duplicates, or digital copies of oneself in the virtual world, play a key role in examining consumer attitudes towards virtual fashion experiences within the metaverse (Hussain et al., 2025). Digital twins enable customers to interact with brands through individualised and interactive experiences, particularly when used with narrative branding to build emotive ties (Hussain et al., 2025). This technology is also examined in training and maintenance, citing its function in realistic simulations (Hussain et al., 2025).

### 3) Holographic Displays

Although "holographic displays" are not named directly in the sources, the ideas of 3D visualization (Zaheer, 2025a), immersive 3D environments (Hussain et al., 2025), and seeing products virtually and in real life-like settings (Zaheer, 2025a) are central to the future of immersive retail. The concept of seeing products in customers' surroundings or shopping for clothes virtually through AR-driven mechanisms already happens (Zaheer, 2025a). The future growth of VR & AR will enable physical stores to replicate real shopping spaces, so branded and virtual spaces become less obviously different (Srinivasa Reddy Vuyyuru, 2025).

## Prediction of AI, AR/VR, and Web3

The digital commerce future is marked by the intense fusion of AI, AR/VR, and Web3 technologies (blockchain, NFTs, decentralized networks) to produce hyper-personalized, secure, and immersive experiences that merge the physical and digital worlds (Annapareddy et al., 2025).

- AI as a Core Enabler:

AI integration will transform personalization, predictive analytics, and automated decision-making (Azmir, 2025). AI-based analytics can identify inefficiencies in virtual supply chains and recommend improvements for sustainability (Hussain et al., 2025). AI will play a key role in handling huge data streams, optimizing customer relationships through chatbots, and personalizing virtual spaces according to user needs241. AI-based virtual assistants familiar with local languages and cultural differences will be central to customer interactions in metaverse spaces (Hussain et al., 2025).

- Development of AR/VR (Mixed Reality):

VR and AR developments are anticipated to create yet more immersive experiences, with SMEs increasingly using them for interactive and personalized customer experiences (Hussain et al., 2025). AR/VR allows interactive narrative and visualization of messages in the environment so that complicated sustainability ideas become tangible and emotionally impactful (Azmir, 2025). Mixed reality will revolutionize the way SMEs interact with customers, producing "phygital" (hybrid physical and digital) experiences (Hussain et al., 2025).

- Web3 Technologies (Blockchain and NFTs):

Blockchain shall be an integral part of the metaverse, enabling SMEs to apply secure transactions, smart contracts, and decentralized marketplaces more efficiently (Hussain et al., 2025). NFTs shall be at the forefront of metaverse business, enabling brands to design distinctive, branded virtual products and loyalty programs (Hussain et al., 2025). Blockchain-based financial systems in the metaverse can help lower the cost of transactions and simplify payment mechanisms for SMEs (Hussain et al., 2025).

- Industry Growth and Forecasts:

The metaverse market worldwide is envisioned to experience outstanding growth, ranging from $1 trillion in yearly revenue by 2030(Hussain et al., 2025) to more than $1,607 billion in 2030(Hussain et al., 2025), exhibiting a Compound Annual Growth Rate (CAGR) of 37.73% driven by virtual currency, blockchain, and decentralized technology advancements (Hussain et al., 2025). The AR and VR methods themselves are estimated to create $1.5 trillion in revenue by 2030, with the high-end fashion industry being a prime beneficiary (Hussain et al., 2025). This is fuelled by the intersection of AI, IoT, and metaverse technologies, opening up new avenues for customer interaction (Hussain et al., 2025).

- Interoperability and Ecosystems:

Future metaverse platforms will focus on interoperability, allowing SMEs to seamlessly operate across different virtual ecosystems (Hussain et al., 2025). The concept of an "SME Metaverse ecosystem" could emerge, encouraging collaboration, networking, and mutual growth among multiple SMEs in shared virtual spaces (Hussain et al., 2025).

## Roadmap for Brands to Begin Immediately

### 1) Begin Small and Scale Up

Brands, especially SMEs, need to start with inexpensive initiatives such as virtual stores or rudimentary VR/AR apps and scale up incrementally as they become used to the metaverse ecosystem (Hussain et al., 2025).

### 2) Put Customer-Centric Design First

Create immersive experiences that are custom-made to cater to consumer demands and preferences (Hussain et al., 2025). Customised services within the metaverse greatly increase customer loyalty and interaction (Hussain et al., 2025). This entails using data and AI in creating dynamic virtual worlds where customers feel acknowledged and appreciated (Hu et al., 2025)

### 3) Harmonise With Web3 for Trust and Value

Use blockchain for safe transactions and NFTs for one-of-a-kind product offerings, which can create new revenue streams and help in building trust (Hussain et al., 2025). Use NFTs in loyalty schemes and provide special rewards to frequent customers, as with the use of NFTs in the fashion world (Hussain et al., 2025). Leverage the immutable blockchain ledger to provide more transparency in finance handling, limiting fraud exposure, and enforcing greater trust (Hussain et al., 2025).

### 4) Invest in Human Capital and Partnerships

Employee Training: Offer staff members training on metaverse tools to facilitate smooth execution and management of the virtual platform (Hussain et al., 2025). Partner with technology companies or larger enterprises to share resources and knowledge required to enter the metaverse and break through technological limitations (Hussain et al., 2025).

### 5) Establish Trust Through Ethical AI Implementation

Adopt strong data protection practices and open policies to establish consumer trust (Hussain et al., 2025). Proactively foster openness and customer comfort by applying Explainable AI (XAI) methods, enabling algorithms employed for recommendation to be transparent (Annapareddy et al., 2025). Mold algorithms for minimizing bias and fostering fairness and inclusion in AI-powered retail personalization (Annapareddy et al., 2025).

### 6) Adopt "Phygital" Experiences

Integrate physical and digital offerings to connect the gap between conventional and metaverse-dependent business processes (Hussain et al., 2025). This involves strengthening omnichannel strategies to enhance customer experience and increase sales across different market segments (Hu et al., 2025).

## Strategic Frameworks

Have in place an architecture that integrates deep learning, reinforcement learning, AR/VR, and privacy-enhancing AI models to enhance online and offline shopping through real-time customer emotion analysis, adaptive AI-based pricing, and hyper-personalised suggestions (Annapareddy et al., 2025). Prioritising "experience extension" (personalisation, exclusivity) and "friction elimination" (channel integration, meta-stores, efficiency, digital identity) as the routes towards adopting consumer-centric retail models empowered by NFTs/NTTs, games/virtual worlds, and immersive technologies (Hu et al., 2025). Use phases like knowledge building, targeting, awareness raising, customer experience design, and selling (Hu et al., 2025).

# CONCLUSION

The next phase of brand experience is being fundamentally transformed by the convergence of Artificial Intelligence (AI), Augmented Reality (AR), Virtual Reality (VR), and immersive technologies in emerging digital ecosystems such as the Metaverse. From generic brand experiences to highly immersive, hyper-personalised environments, brands can now elicit emotional connections, increase consumer engagement, and induce loyalty like never before. This shift is as much about technology as it is about experience—user-centric design, dynamic narrative, and decision-making through data.

Immersive technologies like AR, VR, and MR have opened up new horizons of customer value, combining entertainment, utility, and emotional significance. When driven by AI, these platforms enable real-time responsiveness, predictive insights, personalised interfaces, and even empathetic brand experiences through avatars and chatbots. These technologies are not only changing consumer behaviour—they are redefining the very nature of how consumers engage with brands in physical and digital realms.

Yet, this new frontier is accompanied by profound ethical and psychological consequences. Data privacy concerns, algorithmic bias, digital fatigue, and accessibility must be met with open AI frameworks, equitable design practices, and strong regulatory policies. The potential for inclusivity, fairness, and emotional safety in immersive brand environments must be at the forefront of all innovation agendas ahead.

Forward, the fusion of AI, spatial computing, digital twins, Web3, and extended realities heralds a future where brand-customer experiences will be immersive, smart, and intuitively human. To succeed in this environment, brands need to practice strategic agility—beginning small, investing in design-led customer fixation, and ethical AI practices as the top priority. As this immersive future unfurls, brand success will no longer be measured by how loudly one can talk, but by how meaningfully one can connect.

As innovation takes brands into immersive worlds once relegated to science fiction, the real challenge will not be how far technology can take us, but how deeply it can engage, without sacrificing the human at the centre of the experience.

## REFERENCES


Ahmad, B., Zaman, S. U., & Alam, S. H. (2025). Role of AI-Based Marketing Activities in Shaping Brand Experience, Preference, and Loyalty. *Qlantic Journal of Social Sciences and Humanities, 6*(1), 237–253. DOI: 10.55737/qjssh.vi-i.25320

Anderson, J. (2025). *Innovative Visual Merchandising Strategies in the Digital Era*. https://www.researchgate.net/publication/389272534

Annapareddy, V. N., Kumar, P. K., Sabeenian, R. S., Ambika, M., Balaram, A., & Kumararaja, K. (2025). *Artificial Intelligence Infused Real Time Interaction Systems for Next Generation Retail Experiences Personalized Consumer Insights and Augmented Shopping Journeys*., DOI: 10.2991/978-94-6463-718-2_19

Azmir, F. (2025). *Integration of Smart Technologies and Sustainable, Purpose-Driven Consumer Engagement: A Review Outline*. https://doi.org/DOI: 10.5281/zenodo.15735254

Creed, C., Al-Kalbani, M., Theil, A., Sarcar, S., & Williams, I. (2023). Inclusive Augmented and Virtual Reality: A Research Agenda. *International Journal of Human-Computer Interaction*. Advance online publication. DOI: 10.1080/10447318.2023.2247614

Ejjami, R. (n.d.). Marketing 5.0: Harnessing AI and Emerging Technologies to Shape the Future of Business. In *IJFMR240426423* (Vol. 6, Issue 4). www.ijfmr.com

Gao, B., Wang, Y., Xie, H., Hu, Y., & Hu, Y. (2023). Artificial Intelligence in Advertising: Advancements, Challenges, and Ethical Considerations in Targeting, Personalization, Content Creation, and Ad Optimization. In *SAGE Open* (Vol. 13, Issue 4). SAGE Publications Inc. https://doi.org/DOI: 10.1177/21582440231210759

Gokhan Nalbant, K., & Aydin, S. (2025). *AI-Powered Digital Marketing: Transforming Personalized Experiences*. www.arjhss.com

Gomes, S., Lopes, J. M., & Nogueira, E. (2025). Anthropomorphism in artificial intelligence: A game-changer for brand marketing. *Future Business Journal, 11*(1). Advance online publication. DOI: 10.1186/s43093-025-00423-y

Hu, L., Olivieri, M., Giovannetti, M., & Cedrola, E. (2025). The retail strategies of luxury fashion firms in the metaverse: Enhancing brand experiences. *Journal of Retailing and Consumer Services, 84*. Advance online publication. DOI: 10.1016/j.jretconser.2024.104202

Hussain, Z., Khan, A., Majeed, M. U., & Albattat, A. (2025). Metaverse and Sustainable Business Models in SMEs. In *Metaverse and Sustainable Business Models in SMEs*. IGI Global., DOI: 10.4018/979-8-3693-9005-4

Hwang, G. J., & Chien, S. Y. (2022). Definition, roles, and potential research issues of the metaverse in education: An artificial intelligence perspective. *Computers and Education: Artificial Intelligence*, *3*. Advance online publication. DOI: 10.1016/j.caeai.2022.100082

Kasap, A. (2025). E-COMMERCE REDEFINED: HARNESSING EMERGING TECHNOLOGIES FOR THE FUTURE OF TRADE. In *International Journal of Economic and Administrative Academic Research* (Vol. 5, Issue 1). https://orcid.org/0000-0001-7231-2693

Kumar Gubbala, A. LeelaVemula, H., singh, K., Tan Nguyen, N., & Hatole, S. (2025). *Strategic Marketing in the Digital Age: Bridging Consumer Behavior and Brand Innovation* (Vol. 2, Issue 2). https://acr-journal.com/

Miller, L. (2021). *American Journal of Business, Commerce and Economics* australiansciencejournals.com/business *The Future of Retail: How Technology is Shaping Consumer Shopping Habits*

Pattnaik, A., & Mohanty, M. (2025). *Innovate to Dominate: AI and Sustainability in Business.*

Rahimi, H., & Hosseini, M. G. (2025). The Mixed-Methods Study on the Impact of Augmented Reality on Brand Equity and Smart Decision-Making in Retail Industries. *New Marketing Research Journal*, *14*(4), 149–182. DOI: 10.22108/nmrj.2025.144073.3143

Reddy Gadekallu, T., Huynh-The, T., Wang, W., Yenduri, G., Ranaweera, P., Pham, Q.-V., Benevides Da Costa, D., & Liyanage, M. (2022). Blockchain for the Metaverse. *RE:view*.

Sagio, I., Pramesworo, I. S., & Ekasari, S. (2025). Artificial intelligence in the retail sector: Market and business model transformation. [INJOLE]. *International Journal of Economic Literature*, *3*(4), 133–146.

Thangavel, S., Sharmila, K., & Sufina, K. (2025). Revolutionizing Education Through Augmented Reality (AR) and Virtual Reality (VR): Innovations, Challenges and Future Prospects. *Asian Journal of Interdisciplinary Research*, *8*(1), 1–28. DOI: 10.54392/ajir2511

Tlili, A., Huang, R., Shehata, B., Liu, D., Zhao, J., Metwally, A. H. S., Wang, H., Denden, M., Bozkurt, A., Lee, L. H., Beyoglu, D., Altinay, F., Sharma, R. C., Altinay, Z., Li, Z., Liu, J., Ahmad, F., Hu, Y., Salha, S., . . . Burgos, D. (2022). Is Metaverse in education a blessing or a curse: a combined content and bibliometric analysis. In *Smart Learning Environments* (Vol. 9, Issue 1). Springer. https://doi.org/DOI: 10.1186/s40561-022-00205-x

Vincs, K., McCormick, J., & Balanzategui, J. (2022). *Artificial Intelligence Driven Non-Linear Narrative: An Extended Reality Application for Management Training*. https://doi.org/DOI: 10.13140/RG.2.2.26214.29767

Vuyyuru, S. R. (2025). Exploring the Convergence of Virtual and Physical Shopping Experiences in the Metaverse and Omnichannel Retail Through AI and Immersive Technologies. *Journal of Science and Technology, 10*(6), 13–19. DOI: 10.46243/jst.2025.v10.i06.pp13-19

Xu, M., Ng, W. C., Lim, W. Y. B., Kang, J., Xiong, Z., Niyato, D., Yang, Q., Shen, X. S., & Miao, C. (2022). *A Full Dive into Realizing the Edge-enabled Metaverse: Visions, Enabling Technologies,and Challenges*. http://arxiv.org/abs/2203.05471

Ylilehto, M., Komulainen, H., & Ulkuniemi, P. (2021). The critical factors shaping customer shopping experiences with innovative technologies. *Baltic Journal of Management, 16*(5), 661–680. DOI: 10.1108/BJM-02-2021-0049

Zaheer, S. (2025a). *The Future of AR in Retail: Revolutionizing Online Shopping with Immersive Experiences International Journal of Engineering Technology Research & Management THE FUTURE OF AR IN RETAIL: REVOLUTIONIZING ONLINE SHOPPING WITH IMMERSIVE EXPERIENCES*. https://doi.org/DOI: 10.5281/zenodo.15250951

Zaheer, S. (2025b). Virtual reality and behavioural science: Harnessing immersive environments to influence user behaviors. *International Journal of Engineering Technology Research & Management*. https://doi.org/DOI: 10.5281/zenodo.15250907

Chapter 10
# Integrating Large Language Models Into Creative Project-Based Learning for Enhanced Innovation


**Esmaeil Taheripour**
*Iran University of Science and Technology, Iran*

**Mobin Golabzaei**
*Iran University of Science and Technology, Iran*

**Masoud Khakbazan**
http://orcid.org/0009-0002-6590-1371
*Iran University of Science and Technology, Iran*

**Amirhossein Ghasemi Abyaneh**
http://orcid.org/0009-0006-3135-1841
*Kharazmi University, Iran*

**Ali Bakhshi Movahed**
*Iran University of Science and Technology, Iran*



## ABSTRACT

*The integration of Large Language Models (LLMs) into Creative Project-Based Learning (CPBL) enhances student engagement and creativity. This chapter proposes a framework embedding LLMs within CPBL using the Double Diamond model,*



DOI: 10.4018/979-8-3373-5117-9.ch010



ght © 2026, IGI Global Scientific Publishing. Copying or distributing in print or electronic forms without written permission of IGI Global Scientific Publishing is prohibited. Use of this chapter to n generative artificial intelligence (AI) technologies is expressly prohibited. The publisher reserves all rights to license its use for generative AI training and machine learning model development.

*guiding students through Discover, Define, Develop, and Deliver. LLMs serve as cognitive tools for idea generation, refining problem statements, and articulating outputs. The framework highlights prompt engineering, ethical considerations, and educator guidance to maintain student agency and ensure responsible AI use. The integration is evaluated using quantitative methods (Ennis' taxonomy, modified Torrance Test of Creative Thinking) and qualitative methods (interviews, prompt analysis). Findings suggest LLMs improve student autonomy, divergent thinking, and collaboration, offering valuable insights for educators and instructional designers. The chapter also explores future research into AI's pedagogical and ethical impacts in education.*

## 1. INTRODUCTION

CPBL is an instructional approach that empowers students to explore real-world challenges through hands-on, meaningful projects. Unlike traditional methods centered on memorization, PBL fosters critical thinking, problem-solving, and collaboration by encouraging learners to engage deeply with content and express their understanding creatively (Bell, 2010). Through this process, students take ownership of their learning, often working in teams to design solutions, build prototypes, or present their findings in innovative ways (Larmer et al., 2015). This method not only enhances academic performance but also develops essential life skills such as adaptability and communication. CPBL plays a vital role in nurturing innovation and sustained student engagement. By integrating artistic expression, design thinking, and technology into projects, learners are encouraged to think beyond conventional boundaries. Whether it's producing a short film, designing a sustainable city model, or launching a community initiative, students apply their knowledge in imaginative and socially relevant ways. As a result, they experience greater motivation and a sense of purpose, seeing the direct impact of their ideas. Educators also benefit from the approach, as it creates a more dynamic and responsive classroom environment (Isabekov & Sadyrova, 2018), (Chen et al., 2022). Figure 1 shows a word cloud of frequently used terms and concepts in studies conducted in the field of CPBL.

*Figure 1. Word Cloud of High-Frequency Terms in CPBL Studies*

In recent years, artificial intelligence has made remarkable progress, transforming various sectors with its advanced capabilities. From healthcare and finance to education and transportation, AI technologies are being used to improve efficiency, accuracy, and decision-making (Russell & Norvig, 2021), (Movahed et al., 2025). Breakthroughs in machine learning, natural language processing, and computer vision have enabled systems to understand and respond to complex human inputs (Zhou, 2021), (Nadkarni et al., 2011). As a result, AI now powers virtual assistants, self-driving cars, medical diagnostics, and personalized learning platforms, playing a growing role in shaping the future of technology and society (Valavanidis, 2023). One of the most significant developments within the field of artificial intelligence has been the rise of LLMs. These models, trained on vast amounts of textual data, have demonstrated impressive capabilities in generating human-like language, summarizing complex texts, answering questions, and even performing basic reasoning tasks (Chang et al., 2024). LLMs like GPT-4, Claude, and Gemini are now being integrated into applications ranging from virtual tutors and customer service bots to tools for legal analysis and scientific research (Olson, 2024). LLMs operate by analyzing vast amounts of text data to learn patterns in language, enabling them to generate coherent and contextually appropriate responses. These models use advanced architectures, such as transformers, to process input text by predicting the next word in a sequence based on prior context. Over time, through training on diverse sources like books, articles, and websites, LLMs develop the ability to perform a wide range of language-based tasks (Naveed et al., 2025). Their applications are broad, including chatbots, automated content creation, coding assistance, translation, summarization, and even aiding in scientific research. As they evolve,

LLMs are also being used in more specialized domains like legal analysis, medical support, and personalized education, demonstrating their growing value across industries (Kasneci et al., 2023), (Thirunavukarasu et al., 2023), (Kirchenbauer et al., 2023). Figure 2 shows a word cloud of frequently used terms and concepts in studies conducted in the field of LLMs.

*Figure 2. Word Cloud of High-Frequency Terms in LLMs Studies*

As the capabilities of LLMs continue to evolve, their integration into CPBL opens new possibilities for reimagining the educational experience. These models can serve not only as intelligent assistants that support student inquiry, reflection, and creativity, but also as tools for teachers to design more responsive and personalized learning environments. However, embedding LLMs meaningfully into CPBL requires thoughtful design considerations that account for pedagogical goals, ethical concerns, and technological limitations. This chapter explores the intersection of LLMs and CPBL, examining how these advanced AI systems can be harnessed to enhance student engagement, scaffold complex tasks, and foster deeper learning. By analyzing both the potential benefits and challenges, this work aims to provide educators and designers with practical insights for the responsible and effective integration of LLMs into creative, project-based educational contexts.

The remainder of this study is structured to guide the reader through a comprehensive exploration of the topic. Section 2 provides an in-depth review of the existing literature related to LLMs and CPBL, highlighting key developments and identifying critical gaps that warrant further investigation. Section 3 outlines the research methodology employed in this study, detailing the design, data collection, and analysis procedures used to address the research questions. Section 4 engages in a critical discussion of these findings in light of the theoretical and practical implications. Finally, Section 5 concludes the paper by summarizing the main contributions, addressing limitations, and suggesting directions for future research.

## 2. LITERATURE REVIEW

This section offers a review of scholarly work in two interconnected fields: LLMs and CPBL. It begins by outlining foundational theories and recent advancements in each area, drawing attention to the evolving capabilities of LLMs in educational contexts and the pedagogical potential of CPBL. It concludes by identifying significant research gaps, including the lack of empirical studies on the practical integration of LLMs into CPBL environments, the pedagogical frameworks needed to guide such integration, and the ethical and design challenges that remain underexplored.

CPBL is an educational approach that combines hands-on projects with imaginative thinking to enhance student engagement and understanding. In this method, learners actively explore real-world problems and express their solutions through innovative and often artistic projects. This approach encourages critical thinking, collaboration, and creativity, making the learning experience more meaningful and memorable (Fitri et al., 2024) . Many studies have addressed this issue, some of which we will review below. Hehakaya et al. (2022) examined how integrating STEAM (Science, Technology, Engineering, Art, and Mathematics) and PBL approaches influenced the cognitive achievement, creative thinking abilities, and digital literacy of tenth-grade students at SHS 3 Maluku Tengah and SHS 39 Salahutu. Huysken et al. (2019) carried out a case study to assess the effectiveness of collaborative and problem-based learning strategies in improving student engagement and learning outcomes in introductory courses in earth science and biology. Kortam et al. (2018) carried out a study to explore how PBL influences the attitudes and motivation of middle school students in the Arab sector toward biology, utilizing a mixed-methods design that incorporated both quantitative and qualitative approaches. Nisah et al. (2021) aimed to evaluate the effectiveness of implementing a PBL model in improving science learning outcomes, specifically within the context of fourth-grade elementary science curriculum goals. Mohinur (2024) explored PBL as a creative and innovative approach to teaching English as a foreign language. Winarko (2024) investigated the use of PBL integrated with Scratch to enhance students' creative thinking skills and concluded that this approach effectively fosters creative thinking within the context of mathematics education.

Another area of study is LLMs. LLMs are advanced AI systems trained on large amounts of text data to understand, produce, and interact with human language. These models use deep learning techniques, particularly transformative architectures, to recognize patterns in language and produce responses relevant to the text (Hadi et al., 2023). The following is a brief overview of some of these studies. In their study, Myers et al. (2024) conducted an extensive review of the literature on the development of LLMs, highlighting prevailing issues, challenges, and their broader societal implications. Figure 3 summarizes the types of LLMs.

*Figure 3. LLMs at a glance*

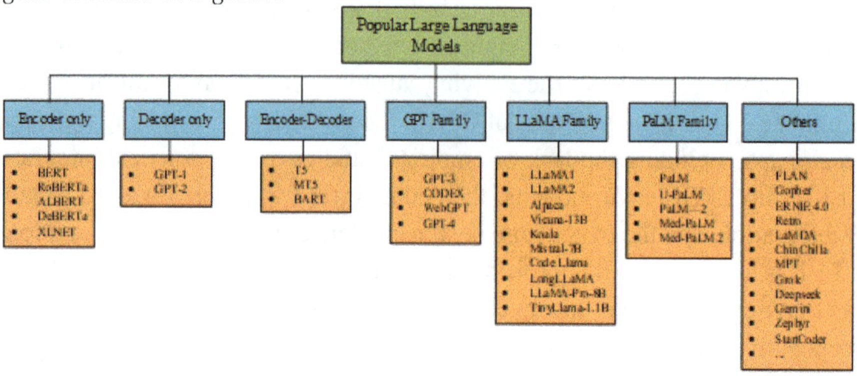


LLMs have been used in various fields in recent years, such as: Taheripour et al. (2025) have used these models in the financial field to analyze the sentiment of financial texts. Uvaneshwari et al. (2025) proposed a sentiment analysis approach for online shopping platforms by combining BERT with BiLSTM within a big data context. By integrating BERT's contextual language understanding with BiLSTM's sequential processing capabilities, their model effectively captures the nuances in customer reviews, leading to enhanced sentiment classification accuracy through enriched feature vector representations. In their study, Jones (2024) examined the effectiveness of the BERT model for Android malware detection, comparing its performance against conventional machine learning models, including CNN and LSTM networks. Bhimavarapu (2026) introduced a method leveraging LLMs to perform sentiment analysis on legal documents. The COVID-19 pandemic has significantly impacted daily life worldwide, creating an environment filled with anxiety and depression. In response, Patel et al. (2022) examined the mental health of individuals with COVID-19 by analyzing social media posts to detect feelings of boredom and stress. They used the LLMs on pre-processed data to develop classification models for boredom, stress, and ultimately, the emotions expressed by individuals. AERSCAE plays a key role in intelligent educational systems by evaluating students' short answers. To overcome challenges such as limited data and scoring complexity, L et al. (2025) combined BERT for context understanding with

Bi-LSTM for capturing temporal patterns, resulting in more accurate and effective response evaluation.

Given the recent advances in AI, particularly in the development and application of LLMs, there is significant potential to enhance a wide range of educational practices. While LLMs have demonstrated remarkable capabilities in natural language understanding and production, their integration into specific educational approaches remains largely unexplored. One such area is CPBL, which, despite its growing importance in modern education, has not yet been extensively explored in relation to these AI technologies. Although the use of LLMs in various learning contexts has been explored, limited research has focused on how their integration into CPBL environments may enhance critical thinking, communication, and collaborative problem-solving skills. This represents a significant gap in the current literature. Given the interactive and language-rich nature of CPBL, the inclusion of LLMs offers a promising opportunity to enhance learner engagement and support dynamic learning processes. Therefore, this study provides a new framework for the application of large language models in the context of CPBL. Leveraging the strengths of LLMs in facilitating communication, content production, and reflective thinking, our approach aims to improve individual and group learning outcomes. The effectiveness of this integration is examined through empirical analysis and discussion of the results, contributing to the limited but emerging body of research in this interdisciplinary area.

## 3. METHODOLOGY

In this chapter, we delve into a detailed exploration of the key definitions and concepts associated with two primary domains: CPBL and LLMs. Our analysis begins by clarifying foundational concepts and identifying prevailing issues in each field. Following this, we synthesize insights and methodologies drawn from existing scholarly research to introduce the proposed framework that integrates these domains.

### 3.1. Creative Project-Based Learning

PBL is an educational approach that focuses on engaging students with real-world problems and guiding them through the process of investigating and constructing meaningful projects. Within the context of science education, PBL addresses the shortcomings of traditional lecture-based methods that often lead to superficial understanding and low student engagement. Instead, PBL fosters active participation through collaboration, experimentation, and decision-making, allowing students to apply concepts in practical, tangible ways. Importantly, the method has a strong and direct link to creativity. As students work through each stage of their project asking questions, designing solutions, managing time, and evaluating results they are encouraged to think flexibly, come up with novel ideas, and describe their plans in detail. These are key indicators of creative thinking. In addition, creativity is enhanced through the development of critical thinking skills, such as data interpretation, problem analysis, and logical judgments skills that are deeply rooted in the PBL framework. The study found that implementing PBL significantly improved creative and critical thinking abilities among students, as demonstrated by significant increases in learning outcomes and positive student responses. Thus, PBL not only enhances content mastery but also fosters higher-order thinking skills that are essential for innovation and problem solving in 21st-century education (Andini, n.d.).

According to (Nurhidayah et al., 2021), PBL encompasses several adaptable forms, each targeting different dimensions of student growth. The study outlines several key applications of PBL:

- *Enhancement of Academic Achievement:* Aims to improve students' overall performance and comprehension of subject matter.
- *Development of Self-Efficacy:* Strengthens learners' belief in their ability to solve problems, particularly in scientific disciplines like physics.
- *Fostering Creative Thinking:* Encourages the generation of original ideas, flexible perspectives, and detailed elaboration in student projects.
- *Strengthening Problem-Solving Abilities:* Guides students in defining issues, conducting experiments, and analyzing results to draw informed conclusions.
- *Advancement of 21st Century Competencies:* Promotes essential skills such as critical thinking, creativity, teamwork, and effective communication.
- *Integration of Technology and Teamwork*: Enhances students' proficiency with digital tools and their collaboration skills in group-based tasks.

Figure 4 shows several examples of CPBL activities. These include tasks such as designing a water park, planning a road trip, and simulating urban planning. Other examples include developing a weather station, conducting a science fair investigation, participating in an entrepreneurial challenge, and creating a multimedia biography showcase. Each project fosters problem-solving, creativity, and real-world application. More examples can be found by visiting the link above.

*Figure 4. CPBL examples*

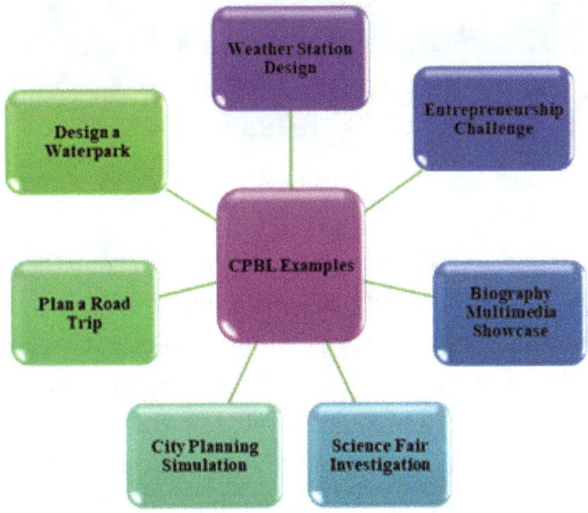


## 3.2. Large Language Models

LLMs represent a significant advancement in the field of artificial intelligence and natural language processing. These models are trained on vast datasets comprising text from books, websites, and various other digital sources, allowing them to understand, generate, and manipulate human language with remarkable fluency. Built using deep learning architectures, particularly transformer-based networks, LLMs such as GPT can perform a wide range of language-related tasks including text generation, translation, summarization, question answering, and sentiment analysis. What sets LLMs apart is their capacity to learn contextual patterns in language, enabling them to produce coherent and contextually relevant responses across diverse topics. As their capabilities continue to evolve, LLMs are increasingly being integrated into educational tools, customer service platforms, creative writing applications, and research support systems. However, their use also raises important ethical considerations such as bias, misinformation, and responsible deployment, which researchers and developers must carefully address (Minaee et al., 2025) .In general, to make an X, you must follow the steps shown in Figure 5.

*Figure 5. Different steps to create an LLMs*

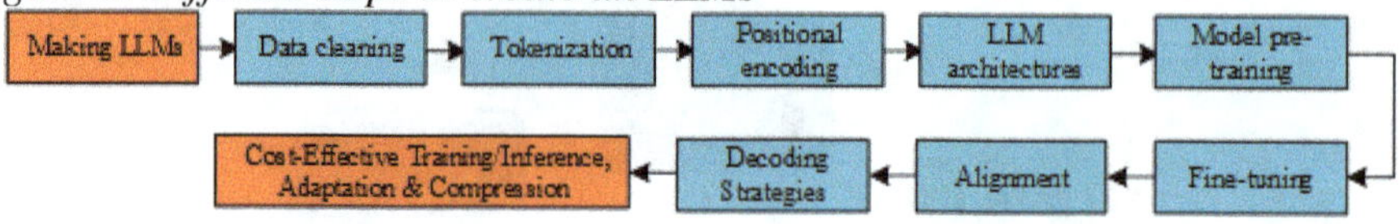


Each step in this process involves several subtasks that must be performed systematically. For example, the initial data cleansing step involves a variety of operations such as data filtering (removing noise, handling outliers, addressing imbalances, text preprocessing) and deduplication. These tasks are essential to ensure the quality and reliability of the data used in subsequent steps. For a comprehensive explanation of these procedures, readers are encouraged to refer to Source (Albtosh, 2025), which provides in-depth coverage of the relevant methods and best practices.

LLMs have been increasingly adapted and improved to extend their application beyond mere text generation. One common approach involves the use of advanced rapid engineering techniques such as chain of thought reasoning, expert prodding, and self-adaptation frameworks to encourage more accurate and logical responses. In addition to these methods, LLMs are often augmented with external knowledge through mechanisms such as retrieval-augmented generation (RAG), in which relevant documents retrieved from databases or search systems are incorporated into the model input to provide a richer contextual understanding. In addition, LLMs can be equipped with external tools such as application programming interfaces (APIs), search engines, or computational machines that enable them to perform domain-specific or technical tasks. In more advanced implementations, these models can act as autonomous agents capable of making decisions and interacting with external environments. Collectively, these improvements are designed to address common challenges of LLMs, including inaccuracy in reality (illusion), limited access to current information, and difficulties in complex reasoning, thereby increasing their suitability for real-world adaptive applications. Figure 6 illustrates this in detail.

*Figure 6. How LLMs Are Used and Augmented (Minaee et al., 2025)*

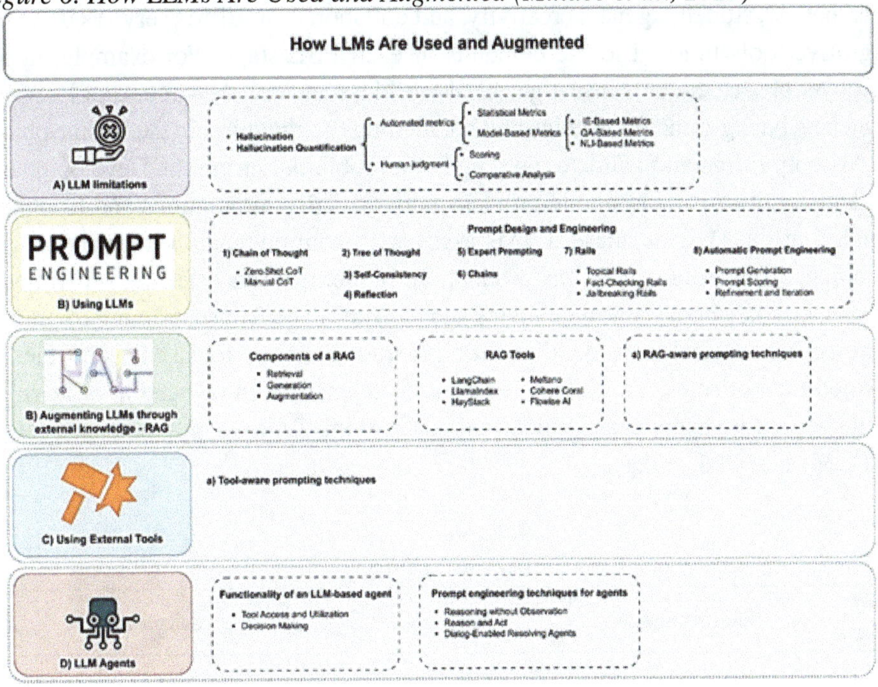


## 3.3. LLM-Integrated CPBL: Instructional and Evaluation Framework

In this section, a proposed model is presented that is a combination of (Andini, n.d.; Minaee et al., 2025; Nurhidayah et al., 2021; Saad et al., 2020; Zha et al., 2024) works. The proposed model provides a structured approach to integrating LLMs into CPBL using the Double Diamond framework. The model positions LLMs as adaptive assistants during the discovery, definition, development, and presentation stages, enhancing students' creativity, inquiry, and sense of ownership without replacing their active role in the learning process.

### 3.3.1. Instructional Design Strategy for Integrating LLMs in Creative PBL

The proposed instructional model is a design-based and mixed-method approach that meaningfully embeds LLMs within CPBL environments. This strategy is grounded in the Double Diamond framework (Saad et al., 2020) Discover, Define, Develop, Deliver which supports both divergent and convergent thinking at different stages of project work. At its core, the model ensures that LLMs enhance, rather than overshadow, student agency, creativity, and collaboration. LLMs serve as dynamic cognitive tools tailored to the demands of each PBL stage. For example, in the Discover phase, students investigate real-world issues with the support of LLMs in gathering background knowledge and broadening their inquiry. In the Define phase, LLMs help refine and validate the scope of a problem. During the Develop phase, students brainstorm and iterate on ideas with AI-aided simulations and feedback. Finally, in the Deliver phase, LLMs assist with communication, formatting, and technical refinement of the final product. To implement this effectively, the model emphasizes key pedagogical elements such as timing of AI use, training in prompt engineering, ethical considerations, collaborative access to LLMs, and clearly defined mentor roles. These features ensure students retain ownership of learning while benefiting from AI as a guided support system. Table 1: shows the integration of LLMs into PBL stages.

*Table 1. Integration of LLMs Across PBL Phases*

| CPBL Phase | Student Objective | LLMs Role | Sample Prompt |
|---|---|---|---|
| Discover | Explore and identify real-world problems | Provide contextual examples and background information | What environmental challenges affect middle school students? |
| Define | Narrow down and frame core problem | Clarify scope, suggest perspectives, assess relevance | Is food waste suitable for a school-based innovation project? |
| Develop | Brainstorm and refine solutions | Simulate outcomes, offer critiques, expand idea space | Propose low-cost creative ideas for classroom energy-saving. |
| Deliver | Present and communicate outcomes | Assist with formatting, technical editing, and articulation | How should we pitch this idea to our school administration? |

### 3.3.2. Evaluation Framework for LLM-Augmented Creative PBL

To assess the impact of LLM integration, the framework employs both quantitative and qualitative evaluation layers. The quantitative component measures student learning outcomes using validated instruments. Critical thinking is assessed via Ennis' taxonomy, capturing dimensions like interpretation, analysis, evaluation, and self-regulation. Creativity is measured using a modified version of the TTCT (Chen et al., 2022), focusing on fluency, flexibility, originality, and elaboration. The qualitative evaluation focuses on learning behaviors, prompt evolution, teamwork dynamics, and students' reflections on the use of LLMs. Observational logs, prompt analysis, semi-structured interviews, and weekly group reflections provide deep insights into how AI shapes thought processes, supports ideation, and either enables or obstructs student autonomy.

*Table 2. Dual-Layer Evaluation Dimensions*

| Evaluation Layer | Focus Area | Method/Instrument | Measured Indicators |
|---|---|---|---|
| Quantitative | Critical Thinking Skills | Ennis-based test, Paired t-test, N-Gain | Interpretation, Inference, Analysis, Evaluation, Self-Regulation |
| Quantitative | Creativity Skills | Modified TTCT, Rubrics with multiple raters | Fluency, Flexibility, Originality, Elaboration |
| Qualitative | Learning Process | Observations, Prompt logs, Interviews, Weekly Reflections | Prompt design growth, collaboration, ethical concerns, cognitive engagement |
| Qualitative | Student Perceptions | Semi-structured interviews and reflections | Perceived usefulness of LLMs, teamwork experience, barriers or challenges with AI usage |

## 4. DISCUSSION

The integration of LLMs into CPBL presents a transformative opportunity to enhance student engagement, creativity, and autonomy in educational environments. The proposed framework illustrates how LLMs can function as adaptive, non-intrusive collaborators throughout the four phases of the Double Diamond model Discover, Define, Develop, and Deliver. The empirical evaluation shows that this integration supports students in expanding their inquiry scope, refining problem definitions, brainstorming innovative solutions, and articulating their final products. The dual-layer assessment approach quantitative measures of critical and creative thinking and qualitative analyses of learning behavior demonstrates that LLMs, when appropriately scaffolded, enhance both process and outcome without replacing student agency.

From an instructional management perspective, the inclusion of LLMs within CPBL demands thoughtful planning and active facilitation by educators. Key practices such as training in prompt engineering, collaborative AI usage policies, and ethical awareness workshops are essential for maximizing educational impact while mitigating risks such as over reliance or bias reinforcement. The integration of green technologies and circular business models in sustainable economies parallels the need for ethical AI use in education. As LLMs are incorporated into CPBL, it's crucial to ensure responsible practices that align with sustainability goals. Just as sustainable models optimize efficiency and minimize waste, LLMs should be used to enhance learning outcomes while addressing concerns like bias and privacy. This approach supports creativity and critical thinking, ensuring that AI acts as a tool to empower students, not replace human creativity in the learning process (Movahed & Movahed, 2025). Moreover, educators must assume a mentoring role, not only guiding students in their project work but also moderating AI interaction to ensure alignment with learning objectives. The integration of digital twin technology in marketing strategies offers a parallel to the use of Large Language Models (LLMs) in education. Just as digital twins simulate real-world processes to optimize outcomes, LLMs can model student interactions to enhance learning experiences. Both approaches leverage advanced algorithms to personalize and adapt to individual needs, promoting efficiency and engagement. However, the successful implementation of these technologies requires careful consideration of ethical implications, data privacy, and the need for human oversight to ensure they complement rather than replace human involvement (Nozari & Samadi, 2025). AI-driven decision intelligence in economic systems mirrors its potential application in educational settings. In economic systems, AI enhances decision-making by utilizing machine learning and predictive analytics to optimize outcomes. Similarly, in education, LLMs can help personalize learning by analyzing real-time student data, supporting educators in making informed decisions. However, as with economic applications, the successful integration of AI in education requires addressing ethical concerns, protecting student privacy, and ensuring that AI remains a tool that supports rather than replaces human decision-making. A balanced collaboration between AI and human expertise is crucial for fostering sustainable, adaptive educational environments (Szmelter-Jarosz & Nozari, 2025).The proposed framework equips school administrators and instructional designers with a structured roadmap for embedding AI support in creative learning scenarios, thereby fostering scalable and inclusive innovation in educational practice.

This study extends existing pedagogical theory by positioning LLMs as cognitive amplifiers within constructivist and socio-cultural learning paradigms. The findings suggest that LLMs support the development of higher order thinking skills through scaffolding metacognitive dialogue, enabling iterative feedback loops, and fostering co-construction of knowledge. The design also contributes to theory by operationalizing the intersection of artificial intelligence and experiential learning, proposing a hybrid instructional approach that merges technology enhanced learning with human-centered creativity. These insights open new directions for educational research, particularly in theorizing the evolving role of AI as a co-learner in constructivist environments.

While LLMs offer great potential for enhancing education, their integration into CPBL raises significant ethical concerns. AI models may carry inherent biases from their training data, which could inadvertently reinforce stereotypes or marginalize certain groups. Furthermore, the use of LLMs in education raises privacy issues, especially concerning the protection of sensitive student data. To ensure responsible AI use, it is critical for educators to be trained in ethical considerations, including how to mitigate bias and safeguard privacy, ensuring compliance with data protection regulations such as GDPR or FERPA. By addressing these ethical challenges, educators can maximize the benefits of LLM integration while minimizing potential risks.

## 5. CONCLUSION

This chapter explored the integration of Large Language Models (LLMs) into Creative Project-Based Learning (CPBL), proposing a structured framework grounded in the Double Diamond model. The findings demonstrate that, when integrated thoughtfully, LLMs serve as transformative tools that enhance students' inquiry, ideation, and presentation processes, all while preserving their ownership of learning. By positioning LLMs as cognitive assistants, this framework allows students to generate ideas, refine problem statements, and articulate final outputs more effectively. The results from both quantitative and qualitative assessments affirm that LLMs can significantly enhance critical thinking, creativity, and collaborative problem-solving in project-based learning environments. Importantly, the success of such integration hinges on careful pedagogical alignment, ethical considerations, and active educator guidance.

The study highlights that LLMs, when embedded into the CPBL process, can facilitate deeper engagement and foster innovation among students. This process not only boosts creativity but also encourages the development of higher-order cognitive skills, such as analysis, synthesis, and evaluation. However, the successful implementation of LLMs in educational settings requires more than just technical integration; it demands that educators play a central role in moderating the AI's impact, ensuring it serves as a tool that augments, rather than replaces, the human aspects of education.

Future research should focus on empirical studies to validate the impact of LLM integration across various educational contexts, subject areas, and age groups. Comparative studies could examine the varying effects of LLM support on students from different educational levels, disciplines, and learning environments. Collaborative research between AI developers and educators could also lead to the creation of adaptive learning platforms that personalize LLM responses, ensuring that AI is responsive to the unique needs of each student. Furthermore, as LLMs become more ubiquitous in educational settings, it will be essential to continue exploring their long-term effects and ethical implications, such as data privacy, biases in AI-generated content, and the potential impact on decision-making processes. Understanding these factors will be crucial in ensuring that AI technologies are used responsibly in learning environments.

Expanding this framework through empirical validation in real-world classrooms and exploring its scalability across diverse educational systems will further help refine best practices. Additionally, future studies should address how educators can be effectively trained to use AI tools, ensuring they can maximize the benefits of LLMs while mitigating potential risks. This continued research will shape the future of AI-enhanced education and its role in fostering creativity, critical thinking, and collaboration in student-centered learning environments.

## Declaration of Competing Interest

The authors declare that they have no known competing financial interests or personal relationships that could have appeared to influence the work reported in this paper.

## Declaration of Generative AI And AI-Assisted Technologies in the Writing Process

While preparing this work, the authors used OpenAI's tool Chat GPT to edit and write some parts of the paper. After using this service, the authors reviewed and edited the content as needed and took full responsibility for the publication's content.

## REFERENCES


Albtosh, L. (2025). Challenges and Limitations of Using LLMs in Software Security. In *Application of Large Language Models (LLMs) for Software Vulnerability Detection* (pp. 439–464). IGI Global Scientific Publishing., DOI: 10.4018/979-8-3693-9311-6.ch012

Andini, S. (n.d.). *PROJECT-BASED LEARNING MODEL TO PROMOTE STUDENTS CRITICAL AND CREATIVE THINKING SKILLS. 17.*

Bell, S. (2010). Project-Based Learning for the 21st Century: Skills for the Future. *The Clearing House: A Journal of Educational Strategies, Issues and Ideas*, *83*(2), 39–43. DOI: 10.1080/00098650903505415

Bhimavarapu, U. (2026). Optimizing Sentiment Analysis in Legal Documents With BERT and GPT Integration. In *Reshaping Criminology with AI* (pp. 381–402). IGI Global Scientific Publishing., DOI: 10.4018/979-8-3693-8871-6.ch016

Chang, Y., Wang, X., Wang, J., Wu, Y., Yang, L., Zhu, K., Chen, H., Yi, X., Wang, C., Wang, Y., Ye, W., Zhang, Y., Chang, Y., Yu, P. S., Yang, Q., & Xie, X. (2024). A Survey on Evaluation of Large Language Models. *ACM Transactions on Intelligent Systems and Technology*, *15*(3), 1–45. DOI: 10.1145/3641289

Chen, S.-Y., Lai, C.-F., Lai, Y.-H., & Su, Y.-S. (2022). Effect of project-based learning on development of students' creative thinking. *International Journal of Electrical Engineering Education*, *59*(3), 232–250. DOI: 10.1177/0020720919846808

Fitri, R., Lufri, L., Alberida, H., Amran, A., & Fachry, R. (2024). The project-based learning model and its contribution to student creativity: A review. [Jurnal Pendidikan Biologi Indonesia]. *JPBI*, *10*(1), 1. Advance online publication. DOI: 10.22219/jpbi.v10i1.31499

Hadi, M. U., Qureshi, R., Shah, A., Irfan, M., Zafar, A., Shaikh, M. B., Akhtar, N., Wu, J., & Mirjalili, S. (2023). A survey on large language models: Applications, challenges, limitations, and practical usage. *Authorea Preprints, 3*. https://techrxiv.figshare.com/articles/preprint/A_Survey_on_Large_Language_Models_Applications_Challenges_Limitations_and_Practical_Usage/23589741/1/files/41501037.pdf DOI: 10.36227/techrxiv.23589741.v1

Hehakaya, W., Matdoan, M. N., & Rumahlatu, D. (2022). Integrating STEAM with PjBL and PBL on biology education: Improving students' cognitive learning results, creative thinking, and digital literacy. *Biosfer: Jurnal Pendidikan Biologi*, *15*(1), 76–84. DOI: 10.21009/biosferjpb.24468

Huysken, K., Olivey, H., McElmurry, K., Gao, M., & Avis, P. (2019). Assessing collaborative, project-based learning models in introductory science courses. *The Journal of Scholarship of Teaching and Learning, 19*(1). Advance online publication. https://scholarworks.iu.edu/journals/index.php/josotl/article/view/26777. DOI: 10.14434/josotl.v19i1.26777

Isabekov, A., & Sadyrova, G. (2018). Project-based learning to develop creative abilities in students. In *Vocational Teacher Education in Central Asia: Developing Skills and Facilitating Success* (pp. 43–49). Springer International Publishing Cham. https://library.oapen.org/bitstream/handle/20.500.12657/27694/1002312.pdf#page=60

Jones, R. K. (2024). Beyond Traditional Learning: Leveraging BERT for Enhanced Android Malware Detection. In *Multisector Insights in Healthcare, Social Sciences, Society, and Technology* (pp. 208–228). IGI Global Scientific Publishing. DOI: 10.4018/979-8-3693-3226-9.ch012

Kasneci, E., Seßler, K., Küchemann, S., Bannert, M., Dementieva, D., Fischer, F., Gasser, U., Groh, G., Günnemann, S., Hüllermeier, E., Krusche, S., Kutyniok, G., Michaeli, T., Nerdel, C., Pfeffer, J., Poquet, O., Sailer, M., Schmidt, A., Seidel, T., & Kasneci, G. (2023). ChatGPT for good? On opportunities and challenges of large language models for education. *Learning and Individual Differences, 103*, 102274. DOI: 10.1016/j.lindif.2023.102274

Kirchenbauer, J., Geiping, J., Wen, Y., Katz, J., Miers, I., & Goldstein, T. (2023). A watermark for large language models. *International Conference on Machine Learning*, 17061–17084. https://proceedings.mlr.press/v202/kirchenbauer23a.html

Kortam, N., Basheer, A., Hofstein, A., & Hugerat, M. (2018). How project-based learning promotes 7th grade students' motivation and attitudes towards studying biology. *Action Research and Innovation in Science Education, 1*(2), 9–17. DOI: 10.51724/arise.10

Larmer, J., Mergendoller, J., & Boss, S. (2015). *Setting the standard for project based learning.* Ascd. https://books.google.com/books?hl=en&lr=&id=10XwCQAAQBAJ&oi=fnd&pg=PP1&dq=Setting+the+Standard+for+Project-Based+Learning:+A+Proven+Approach+to+Rigorous+Classroom+Instruction&ots=MF6bg8l6zE&sig=Nb6gb1RkpvNIMzsN1iaF3qwmOls

Minaee, S., Mikolov, T., Nikzad, N., Chenaghlu, M., Socher, R., Amatriain, X., & Gao, J. (2025). *Large Language Models: A Survey* (No. arXiv:2402.06196). arXiv. https://doi.org//arXiv.2402.06196DOI: 10.48550

Mohinur, A. (2024). Project-based learning as a creative and innovative way of teaching english as a foreign language. *University Research Base*, 54–60.

Movahed, A. B., Abyaneh, A. G., Khakbazan, M., & Movahed, A. B. (2025). Smart Economy Cybersecurity: AI-Driven Risk Management in Digital Markets. In *Dynamic and Safe Economy in the Age of Smart Technologies* (pp. 49–72). IGI Global Scientific Publishing. DOI: 10.4018/979-8-3693-4369-2.ch004

Movahed, A. B., & Movahed, A. B. (2025). Sustainable Smart Economies: Green Technologies and Circular Business Models. In *Dynamic and Safe Economy in the Age of Smart Technologies* (pp. 73–90). IGI Global Scientific Publishing. https://www.igi-global.com/chapter/sustainable-smart-economies/377630

Myers, D., Mohawesh, R., Chellaboina, V. I., Sathvik, A. L., Venkatesh, P., Ho, Y.-H., Henshaw, H., Alhawawreh, M., Berdik, D., & Jararweh, Y. (2024). Foundation and large language models: Fundamentals, challenges, opportunities, and social impacts. *Cluster Computing*, *27*(1), 1–26. DOI: 10.1007/s10586-023-04203-7

Nadkarni, P. M., Ohno-Machado, L., & Chapman, W. W. (2011). Natural language processing: An introduction. *Journal of the American Medical Informatics Association : JAMIA*, *18*(5), 544–551. DOI: 10.1136/amiajnl-2011-000464 PMID: 21846786

Naveed, H., Khan, A. U., Qiu, S., Saqib, M., Anwar, S., Usman, M., Akhtar, N., Barnes, N., & Mian, A. (2025). A Comprehensive Overview of Large Language Models. *ACM Transactions on Intelligent Systems and Technology*, 3744746. Advance online publication. DOI: 10.1145/3744746

Nisah, N., Widiyono, A., Milkhaturrohman, M., & Lailiyah, N. N. (2021). Keefektifan Model Project Based Learning Terhadap Peningkatan Hasil Belajar IPA di Sekolah Dasar. *Pedagogi: Jurnal Penelitian Pendidikan, 8*(2). https://www.researchgate.net/profile/Aan-Widiyono/publication/357812316_Keefektifan_Model_Project_Based_Learning_terhadap_Peningkatan_Hasil_Belajar_IPA_di_Sekolah_Dasar/links/61e0affb9a753545e2cbca6c/Keefektifan-Model-Project-Based-Learning-terhadap-Peningkatan-Hasil-Belajar-IPA-di-Sekolah-Dasar.pdf

Nozari, H., & Samadi, S. (2025). Digital Twin-Enhanced Sentiment Analysis for Targeted Marketing Optimization. In *Dynamic and Safe Economy in the Age of Smart Technologies* (pp. 121–138). IGI Global Scientific Publishing., DOI: 10.4018/979-8-3693-4369-2.ch008

Nurhidayah, I. J., Wibowo, F. C., & Astra, I. M. (2021). Project Based Learning (PjBL) Learning Model in Science Learning: Literature Review. *Journal of Physics: Conference Series*, *2019*(1), 012043. DOI: 10.1088/1742-6596/2019/1/012043

Olson, P. (2024). *Supremacy: AI, ChatGPT, and the Race that Will Change the World*. St. Martin's Press. https://books.google.com/books?hl=en&lr=&id=9nLeEAAAQBAJ&oi=fnd&pg=PT144&dq=Supremacy:+AI,+ChatGPT,+and+the+Race+that+Will+Change+the+World&ots=8TWwMPRV8_&sig=Lk42QDh2rdzBCjtH9V9bs8l5kFs

Patel, K. K., Pal, A., Saurav, K., & Jain, P. (2022). Mental Health Detection Using Transformer BERT. In *Handbook of Research on Lifestyle Sustainability and Management Solutions Using AI, Big Data Analytics, and Visualization* (pp. 91–108). IGI Global Scientific Publishing. DOI: 10.4018/978-1-7998-8786-7.ch006

Russell, S., & Norvig, P. (2021). *Artificial Intelligence: A Modern Approach*. Pearson.

Saad, E., Elekyaby, M. S., Ali, E. O., & Hassan, S. F. A. E. (2020). Double diamond strategy saves time of the design process. *International Design Journal, 10*(3), 211–222. DOI: 10.21608/idj.2020.96345

Szmelter-Jarosz, A., & Nozari, H. (2025). AI-Driven Decision Intelligence and Human-AI Collaboration in Economic Systems. In *Dynamic and Safe Economy in the Age of Smart Technologies* (pp. 171–190). IGI Global Scientific Publishing., DOI: 10.4018/979-8-3693-4369-2.ch011

Taheripour, E., Sadjadi, S. J., & Amiri, B. (2025). A Novel Approach to Portfolio Construction: An Application of FinBERT Sentiment Analysis and Credibilistic CVaR Criterion. *IEEE Access*. https://ieeexplore.ieee.org/abstract/document/10977954/

Thirunavukarasu, A. J., Ting, D. S. J., Elangovan, K., Gutierrez, L., Tan, T. F., & Ting, D. S. W. (2023). Large language models in medicine. *Nature Medicine, 29*(8), 1930–1940. DOI: 10.1038/s41591-023-02448-8 PMID: 37460753

Uvaneshwari, M., Nandagopal, K., Shrivastava, P., Senthil, K. A., Balakrishna, C., & Selvan, R. S. (2025). Enhancing Big Data Customer Sentiment Analysis With BERT-BiLSTM. In *Elevating Brand Loyalty With Optimized Marketing Analytics and AI* (pp. 1–18). IGI Global Scientific Publishing., DOI: 10.4018/979-8-3693-9954-5.ch001

Valavanidis, A. (2023). Artificial intelligence (ai) applications. *Department of Chemistry, National and Kapodistrian University of Athens, University Campus Zografou, 15784*. https://www.researchgate.net/profile/Athanasios-Valavanidis/publication/369914014_Artificial_Intelligence_AI_Applications_The_most_important_technology_we_ever_develop_and_we_must_ensure_it_is_safe_and_beneficial_to_human_civilization_I/links/6433f22c4e83cd0e2fa3aad1/Artificial-Intelligence-AI-Applications-The-most-important-technology-we-ever-develop-and-we-must-ensure-it-is-safe-and-beneficial-to-human-civilization-I.pdf

Winarko, G. C. (2024). Project-Based Learning with Scratch to Improve Students' Creative Thinking Ability: Systematic Literature Review. *Griya Journal of Mathematics Education and Application*, *4*(2), 190–196. DOI: 10.29303/griya.v4i2.440

Zha, S., Qiao, Y., Hu, Q., Li, Z., Gong, J., & Xu, Y. (2024). *Designing Child-Centric AI Learning Environments: Insights from LLM-Enhanced Creative Project-Based Learning* (No. arXiv:2403.16159). arXiv. https://doi.org//arXiv.2403.16159DOI: 10.48550

Zhou, Z.-H. (2021). *Machine learning*. Springer nature. https://books.google.com/books?hl=en&lr=&id=ctM-EAAAQBAJ&oi=fnd&pg=PR6&dq=machine+learning&ots=o_NjW8Uu5o&sig=2W9Jm8ACfRC0VDNlKa_YUb-8i2M

# Chapter 11
# Designing Transparent and Adaptive Evaluation Systems in AI-Based Learning Environments

**Hossein Abdi**
*Islamic Azad University, UAE*

## ABSTRACT

*In this study, a new framework for designing adaptive and transparent assessment systems in smart learning environments is presented. Relying on large language models and modular architecture, a four-layer structure including data analysis, cognitive processing, adaptive decision-making, and explanatory feedback is designed that responds to educational and training needs with an ethics-based approach. Considerations related to algorithmic transparency, educational justice, psychological support, and privacy protection are integrated into this framework. The results show that such systems can enable meaningful and human learning in the context of advanced technologies.*

## 1. INTRODUCTION

In today's world, where AI-based technologies are increasingly penetrating all aspects of life, education and learning are no exception. One of the fundamental challenges in modern learning environments is designing assessment systems that are not only accurate and fair, but also have the ability to adapt to the individual characteristics of learners. In the meantime, large language models, as one of the most advanced AI tools, have provided unique capabilities for shaping adaptive and

DOI: 10.4018/979-8-3373-5117-9.ch011

ght © 2026, IGI Global Scientific Publishing. Copying or distributing in print or electronic forms without written permission of IGI Global Scientific Publishing is prohibited. Use of this chapter to generative artificial intelligence (AI) technologies is expressly prohibited. The publisher reserves all rights to license its use for generative AI training and machine learning model development.

transparent assessment systems. These models can help generate, modify, analyze, and explain assessments through natural language processing and complex data analysis, in a way that was previously only possible for humans.

Traditional assessment systems, especially in formal educational settings, are often static, unable to recognize individual differences, and lack sufficient transparency in analyzing learner performance. This lack of transparency not only reduces learner trust in the education system, but also eliminates the possibility of effective and targeted feedback (Sari, Tumanggor, & Efron, 2024). On the other hand, in many cases, existing tests and assessment methods are designed to measure only low-level cognitive abilities and do not pay attention to deeper analyses such as critical thinking, moral reasoning, or problem-solving ability (Nozari, Ghahremani-Nahr, & Najafi, 2023). In contrast, data-driven intelligent learning environments have the capacity to not only dynamically and adaptively implement the assessment process by leveraging artificial intelligence, but also to improve transparency in the production of results, model interpretability, and the quality of feedback (Rahmaty & Nozari, 2023).

With the advent of large language models, it has become possible to design assessments that adapt to learner responses in real time, adjust the difficulty of questions to the current level of knowledge, and at the same time provide explanations for the results that are understandable to the learner. This explainability is a key element of transparency in AI-based assessment systems (Movahed, Movahed, & Nozari, 2024). Unlike traditional algorithms, whose inner workings remain a black box to users, LLMs can provide natural language explanations that help the audience better understand the assessment process and communicate with its results (Movahed, Movahed, & Nozari, 2024). At the same time, these systems have the ability to analyze behavioral, temporal, and conceptual patterns in the learner's responses and are able to build a mental and cognitive model of the learner over time and use it as the basis for future assessments (Nozari, 2023).

The issue of transparency in assessment is not only a technical issue, but also a serious ethical concern. When the results of an assessment are the basis for educational, employment, or even social decisions, it is essential that the assessment process is traceable and explainable to all stakeholders. Lack of transparency can lead to bias, inequality, and ultimately distrust in educational systems (Strielkowski et al., 2025). In this regard, the use of LLMs should be done in a way that is ethically justifiable and does not make the audience a mere passive consumer of technology, but rather an active part of the learning and assessment process. Especially in environments where education is linked to transformative goals and deep learning, transparency and adaptability of assessments are recognized as critical criteria for educational quality (Szmelter-Jarosz, Ghahremani-Nahr, & Nozari, 2021).

On the other hand, the adaptability of assessments to the needs and cognitive characteristics of the learner allows for the personalization of the assessment process. This adaptability not only leads to increased accuracy and effectiveness of assessment, but can also help reduce learner anxiety, increase active participation in the learning process, and improve the quality of feedback (Tan, Hu, Yeo, & Cheong, 2025). Large language models, with the ability to understand context, analyze concepts, and provide appropriate content, can serve as the core of adaptive assessment systems, generating or selecting content appropriate to the learning situation in real time. This type of assessment, unlike standard methods, allows the individual to receive immediate and relevant feedback during interaction with the system and gradually improve their skill level.

In summary, what this chapter seeks to do is to provide a conceptual and practical framework for designing transparent and adaptive assessment systems using large language models. By combining new artificial intelligence technologies, educational requirements, and ethical considerations, this approach seeks to redefine the role of assessment in the intelligent learning process. By reviewing the theoretical foundations, technical architecture, challenges, and exemplary applications, this chapter attempts to provide a vision for a transformation in educational assessment systems; a transformation in which measurement becomes a tool for meaningful and human learning instead of a control tool.

## 2. BACKGROUND AND RELATED WORK

With the development of smart technologies in education, numerous studies have examined various aspects of adaptive and transparent assessment. Although the concept of adaptive assessment was also discussed in computer-based learning environments before the advent of artificial intelligence, today's capabilities of large language models have fundamentally changed the way we look at educational assessment. In the past, adaptive assessment systems were mainly designed based on multiple-choice tests that determined the difficulty level of questions based on previous answers. However, such systems often remained limited to low-level cognitive skills and lacked the ability to analyze semantics or understand context (Aliahmadi & Nozari, 2023).

Research has shown that one of the main limitations of these systems has been the lack of transparency in the assessment and feedback process. Often, students and teachers remain unaware of the mechanism of question selection, response analysis, and scoring, which reduces trust and effective participation (Gyonyoru & Katona, 2025). This challenge is more pronounced in online and distance learning environments, where there is less human interaction. For this reason, explainable

AI approaches that attempt to explain the decision-making process of intelligent models in natural language have become increasingly important (Najafi, Nozari, & Edalatpanah, 2022).

On the other hand, recent research analysis suggests that the use of LLMs in adaptive assessment systems has enabled deeper analysis of text responses, simulation of educational conversations, and generation of dynamic and personalized feedback. Unlike previous systems that relied on rigid rules and a bank of predetermined questions, language models can generate content and even assess conceptual responses according to the learner's level (Ezzaim, Dahbi, Haidine, & Aqqal, 2023). This is especially important in assessing writing skills, critical thinking, and moral reasoning; areas that were previously difficult to measure automatically (Bathaee, Nozari, & Szmelter-Jarosz, 2023).

Along with technological advances, there are also challenges in using AI in assessment. The issue of algorithmic bias, the quality of training data, and the interpretability of results are among the issues discussed in the research literature (Meylani, 2024). Some studies have warned that the use of language models without human control and without ethical design can lead to misleading, unfair, or inappropriate feedback. Hence, hybrid frameworks in which AI works alongside human judgment have attracted the most attention (Aliahmadi, Ghahremani-Nahr, & Nozari, 2023).

Large language models also play a key role in the design of adaptive and explanatory prompts. These prompts can be designed based on the cognitive, linguistic, or psychological characteristics of the learner and guide him/her through the learning process in such a way that the assessment process becomes a learner-centered and interactive experience. In this regard, research is increasingly emphasizing the role of meta-adaptive models, models that not only adapt to user responses but also use past behaviors and performances to predict future needs (Demartini, Sciascia, Bosso, & Manuri, 2024).

From a technical architecture perspective, various studies have also proposed frameworks for implementing transparent and adaptive assessment systems. These frameworks usually consist of several layers: a learner analysis layer that collects behavioral and cognitive data; a decision layer that performs analysis with the help of linguistic models; and a feedback layer that displays the outputs in human-understandable language (Najafi, Nozari, & Edalatpanah, 2022). In the meantime, the explanatory and interaction-oriented design of educational graphs, feedbacks, and dashboards plays an important role in understanding the assessment process.

Finally, it can be said that the existing literature has provided a rich ground for the development of new assessment systems. However, there is a significant gap between the potential capabilities of LLMs and their actual implementation in educational settings. The present chapter, drawing on theoretical and empirical findings, attempts to take a step towards closing this gap and, by introducing a hybrid framework, helps create assessment systems that are not only accurate and intelligent, but also fair, transparent, and humane.

## 3. CONCEPTUAL FRAMEWORK

To design an adaptive and transparent assessment system in the context of smart learning, it is necessary to develop a conceptual framework that can simultaneously benefit from the capabilities of advanced technologies, cognitive psychology principles, and ethical and educational requirements. In this regard, the framework introduced in this section is based on the dynamic interaction between four main components: the learner profile, the adaptive engine, the large language model core, and the transparent feedback interface. Inspired by the architecture of adaptive learning systems and relying on the characteristics of LLMs, this framework is designed in a way that, while maintaining functional coherence, it also has the flexibility necessary to personalize assessment paths (Aliahmadi, Nozari, Ghahremani-Nahr, & Szmelter-Jarosz, 2022).

At the starting point, there is the learner profile, which includes a dynamic set of information about the learner. This information may include learning style, knowledge level, performance history, response time patterns, and behavioral or linguistic data. The learner profile does not simply provide a static picture of the learner's abilities, but is continuously updated and enriched with each new response (Aliahmadi, Nozari, Ghahremani-Nahr, & Szmelter-Jarosz, 2022). The data in this profile is collected through the learner's interaction with the learning platform and forms the basis for subsequent analyses.

The second component is the adaptive engine, which plays a central role in the system architecture. It combines the information in the learner profile with the real-time analysis of the responses and, with the help of the language model core, decides what the next step of the assessment should be. The adaptive engine is involved not only in the selection of questions, but also in adjusting the difficulty level, language structure, presentation format, and even the timing of the question presentation. The engine's operation is based on machine learning algorithms that are capable of feedback-based adjustment, so that with each iteration, the assessment becomes more accurate and more aligned with the learner's needs (Gligorea et al., 2023).

At the bottom of this structure is the core of the large language model. This part acts as the computational brain of the system and is responsible for generating content, analyzing text responses, rewriting questions, and providing linguistic explanations. In this framework, LLMs are not only question generators, but also play the role of semantic analyzers; that is, they are able to evaluate the learner's written or verbal responses in terms of coherence, reasoning, creativity, or conceptual correctness and return the result to the system in a transparent language format (Fallah & Nozari, 2021). The important point is that, unlike traditional approaches, the assessment is not based solely on numerical scoring, but is considered a combination of quantitative and qualitative analysis in natural language.

At the top layer, there is the feedback interface, which plays the role of communication between the system and the learner. This interface not only displays the assessment results, but also provides accurate, understandable, and educationally valuable feedback. The feedback generated can include explanations of errors, suggestions for improvement, reminders of concepts, and even examples of desired responses. The feedback interface, using interactive visual design, attempts to facilitate the learner's understanding of the assessment process and increase his or her sense of active participation (Sayed et al., 2023).

Figure 1 graphically illustrates this framework. As can be seen in the figure, there is a constant interaction between the components: response data from the learner's profile is sent to the adaptive engine; the adaptive engine selects the appropriate question based on information from the LLM; the question is then displayed to the learner and the new answer is fed back into the loop as input. At the same time, the language model generates an explanation of the results and provides it to the learner through the feedback interface. This cycle continues dynamically until the level of confidence in the assessment reaches an acceptable level or the learning objective is achieved.

*Figure 1. Conceptual model of transparent adaptive assessment in a smart learning environment*

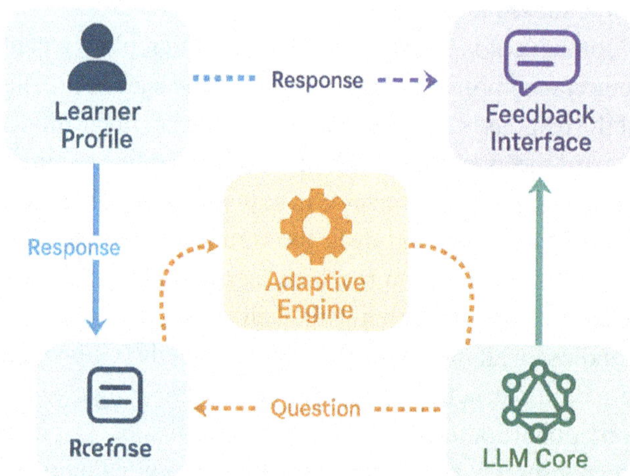

This framework also has the potential to be integrated with other digital learning systems such as analytical learning dashboards, personalized learning modules, and even augmented reality environments. The important point in this model is the emphasis on the coexistence of humans and machines, meaning that human judgment and teacher intuition still maintain their place and language models act as complementary tools to increase accuracy, transparency, and speed (Nozari, Fallah, Szmelter-Jarosz, & Krzemiński, 2021).

In conclusion, it can be said that the proposed framework not only provides an advanced structure for adaptive assessment by utilizing LLM technology, but also has taken an effective step towards humanizing the assessment and teaching process with its explanatory and transparent design. This model can be the basis for developing systems in which learning, assessment, and feedback are integrated in a continuous, meaningful, and tailored manner to the individual characteristics of the user.

## 4. TECHNICAL ARCHITECTURE OF THE EVALUATION SYSTEM

Following the development of a conceptual framework for adaptive and transparent assessment in smart learning environments, it is essential that the technical architecture of this system is also designed in a way that allows its practical implementation in real contexts. This architecture should be able to use input data related to learner performance, analyze them, generate relevant content and questions, interpret the results, and provide clear and effective feedback. The aforementioned system is built on a layered and modular structure in which effective interaction between technical and data components is considered the key to successful performance (Sajja, Sermet, Cikmaz, Cwiertny, & Demir, 2024).

The proposed technical architecture consists of four main layers: data layer, processing layer, decision layer, and interaction layer. In the first layer, the data layer, various types of raw information about learner performance are stored. This data includes written or spoken responses, duration of interaction with content, patterns of choice of options, linguistic cues, reading speed, and other behavioral indicators. This data is collected through digital user interfaces or intelligent learning platforms and fed into a central data warehouse. The data is not simply stored in raw form at this stage, but is prepared for advanced analytics using preprocessing, filtering, normalization, and labeling algorithms (Lotfi, Najafi, & Nozari, 2016).

In the second layer, the processing layer, the prepared data is fed into the analysis engine. This part of the system plays a vital role in interpreting the cognitive, behavioral, and linguistic state of the learner. In this part, models based on machine learning and natural language analysis are implemented on the LLM platform. One of the most important features of this layer is the ability to analyze the text of open-ended responses, so that the system can extract the meaning of the responses, the level of reasoning, conceptual coherence, and the level of understanding of concepts. This allows the system to assess not only the level of knowledge, but also deeper dimensions of learning such as critical thinking, ethical analysis, or creativity (Algahtani, 2024).

The third layer, known as the decision-making layer, is responsible for generating adaptive content, designing subsequent questions, and guiding the assessment process based on the outputs of the processing layer. In this layer, the system estimates the appropriate level of difficulty based on previous analyses, selects the desired question type, and generates content to display to the learner. These decisions can be adjusted based on indicators such as previous conceptual errors, response level, learning speed, and predetermined educational goals. Importantly, the decision-making process is carried out using a configurable and explainable rules engine, the output of which is not only technically appropriate but also educationally meaningful and goal-oriented (Nozari, Tavakkoli-Moghaddam, & Gharemani-Nahr, 2022).

The fourth layer, the interaction layer, is the interface between the system and the learner. In this layer, the generated questions are displayed to the user, their answers are received, and clear, precise, and personalized feedback is provided. The user interface of this section should be designed in a way that is both graphically attractive and successful in conveying complex analytical information in simple and understandable language for the learner. In this section, LLM language algorithms are used to provide explanatory, corrective, and motivational feedback. It is also possible to use a conversation-based system so that the learner can ask questions about his assessment and receive real-time answers (Rahmaty, 2024).

Figure 2 again shows this architecture in a colorful and modular image. In this figure, the vertical relationship between the four layers as well as the flow of data and interpretations are shown with clear arrows. For example, data is transmitted from the user to the first layer, then analyzed in the second layer, sent to the decision-making layer, and finally returned to the user in the form of a question or feedback.

*Figure 2. Layered technical architecture of the adaptive and transparent assessment system in the smart learning environment*

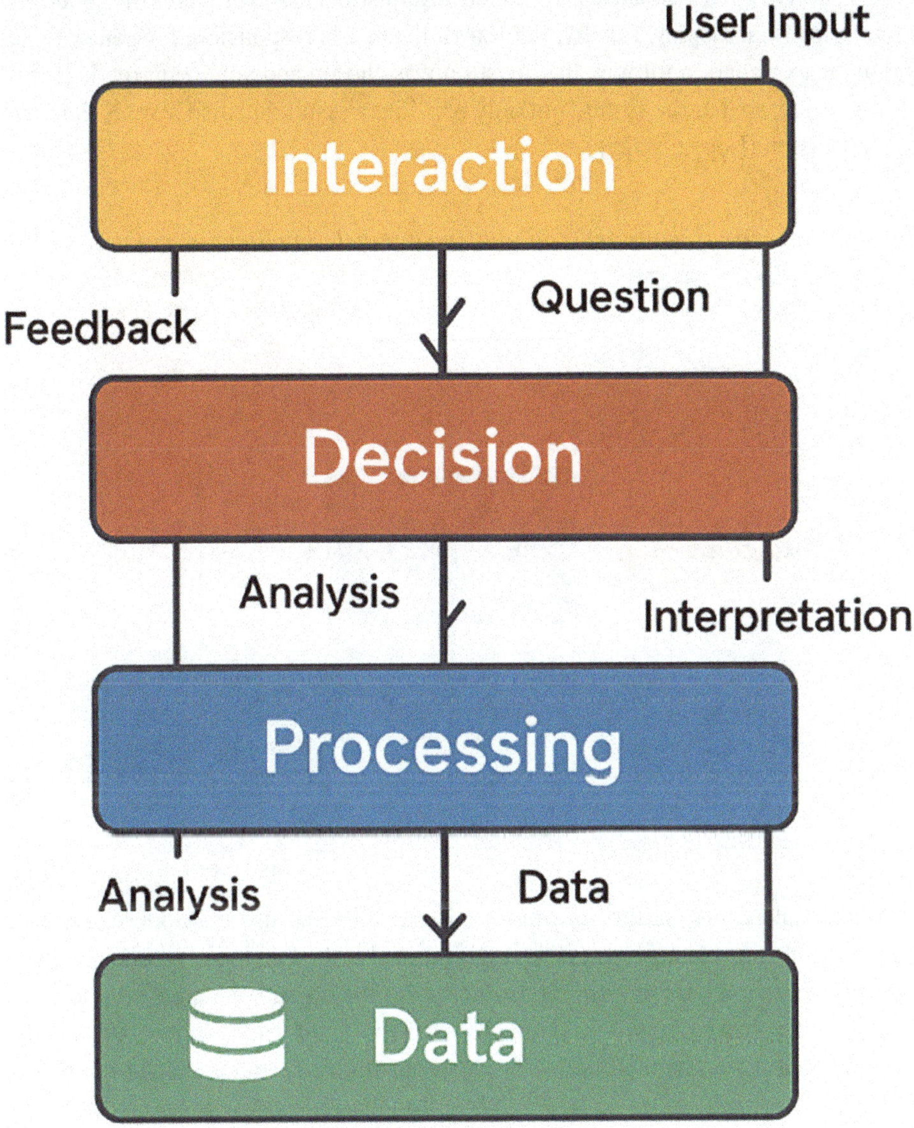


On the other hand, Figure 3 shows the internal structure of the adaptive engine in a more detailed and discrete manner. This engine consists of four submodules: the answer analyzer, the question generator, the difficulty level adjuster, and the decision explanation module. The first module extracts the linguistic and cognitive features of the answer using NLP algorithms. Then, the question generator generates a new question based on the previous analysis that is not only conceptually relevant but also consistent with the learner's current level. The third submodule, using adaptive models, makes difficulty level adjustments and prepares the generated content for final display. Finally, the fourth module is responsible for generating a linguistic explanation for why the question was chosen and analyzing the learner's performance, so that the system not only provides a result, but also reveals the logic of its decision (Lopez, 2025).

*Figure 3. Internal structure of the adaptive engine in the intelligent evaluation system*

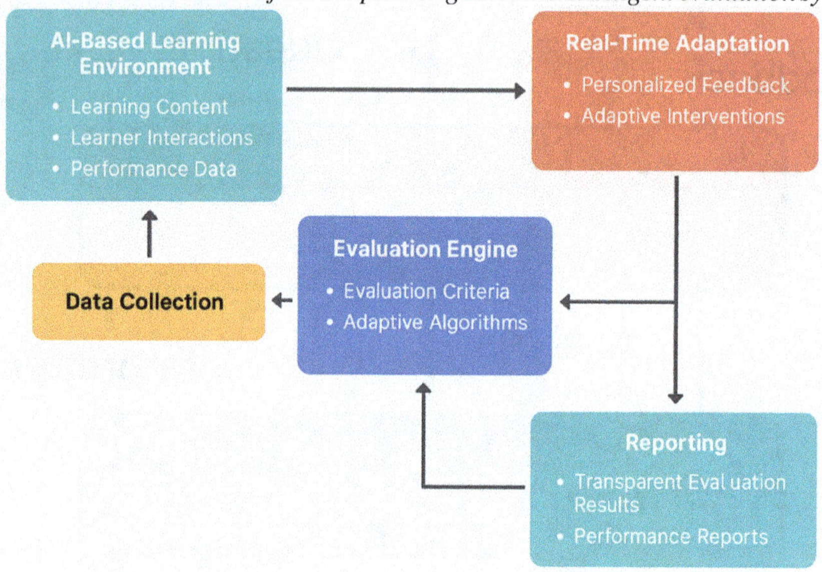


What makes this architecture unique is not only the use of modern machine learning and natural language technologies, but also the emphasis on transparency, human interaction, and real-time adaptability to the cognitive state of the learner. This structure can be easily implemented in formal, informal, and organizational learning contexts and integrated with other educational modules such as analytical dashboards, recommender systems, and multimodal learning environments.

## 5. ETHICAL AND PEDAGOGICAL CONSIDERATIONS

In the development and implementation of adaptive and transparent assessment systems in smart learning environments, it is essential and inevitable to pay attention to ethical and pedagogical considerations. These considerations are not only related to protecting the rights of learners and ensuring fairness in assessment, but also directly affect the social acceptance and educational success of these systems. The design of any technological tool that deals with cognitive, behavioral, or linguistic data of individuals without an ethics-based framework can lead to unintended effects that go beyond the field of education and harm privacy, human dignity, and social justice (Nozari, Najafi, Jafari-Eskandari, & Aliahmadi, 2016).

One of the important challenges in the field of ethics is the issue of transparency of algorithmic performance. In many smart assessment systems, decision-making is based on models that operate as black boxes. The inability to explain decisions made, especially when assessment results have educational or career implications, can lead to distrust, stress, and feelings of injustice in learners. Therefore, it is an ethical principle to use explainable models and promote algorithms that can express their decision logic in natural and understandable language (Raza, 2025).

Another issue is the issue of algorithmic bias. Large language models, due to being trained on large amounts of human data, may carry cultural, gender, linguistic, or class-based assumptions. If such biases are not taken into account in the design of the assessment system, some groups of learners may be judged unfairly. For example, the response language of a learner with a particular cultural background may be incorrectly perceived by the model as inconsistent or weak. Therefore, designing models with the ability to adapt linguistically, culturally, and examine responses in a multifaceted manner is an essential step to mitigate this risk (Mohammadi, Ghazanfari, Nozari, & Shafiezad, 2015).

From an educational perspective, the use of adaptive assessments should also be aimed at supporting deep, human learning, not simply optimizing system performance. Although AI can make the assessment process faster, more accurate, and more personalized, it should not replace the teacher's role as a human observer, educational coach, and contextual analyst. Rather than eliminating human judgment, it is necessary to engage the system so that final decisions are not based solely on data, but on an educational, ethical, and humane context (Memarian & Doleck, 2023).

Special attention should also be paid to the issue of informed consent in the use of these systems. Learners should know how their data is being collected, what kind of analysis is being performed on it, and how the results are being used. Without transparency in this process, even the most rigorous systems lose their moral legitimacy. Implementing clear privacy policies, the right to access personal data, the ability to object to machine decisions, and providing a copy of the analysis to the user are among the fundamental principles in the design of such systems (Movahed, Aliahmadi, Parsanejad, & Nozari, 2023).

On the other hand, the design of system feedback should also be accompanied by psychological and motivational considerations. Feedback that is presented solely in the form of numbers or performance levels may have a negative impact on individuals' self-efficacy or motivation to learn. In contrast, explanatory feedback that is accompanied by constructive suggestions, a representation of the path of progress, and an analysis of strengths can lead the learner to actively participate in the process of self-assessment and self-regulation. Such feedback not only helps to develop cognitive skills, but also strengthens the learner's sense of growth, belonging, and worth (Chandramma et al., 2025).

Another important point is the accountability of educational institutions and system designers for the performance of algorithms. In cases where errors, biases, or unfair results are observed in assessments, it is necessary to foresee mechanisms for accountability, correction, and compensation. Without these mechanisms, the use of AI in assessment may lead to the reinforcement of inequality, the elimination of human experience, and the reduction of educational justice (Movahed, Movahed, & Nozari, 2024).

In Figure 4, a set of key ethical and educational principles that should be considered in the design of intelligent assessment systems is presented in the form of a colorful and interactive diagram. The diagram includes four main areas: transparency and explanation, fairness and impartiality, psychological and educational support, and privacy. Each of these areas has sub-indicators that, together, provide a roadmap for the responsible and humane design of intelligent assessment systems.

*Figure 4. Ethical and educational dimensions in designing adaptive and transparent assessment systems*

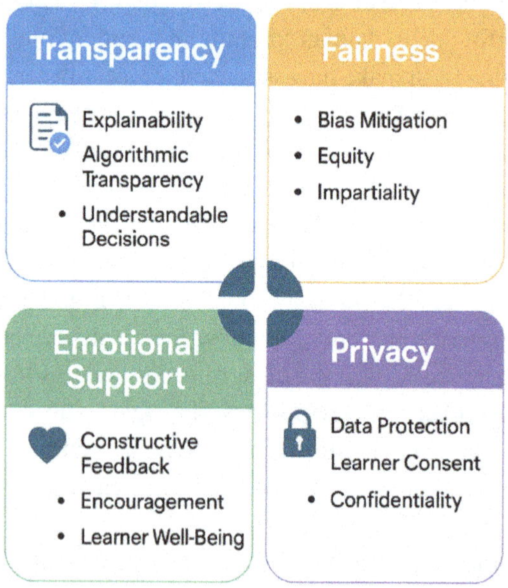

In conclusion, although new technologies offer extraordinary capabilities to improve the quality of educational assessment, these capabilities will only be valuable when they are used within an ethical, educational, and humane framework. Otherwise, the very technology that can enable learning may inadvertently become a tool for control, discrimination, or harm. Therefore, maintaining a balance between the analytical power of AI and human ethics is the most important responsibility in designing the future of smart education.

## 6. CONCLUSION

In today's world, where artificial intelligence technologies are rapidly penetrating all aspects of human life, education has also become an arena for redefining traditional concepts. One of the most important of these concepts is learning assessment; a concept that has played a role in educational systems for centuries as a tool for measuring knowledge, skills, and competence, but has always been accompanied by fundamental challenges. In the meantime, the design of comparative and transparent assessment systems based on large language models has opened new horizons for educational thinkers; horizons that enable the simultaneous analytical accuracy of the machine and the educational sensitivity of humans.

In this research, an attempt was made to analyze the theoretical foundations, technical architecture, and ethical considerations, and to present a combined framework for designing such a system; a framework that can, on the one hand, respond to the technological needs and cognitive complexities of learners, and on the other hand, maintain the fundamental principles of education such as fairness, meaning, interaction, and growth. Theoretical findings and proposed designs showed that large language models, especially in interaction with adaptive engines and cognitive analyzers, can serve as the backbone of future assessment systems. These models are able to process multi-layered data on learner behavior, language, and responses and, based on them, not only design questions appropriate to the level and need, but also provide accurate, explanatory, and motivating feedback.

On the other hand, the importance of transparent design as one of the pillars of trust-building in intelligent assessment was emphasized. In a world where machine decisions have increasingly penetrated everyday life, only explainability can help maintain the legitimacy of decision-support systems. This means that assessment models must be able to express the logic of their decisions in a language understandable to users, teachers, and policymakers. Also, in the context of educational justice, the design of these systems should be such that they prevent the reproduction of algorithmic biases while allowing adaptation to the cultural, linguistic, and cognitive diversity of learners.

At the educational level, the results of this study also showed that adaptive assessment, if combined with a humanistic and growth-oriented approach, can become a powerful tool for meaningful learning. Systems that, instead of focusing solely on grading, follow the learning path, explain errors, and provide suggestions for improvement will be able to strengthen the sense of self-regulation, intrinsic motivation, and self-confidence in learners. This feature can greatly compensate for the gap in human support, especially in digital learning environments where the distance between teacher and student has increased.

However, the design of such systems is not without challenges. Issues related to privacy, informed consent, institutional accountability, as well as technical considerations such as the quality of educational data, the accuracy of language models, and the stability of algorithms, all require serious attention. This requires that developers of these technologies, in addition to technical knowledge, benefit from interdisciplinary knowledge in the fields of educational sciences, cognitive psychology, technological ethics, and human-centered design. Only then can we achieve the creation of systems that are not only intelligent, but also fair, transparent, and humane.

Overall, we can conclude that adaptive and transparent assessment systems based on LLM are not just a technological tool, but represent a new vision of education; one in which the learner is at the center of the process, learning is personalized and dynamic, and assessment becomes a learner-centered experience. This approach, if designed with wisdom, care, and responsibility, could be one of the most fundamental transformations in education in the coming decade. Therefore, it is the duty of researchers, teachers, designers, and policymakers to view this transformation path not as a technological threat but as an opportunity to rethink the principles and goals of education.

Finally, it must be emphasized that the move toward smart learning and adaptive assessment is not possible by relying solely on technology. What makes this path meaningful is a commitment to the dignity of the learner, social responsibility in the use of technology, and loyalty to the philosophy of humane education. If these values remain at the heart of design, we can hope for a future in which assessment is not a tool for differentiation, but a bridge between learning, understanding, and growth.

## REFERENCES


Algahtani, A. M. I. R. A. H. (2024). A Comparative Study of AI-Based Educational Tools: Evaluating User Interface Experience and Educational Impact. *Journal of Theoretical and Applied Information Technology*, *102*(5).

Aliahmadi, A., Ghahremani-Nahr, J., & Nozari, H. (2023). Pricing decisions in the closed-loop supply chain network, taking into account the queuing system in production centers. *Expert Systems with Applications*, *212*, 118741. DOI: 10.1016/j.eswa.2022.118741

Aliahmadi, A., & Nozari, H. (2023, January). Evaluation of security metrics in AIoT and blockchain-based supply chain by Neutrosophic decision-making method. In Supply chain forum: an international journal (Vol. 24, No. 1, pp. 31-42). Taylor & Francis. DOI: 10.1080/16258312.2022.2101898

Aliahmadi, A., Nozari, H., Ghahremani-Nahr, J., & Szmelter-Jarosz, A. (2022). Evaluation of key impression of resilient supply chain based on artificial intelligence of things (AIoT). arXiv preprint arXiv:2207.13174.

Bathaee, M., Nozari, H., & Szmelter-Jarosz, A. (2023). Designing a new location-allocation and routing model with simultaneous pick-up and delivery in a closed-loop supply chain network under uncertainty. *Logistics (Basel)*, *7*(1), 3. DOI: 10.3390/logistics7010003

Chandramma, R., Babu, K. S., Ranjith, K. S., Sinha, A. K., Neerugatti, V., & Reddy, D. S. (2025, January). Enhancing E-learning Accessibility through AI (Artificial Intelligence) and Inclusive Design. In 2025 6th International Conference on Mobile Computing and Sustainable Informatics (ICMCSI) (pp. 1466-1471). IEEE.

Demartini, C. G., Sciascia, L., Bosso, A., & Manuri, F. (2024). Artificial intelligence bringing improvements to adaptive learning in education: A case study. *Sustainability (Basel)*, *16*(3), 1347. DOI: 10.3390/su16031347

Ezzaim, A., Dahbi, A., Haidine, A., & Aqqal, A. (2023). AI-based adaptive learning: A systematic mapping of the literature. *Journal of Universal Computer Science*, *29*(10), 1161–1198. DOI: 10.3897/jucs.90528

Fallah, M., & Nozari, H. (2021). Neutrosophic mathematical programming for optimization of multi-objective sustainable biomass supply chain network design. *Computer Modeling in Engineering & Sciences*, *129*(2), 927–951. DOI: 10.32604/cmes.2021.017511

Gligorea, I., Cioca, M., Oancea, R., Gorski, A. T., Gorski, H., & Tudorache, P. (2023). Adaptive learning using artificial intelligence in e-learning: A literature review. *Education Sciences*, *13*(12), 1216. DOI: 10.3390/educsci13121216

Gyonyoru, K. I. K., & Katona, J. (2025). Comprehensive Overview of the Concept and Applications of AI-based Adaptive Learning. *Acta Polytechnica Hungarica*, *22*(3), 167–186. DOI: 10.12700/APH.22.3.2025.3.9

Lopez, S. (2025). *Integrating Artificial Intelligence in Regional Education: A Holistic Framework for Inclusive, Adaptive, and Community-Centric Learning* (Vol. 6). Electronic Journal of Social and Strategic Studies.

Lotfi, F. H. Z., Najafi, S. E., & Nozari, H. (Eds.). (2016). *Data envelopment analysis and effective performance assessment*. IGI Global.

Memarian, B., & Doleck, T. (2023). Fairness, Accountability, Transparency, and Ethics (FATE) in Artificial Intelligence (AI) and higher education: A systematic review. *Computers and Education: Artificial Intelligence*, *5*, 100152.

Meylani, R. (2024). A Critical Glance at Adaptive Learning Systems Using Artificial Intelligence: A Systematic Review and Qualitative Synthesis of Contemporary Research Literature. *Batı Anadolu Eğitim Bilimleri Dergisi*, *15*(3), 3518–3546. DOI: 10.51460/baebd.1525452

Mohammadi, H., Ghazanfari, M., Nozari, H., & Shafiezad, O. (2015). Combining the theory of constraints with system dynamics: A general model (case study of the subsidized milk industry). International journal of management science and engineering management, 10(2), 102-108.

Movahed, A. B., Aliahmadi, A., Parsanejad, M., & Nozari, H. (2023). A systematic review of collaboration in supply chain 4.0 with meta-synthesis method. *Supply Chain Analytics*, *4*, 100052.

Movahed, A. B., Movahed, A. B., & Nozari, H. (2024). Marketing 6.0 Conceptualization. In Advanced Businesses in Industry 6.0 (pp. 15-31). IGI Global.

Movahed, A. B., Movahed, A. B., & Nozari, H. (2024). Opportunities and challenges of smart supply chain in Industry 5.0. Information Logistics for Organizational Empowerment and Effective Supply Chain Management, 108-138.

Movahed, A. B., Movahed, A. B., & Nozari, H. (2024). Opportunities and challenges of marketing 5.0. Smart and Sustainable Interactive Marketing, 1-21.

Najafi, S. E., Nozari, H., & Edalatpanah, S. A. (2022). Investigating the key parameters affecting sustainable IoT-based marketing. In *Computational Intelligence Methodologies Applied to Sustainable Development Goals* (pp. 51–61). Springer International Publishing. DOI: 10.1007/978-3-030-97344-5_4

Najafi, S. E., Nozari, H., & Edalatpanah, S. A. (2022). Artificial Intelligence of Things (AIoT) and Industry 4.0–Based Supply Chain (FMCG Industry). A roadmap for enabling industry 4.0 by artificial intelligence, 31-41.

Nozari, H. (Ed.). (2023). *Building Smart and Sustainable Businesses with Transformative Technologies*. IGI Global. DOI: 10.4018/979-8-3693-0210-1

Nozari, H., Fallah, M., Szmelter-Jarosz, A., & Krzemiński, M. (2021). Analysis of security criteria for IoT-based supply chain: a case study of FMCG industries. Central European Management Journal, 29(4).

Nozari, H., Ghahremani-Nahr, J., & Najafi, E. (2023). The role of Internet of things and Blockchain in the development of agile and sustainable supply chains. In Digital Supply Chain, Disruptive Environments, and the Impact on Retailers (pp. 271-282). IGI Global. DOI: 10.4018/978-1-6684-7298-9.ch015

Nozari, H., Najafi, S. E., Jafari-Eskandari, M., & Aliahmadi, A. (2016). Providing a model for virtual project management with an emphasis on IT projects. In *Strategic Management and Leadership for Systems Development in Virtual Spaces* (pp. 43–63). IGI Global Scientific Publishing. DOI: 10.4018/978-1-4666-9688-4.ch003

Nozari, H., Tavakkoli-Moghaddam, R., & Gharemani-Nahr, J. (2022). A neutrosophic fuzzy programming method to solve a multi-depot vehicle routing model under uncertainty during the covid-19 pandemic. *International Journal of Engineering*, *35*(2), 360–371.

Rahmaty, M. (2024). Presenting a conceptual model to identify the dimensions, components, and applications of a resilient green supply chain. *Journal of Industrial and Systems Engineering*, *16*(1), 157–164.

Rahmaty, M., & Nozari, H. (2023). Optimization of the hierarchical supply chain in the pharmaceutical industry. *Edelweiss Applied Science and Technology*, *7*(2), 104–123. DOI: 10.55214/25768484.v7i2.376

Raza, A. (2025). Personalized Learning through AI: Opportunities and Challenges in Adaptive Educational Technologies. *Journal of AI Integration in Education*, *2*(1), 21–28.

Sajja, R., Sermet, Y., Cikmaz, M., Cwiertny, D., & Demir, I. (2024). Artificial intelligence-enabled intelligent assistant for personalized and adaptive learning in higher education. *Information (Basel)*, *15*(10), 596. DOI: 10.3390/info15100596

Sari, H. E., Tumanggor, B., & Efron, D. (2024). Improving educational outcomes through adaptive learning systems using ai. *International Transactions on Artificial Intelligence*, *3*(1), 21–31. DOI: 10.33050/italic.v3i1.647

Sayed, W. S., Noeman, A. M., Abdellatif, A., Abdelrazek, M., Badawy, M. G., Hamed, A., & El-Tantawy, S. (2023). AI-based adaptive personalized content presentation and exercises navigation for an effective and engaging E-learning platform. *Multimedia Tools and Applications*, *82*(3), 3303–3333. DOI: 10.1007/s11042-022-13076-8 PMID: 35789938

Strielkowski, W., Grebennikova, V., Lisovskiy, A., Rakhimova, G., & Vasileva, T. (2025). AI-driven adaptive learning for sustainable educational transformation. *Sustainable Development (Bradford)*, *33*(2), 1921–1947. DOI: 10.1002/sd.3221

Szmelter-Jarosz, A., Ghahremani-Nahr, J., & Nozari, H. (2021). A neutrosophic fuzzy optimisation model for optimal sustainable closed-loop supply chain network during COVID-19. *Journal of Risk and Financial Management*, *14*(11), 519. DOI: 10.3390/jrfm14110519

Tan, L. Y., Hu, S., Yeo, D. J., & Cheong, K. H. (2025). Artificial Intelligence-Enabled Adaptive Learning Platforms: A Review. Computers and Education: Artificial Intelligence, 100429.

# Chapter 12
# Artificial Intelligence and the Development of Creative Skills in STEM Education

**Maryam Rahmaty**
http://orcid.org/0000-0003-3772-4216
*Department of Management, Islamic Azad University, Chalus, Iran*

## ABSTRACT

*This chapter examines the role of artificial intelligence in promoting educational creativity in STEM and shows how AI tools can transform the learning process from a traditional one to a dynamic, problem-based, and personalized experience. By analyzing various dimensions such as fostering divergent and convergent thinking, designing creative scenarios, and ethical and technical challenges, the present study provides a comprehensive picture of the opportunities and limitations of this transformation. Finally, the need for purposeful design, teacher preparation, and an interdisciplinary approach to effectively utilize AI in education is emphasized.*

## 1. INTRODUCTION

In recent decades, the role of creative skills in science, technology, engineering, and mathematics (STEM) education has been recognized as one of the main axes of the transformation of educational systems. While traditional educational systems have often focused on the transfer of knowledge and strengthening analytical and logical capabilities, global developments in the fields of industry, technology, and the humanities have made the cultivation of creativity, innovative thinking, and the ability

DOI: 10.4018/979-8-3373-5117-9.ch012

ight © 2026, IGI Global Scientific Publishing. Copying or distributing in print or electronic forms without written permission of IGI Global Scientific Publishing is prohibited. Use of this chapter to n generative artificial intelligence (AI) technologies is expressly prohibited. The publisher reserves all rights to license its use for generative AI training and machine learning model development.

to solve complex problems independently a fundamental necessity in educating the next generation (Giang et al., 2024). With the entry of artificial intelligence into the field of education, new perspectives have emerged in the field of creating creative, interactive, and personalized learning experiences; perspectives that can significantly reduce the limitations of traditional STEM education structures (Alangari, 2022).

Unlike creativity in the arts, creativity in STEM often manifests itself in the form of generating new solutions, designing innovative concepts, or discovering complex patterns in scientific data. In this context, AI can not only provide new tools for data analysis and process simulation, but also provide opportunities to foster individual and group creativity by creating interactive learning environments (Nozari, Abdi, & Szmelter-Jarosz, 2025). In particular, advanced language models, machine learning algorithms, and machine vision systems have enabled students to go beyond conventional numerical analysis formats and, instead of repeating formulas, build and test new ideas in virtual environments (Sirajudin & Suratno, 2021).

On the other hand, the emergence of automated design tools, generative modeling, and AI-powered computing platforms have expanded teaching methods in which students can develop their own experimental prototypes, engineering designs, and scientific predictions with high accuracy without deep programming or computing knowledge (Kalogeras, Mejri, & Efthimiou, 2022). This development has, on the one hand, increased the level of access to scientific innovation for students at younger ages, and on the other hand, has narrowed the boundary between the role of knowledge receiver and knowledge producer (Pramesti, Probosari, & Indriyanti, 2022). In other words, in environments equipped with artificial intelligence, the learner can simultaneously act as a learner and a designer of creative ideas.

An important point to note in this regard is the change in the nature of the role of the teacher and the learning environment. In the traditional educational environment, the teacher was generally considered the main source of knowledge and learners were placed in a hierarchical structure. However, in the AI-driven environment, the teacher's role has evolved into a guide, facilitator, and designer of the learning experience. In such an environment, the learner will be able to discover personalized paths to develop their creative skills through interaction with intelligent systems (Nozari, Abdi, & Jahangard, 2025). This structural transformation is important because STEM education requires not only strengthening basic knowledge, but also developing "innovative design capacities" on a global scale.

However, the use of AI in creative STEM education also comes with challenges. One of the main concerns is the reduction of independent thinking in students due to excessive dependence on suggestive and generative systems. In addition, assessing the originality of ideas generated by students using AI tools has become a methodological and pedagogical issue in itself (García Aranda et al., 2020). Despite these challenges, research evidence shows that if learning environments are properly designed, the targeted use of AI can lead to improved creative performance in solving interdisciplinary problems, strengthening divergent thinking, and increasing scientific self-confidence in students (Saputri & Syukri, 2022).

In the context of STEM education, creativity is considered a key tool for moving beyond memorization-based education to a space of construction, analysis, and improvement-based education. In this path, AI acts as a powerful accelerator that guides the learner from the observation stage to the production stage by providing rapid feedback, providing simulated data, and designing personalized paths (Rifandi & Rahmi, 2019). This conceptual transition from "learning about science" to "learning in the context of creating science" is considered the basis of the future-oriented approach in STEM education.

In conclusion, it can be said that the integration of creativity and AI in science, technology, engineering, and mathematics education is not only a necessity to respond to the conditions of the modern world, but also a path to reinvent education in a participatory, dynamic, and creative way. This futuristic approach allows teachers, educational policymakers, and intelligent systems designers to cultivate a generation of learners who, in addition to academic skills, are equipped with creative insights to confront complex global issues (Cooper & Heaverlo, 2013).

## 2. REDEFINING CREATIVITY IN STEM EDUCATION WITH THE PRESENCE OF ARTIFICIAL INTELLIGENCE

In traditional science, technology, engineering, and mathematics (STEM) education, creativity has often been seen as an optional feature rather than a core requirement. The focus on precise concepts, rigid rules, and numerical analysis has left little room for creativity to emerge. However, in the last decade, with the advent of artificial intelligence in learning and teaching, a profound redefinition of the nature of creativity in STEM has begun; a redefinition that has not only transformed the traditional boundaries between analysis and innovation, but also created a new perspective on the role of humans in the process of knowledge generation and problem solving (Szmelter-Jarosz & Nozari, 2025).

At the heart of this transformation is the question of whether creativity can be reproduced in an algorithmic context. The answer to this question lies not in an absolute rejection or acceptance, but in examining the role of AI as an "accelerator" of creativity. By leveraging its rapid processing capacity, predictive capabilities based on big data, and generation of novel content based on implicit patterns, AI enables learners to transcend mental constraints and think in previously unimaginable structures (Hasibuan et al., 2022). Thus, creativity in STEM no longer simply means having a new idea, but rather the ability to interact with intelligent systems to nurture, refine, and expand these ideas in hybrid human-machine environments.

AI has also enabled a form of "co-creation" creativity. In this model, the student or researcher, rather than being the sole producer of content or solutions, engages in a creative dialogue with AI-based linguistic, visual, or numerical systems. This dialogue can take the form of suggesting new concepts, generating simulated designs, or automatically analyzing raw ideas. For example, a student designing a clean energy system can consult an AI model, compare different scenarios, and, with the help of machine vision, come up with a new model that they had not initially thought of (Chen, Lin, & Chung, 2023).

What is important here is the shift in focus from the end product of creativity to the "process of creativity." In the past, STEM education focused more on the correctness of the final answer. But now, dynamic interactions with AI have led to the process of arriving at an answer itself—including posing questions, testing hypotheses, cross-data analysis, and generating multiple solutions—being considered a key part of creativity (Wang & Li, 2024). This shift in approach has also made it possible to teach higher-level thinking skills such as conceptual design, systems analysis, and multi-criteria evaluation alongside classic STEM concepts.

In addition, AI has expanded the possibility of linking individual creativity with collective learning. In AI-powered digital learning environments, students can share their ideas with other learners or intelligent models, get feedback, and eventually reproduce optimized versions. This social-machine learning cycle leads to what can be called "networked interactive creativity," a concept in which learners simultaneously leverage human and artificial intelligence to create new knowledge (Widyasmah & Herlina, 2020).

To better understand how creativity is redefined in the new context of STEM education, a hybrid framework can be used in which three main layers play a fundamental role: Cognitive Creativity, Generative Creativity, and Collaborative Creativity. The figure below shows a representation of this structure.

*Figure 1. AI-Augmented Creativity Framework in STEM Education*

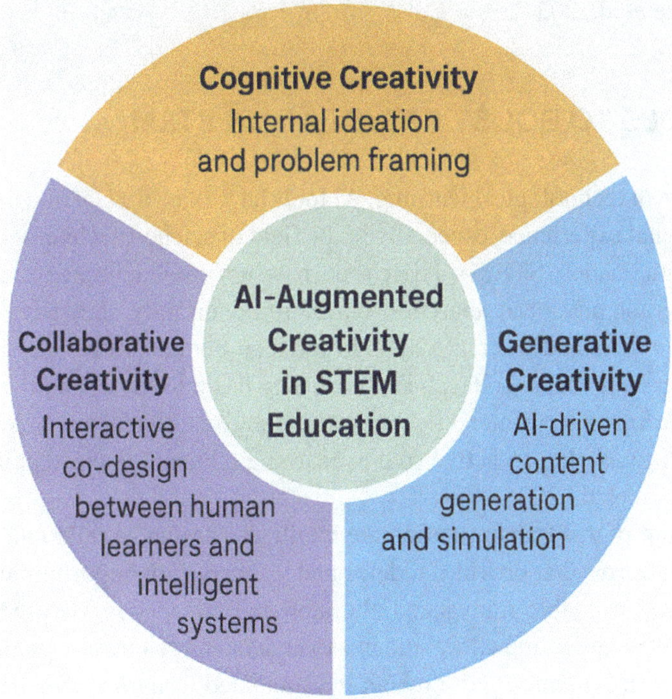


In this model, "cognitive creativity" refers to the basic ability of an individual to identify problems, generate hypotheses, and analyze information. "Generative creativity" refers to the use of AI tools to generate designs, data, or solutions that go beyond human mental capacity. Finally, "interactive creativity" is the result of collaboration between humans and machines, or between multiple learners, who can use AI technologies to reach multidimensional and creative solutions (Nozari, 2025).

It is noteworthy that these layers not only interact with each other, but also gradually strengthen in the course of progressive STEM education. The learner initially acquires the ability to understand the structure of the problem through cognitive exercises. Then, by interacting with AI-generated tools, he or she tries out creative paths. Finally, by entering interactive environments (such as group design platforms or intelligent learning networks), it improves its skill in combining human insight and machine ability (Larkin, 2015).

Therefore, redefining creativity in STEM education is not just a change in tools, but a change in attitude; from an approach that considered creativity as an individual and subjective phenomenon to an approach that sees creativity as a collaborative, dynamic, and technology-enhanced process. This transformation will not only make education more effective, but will also pave the way for the education of a generation that will be prepared to face multidisciplinary, global, and technological challenges (Tavdgiridze et al., 2024).

## 3. AI TOOLS TO BOOST CREATIVITY IN STEM

In the era of technological learning, AI tools have played a key role in redefining the educational experience, especially in the field of science, technology, engineering, and mathematics (STEM). These tools have not only facilitated access to data, simulations, and advanced analytics, but more importantly, they have provided a platform in which student creativity is fostered as a collaborative, productive, and problem-driven process. Today, STEM learning has moved beyond the traditional transferrable format to an interactive, generative, and intelligently modeled paradigm in which AI tools play an active role as learning companions in shaping creative thinking (Ram et al., 2025).

At the root of this transformation are intelligent design, simulation, and manufacturing platforms that provide students and teachers with opportunities that were previously only available in advanced laboratories. Tools such as AI-based simulators in physics and engineering allow students to understand scientific concepts through interaction with dynamic environments and simulated scenarios, rather than memorizing formulas (Nozari, 2025). For example, software designed to model fluid flow, heat transfer, or power transfer can use deep learning algorithms to create visual, scalable models for testing hypotheses, a process that clearly enhances students' design, analysis, and engineering creativity skills (Mukaromah & Wusqo, 2020).

Another transformative tool is advanced language models that act as "intelligent learning assistants." These models can help automatically generate hypotheses, formulate research questions, or even create basic programming code in STEM environments. The key difference between these tools and traditional methods is that they are not just sources of information, but also intellectual partners of the learner who can suggest creative paths to problem solving with interactive responses (He et al., 2023). This capacity strengthens divergent thinking skills in students, as each question or input to an AI model can lead to a range of creative, unique, and testable answers.

On the other hand, in the field of data science education, intelligent visualization tools have made a significant difference in shaping analytical creativity. Using these tools, instead of examining dry numerical tables, students can identify patterns, correlations, and hidden behaviors in data and propose new hypotheses based on them. Combining these analyses with predictive or classifier models based on machine learning turns the research process into a creative and exploratory experience (Pinasa, Siripun, & Yuenyong, 2018).

In the mathematics education space, AI-based tools have enabled students to adapt their solutions to the model step by step and receive personalized feedback. This feedback goes beyond right or wrong answers and offers suggestions for alternative paths or improvements by analyzing the student's mental process. Such tools not only improve problem-solving skills, but also pave the way for the creation of creative problem-solving paths (Hasançebi et al., 2021).

The figure below shows how AI tools, in interaction with the learner, shape the creative process in STEM in three main stages: discovery, generation, and refinement.

*Figure 2. AI Tools Driving Creativity in STEM Learning*

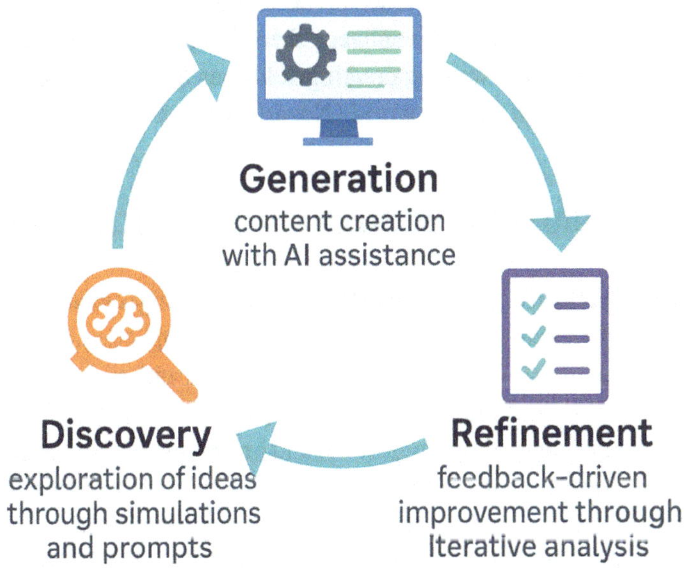


In the "discovery" phase, AI tools stimulate the learner's mind to think beyond previous frameworks by presenting data, simulated patterns, or even challenging questions. In the "production" phase, generative models (such as text, code, images, or engineering drawings) allow the learner to build early versions of their solution or product. Finally, in the "refine" phase, intelligent analytics tools provide constructive feedback that helps the learner improve, complete, or change their approach (Özsoy & Özyer, 2018).

In group learning environments, AI-powered tools also help facilitate creative collaboration. Platforms that enable sharing of AI-generated designs have made it possible for students to combine their ideas, build hybrid patterns, or choose the best path through intelligent voting. These processes not only foster individual creativity, but also lead to the growth of collective creativity (Üret & Ceylan, 2021)

design personalized pathways that will lead to deeper and more creative learning (Stylianidou et al., 2018).

In some schools and universities, AI-based creative scenarios have even been implemented internationally and in groups; so that students from different countries collaborate on an environmental or engineering project with the help of an intelligent platform. In addition to improving STEM skills, these experiences have also strengthened the communication, intercultural and ethical capabilities of learners (Wilis et al., 2023).

Overall, AI-supported creative learning scenarios provide a unique opportunity to move from one-way and static education to active, problem-based and collaborative learning. What distinguishes these scenarios from traditional education is the design of environments in which errors, testing, failure and correction are considered part of the creative learning process. In this space, creativity is recognized not as an exceptional characteristic, but as a capability that can be cultivated for all students (Yıldırım & Selvi, 2016).

## 5. THE IMPACT OF AI ON DIVERGENT AND CONVERGENT THINKING SKILLS IN STEM

In the context of modern STEM education, the development of high-level cognitive skills such as divergent and convergent thinking is recognized as one of the main educational goals. These two types of thinking complement each other in the process of creative problem solving. Divergent thinking, by emphasizing the production of numerous, new and diverse ideas, paves the way for innovation and discovery; while convergent thinking, by focusing on choosing the best option based on logical analysis and available data, leads to effective decision-making. Meanwhile, the introduction of artificial intelligence into the learning process has enabled the simultaneous strengthening of these two skills; in an environment where the combination of knowledge, creativity and decision-making is dynamically ongoing (Thingwiangthong, Termtachatipongsa, & Yuenyong, 2021).

In traditional educational environments, excessive focus on the correct answer or the use of predetermined paths reduced the opportunity for divergent thinking. Students often looked for a specific pattern to arrive at the final answer based on it. However, in learning environments equipped with artificial intelligence, there is no longer a single answer; Rather, the path to the answer is part of the learning process. By providing diverse suggestions, alternative scenarios, and creative feedback, AI tools free the learner's mind from closed frames and encourage him to explore new paths (Dewi, Mayasari, & Handhika, 2019).

For example, when an intelligent language model in response to a technical problem offers several possible paths to a solution, the learner enters a process of selection, adaptation, and evaluation. This interaction first stimulates divergent thinking to generate alternative solutions, and then uses convergent thinking to select the best possible option by analyzing data, applying logical constraints, and using simulation tools (Han et al., 2022).

Also, in the engineering design process or research-based projects, AI models can act as an analytical partner, examining initial outputs and providing suggestions for improving performance or modifying the structure. This type of feedback is far from being closed and right/wrong, and instead offers a range of corrections, recommendations, and follow-up questions. Such an approach creates a learning-oriented environment in which the student simultaneously engages in creative exploration (divergent) and purposeful analysis (convergent) (Nozari & Samadi, 2025).

The role of intelligent algorithms in visual visualization and modeling is also significant. Machine vision tools, graphical neural networks, and simulation platforms can represent complex processes in an understandable way. When a student graphically understands the heat transfer process in a system and sees how the flow pattern changes when a parameter is changed, both his or her discovery (divergent) and numerical analysis (convergent) capacities are simultaneously activated (Hanfy et al., 2022).

The figure below shows how AI tools enable divergent and convergent skills at different stages of problem solving, allowing the learner to experience a full cycle of thinking, from idea discovery to solution selection.

*Figure 3. AI-Enhanced Divergent and Convergent Thinking Cycle in STEM*

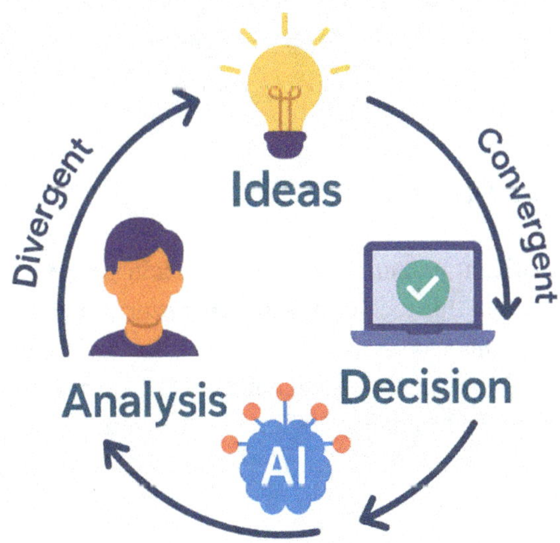

In this cycle, AI tools first play the role of stimulating creativity; where they force the student to generate new ideas by generating questions, simulating scenarios, or presenting unexpected data. Then, analytical tools come into play and facilitate the process of evaluation and choosing the optimal path with the help of precise algorithms. In the meantime, the feedback process also plays a role, because the student can return to generating ideas and correct previous paths based on the model analysis. This continuous return between divergence and convergence indicates deep, adaptive, and creative learning in AI-driven environments (Kencana & Syukri, 2020).

Some studies have shown that in environments where students interact with AI models repeatedly, not only the variety of their proposed answers increases, but also their accuracy in choosing the right answer improves. This simultaneous growth in diversity and rigor is precisely what creative and analytical STEM education seeks (Kwon & Lee, 2025).

Of course, it should be noted that the full realization of this cycle requires the conscious design of learning environments. If AI tools are used solely to display information or perform calculations, the opportunity for divergent thinking is reduced. Conversely, if these tools are defined as constructive, suggestive, and analytical, they can create a bridge between raw creativity and structured thinking; a bridge in which the learner is not just a recipient of content, but also a producer of knowledge (Marsono, Khasanah, & Yoto, 2019).

Finally, the integration of divergent and convergent thinking in STEM education with the support of artificial intelligence is a fundamental step in cultivating flexible, analytical, and innovative minds. This type of learning prepares students to first identify different creative paths in the real world, when faced with complex problems, and then make informed and effective decisions with logic and evidence. What makes this process possible is the intelligent and designed presence of AI in all stages of learning; from idea discovery to solution selection (Hanif, Wijaya, & Winarno, 2019).

## 6. CHALLENGES AND LIMITATIONS

Despite the significant potential of AI in enhancing creativity and learning in STEM, the reality is that this technological transformation comes with challenges and limitations that cannot be ignored. Incorrect use or inappropriate design of smart tools can not only reduce the effectiveness of the learning process, but in some cases lead to a decrease in the quality of thinking, reduced mental independence and weakened intrinsic motivation of the learner (Raksapoln & Suttiwan, 2021). Therefore, a careful analysis of the limitations and possible consequences is an integral part of the design and implementation of AI-based learning in STEM education.

One of the most important challenges is the risk of cognitive dependence on smart tools. When AI models are used as content generators, problem solvers or performance assessors, learners may rely solely on the outputs provided by the system instead of trying to understand the concepts. This can lead to a weakening of independent analysis, a reduced ability to search for alternative solutions, and a sense of "adequacy" in the face of complexity. Effective teaching should first and foremost promote learner self-efficacy, and this can only be achieved if AI tools are supportive of learning rather than a substitute (Hacıoğlu & Gülhan, 2021).

Another challenge is the ambiguity of intellectual property and originality of creativity in AI-based creative learning environments. When a student presents a solution, essay, or concept design with the help of a text or image generative model, it is difficult to distinguish between what originated in his or her mind and what was suggested by the algorithm. This situation can undermine the process of assessing originality, individual creativity, and even trust in educational fairness. Traditional assessment systems are not designed for this level of human-machine integration and need to be redesigned (Oner et al., 2016).

Other obstacles include algorithmic discrimination and data bias. Many AI models are trained on specific educational data and cultural constructs. When these models are used in educational settings with cultural or social diversity, they may provide inconsistent, irrelevant, or even biased recommendations. These biases can limit choices, unconsciously guide learners, and even reproduce inequalities in education (Othman, Iksan, & Yasin, 2022).

Another limitation is the inequality in access to smart technologies. In many regions, especially in underserved communities, the infrastructure needed to use AI tools in education is lacking or limited. This digital divide leaves some learners deprived of the creative benefits of AI, while others widen their cognitive gap with access to advanced tools. As a result, not only is educational equity at risk, but the playing field is also unfair (Chanthala, Santiboon, & Ponkham, 2018).

Figure 4 shows a classification of key AI challenges in STEM education into four main categories.

*Figure 4. Key Challenges of AI Integration in Creative STEM Learning*

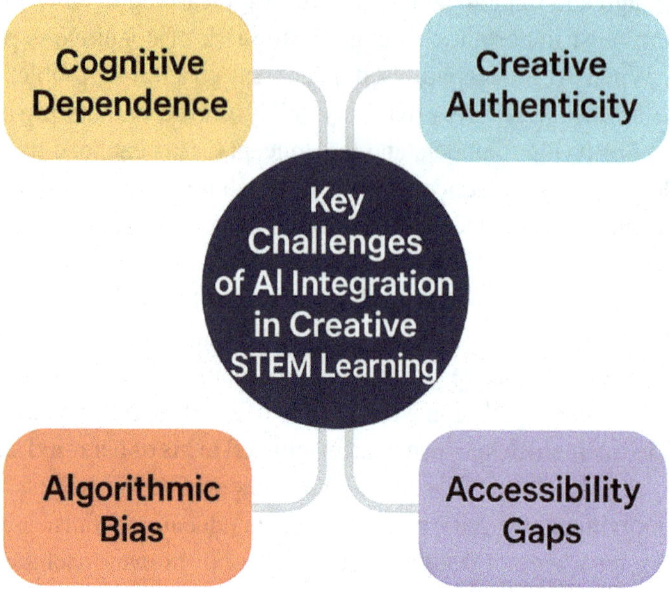


In addition to these challenges, the lack of teacher preparation is also a significant barrier to the proper use of AI in the classroom. Many teachers either lack the knowledge to use these tools pedagogically, or lack confidence in their ability to integrate them into the curriculum. Without proper professional training, teachers may use AI tools as superficial embellishments or, worse, see them as a threat to their role. This is while the role of the teacher, in AI-driven environments, is increasingly important as a designer of the learning experience, a facilitator of creativity, and a quality monitor of performance (Sutaphan & Yuenyong, 2023).

Finally, the lack of clear ethical and legal frameworks for the use of AI in education can lead to misuse or irresponsible decision-making. How much content production to entrust to AI, what data to use to train models, and how to protect learner privacy and rights all require clear and responsible policymaking (Astawan et al., 2023).

In conclusion, the use of AI to enhance educational creativity in STEM has unique potential, but without design based on pedagogical principles, social justice, and ethical transparency, it may lead to counterproductive results. Addressing these challenges will only be possible through collaboration among teachers, instructional designers, policymakers, and technology developers, with the goal of building a smart, creative, and equitable future for education.

## 7. CONCLUSION

By the end of this chapter, it becomes clear that the role of AI in enhancing educational creativity in STEM is not only a technical tool, but also a transformative educational and cognitive force. AI is fundamentally redefining learning paths; a path that is guided from education based on the transfer of information and repetitive exercises, to problem-based, experiential, and creative learning. This transition is not only effective at the level of learning tools, but also in the intellectual and philosophical structure of education. Learning is no longer simply about getting the right answers, but has become a process of discovering, testing, rethinking, and producing diverse solutions that continuously interact with AI.

One of the main achievements of integrating AI in STEM education is the strengthening of divergent and convergent thinking simultaneously. In an intelligent learning environment, students have the opportunity to first brainstorm and explore diverse paths, then evaluate options and choose the best path with the support of AI-based analytical tools. This cycle of creativity and evaluation, repeated many times throughout a project, will foster a dynamic, flexible, and problem-solving mindset. On the other hand, AI can create adaptive and personalized environments in which each learner follows a unique path for creative growth, a path shaped by data, feedback, and human-machine interactions.

However, as noted in this chapter, these new approaches also come with serious challenges. These include concerns such as cognitive dependency on machines, reduced originality in creative processes, algorithmic biases, and digital divides in access. If ignored without intervention and redesign, these obstacles can negatively impact the quality of education, educational equity, and even students' intrinsic motivation. Therefore, success in using AI to promote educational creativity will be conditional on purposeful design, ongoing monitoring, and adherence to ethical and pedagogical principles.

In this regard, the role of teachers and instructional designers is of particular importance. They must have the ability to interpret the results of interaction with AI, recognize the creative needs of each student, and select the most appropriate tools. This means redefining the role of the teacher in the age of artificial intelligence; a role that has changed from a knowledge transmitter to a learning designer and facilitator of creative thinking. It is also necessary to redesign educational systems, assessments, and educational policies in a way that recognizes these capabilities and enables their realization at the classroom, school, and macro-educational levels.

Looking ahead, we can say that artificial intelligence is creating a platform for a kind of collaborative and constructive learning between humans and machines. In this context, the boundary between human and machine production is becoming less clear, but the importance of the human observer and educational responsibility is increasing. This new paradigm requires interdisciplinary thinking, synergy between educational sciences, data sciences, and cognitive sciences. Developing frameworks for assessing creativity in AI-driven environments, designing learning scenarios compatible with smart tools, and developing methods for fostering ethical and responsible creativity are among the paths that researchers and policymakers should seriously pursue.

Ultimately, AI-supported creativity in STEM not only enhances the ability to generate new ideas, but also the capacity to face complex problems, think systems, and make decisions under uncertainty. These abilities are exactly the skills that the next generation will need to face technological, environmental, and social challenges. Therefore, the purposeful, balanced, and informed use of AI in education is an opportunity to redesign a future in which creativity is not an exceptional privilege, but a shared identity in the context of smart learning.

## REFERENCES


Akcanca, N. (2020). 21st Century Skills: The Predictive Role of Attitudes Regarding STEM Education and Problem-Based Learning. *International Journal of Progressive Education, 16*(5), 443–458. DOI: 10.29329/ijpe.2020.277.27

Alangari, T. S. (2022). Online STEM education during COVID-19 period: A systematic review of perceptions in higher education. *Eurasia Journal of Mathematics, Science and Technology Education, 18*(5), em2105. DOI: 10.29333/ejmste/11986

Astawan, I. G., Suarjana, I. M., Werang, B. R., Asaloei, S. I., Sianturi, M., & Elele, E. C. (2023). STEM-Based Scientific Learning and Its Impact on Students' Critical and Creative Thinking Skills: An Empirical Study. *Jurnal Pendidikan IPA Indonesia, 12*(3), 482–492. DOI: 10.15294/jpii.v12i3.46882

Chanthala, C., Santiboon, T., & Ponkham, K. (2018, January). Instructional designing the STEM education model for fostering creative thinking abilities in physics laboratory environment classes. In AIP Conference Proceedings (Vol. 1923, No. 1). AIP Publishing. DOI: 10.1063/1.5019501

Chen, T. I., Lin, S. K., & Chung, H. C. (2023). Gamified Educational Robots Lead an Increase in Motivation and Creativity in STEM Education. *Journal of Baltic Science Education, 22*(3), 427–438. DOI: 10.33225/jbse/23.22.427

Cooper, R., & Heaverlo, C. (2013). Problem Solving and Creativity and Design: What Influence Do They Have on Girls' Interest in STEM Subject Areas? *American Journal of Engineering Education, 4*(1), 27–38. DOI: 10.19030/ajee.v4i1.7856

Dewi, H. R., Mayasari, T., & Handhika, J. (2019). Increasing creative thinking skills and understanding of physics concepts through application of stem-based inquiry. [Jurnal Penelitian Pendidikan IPA]. *JPPIPA, 4*(1), 25–30.

Fajrina, S., Lufri, L., & Ahda, Y. (2020). Science, technology, engineering, and mathematics (STEM) as a learning approach to improve 21st century skills: A review. *International Journal of Online & Biomedical Engineering, 16*(7), 95–104. DOI: 10.3991/ijoe.v16i07.14101

García Aranda, C., Molina García, A., Morillo Balsera, M., Martínez Cuevas, S., Rodríguez Hurtado, M. E., Pérez Rodríguez, J., ... & Izquierdo García, P. C. (2020). Creativity and innovation skills in university stem education: The chet project approach.

Giang, N. T. C., Anh, N. T. Q., Dao, T. T., Tuan, P. A., Linh, C. T. H., & Chau, P. T. H. (2024). A systematic review of problem-solving skill development for students in STEM education. International Journal of Learning. *Teaching and Educational Research, 23*(5), 1–20.

Hacıoğlu, Y., & Gülhan, F. (2021). The effects of STEM education on the students' critical thinking skills and STEM perceptions. *Journal of Education in Science, Environment and Health, 7*(2), 139–155. DOI: 10.21891/jeseh.771331

Han, J., Park, D., Hua, M., & Childs, P. R. (2022). Is group work beneficial for producing creative designs in STEM design education? *International Journal of Technology and Design Education, 32*(5), 2801–2826. DOI: 10.1007/s10798-021-09709-y

Hanfy, H., Daleure, G., Abuquad, K., & Al Hosani, S. (2022). Enhancing critical and creative thinking skills in math at post-secondary level: Examining STEM versus STeM for efficiency and effectiveness. In *English language and general studies education in the united arab emirates: Theoretical, empirical and practical perspectives* (pp. 129–144). Springer Nature Singapore. DOI: 10.1007/978-981-16-8888-1_9

Hanif, S., Wijaya, A. F. C., & Winarno, N. (2019). Enhancing Students' Creativity through STEM Project-Based Learning. Journal of science Learning, 2(2), 50-57.

Hasançebi, F., Güner, Ö., Kutru, C., & Hasancebi, M. (2021). Impact of STEM integrated argumentation-based inquiry applications on students' academic success, reflective thinking and creative thinking skills. *Participatory Educational Research, 8*(4), 274–296. DOI: 10.17275/per.21.90.8.4

Hasibuan, M. P., Sari, R. P., Syahputra, R. A., & Nahadi, N. (2022). Application of integrated project-based and STEM-based E-learning tools to improve studentsâ€™ creative thinking and self-regulation skills. *Jurnal Penelitian Pendidikan IPA, 8*(1), 51–56. DOI: 10.29303/jppipa.v8i1.1050

He, W., Yan, J., Wang, C., Liao, L., & Hu, X. (2023). Exploring the impact of the design thinking model on fifth graders' creative self-efficacy, situational interest, and individual interest in STEM education. *Thinking Skills and Creativity, 50*, 101424. DOI: 10.1016/j.tsc.2023.101424

Holik, I., & Sanda, I. D. (2023). The possibilities of developing STEM skills in higher education. *Athens Journal of Technology & Engineering, 10*(1), 9–26. DOI: 10.30958/ajte.10-1-1

Kalogeras, S., Mejri, S., & Efthimiou, F. (2022). The neuroscience of student engagement: Case studies in narrative pedagogies in mathematics, science, and technology. [IJOPCD]. *International Journal of Online Pedagogy and Course Design, 12*(1), 1–19. DOI: 10.4018/IJOPCD.311440

Kencana, M. A., & Syukri, M. (2020, February). The effect of science, technology, engineering, and mathematics (STEM) on students' creative thinking skills. [). IOP Publishing.]. *Journal of Physics: Conference Series, 1460*(1), 012141. DOI: 10.1088/1742-6596/1460/1/012141

Kwon, H., & Lee, Y. (2025). A meta-analysis of STEM project-based learning on creativity. *STEM Education, 5*(2), 275–290. DOI: 10.3934/steme.2025014

Larkin, T. L. (2015, September). Creativity in STEM education: Reshaping the creative project. In 2015 international conference on interactive collaborative learning (ICL) (pp. 1184-1189). IEEE.

Marsono, M., Khasanah, F., & Yoto, Y. (2019, January). Integrating STEM (Science Technology Engineering and Mathematics) education on advancing vocational student's creative thinking skills. In 2nd international conference on vocational education and training (ICOVET 2018) (pp. 170-173). Atlantis Press.

Mukaromah, S. H., & Wusqo, I. U. (2020, March). The influence of PjBL model with stem approach on global warming topic to students' creative thinking and communication skills. [). IOP Publishing.]. *Journal of Physics: Conference Series, 1521*(4), 042052. DOI: 10.1088/1742-6596/1521/4/042052

Nozari, H. (2025). Cognitive Targeting and Neuromarketing Applications in AI-Driven Digital Advertising. *Applied Innovations in Industrial Management, 5*(2), 52–58. DOI: 10.63630/aiim.52.52

Nozari, H. (Ed.). (2025). *Dynamic and Safe Economy in the Age of Smart Technologies*. IGI Global. DOI: 10.4018/979-8-3693-4369-2

Nozari, H., Abdi, H., & Jahangard, S. (2025). Quantum Cognitive Intelligence Network Q-CIN as a Transformative Framework for Industry 6.0. *ALL Bioscience, 1*(1), 27–37.

Nozari, H., Abdi, H., & Rafiei, K. (2025). Edge Computing and Marketing in the Smart Economy: Processing Consumer Data in Real-Time. In Dynamic and Safe Economy in the Age of Smart Technologies (pp. 191-208). IGI Global Scientific Publishing.

Nozari, H., Abdi, H., & Szmelter-Jarosz, A. (2025). A Neuromorphic and Bio-Inspired Framework for Optimization in Multi-Echelon Supply Networks. *Transformative Science*, *1*(1), 9–17.

Nozari, H., & Samadi, S. (2025). Digital Twin-Enhanced Sentiment Analysis for Targeted Marketing Optimization. In Dynamic and Safe Economy in the Age of Smart Technologies (pp. 121-138). IGI Global Scientific Publishing. DOI: 10.4018/979-8-3693-4369-2.ch008

Oner, A. T., Nite, S. B., Capraro, R. M., & Capraro, M. M. (2016). From STEM to STEAM: Students' beliefs about the use of their creativity. *The STEAM Journal*, *2*(2), 6. DOI: 10.5642/steam.20160202.06

Othman, O., Iksan, Z. H., & Yasin, R. M. (2022). Creative Teaching STEM Module: High School Students' Perception. *European Journal of Educational Research*, *11*(4), 2127–2137. DOI: 10.12973/eu-jer.11.4.2127

Özsoy, N., & Özyer, S. (2018). Creative drama and example of activity plan in STEM. *European Journal of Education Studies*.

Pinasa, S., Siripun, K., & Yuenyong, C. (2018, January). Developing design-based STEM education learning activities to enhance students' creative thinking. In AIP Conference Proceedings (Vol. 1923, No. 1). AIP Publishing.

Pramesti, D., Probosari, R. M., & Indriyanti, N. Y. (2022). Effectiveness of project based learning low carbon STEM and discovery learning to improve creative thinking skills. *Journal of Innovation in Educational and Cultural Research*, *3*(3), 444–456. DOI: 10.46843/jiecr.v3i3.156

Raksapoln, K., & Suttiwan, W. (2021, November). Enhancing creativity and collaboration by learning management in STEM Education. In 2021 2nd SEA-STEM International Conference (SEA-STEM) (pp. 116-118). IEEE. DOI: 10.1109/SEA-STEM53614.2021.9667983

Ram, I., Rosenberg-Kima, R., Lewin, D. R., Barzilai, A., Chumtonov, O., & Roll, I. (2025). Active Learning and the Development of 21st Century Skills in Online STEM Education: A Large-Scale Survey. *Online Learning : the Official Journal of the Online Learning Consortium*, *29*(1), 4–29. DOI: 10.24059/olj.v29i1.3533

Rifandi, R., & Rahmi, Y. L. (2019, October). STEM education to fulfil the 21st century demand: A literature review. [). IOP Publishing.]. *Journal of Physics: Conference Series*, *1317*(1), 012208. DOI: 10.1088/1742-6596/1317/1/012208

Saputri, M., Syukri, M., & Elisa, . (2022, February). Analysis of momentum and impulse on students' creative thinking skill through project based learning integrated STEM (science, technology, engineering, mathematics). []. IOP Publishing.]. *Journal of Physics: Conference Series, 2193*(1), 012066. DOI: 10.1088/1742-6596/2193/1/012066

Sawu, M. R. F., Sukarso, A. A., Lestari, T. A., & Handayani, B. S. (2023). The effect of STEM learning in building creative dispositions and creative thinking skills of junior high school students. *Jurnal Penelitian Pendidikan IPA, 9*(8), 6219–6229. DOI: 10.29303/jppipa.v9i8.4180

Sirajudin, N., Suratno, J., & Pamuti, . (2021, March). Developing creativity through STEM education. []. IOP Publishing.]. *Journal of Physics: Conference Series, 1806*(1), 012211. DOI: 10.1088/1742-6596/1806/1/012211

Stylianidou, F., Glauert, E. B., Rossis, D., Compton, A., Cremin, T., Craft, A., & Havu-Nuutinen, S. (2018). Fostering inquiry and creativity in early years STEM education: Policy recommendations from the Creative Little Scientists Project. *European Journal of STEM Education, 3*(3). Advance online publication. DOI: 10.20897/ejsteme/3875

Sutaphan, S., & Yuenyong, C. (2023). Enhancing grade eight students' creative thinking in the water stem education learning unit. Cakrawala Pendidikan. *Jurnal Ilmiah Pendidikan, 42*(1), 120–135.

Szmelter-Jarosz, A., & Nozari, H. (2025). AI-Driven Decision Intelligence and Human-AI Collaboration in Economic Systems. In Dynamic and Safe Economy in the Age of Smart Technologies (pp. 171-190). IGI Global Scientific Publishing.

Tavdgiridze, L., Didmanidze, I., KHASAIA, I., SHEROZIA, N., DOBORDGINIDZE, D., AKHVLEDIANI, D., & AKHVLEDIANI, Z. (2024). STEM teaching in contemporary education. Challenges to National Defence in Contemporary Geopolitical Situation, 1(1).

Thingwiangthong, P., Termtachatipongsa, P., & Yuenyong, C. (2021, March). Status quo and needs of STEM Education curriculum to enhance creative problem solving competency. []. IOP Publishing.]. *Journal of Physics: Conference Series, 1835*(1), 012089. DOI: 10.1088/1742-6596/1835/1/012089

Tytler, R. (2020). STEM education for the twenty-first century. Integrated approaches to STEM education: An international perspective, 21-43.

Üret, A., & Ceylan, R. (2021). Exploring the effectiveness of STEM education on the creativity of 5-year-old kindergarten children. *European Early Childhood Education Research Journal, 29*(6), 842–855. DOI: 10.1080/1350293X.2021.1913204

Villán-Vallejo, A., Zitouni, A., García-Llamas, P., Fernández-Raga, M., Suárez-Corona, A., & Baelo, R. (2022). Soft Skills and STEM education: Vision of the European university EURECA-PRO. *BHM. Berg- und Hüttenmännische Monatshefte, 167*(10), 485–488. DOI: 10.1007/s00501-022-01275-7 PMID: 36118302

Wang, B., & Li, P. P. (2024). Digital creativity in STEM education: The impact of digital tools and pedagogical learning models on the students' creative thinking skills development. *Interactive Learning Environments, 32*(6), 2633–2646.

Widyasmah, M., & Herlina, K. (2020, February). Implementation of STEM Approach Based on Project-based Learning to Improve Creative Thinking Skills of High School Students in Physics. []. IOP Publishing.]. *Journal of Physics: Conference Series, 1467*(1), 012072. DOI: 10.1088/1742-6596/1467/1/012072

Wilis, R., Prayitno, B. A., Sunarno, W., & Anjirawaroj, S. (2023). Improving students' metacognitive abilities and creative thinking skills through STEM-based in online learning. [Jurnal Pendidikan Biologi Indonesia]. *JPBI, 9*(1), 90–102. DOI: 10.22219/jpbi.v9i1.22994

Yıldırım, B., & Selvi, M. (2016). Examination of the effects of STEM education integratedas a part of science technology society and environmentcourses. *International Journal of Human Sciences, 13*(3), 3684. DOI: 10.14687/jhs.v13i3.3876

# Chapter 13
# Merging AIoE technology With Brain-Inspired Computing in Education

**Zornitsa Yordanova**
http://orcid.org/0000-0002-6056-8445
*University of National and World Economy, Bulgaria*

## ABSTRACT

*This research explores the convergence of Artificial Intelligence of Everywhere (AIoE) and neuromorphic computing in intelligent learning analytics. By explaining the theoretical concepts, system architecture, application scenarios, and ethical challenges, it is shown that this combination can transform educational environments into adaptive, human centered, and personalized systems through real-time processing of cognitive and biological data. Along with the opportunities, issues such as cognitive privacy, informed consent, and algorithmic bias are also analyzed. The research emphasizes the necessity of responsible and human-centered design of these technologies for the future of education.*

## 1. INTRODUCTION

In the present era, education is no longer a passive and linear activity, but has become a complex, dynamic, and multi-agent system that involves continuous interaction between the learner, content, digital platforms, and the surrounding environment. With the explosive growth of smart technologies, especially the Internet of Things, edge computing, and embedded artificial intelligence, a new concept called "Artificial Intelligence of Everything" (AIoE) is emerging; a concept in which all components of the digital environment have the ability to process, learn, and make

DOI: 10.4018/979-8-3373-5117-9.ch013

ght © 2026, IGI Global Scientific Publishing. Copying or distributing in print or electronic forms without written permission of IGI Global Scientific Publishing is prohibited. Use of this chapter to
generative artificial intelligence (AI) technologies is expressly prohibited. The publisher reserves all rights to license its use for generative AI training and machine learning model development.

decisions (Szmelter-Jarosz & Nozari, 2025). This fundamental transformation has created a new perspective for learning analytics and the development of intelligent educational systems; a perspective in which not only traditional educational data but also biological, behavioral, emotional, and even cognitive data are collected, processed, and analyzed in real time.

Alongside these developments, brain-inspired computing, or neuromorphic computing, is also emerging as a key component of future technologies. This approach attempts to recreate the neural structure and functions of the brain at the hardware and software levels, rather than simply imitating classical AI algorithms (Li, G., Deng, L., Tang, H., Pan, G., Tian, Y., Roy, K., & Maass, W. (2024). Using traditional neural circuits, spiking circuits, and event-driven neural networks, neuromorphic systems are capable of very fast, low-power, and instantaneous processing of data coming from sensors or the surrounding environment (Nozari & Szmelter-Jarosz, 2024). From this perspective, neuromorphic computing is considered a powerful complement to the AIoE ecosystem, as it can provide deeper analyses of the learning process with high adaptability and low energy, especially in sensitive and real-time educational environments. One of the serious gaps in today's learning analytics is the inability to understand the cognitive and neural layers of learner behavior. While many learning analytics systems are built on clicks, superficial interactions, or performance scores, AIoE and neuromorphic-based systems are able to understand and analyze brain data such as EEG, galvanic skin responses, eye movements, and heart rate (Rahmaty & Nozari, 2023). This capability allows learning analytics to achieve a more dynamic, multi-layered, and perceptual model of an individual's learning and mental processes rather than a superficial and static picture. Accordingly, an intelligent learning environment can automatically adjust the content and learning path by understanding the cognitive load, fatigue, excitement, or momentary focus of the learner (Szmelter-Jarosz, Ghahremani-Nahr, & Nozari, 2021).

The convergence of AIoE and neuromorphic computing not only creates new technical possibilities in learning analytics, but also is revolutionary in terms of educational philosophy. In this approach, the learner is not only considered as a recipient of content but also as an intelligent node in a connected perceptual network; a node capable of two-way data exchange (Guo, X. 2022), biocompatibility, and mutual influence on the educational system. Such a view will lead to the formation of a new generation of "cognitive twins"; digital representations of the individual's neural, emotional, and cognitive state that can play a key role in the design of personalized educational experiences (Nozari, 2023). However, the realization of such systems is not possible without considering ethical challenges and concerns. Although the collection and analysis of neural data is aimed at improving education, it faces issues such as cognitive privacy, informed consent, and the risk of biased analyses (Aliahmadi & Nozari, 2023). For this reason, the convergence of AIoE and neuromorphic in education must include ethical and legal infrastructures, along with the design of technical mechanisms, so that it can be developed in a sustainable, transparent, and responsible manner.

In this chapter, we advance a conceptual framework for integrating AIoE and brain-inspired (neuromorphic) computing in education, specify a layered system architecture (sensing-edge neuromorphic analytics-adaptive orchestration-human-in-the-loop oversight), and map high-value use cases across smart classrooms, XR, distance learning, and inclusion. Beyond technical design, we articulate managerial and policy implications (governance, readiness, teacher roles) and foreground ethical guardrails—dynamic consent, cognitive privacy, bias mitigation, and transparency—aligned with international guidance (UNESCO, 2021; OECD, 2019; European Parliament & Council, 2024).

The chapter is structured to (i) synthesize technological and theoretical foundations, (ii) present a reference architecture with data flows and decision points, (iii) examine application scenarios and evaluation criteria, and (iv) propose a research agenda (multicultural datasets, edge-AI evaluation protocols, cognitive-twin ethics). Taken together, it aims to provide an interdisciplinary platform at the nexus of learning sciences, AI systems, and neuroscience, enabling responsible, human-centered deployment at scale.

## 2. THEORETICAL BACKGROUND AND CONCEPTUAL FOUNDATIONS

Intelligent learning analytics in new technological contexts requires a deep understanding of the theoretical concepts and technological architectures that lie at the heart of this transformation. The convergence of Artificial Intelligence Ubiquitous (AIoE) and Brain-Inspired Computing is not only a technological link, but also a conceptual and philosophical structure between two macro-views of education and intelligence. To understand this integration, we must first redefine the core concepts and then design a theoretical model that explains the interactions of different layers in modern learning analytics.

Artificial Intelligence Ubiquitous (AIoE) is a concept that has emerged from the evolution of the Internet of Things, edge computing, distributed machine learning, and intelligent communications. Unlike the traditional approach to AI that relies on centralized processing and central data, AIoE aims to extend the processing, understanding, and decision-making capabilities to all objects, devices, and sensors in the environment. In such an ecosystem, each element, whether it is a sensor in a smart classroom or a wearable device on the learner's body, has the ability to interpret and transmit information independently and embedded (Nozari, Abdi, & Jahangard,

2025). This new paradigm has changed the flow of data from classical paths to a multi-center and self-organizing network in which processing takes place not only in the cloud, but also at the edge, in real time and with respect to the environmental context (Najafi, Nozari, & Edalatpanah, 2022).

In this context, learning analytics also changes from a posteriori data collection to a continuous process of real-time sensing, interpretation, and decision-making. Data such as eye movements, biological responses, type of interaction with educational content, and even location in the learning space can be analyzed continuously. At the same time, this data is processed in small processing units at the edge of the network (Edge Nodes) with embedded learning models, and its results are provided to educational decision support systems (Nozari, Abdi, & Szmelter-Jarosz, 2025). In such a case, educational analysis is not only faster and more accurate, but also more contextual, personalized, and more adaptable to the learner's immediate circumstances.

However, the ability to analyze such data is not possible using classical machine learning approaches alone. Brain-inspired computing, or neuromorphic computing, provides a new path for understanding and processing biological and cognitive educational data. This type of computing, which is designed based on the neuronal structure of the brain, uses models that transmit neuronal activity in the form of spikes or event-driven signals instead of using traditional weight- and layer-based neural networks. This type of processing is not only very low-power and fast, but also very suitable for analyzing temporal and sequential data such as EEG or biological signals (Bathaee, Nozari, & Szmelter-Jarosz, 2023).

The main feature of neuromorphic computing is its similarity to the way the human brain processes data at the hardware and software levels. Unlike the sequential processing of traditional computers, neuromorphic architectures take advantage of massive parallelism and event-driven processing. In these architectures, memory and processing are not separated; neurons and synapses store and process information, and therefore, it is possible to build systems that respond to stimuli in real time (Nozari, 2024). Such features make this type of computing an ideal option for real-time analysis of sensory, cognitive, and behavioral data in educational environments.

The conceptual integration of AIoE and neuromorphic computing in education could lead to the formation of a new generation of learning systems in which each sensor is an intelligent processing unit and each learner is a dynamic cognitive node in a learning network. In these systems, biological data is received directly from the learner's body, processed on the spot, and analyzed using spiking neural networks. The results of these analyses can include levels of mental engagement, cognitive load, momentary emotions, and personalized learning patterns (Aliahmadi, Ghahremani-Nahr, & Nozari, 2023). Such a model of analysis not only adapts educational content more intelligently, but also allows instructional designers to fine-tune learning paths with neural precision.

To better understand this conceptual structure, a multi-layered model of the convergence of AIoE and neuromorphic in learning analytics can be proposed. In the first layer, raw data is collected through sensors and wearables. In the second layer, this data is analyzed using neuromorphic models in the Edge Device or Node. In the third layer, the analysis results are combined with other data sources (such as digital interactions or learning history) and finally, in the fourth layer, educational content, suggestions, or learning environment settings are modified in real-time and adaptively. This model can be implemented in environments such as virtual reality, smart physical classrooms, or even distance learning platforms (Nozari, Rahmaty, & Szmelter-Jarosz, 2024).

Finally, it should be emphasized that this integration is not just a technical change, but a completely new approach to the learning process and its analysis. In this view, cognitive and neural data are not just peripheral information, but part of the core of learning analysis. Also, educational systems are no longer simply content distribution systems, but living, adaptive, and interactive environments that have the ability to interpret and respond to the biological, cognitive, and emotional states of the learner. This is what makes AIoE and neuromorphic computing the core of future smart education.

## 3. ARCHITECTURE OF NEUROMORPHIC AIoE-ENHANCED LEARNING SYSTEMS

The architecture of intelligent learning systems based on the convergence of AIoE and neuromorphic computing depicts the intersection of environmental perception, cognitive processing, and real-time educational responsiveness. Such an architecture should be able to receive, process, and interpret multi-source data from complex educational environments, with the ability to recognize context, save energy, and process very quickly. In this framework, the goal is to create an intelligent platform in which the educational system is not only responsive but also cognitive, adaptive, and self-learning.

At the first level of this architecture, the data acquisition layer, a set of sensors embedded in the environment or on the learner's body play a key role. These sensors may include EEG sensors, facial recognition cameras, eye movement sensors, heart rate monitors, or smart wearable devices. In this layer, the system is involved in the continuous reception of signals that reflect indicators of the learner's cognitive, emotional, and behavioral state. This data, unlike traditional information such as test responses or time spent studying, is dynamic, continuous, and instantaneous (Najafi, Nozari, & Edalatpanah, 2022).

The second layer, the Edge Processing layer, is where the neuromorphic architecture comes into play. In this layer, the received data is sent not to central servers but to neuromorphic processing units designed based on spiky neural networks (SNNs). Modeled after biological neurons, these units are able to analyze data in an event-driven manner with very low energy consumption. The main advantage of using such an architecture is its high ability to process sensitive data such as brain signals and biological reactions in real time, something that is not achievable in traditional learning systems (Nozari, 2024).

In the third layer, the data processed by the neuromorphic units enters an adaptive analysis layer. This layer uses embedded learning models that can adapt to individual learning patterns. For example, if a pattern in a learner's behavior indicates cognitive fatigue or decreased concentration, this layer can simultaneously analyze different inputs to provide a warning signal or correction to the educational system. The output of this analysis can include suggesting a break, changing the type of content, or adjusting the intensity of interaction (Aliahmadi, Nozari, Ghahremani-Nahr, & Szmelter-Jarosz, 2022).

The fourth layer is the adaptive feedback and interaction layer. At this level, the system applies the results of the analysis in the form of instantaneous changes to the learning environment. This feedback can take the form of changes to the user interface, modifying the content flow, activating a teaching assistant, or even changing the physical conditions of the classroom environment such as lighting or sound. In this way, the system truly becomes an intelligent, sensitive, and responsive learning environment (Nozari, Ghahremani-Nahr, & Najafi, 2023).

To better understand the structure of this architecture, Figure 1 has been designed to simplify the different layers of the system graphically and with colored icons. In this diagram, the information flow is depicted from sensors to neuromorphic units, then to adaptive analysis, and finally to the training response. Each of the sections is represented by icons such as the digital brain, eye sensor, neuromorphic unit, and feedback icons. This image clearly shows the hierarchical, but nonlinear, and feedback nature of the system.

*Figure 1. Conceptual architecture of intelligent learning systems based on AIoE and neuromorphic computing*

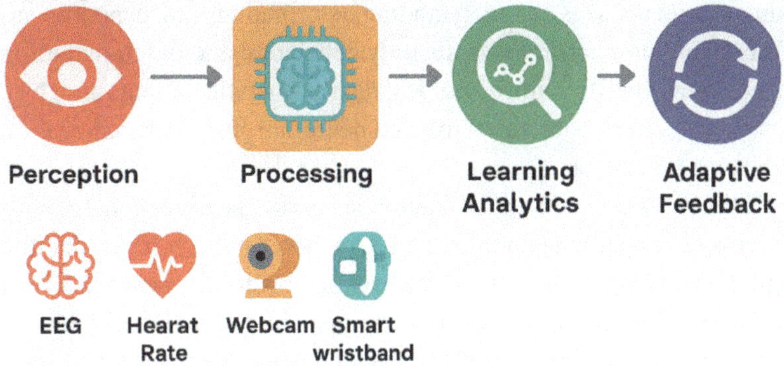


An important point in this architecture is its embeddability and scalability. Unlike central server-based training systems, the present architecture is designed to be easily deployed in real classrooms, virtual reality environments, or online learning platforms. Also, since most of the processing is done at the edge, latency is minimized and data security is better maintained, as the need to constantly send sensitive information to the cloud is reduced (Fallah & Nozari, 2021).

Another aspect that distinguishes this architecture is its ability to adapt to individual learners. Each neuromorphic unit can adapt to its previous data and locally modify its learning algorithms. This means that the learning system is not only responsive, but also able to identify and optimize individual learning patterns. This feature will have a significant impact on the design of personalized systems for learners with special needs (Movahed, Movahed, & Nozari, 2024).

Finally, this architecture can also interact bidirectionally with digital or cognitive twin models of the learner. That is, not only instantaneous analyses, but also long-term data about the individual's cognitive and behavioral processes are stored in the memory of these twins. Such a link between the neuromorphic system and the cognitive twin provides the infrastructure for designing intelligent adaptive learning in the long term; An infrastructure that can lead to lifelong and dynamic learning in the era of ubiquitous artificial intelligence (Nozari, Fallah, Szmelter-Jarosz, & Krzemiński, 2021).

## 4. APPLICATION SCENARIOS IN SMART EDUCATION

In the future educational space, application scenarios of the convergence of AIoE and neuromorphic computing go beyond the theoretical level and take shape as real systems in various educational contexts. The implementation of these technologies in smart education can create environments that are very similar to the functioning of the human brain in terms of understanding, interpreting, and responding to learner states. These environments receive not only behavioral and functional information, but also real-time cognitive and biological data as analytical inputs and, by utilizing intelligent architectures based on AIoE and neuromorphic, personalize the learning path with neural precision.

One of the most prominent application scenarios is educational environments based on virtual or augmented reality (XR). In these spaces, the learner interacts in a 3D digital environment that simultaneously adapts to his movements, eye focus, biological and emotional responses. For example, in a virtual reality biology class, the system can analyze EEG signals to detect when a learner's attention span has dropped and immediately increase the level of cognitive engagement with changes in narration, audio, or visuals (Ghahremani-Nahr, Najafi, & Nozari, 2022). This approach not only increases learning effectiveness, but also makes the learning experience much more natural and interactive.

In another scenario, smart physical classrooms involve the use of a wide range of environmental and wearable sensors. In these environments, every desk or chair can be equipped with sensors that record the student's biological and behavioral information. Neuromorphic processing units installed in the classroom or even inside wearable devices are responsible for processing this information in real time. If the system detects a decrease in the level of alertness, anxiety or distraction in the student, it can immediately change the type of content or teaching method adaptively through smart boards, sound or lighting in the classroom (Lotfi, Najafi, & Nozari, 2016).

This technology can also be widely used in the field of distance education. One of the main problems in virtual education is the lack of physical presence and the reduction of emotional and behavioral understanding of the learner by the teacher or the educational system. By using AIoE-based sensors in the learner's home, including webcams, smart wristbands or even EEG headsets, the educational system can monitor the learner's real-time state and provide an experience similar to an in-person class. This information is transmitted in the form of signals to the neuromorphic unit, which, through real-time analysis, offers suggestions for changing the content, adding interaction or even suggesting a pause in the educational session (Aliahmadi, Movahed, & Nozari, 2024).

Also, in skill or technical training scenarios, the combination of AIoE and neuromorphic can be used to accurately analyze the learner's movements, stress, and accuracy. For example, in practical training such as virtual surgery or industrial assembly, the system can record movement data, stress signals, and concentration status to analyze the individual's performance in real time and provide intelligent warnings if a potential error is detected. This type of feedback not only reduces errors but also makes learning deeper and safer (Nozari, Tavakkoli-Moghaddam, & Gharemani-Nahr, 2022).

In a more advanced scenario, AIoE-based cognitive twins can be used to continuously model the learner's mental and biological state. These twins, by combining long-term learning data, cognitive history, current neural state, and moment-to-moment analysis, are able to design personalized learning paths for each individual. For example, a student who has lower concentration at certain times of the day or experiences cognitive fatigue when learning abstract concepts will be better served by offering more graphic content or using gamification (Movahed, Movahed, & Nozari, 2024).

In a more specific scenario, this technology can also be used for inclusive education and supporting learners with special needs. For example, children on the autism spectrum or with learning disabilities may react differently to certain environmental stimuli. By analyzing the biological and cognitive responses of these individuals in real time, the system can adjust the conditions in such a way that the learning environment is less stressful for them and at the same time effective. This type of deep personalization has not been achieved in any traditional system (Nozari, Najafi, Jafari-Eskandari, & Aliahmadi, 2016).

Meanwhile, Figure 2 graphically depicts the diversity of AIoE and neuromorphic-based educational scenarios and clearly demonstrates the relationships between key components such as virtual reality, smart classroom, distance learning, skill training, cognitive twins, and neuromorphic processing units.

*Figure 2. Application scenarios of AIoE and neuromorphic computing in smart education*

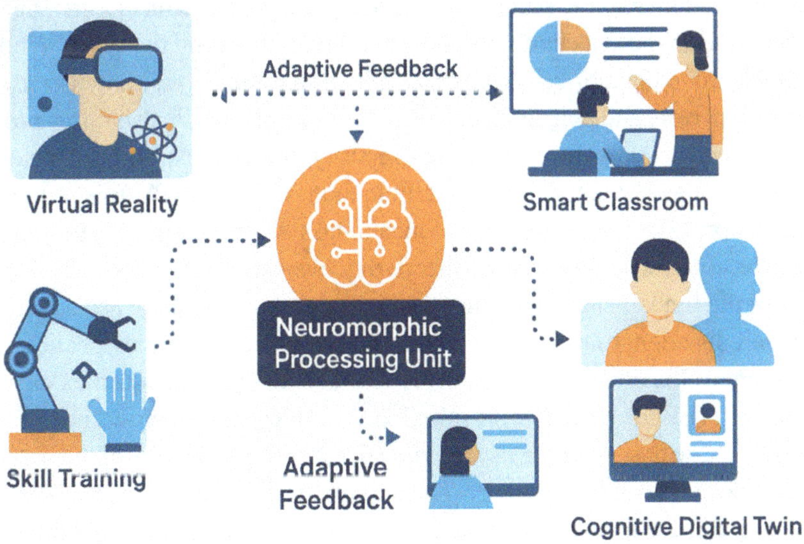

Overall, what all these scenarios have in common is the ability to multimodal perception, real-time processing, cognitive analytics, and adaptive feedback; features that are only possible with the integration of AIoE and neuromorphic computing. These features have led to the creation of environments that are not only technologically advanced, but also cognitively and humanly designed much closer to the functioning of the human mind.

Importantly, the successful implementation of these scenarios requires synergy between hardware, algorithms, learning design, and ethical frameworks. For example, the storage of biological data should be encrypted and under informed consent, and the analysis systems should be resistant to bias. Also, the design of the learning experience should be carried out in collaboration with cognitive psychologists, intelligent systems engineers, and education specialists to provide a comprehensive and sustainable experience (Ghahremani-Nahr et al., 2023).

In conclusion, the above scenarios show that the use of AIoE and neuromorphic is not just a technical tool, but a comprehensive approach to redesigning the learning and teaching process. This approach leads to more meaningful, human, and personalized education by enabling deep analysis, real-time response, and neural understanding of the learner. The expansion of these applications in the coming decade can upgrade educational systems from one-sided and general to dynamic, cognitive, and human-friendly ecosystems.

## 5. CHALLENGES AND ETHICAL CONSIDERATIONS

As the use of Artificial Intelligence of Everywhere (AIoE) and neuromorphic computing in education expands, the need to address the ethical challenges and considerations of these technologies becomes more important than ever. While this technological combination offers unprecedented opportunities for designing adaptive, cognitively-driven, and personalized learning environments, it also raises profound questions about cognitive privacy, data security, the responsibility of automated decision-making, and algorithmic discrimination. If these challenges are ignored, not only will public trust in intelligent educational systems decline, but the outcomes they produce may also be severely distorted or even harmful.

One of the fundamental challenges is the concept of "cognitive privacy." Unlike traditional educational data, which includes grades, connection times, or clicks, AIoE and neuromorphic computing systems record and analyze data such as electroencephalogram (EEG), heart rate, respiration, eye micromovements, and emotional responses. These data enter the psychological and biological realm of the individual at a much deeper level than privacy. The question is, does analyzing this data, even with consent, mean entering the unconscious layers of the individual's mind? And can a clear boundary be established for "authorized educational information"? (Mohammadi, Ghazanfari, Nozari, & Shafiezad, 2015)

Furthermore, the issue of informed consent also arises. Obtaining consent from learners, especially children or individuals with special needs, can be very challenging when their level of understanding of the nature of biological data or neuromorphic analytics is low. Can a teenage student understand the depth of the implications of sharing their brain data? Answering this question requires a serious rethinking of traditional models of educational consent. Mechanisms must be designed that not only receive consent symbolically, but also continuously, auditably, and with safe exit options (Tavakkoli-Moghaddam, Nozari, Bakhshi-Movahed, & Bakhshi-Movahed, 2024).

From a technical perspective, another important challenge is related to sustainability and energy consumption. Although neuromorphic units are much more energy-efficient than classical processors, at large scales, a network of thousands of sensors, wearables, and processing nodes imposes a high energy pressure on the educational environment. Especially in underserved areas or developing countries, providing continuous and stable energy for such infrastructure can be a serious implementation obstacle. Consequently, the successful implementation of these technologies requires the development of low-power, portable, and resilient architectures against frequent outages (Movahed, Aliahmadi, Parsanejad, & Nozari, 2023).

Another serious challenge is the risk of algorithmic bias in cognitive data analysis. Machine learning algorithms may be trained on data that is not representative of the cultural, gender, ethnic, or neural spectrum. In this case, the interpretation of the mental or emotional state of learners may be inaccurate, discriminatory, or even harmful. For example, signals that are interpreted as anxiety in one culture may indicate high concentration in another. If such differences are not taken into account in the model design, the learning results will be severely biased (Nozari, Tavakkoli-Moghaddam, Rohaninejad, & Hanzalek, 2023).

In the meantime, Figure 3 visually represents the key challenges of AIoE and neuromorphic learning systems along four main axes: cognitive privacy, algorithmic bias, energy consumption, and informed consent. Each axis is marked with a colored symbolic icon and initial solutions to mitigate the negative effects are included next to it. This diagram helps the audience more quickly understand the ethical-technical complexities of these systems and shifts the position of decision-making from a purely technical to an interdisciplinary area.

*Figure 3. Ethical challenges and considerations in AIoE and neuromorphic computing-based learning systems*

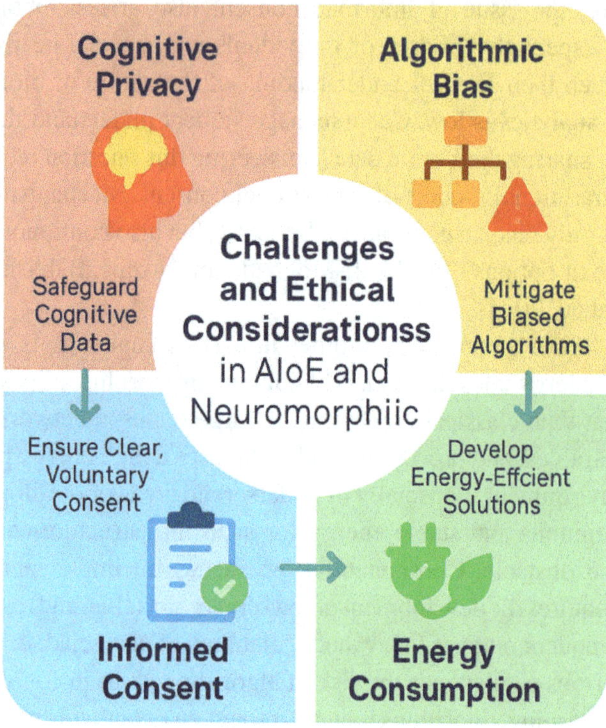


In addition to individual issues, there are also challenges at the organizational level and in the larger educational systems. For example, the compatibility of legal and institutional infrastructures with brain data analysis is still not well defined in many countries. Data protection laws are usually limited to textual or behavioral information and do not fully cover biological, neurological, and emotional data. Therefore, there is a possibility of legal loopholes, institutional abuse, or unfair commercialization of students' cognitive information (Movahed, Movahed, & Nozari, 2024).

On the other hand, the increasing educational dependence on technology should also be considered as a strategic challenge. By transforming learning into a process that is completely in the hands of algorithms, sensors, and intelligent analytics, the risk of removing the human element increases, teachers' authority decreases, and learners' cognitive dependence on machine feedback increases. This dependence can lead to the weakening of self-regulation, critical thinking, and intellectual independence in the long run; Because the learner waits for automated and algorithmic feedback to adjust the learning path, rather than based on individual understanding, experience, or reflection (Nozari & Edalatpanah, 2023).

A delicate point to consider is the balance between humans and machines in an intelligent learning environment. Although neuromorphic computing has brought the ability to analyze biological data to an unprecedented level, it should not be forgotten that learning is also an emotional, social, and cultural process. Therefore, the design of such systems should maintain the principles of human participation, the transparency of AI decisions, and the comprehensibility of the analyses for teachers and learners. This approach will not only help increase user trust, but will also strengthen mutual understanding and accountability (Nozari & Edalatpanah, 2023).

Ultimately, addressing these challenges requires a multi-layered approach. On the one hand, new ethical standards for cognitive data analysis need to be defined. On the other hand, algorithms need to be designed to be open, auditable, and based on diverse data. It is also crucial to train teachers to understand how these systems work, understand the outputs, and provide human oversight of automated decisions. These actions can lead to an educational ecosystem that leverages AIoE and neuromorphic capabilities while remaining true to humane, ethical, and responsible principles.

## 6. CONCLUSION

By the end of this chapter, what becomes clear is the need for a fundamental rethinking of learning paradigms in light of emerging technologies such as Artificial Intelligence of Everywhere (AIoE) and neuromorphic computing. What was considered a dream or scientific fantasy just a few decades ago is now being realized in the form of powerful, adaptive, and almost perceptual systems. Education, inherently a complex, multi-layered, human process, is now intertwined with technologies that penetrate deeply into the mind, body, and behavior of the learner, understanding him or her not just as a recipient of content but as a cognitive being with unique patterns. This transformation is considered a turning point in the history of modern education not only from a technical and pedagogical perspective, but also from a philosophical and ethical perspective.

This chapter first describes the theoretical and conceptual background to show how AIoE, as a platform of intelligent communications, connected sensors, edge computing, and embedded learning, has created a technological ecosystem for continuous, contextual, and multi-source learning analysis. In addition, neuromorphic computing, with its neural-inspired structure, has enabled real-time processing of biological and cognitive data; a processing that is not only fast and low-power, but also, due to its similarity to the functioning of the human brain, allows for the understanding of the complexities of learner behavior.

Next, by presenting the architectural structure of such systems, it was shown how the layers of perception, neuromorphic analysis, adaptive learning, and real-time feedback are seamlessly interconnected and can manage from the level of biological signals to the level of educational content regulation in real time. Designing this architecture is important not only from a system engineering perspective, but also from a learning design perspective and its human recognizability. Creating such a structure, especially in virtual reality training platforms, smart physical classrooms, distance learning environments, and skill systems, brings unique capabilities to improve effectiveness, personalization, and reduce learning inequalities.

On the other hand, examining application scenarios showed that the convergence of AIoE and neuromorphic can transform various aspects of education. These systems are able to analyze levels of fatigue, focus, cognitive engagement, and emotional state in real time and adapt the content, time, intensity, or type of education in response to it. In skill learning environments, these systems can increase safety and provide a more humane experience for learners with special needs in inclusive education. The design of digital cognitive twins also enables longitudinal analysis of learner behavior and the construction of unique learning paths.

However, it is clear that such technological power is not without consequences. The ethical considerations raised in this chapter have clearly shown that accessing human cognitive and neural data, without defining precise ethical, legal, and technical frameworks, can lead to privacy violations, deepening algorithmic discrimination, and psychological or social harm. Privacy in such systems no longer means simply identifying or behavioral information, but extends to the depths of individuals' minds and emotions. Therefore, the concept of "cognitive privacy" should be considered as one of the key concepts in the future design of these systems.

In addition, the issue of informed consent must also be redefined. It is no longer possible to obtain students' consent to analyze their brain data with a simple checkbox on registration forms. This consent must be dynamic, reviewable, revocable, and conceptually understandable. From an algorithmic perspective, learning models must be designed based on diverse, equitable, and multicultural data to avoid cognitive or cultural biases. Underlying challenges such as energy consumption, technology dependency, and reduced human agency are also issues that must be addressed with forward-looking, flexible, and multidisciplinary designs.

Overall, what emerges from this review is a need to develop a new paradigm in education; one in which technology acts not as a substitute for humans but as a tool to enhance human capabilities. This paradigm must be designed based on principles such as transparency, human participation, adaptability, cognitive security, and explainability. Intelligent learning systems must grow not only based on what they learn from data, but also by understanding the complex human, cultural, and social layers of learners.

It is suggested that in future steps, researchers focus on developing algorithms that can be context-aware, multicultural, and adaptive. Also, designing international ethical frameworks for the use of brain and cognitive data in educational settings is a key priority. Linking these technologies with fields such as educational neuroscience, cognitive psychology, philosophy of mind, and cultural studies can also help deepen and better understand their implications.

Finally, it can be concluded that the combination of AIoE and neuromorphic computing in education is not only a technological choice, but also an anthropological decision. A choice that, if accompanied by insight, interdisciplinary knowledge, and ethical commitment, can transform education into a deep, meaningful, personal, and human experience; but if viewed solely from an efficiency and data-driven perspective, it may lead to the reduction of humans to data, and learning to algorithms. The future of smart education depends on how we balance technological capability with human-centered understanding, and how we apply both science and conscience simultaneously to build better learning.

## REFERENCES


Aliahmadi, A., Ghahremani-Nahr, J., & Nozari, H. (2023). Pricing decisions in the closed-loop supply chain network, taking into account the queuing system in production centers. *Expert Systems with Applications*, *212*, 118741. DOI: 10.1016/j.eswa.2022.118741

Aliahmadi, A., Movahed, A. B., & Nozari, H. (2024). Collaboration analysis in supply chain 4.0 for smart businesses. In *Building Smart and Sustainable Businesses With Transformative Technologies* (pp. 103–122). IGI Global Scientific Publishing.

Aliahmadi, A., & Nozari, H. (2023, January). Evaluation of security metrics in AIoT and blockchain-based supply chain by Neutrosophic decision-making method. In Supply chain forum: an international journal (Vol. 24, No. 1, pp. 31-42). Taylor & Francis. DOI: 10.1080/16258312.2022.2101898

Aliahmadi, A., Nozari, H., Ghahremani-Nahr, J., & Szmelter-Jarosz, A. (2022). Evaluation of key impression of resilient supply chain based on artificial intelligence of things (AIoT). arXiv preprint arXiv:2207.13174.

Bathaee, M., Nozari, H., & Szmelter-Jarosz, A. (2023). Designing a new location-allocation and routing model with simultaneous pick-up and delivery in a closed-loop supply chain network under uncertainty. *Logistics (Basel)*, *7*(1), 3. DOI: 10.3390/logistics7010003

Fallah, M., & Nozari, H. (2021). Neutrosophic mathematical programming for optimization of multi-objective sustainable biomass supply chain network design. *Computer Modeling in Engineering & Sciences*, *129*(2), 927–951. DOI: 10.32604/cmes.2021.017511

Ghahremani-Nahr, J., Najafi, S. E., & Nozari, H. (2022). A combined transportation model for the fruit and vegetable supply chain network. *Journal of Optimization in Industrial Engineering*, *15*(2), 131–145.

Ghahremani-Nahr, J., Nozari, H., Rahmaty, M., Zeraati Foukolaei, P., & Sherejsharifi, A. (2023). Development of a novel fuzzy hierarchical location-routing optimization model considering reliability. *Logistics (Basel)*, *7*(3), 64. DOI: 10.3390/logistics7030064

Guo, X. (2022). A Study on Cross-Media Teaching Model for College English Classroom Based on Output-Driven Hypothetical Neural Network. *Computational Intelligence and Neuroscience*, *2022*(1), 5283439.

Li, G., Deng, L., Tang, H., Pan, G., Tian, Y., Roy, K., & Maass, W. (2024). Brain-inspired computing: A systematic survey and future trends. *Proceedings of the IEEE.*

Lotfi, F. H. Z., Najafi, S. E., & Nozari, H. (Eds.). (2016). *Data envelopment analysis and effective performance assessment.* IGI Global.

Mohammadi, H., Ghazanfari, M., Nozari, H., & Shafiezad, O. (2015). Combining the theory of constraints with system dynamics: A general model (case study of the subsidized milk industry). International journal of management science and engineering management, 10(2), 102-108.

Movahed, A. B., Aliahmadi, A., Parsanejad, M., & Nozari, H. (2023). A systematic review of collaboration in supply chain 4.0 with meta-synthesis method. *Supply Chain Analytics, 4,* 100052. DOI: 10.1016/j.sca.2023.100052

Movahed, A. B., Movahed, A. B., & Nozari, H. (2024). Opportunities and challenges of smart supply chain in Industry 5.0. Information Logistics for Organizational Empowerment and Effective Supply Chain Management, 108-138.

Movahed, A. B., Movahed, A. B., & Nozari, H. (2024). Marketing 6.0 Conceptualization. In Advanced Businesses in Industry 6.0 (pp. 15-31). IGI Global.

Movahed, A. B., Movahed, A. B., & Nozari, H. (2024). Opportunities and challenges of marketing 5.0. Smart and Sustainable Interactive Marketing, 1-21.

Najafi, S. E., Nozari, H., & Edalatpanah, S. A. (2022). Investigating the key parameters affecting sustainable IoT-based marketing. In *Computational Intelligence Methodologies Applied to Sustainable Development Goals* (pp. 51–61). Springer International Publishing. DOI: 10.1007/978-3-030-97344-5_4

Najafi, S. E., Nozari, H., & Edalatpanah, S. A. (2022). Artificial Intelligence of Things (AIoT) and Industry 4.0–Based Supply Chain (FMCG Industry). A roadmap for enabling industry 4.0 by artificial intelligence, 31-41.

Nozari, H. (Ed.). (2023). *Building Smart and Sustainable Businesses with Transformative Technologies.* IGI Global. DOI: 10.4018/979-8-3693-0210-1

Nozari, H. (2024). Supply chain 6.0 and moving towards hyper-intelligent processes. In *Information logistics for organizational empowerment and effective supply chain management* (pp. 1–13). IGI Global.

Nozari, H. (2024). Green Supply Chain Management based on Artificial Intelligence of Everything. *Journal of Economics and Management, 46,* 171–188. DOI: 10.22367/jem.2024.46.07

Nozari, H., Abdi, H., & Jahangard, S. (2025). Quantum Cognitive Intelligence Network Q-CIN as a Transformative Framework for Industry 6.0. *ALL Bioscience*, *1*(1), 27–37.

Nozari, H., Abdi, H., & Szmelter-Jarosz, A. (2025). A Neuromorphic and Bio-Inspired Framework for Optimization in Multi-Echelon Supply Networks. *Transformative Science*, *1*(1), 9–17.

Nozari, H., & Edalatpanah, S. A. (2023). Smart systems risk management in IoT-based supply chain. In *Advances in reliability, failure and risk analysis* (pp. 251–268). Springer Nature Singapore. DOI: 10.1007/978-981-19-9909-3_11

Nozari, H., Fallah, M., Szmelter-Jarosz, A., & Krzemiński, M. (2021). Analysis of security criteria for IoT-based supply chain: a case study of FMCG industries. Central European Management Journal, 29(4).

Nozari, H., Ghahremani-Nahr, J., & Najafi, E. (2023). The role of Internet of things and Blockchain in the development of agile and sustainable supply chains. In Digital Supply Chain, Disruptive Environments, and the Impact on Retailers (pp. 271-282). IGI Global. DOI: 10.4018/978-1-6684-7298-9.ch015

Nozari, H., Najafi, S. E., Jafari-Eskandari, M., & Aliahmadi, A. (2016). Providing a model for virtual project management with an emphasis on IT projects. In *Strategic Management and Leadership for Systems Development in Virtual Spaces* (pp. 43–63). IGI Global Scientific Publishing. DOI: 10.4018/978-1-4666-9688-4.ch003

Nozari, H., Rahmaty, M., & Szmelter-Jarosz, A. (2024). A framework for AIoT-based smart sustainable marketing system. In *Artificial Intelligence of Things for Achieving Sustainable Development Goals* (pp. 255–271). Springer Nature Switzerland. DOI: 10.1007/978-3-031-53433-1_13

Nozari, H., & Szmelter-Jarosz, A. (2024). An analytical framework for smart supply chains 5.0. In *Building Smart and Sustainable Businesses With Transformative Technologies* (pp. 1–15). IGI Global Scientific Publishing.

Nozari, H., Tavakkoli-Moghaddam, R., & Gharemani-Nahr, J. (2022). A neutrosophic fuzzy programming method to solve a multi-depot vehicle routing model under uncertainty during the covid-19 pandemic. *International Journal of Engineering*, *35*(2), 360–371.

Nozari, H., Tavakkoli-Moghaddam, R., Rohaninejad, M., & Hanzalek, Z. (2023, September). Artificial intelligence of things (AIoT) strategies for a smart sustainable-resilient supply chain. In IFIP International Conference on Advances in Production Management Systems (pp. 805-816). Cham: Springer Nature Switzerland. DOI: 10.1007/978-3-031-43670-3_56

Rahmaty, M., & Nozari, H. (2023). Optimization of the hierarchical supply chain in the pharmaceutical industry. *Edelweiss Applied Science and Technology*, *7*(2), 104–123. DOI: 10.55214/25768484.v7i2.376

Szmelter-Jarosz, A., Ghahremani-Nahr, J., & Nozari, H. (2021). A neutrosophic fuzzy optimisation model for optimal sustainable closed-loop supply chain network during COVID-19. *Journal of Risk and Financial Management*, *14*(11), 519. DOI: 10.3390/jrfm14110519

Szmelter-Jarosz, A., & Nozari, H. (2025). AI-Driven Decision Intelligence and Human-AI Collaboration in Economic Systems. In Dynamic and Safe Economy in the Age of Smart Technologies (pp. 171-190). IGI Global Scientific Publishing.

Tavakkoli-Moghaddam, R., Nozari, H., Bakhshi-Movahed, A., & Bakhshi-Movahed, A. (2024). A Conceptual framework for the Smart Factory 6.0. In *Advanced Businesses in Industry 6.0* (pp. 1–14). IGI Global. DOI: 10.4018/979-8-3693-3108-8.ch001

# Chapter 14
# Seamless Data Integration for Predictive Learning Environments

**Zornitsa Yordanova**
http://orcid.org/0000-0002-6056-8445
*University of National and World Economy, Bulgaria*

**Hamed Nozari**
http://orcid.org/0000-0002-6500-6708
*Azad University UAE, Dubai, UAE*

## ABSTRACT

*This research explores predictive learning structures in connected environments and shows that seamless integration of multi-purpose data through intelligent architectures enables adaptive and personalized learning. Leveraging the Internet of Things, artificial intelligence, and real-time analytics, educational systems are able to accurately predict learner behavior and performance and deliver targeted interventions. By introducing data-driven frameworks, this study addresses the technical, ethical, and cognitive requirements for designing such environments and outlines a roadmap for future education.*

## 1. INTRODUCTION

In the current era, the spread of emerging technologies such as the Internet of Things (IoT), artificial intelligence (AI), and learning analytics has fundamentally transformed the way we teach and learn. One of the most important approaches in this transformation is the creation of predictive learning environments that contin-

DOI: 10.4018/979-8-3373-5117-9.ch014

ight © 2026, IGI Global Scientific Publishing. Copying or distributing in print or electronic forms without written permission of IGI Global Scientific Publishing is prohibited. Use of this chapter to
generative artificial intelligence (AI) technologies is expressly prohibited. The publisher reserves all rights to license its use for generative AI training and machine learning model development.

uously analyze learner performance and optimize their educational path based on data from the brain. Such environments require the integration of diverse data from heterogeneous sources, including smart sensors, educational platforms, interaction-based systems, and behavioral data, which must be integrated into secure, scalable, and compatible platforms (Moon et al., 2024).

Seamless Data Integration, as a key prerequisite for creating these environments, requires the design of infrastructures that can integrate multi-purpose and time-sensitive data streams with minimal latency and maximum accuracy. In connected education ecosystems, data is received not only from multiple sources but also from different levels – from the edge to the cloud. This data includes physiological information, location, classroom behaviors, learning histories, and even emotional and cognitive data, each of which is incomplete on its own but combined with each other can provide a comprehensive picture of the learning situation (Nozari, Szmelter-Jarosz, & Ghahremani-Nahr, 2022).

In the meantime, artificial intelligence plays a central role in analyzing hidden patterns in educational data. Machine learning models, especially in the field of supervised learning and deep learning, are able to predict learner behavior by training on combined data, warn of potential risks such as academic failure, and dynamically adapt educational content (Lee, 2007). This is especially important when educational systems are faced with cultural, cognitive, and behavioral diversity of learners; conditions that other traditional models are unable to respond to (Nozari, Fallah, Kazemipoor, & Najafi, 2021).

On the other hand, the Internet of Things (IoT) in the form of wearable sensors, smart peripherals, and interactive tools has enabled the continuous collection of precise, location-based data. Unlike traditional data that was collected after the learning event, this data is made available to analytics systems in real time, enabling timely learning decisions (Andrews, Owen, & Oye, 2025). However, the main challenge is integrating this data in a way that not only maintains analytical consistency, but also minimizes system latency and ensures data security (Nozari, Szmelter-Jarosz, & Ghahremani-Nahr, 2021).

In many current approaches, data integration is performed centrally and post-processed, which reduces efficiency in real-time learning environments. In contrast, the design of distributed architectures based on edge computing allows some of the analysis to be performed at the closest point to the data source, resulting in significantly faster decision-making and more accurate responses to learner changes (Aithal & Aithal, 2023). This paradigm shift in architecture also provides a platform for the scalability of educational infrastructures, so that educational environments can function appropriately in diverse conditions without dependence on central infrastructures (Nozari, Ghahremani-Nahr, & Szmelter-Jarosz, 2024).

In the meantime, learning analytics plays a role as a connecting link between data and educational decisions. Learning analytics frameworks that have been developed in recent years attempt to extract meaningful indicators from data streams to provide a dynamic picture of individual and group progress or challenges (Naithani, Raiwani, & Tiwari, n.d.). These analyses become meaningful when raw data is properly aggregated and at the right time. Therefore, seamless data integration is not an option but an infrastructural necessity for the success of learning analytics in intelligent environments (Mills & Khoei, 2024).

From a technical perspective, educational data integration faces challenges such as data format heterogeneity, differences in resource update rates, asynchronous data capture, and lack of cross-platform standards. To overcome these challenges, the use of semantic frameworks, semantic mapping, and API-based technologies have been proposed (Nozari, Ghahremani-Nahr, & Szmelter-Jarosz, 2023). Also, temporal alignment and multimodal fusion algorithms play an effective role in the effective integration of this data (Widiyati et al., 2024).

From a social and ethical perspective, entering environments where behavioral, biological, and cognitive data of learners are recorded and analyzed in real time requires a review of the principles of educational system design. Privacy protection, transparency in data use, and respect for learner autonomy should be considered in the design of these systems. Excessive use of data without control mechanisms may lead to data dependency and unbalanced educational decisions (Udupi, Malali, & Noronha, 2016).

In summary, this chapter explores the role of seamless data integration in predictive learning environments and shows how the combination of AI, IoT, and learning analytics can provide a platform for personalized, dynamic, and effective learning. In this regard, a special focus will be placed on technical challenges, new architectures, and future research in this field. The main goal of this chapter is to provide a theoretical-practical framework for developing environments that not only respond to data, but also use it to shape the future of learning.

## 2. THEORETICAL BACKGROUND

A theoretical understanding of the concept of "seamless data integration" in the context of predictive learning environments requires an exploration of the theoretical foundations of three key areas: learning analytics, artificial intelligence, and the Internet of Things. These three areas have converged in recent years to provide new platforms for personalized, adaptive, and data-driven learning. However, the relationship between them is not simply a matter of technological links, but also involves deeper conceptual layers, analytical, and theoretical logics. This section attempts to explain these theoretical foundations to provide the necessary context for understanding the operational structures in the following chapters.

First, the foundation of learning analytics must be addressed. Learning analytics is the process of collecting, interpreting, and using educational data to better understand and improve learning. At the heart of this process are two key concepts: "accurate representation of the learning process" and "explanatory capacity for educational intervention" (Szmelter-Jarosz, Ghahremani-Nahr, & Nozari, 2021). Without coherent, real-time, and structured data, none of these goals can be achieved. Therefore, traditional analytical frameworks based on data recorded in educational systems such as LMSs have limited effectiveness in the face of the dynamic and real-time realities of connected learning environments (Greven & Schroeder, 2015).

In contrast, new analytical models are based on multi-objective data streams, temporal data, and bio-data. These approaches require the integration and alignment of data from heterogeneous sources, such as sensors, wearables, cameras, conversational systems, and other IoT technologies (Aliahmadi & Nozari, 2023). From a theoretical perspective, such a framework requires a redefinition of the concept of "educational data" so that data not only reflects past performance but also predicts the future state of the learner. This shift in perspective elevates learning analytics from a retrospective tool to a predictive tool.

In the field of artificial intelligence, classical approaches to education were designed based on the analysis of past learner behavior; however, the development of machine learning models, especially deep learning, has enabled real-time data analysis and prediction of future learner responses. In modern machine learning theories, the concept of "adaptive prediction" has been formed based on instantaneous data changes; a model in which the system continuously adjusts itself to new conditions and provides educational solutions based on them (Rehan, 2024). These models will be effective if their information feeding is carried out without interruption, delay, or inconsistency, which precisely defines the key role of seamless integration.

On the other hand, the Internet of Things, as a vast data collection platform, has found a special place in data-driven learning theories. In modern theories of digital learning, technology is not seen as a passive entity, but rather as an active player in the production of learning contexts (Bhosle, 2025). By sensing the environment, physiological state, cognitive engagement, and even emotional states of the learner, connected devices can provide data that is critical for predictive modeling of learning. This data can only be used if the necessary structures are in place to aggregate and analyze it in real time. In other words, without a data integration infrastructure, the potential of the Internet of Things in education will not be realized (Bathaee, Nozari, & Szmelter-Jarosz, 2023).

In this context, the concept of "seamless integration" refers not only to the physical connection of data sources, but also to the semantic, temporal, and operational continuity of data in the analytical context. From a semantic perspective, data must be placed within a common conceptual framework so that their interpretation in learning models can be reliable. From a temporal perspective, data streams must be aligned so that learning events are accurately represented. From an operational perspective, data must be used in educational decision-making processes, not just for observation and reporting (Spaho, Çiço, & Shabani, 2025).

New theories in the design of adaptive learning systems also emphasize the need for data integration. These theories are based on behavioral-cognitive models that view learning not only as the accumulation of knowledge, but also as changes in individual decision-making networks. To understand these decision-making networks, the system must be able to have accurate, continuous, and multimodal information about the behavior and state of the learner (Yeganeh et al., 2025). Such a capability can only be achieved through advanced data integration structures and real-time analytics.

On the other hand, in systems-oriented perspectives, learning environments are considered as intelligent ecosystems in which human, machine and information elements are in constant interaction. These perspectives emphasize the dynamism, self-regulation and adaptation of the system to learner changes (Aliahmadi, Ghahremani-Nahr, & Nozari, 2023). In these models, the seamless integration of data is considered as the bloodstream of this ecosystem: if this flow is disrupted, noisy or delayed, the entire system will fail to adapt to the learner's state.

Also, in recent discussions on personalized learning design, the importance of context-awareness of data has been emphasized. Data has limited analytical value without awareness of the context in which learning occurs. For example, changes in heart rate or physical activity level only make sense when interpreted in the context of a specific learning activity. This kind of advanced interpretation is only possible by aggregating multi-purpose data in real time and aligning it with cognitive constructs (Shinde, 2025).

Ultimately, the theoretical connection between learning analytics, AI, and IoT leads to their synergy in building "adaptive intelligent learning" environments. These environments, unlike traditional systems that are reactive, optimize learning through timely prediction and intervention. This requires a kind of systems, forward-looking, data-driven thinking in which seamless data integration is not a technical tool but a fundamental theoretical principle.

## 3. DATA SOURCES IN CONNECTED LEARNING ECOSYSTEM

In designing predictive learning environments, the variety, volume, and velocity of data play a central role. The data generated in these connected ecosystems originates from multiple sources, each reflecting a part of the learning process. In a general view, these sources can be divided into three main categories: physical and physiological data (sensory and biometric data), behavioral and interactional data (behavioral and interactional data), and instructional and performance data (instructional and performance data). The accurate and real-time integration of these data is the foundation for adaptive and predictive analytics in intelligent learning systems (Ranjan, 2025).

The first and most fundamental source is data from environmental and wearable sensors. This data includes information such as body temperature, heart rate, physical activity level, sleep quality, stress level, respiratory rate, and even brain waves. Wearable sensors such as health bracelets, smart watches, EEG sensors, and motion sensors allow the learning system to understand the current physiological state of the learner. This information is very effective in predicting decreased concentration or fatigue, especially in training that is accompanied by cognitive stress or high mental load (Najafi, Nozari, & Edalatpanah, 2022).

At the same time, environmental sensors such as measuring light, temperature, humidity, noise pollution, or the physical presence and movement of people in the training space provide a basis for understanding the learning environment. Data from these sensors not only help to adjust the physical environment, but also are used in the contextual analysis of behavioral responses. For example, decreased concentration may not be due to cognitive impairment, but rather to environmental changes such as inappropriate lighting or ambient noise (Mehta, Doshi, Butle, Inamdar, & Shinde, 2025).

Figure 1 shows the general architecture of the data flow from physiological and environmental sources in a connected learning environment. In this diagram, the layers of sensing, initial processing at the edge, and data transfer to central analytical systems are clearly identified.

*Figure 1. General structure of environmental and physiological data integration in connected learning environments*

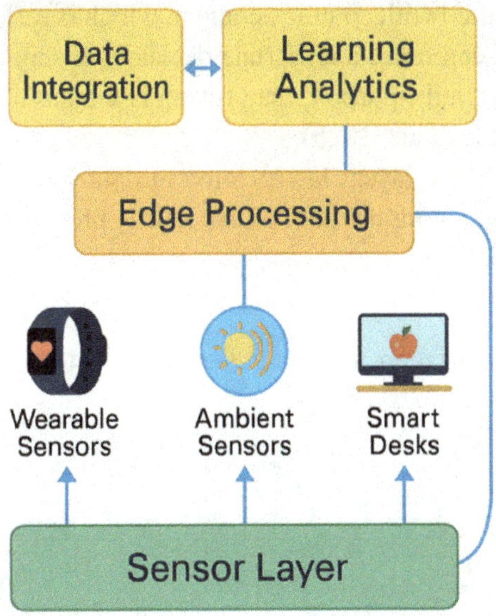


The second category of data is behavioral and interactional data, which is obtained from the learner's interaction with digital platforms and other people. This data includes the duration of study, the pattern of browsing, the order in which they engage with content, participation in group discussions, responses to online assessments, and even the type of mouse or screen touch movements. Analysis of this data can reveal patterns of cognitive engagement, learning strategies, or even test anxiety (Oloruntoba, 2025).

In modern educational systems, this data is often obtained through logs from learning management systems (LMSs), interactive platforms such as discussion boards, learning videos, virtual classrooms, and real-time collaboration tools. One of the main challenges in this category is the heterogeneity of data formats and the asynchronous recording of events. For example, a question may be answered in the LMS, but the reason for the delay in the response can only be explained through real-time analysis of browser activity or interaction with external files (Fallah & Nozari, 2021).

The third category is structured educational data, which includes learner background information (e.g., academic background, major, courses taken), performance data (test scores, homework progress, teacher feedback), and pre-instructional data (entry assessments, prior knowledge level). These data are mostly stored in tables and databases and play a key role in explaining individual differences, personalizing learning paths, and analyzing content effectiveness (Devan, 2025).

The importance of these data is doubled when combined with real-time data. For example, a person with a weak background in a particular subject may experience anxiety when confronted with complex content, which is reflected in physiological data, and the system can make appropriate decisions by combining past and present data. This type of multi-purpose data fusion is the basis of predictive learning environments (Damaševičius, 2025).

Figure 2 shows a three-layer classification of data sources in connected learning environments, indicating the path of data entry, processing, and analysis in an integrated framework.

*Figure 2. Three layers of data sources in the connected learning ecosystem: physiological, interactive, and structured*

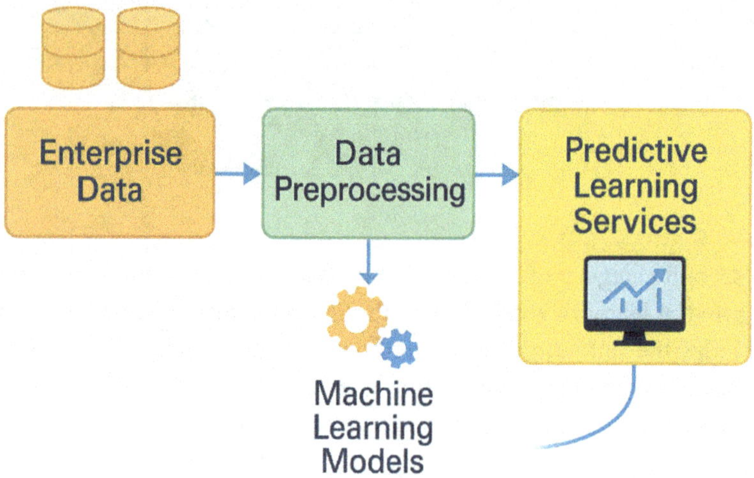


From a data architecture perspective, the successful implementation of a predictive learning system requires integrating these three categories of data in a way that their time, logic, and context are not at odds. Physiological data may be entered at a rate of 10 times per second, while interaction data is recorded discontinuously, and structured data is updated infrequently. Therefore, establishing mechanisms for temporal alignment, data format normalization, and common concept semantics are essential to achieve seamless integration (Aliahmadi, Nozari, Ghahremani-Nahr, & Szmelter-Jarosz, 2022).

Finally, it should be noted that data sources in connected learning environments not only represent the learner's state, but also part of their learning experience. Any analytical design or predictive modeling must be done with respect to the temporal, cognitive, and emotional structure of this data. Only then will intelligent systems be able to correctly understand and respond to educational needs.

## 4. INTEGRATION ARCHITECTURES AND TECHNOLOGIES

In predictive learning environments, having rich and valuable data is not the only guarantee of analytical performance; rather, the architecture and technologies used to integrate this data play a decisive role in the quality of the analysis, the accuracy of predictions, and the response time of the system. Seamless data integration requires the design of architectures that can seamlessly collect, process, and transmit heterogeneous data from different sensor, edge, and cloud layers. This process requires a set of technologies, standards, and technical approaches that are discussed in detail below (Setyadi, Pawirosumarto, Damaris, & Dharma, 2025).

At a basic level, a data integration architecture is usually defined based on three main layers: the Sensor Layer, the Edge Processing Layer, and the Cloud Analytics Layer. Each of these layers performs specific tasks in the data transfer and processing process. The sensor layer is responsible for collecting raw data from physical (e.g., wearables and environmental sensors) and digital (e.g., activity logs) sources. This data often has high sampling rates, high noise, and diverse formats. Therefore, it requires initial filtering, noise reduction, and in some cases compression before being transmitted to higher levels (Nozari, Fallah, Szmelter-Jarosz, & Krzemiński, 2021).

The edge processing layer is essentially the intermediary between the raw data and the central analytical systems. Processing at this layer helps reduce the transmission load, increase the speed of response, and in some cases, analyze the data locally. For example, in scenarios that require real-time detection of concentration loss or stress, one cannot wait for the data to be sent to the cloud servers; rather, the decision must be made at the edge. This logic has led to the edge-fog-cloud architectures as a proposed structure for real-time learning environments (Lu, 2025).

The core analytics layer is responsible for running machine learning models, updating models, storing historical data, and generating long-term insights. In this layer, temporal and conceptual integrity of data is doubly important, as analysis is performed on combined sets of physiological, behavioral, and functional data. If the data structure or timing is inconsistent, the model output will be distorted (Vemula, 2025).

Figure 3 shows a reference architecture for multi-layered data integration in connected learning environments. The diagram includes three main levels (sensor, edge, central analytics) and the data paths between them, which are depicted with distinct colors and icons.

*Figure 3. Proposed architecture for seamless data integration in predictive learning environments*

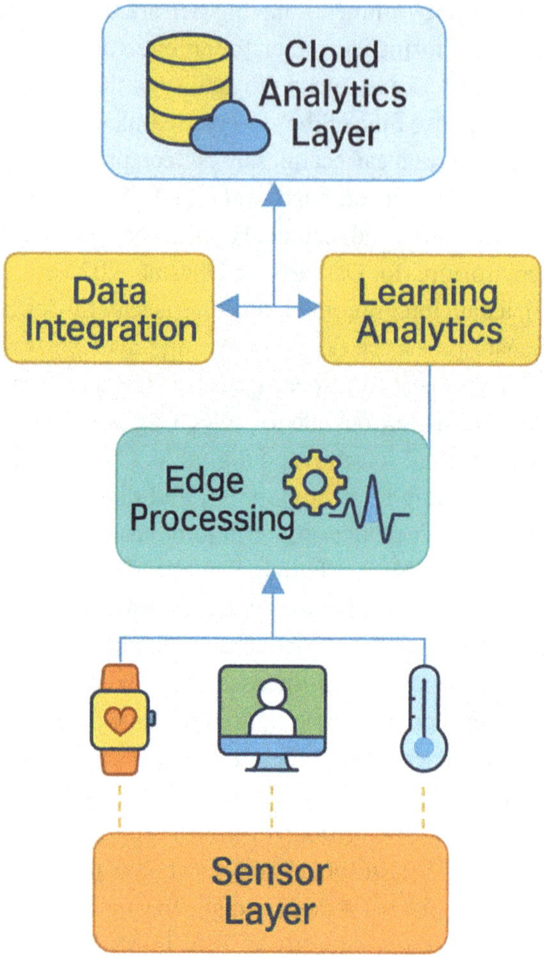


From a technological perspective, tools such as MQTT and CoAP platforms have found widespread use for data transfer from the sensor layer to the edge. These protocols are preferred, especially in environments with limited resources and large data volumes, due to their lightweight nature and ability to work in unstable network conditions. The path from edge to central computing also often uses REST APIs, web services, and in more advanced cases, GraphQL or Kafka-based technologies that provide the ability to manage complex data streams (Lotfi, Najafi, & Nozari, 2016).

In addition to transfer protocols, technologies related to semantic modeling play a crucial role in creating conceptual coherence between data from different sources. Using languages such as RDF or OWL, it is possible to define conceptual relationships between data elements (e.g., the difference between "physiological stress" and "perceived stress") and improve the analytical understanding of the system. This feature is very valuable in systems that need to adapt concepts in different layers (Diameh et al., 2025).

Another important technology is Temporal Alignment. This process, using algorithms such as Dynamic Time Warping or Sliding Window Techniques, aligns data that enters the system at different rates. For example, a 1Hz heartbeat and a minute-long LMS interaction should be overlapped so that the learner's behavior at critical moments can be analyzed (Vetrivel, Vidhyapriya, & Arun, 2025).

Modern architectures also emphasize the use of local learning models (Federated Learning) at the edge layer. In these models, the data remains local and only the model weights are transmitted to the central server. In addition to maintaining privacy, this approach reduces network load and increases the system's response speed. Theoretically, this model is also aligned with the principles of personalized adaptive learning (Mohammadi, Ghazanfari, Nozari, & Shafiezad, 2015).

In addition to the technical infrastructure, data integration architectures must adhere to principles such as scalability, fault tolerance, and data security. Scalability ensures that system performance does not degrade as users or data sources increase. Fault tolerance allows the system to continue to perform satisfactorily in the event of a sensor outage or network latency. And data security, through end-to-end encryption, multi-layered authentication, and role-based access control, maintains user trust in the system (Teles & Moreira, 2025).

Finally, successful integration in these architectures depends on defining transparent workflows. These flows specify how and when each type of data enters the system, what processing is performed on it, and what decisions it contributes to. Accurate documentation of these pathways is important for both developers and educational stakeholders (such as teachers and policymakers) as it helps to explain the mechanism of intelligent decision-making and increases trust in the system (Nozari & Chobar, 2024).

Thus, it can be concluded that data integration architectures in predictive learning environments are not simply technical constructs, but rather multifaceted frameworks that must both meet the analytical needs of AI-driven systems and consider the human, ethical, and practical requirements of education. These architectures connect the layers of data, analytics, and decision-making and are at the heart of the digital transformation of education.

## 5. AI-DRIVEN PREDICTIVE ANALYTICS IN LEARNING ENVIRONMENTS

In connected learning environments, AI has opened up a new path to understanding, modeling, and improving learner performance as a driving force behind predictive analytics. AI-driven predictive analytics is a set of computational approaches that interprets a learner's current state and predicts their future responses using real-time and historical data. These predictions allow the system to dynamically and in real time personalize learning strategies, content levels, or engagement levels, preventing performance decline, cognitive fatigue, or academic failure (Movahed, Aliahmadi, Parsanejad, & Nozari, 2023).

Unlike traditional systems that relied on static statistical data, predictive analytics in modern learning ecosystems leverage sensor data, interaction logs, learning histories, and even psychophysiological data in a multi-purpose and simultaneous manner. This diversity in data has opened up new opportunities for accurate detection of learning patterns. For example, attentional lapses can be detected by aligning heart rate data, eye movements, and decreased engagement with educational content (Venice, Vettriselvan, Rajesh, Suresh, & Abirami, 2025).

In such a context, AI analytics operate in three main layers: (1) behavioral analytics, (2) cognitive analytics, and (3) performance analytics. Behavioral analytics examines how users interact with content, cognitive analytics tracks changes in mental load or attention patterns, and performance analytics focuses on predicting learning outcomes or the likelihood of success in an educational activity (Nozari & Edalatpanah, 2023). Combining these three layers into an intelligent architecture result in the generation of predictive hybrid models that can generate educational interventions in real time.

Figure 4 shows the structure of a predictive analytics system that consists of multi-layered data fusion, machine learning model processing, and real-time feedback generation. This figure highlights four main components: data sources, preprocessing layer, prediction kernel, and intervention systems. Each of these components is clearly and color-coded in the image.

*Figure 4. Conceptual structure of AI-based predictive analytics in connected learning environments*

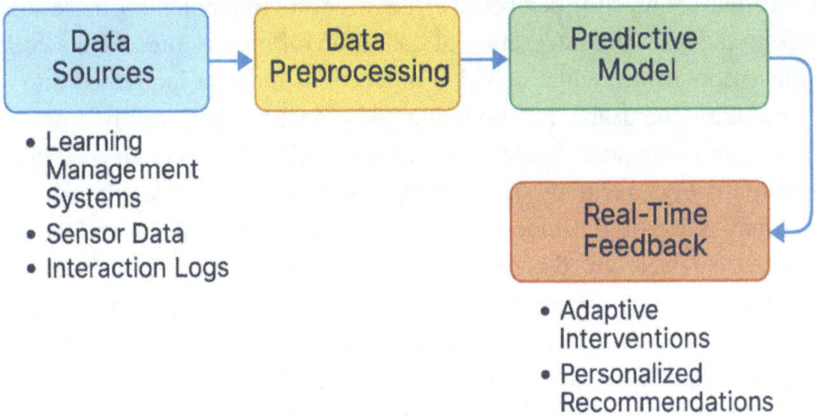


At the core of this architecture are machine learning models such as Random Forest, Gradient Boosting, or deep neural networks that are capable of analyzing complex and nonlinear patterns. These models are trained after a data preprocessing step that includes cleaning, normalization, and feature extraction and are able to predict future learning events. Depending on the nature of the data, temporal models such as LSTM or GRU may be chosen for analyzing time sequences (Isaeva, Karasartova, Dznunusnalieva, Mirzoeva, & Mokliuk, 2025).

Another key capability in these systems is the ability to analyze data in real-time or semi-real-time. In educational environments where learning is changing instantaneously, delays in analysis can lead to missed opportunities for intervention. For this reason, some of the predictive computations are performed at the edge layer to provide a faster response. For example, if a sudden increase in anxiety is detected, the system can pause or simplify the current content without referring to the cloud (Movahed, Movahed, & Nozari, 2024a).

One of the important applications of predictive analytics is to identify learners at risk. This is done by combining behavioral data such as decreased participation, dropping grades, and late submission of assignments. Classification models can estimate the probability of performance decline and alert the teacher. This alert can appear in the form of a dashboard or smart message and help the teacher in decision-making (Nozari, Szmelter-Jarosz, & Rahmaty, 2024).

In addition to predicting negative situations, these analytics are also used to optimize the learning path. For example, if the system detects that the learner has deeper learning when exposed to video content, it will provide more video content in subsequent stages. This process is based on reinforcement learning and educational recommender systems that consider the learner's future behavior (Movahed, Movahed, & Nozari, 2024b).

From a data architecture perspective, the success of implementing these analytics depends on the seamless integration of data from different sources. Data collected from biosensors, LMS, audio or video interactions must be integrated into a uniform structure to be usable for modeling. Otherwise, models will be trained with incomplete or confounded data and predictions will be biased (Bairy, 2025).

Despite the high accuracy of the models, the challenge of "explainability" remains. Many powerful machine learning models (especially deep models) act like black boxes. To overcome this challenge, tools such as SHAP and LIME are used that specify the weight of each feature in the model's prediction. This transparency helps teachers and administrators to understand the reasons for warnings or educational recommendations (Sun, Looi, Yang, & Jia, 2025).

In addition to these technical considerations, the ethical dimension is also important in predictive analytics. Prediction should be accompanied by respect for privacy, informed consent of users, and non-discrimination. The use of sensitive biological and behavioral data can have psychological or social consequences for the learner, if done without their knowledge or consent. Therefore, the responsible design of these systems should be based on transparency, controllability, and interpretability (Rahmaty & Nozari, 2023).

In conclusion, predictive analytics based on artificial intelligence are a powerful tool for transforming education in digital and connected environments. With the ability to understand and predict learner behavior, these systems personalize the learning path and enable targeted and effective interventions. By developing robust architectures, employing accurate models, and adhering to ethical principles, we can expect these technologies to become the core of intelligent learning environments in the near future.

## 6. INTELLIGENT ORCHESTRATION OF MULTIMODAL LEARNING DATA

In predictive and connected learning environments, a huge amount of diverse data is continuously generated from various sources. This data includes physiological, behavioral, cognitive, interactional, environmental, and performance information, each of which is meaningful and capable of extracting knowledge from an analytical perspective. However, the main challenge lies not in collecting this data, but in intelligently orchestrating it; a process known as Intelligent Orchestration of Multimodal Learning Data. In this framework, the goal is for the learning system to be able to select the most relevant and high-quality information from among the multimodal data at the right time, weight it, and enter it into the analytical or decision-making model (Rafiq, Abdelali, Amraouy, Nouh, & Bennane, 2025).

Understanding this process requires first defining the concept of "multimodality" of data. Multi-purpose data in educational environments can include biological signals (such as heart rate or body temperature), digital interactions (such as clicks, page scrolling, time spent on content), speech and audio (tone of voice, pauses), visuals (facial expressions, eye movements), texts (written responses, questions), and performance scores. Each of these data enters the system with a different frequency and format, and their convergence without a coordinating mechanism will lead to analytical chaos (Rathee, Vats, & Sharma, 2025).

This is where the concept of orchestration comes in. Orchestration means consciously integrating data with an understanding of the context of learning and the analytical goal. For example, in a language learning scenario, if the system detects that the learner is experiencing mental fatigue, it may prioritize visual data (such as blinking or unfocused gaze) over digital interaction data in the analysis. This decision is made not based on static weights, but on the context of the learning process at the moment (Nozari, Ghahremani-Nahr, & Najafi, 2023).

Figure 5 illustrates an example of an intelligent multi-objective data orchestration architecture. In this architecture, five main data sources are fed into a pre-processing layer, where context-aware filters and feature selection analyzers are active. The data is then fed into the Orchestration Engine layer and, after weighting and temporal matching, is sent to analytical modules such as machine learning, cognitive models, or adaptive intervention systems.

*Figure 5. Conceptual architecture of intelligent coordination of multi-purpose data in connected learning systems*

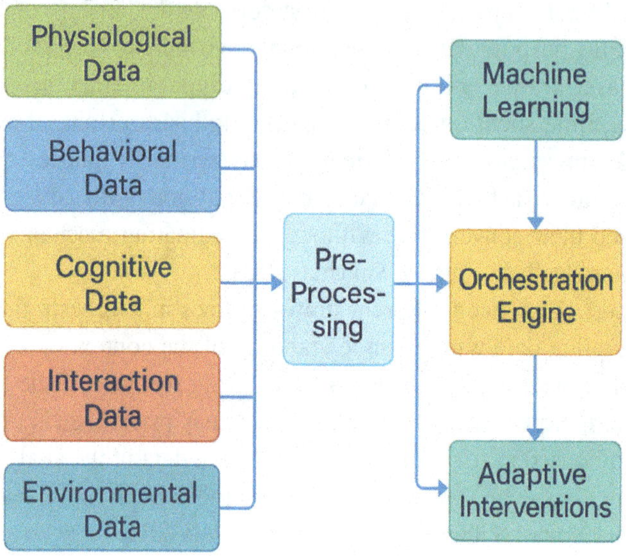


In the Orchestration Engine, decisions about the weight and importance of each data source are made dynamically, based on contextual analysis. For example, if the system detects that the user is interacting with mathematically challenging content, it may prioritize physiological data (such as increased heart rate or nervous tension), but during free browsing, digital interactions or scrolling speed may become more important (Cavus, Dissanayake, & Bell, 2025).

In this regard, advanced technologies such as multi-modal reinforcement learning algorithms, attention networks in deep learning models, and transfer learning approaches are used to translate the meaning of heterogeneous data into a common analytical framework. These algorithms have the ability to teach the learning system what data to enter into the analytical model, when, with what weight, and in what structure (Movahed, Movahed, & Nozari, 2024c).

On the other hand, intelligent orchestration is not limited to data selection, but also includes the timing of their delivery to the analysis core. This process is particularly useful in time-sensitive systems such as surgical skills training, flight control, or live language training. In such scenarios, delays in data processing can lead to the loss of effective educational intervention opportunities. Therefore, the orchestration architecture also needs to support distributed and edge-based computing so that, if needed, the analysis can be performed at the nearest computing node (Dhiman, 2025).

Another important point is to create a common language between the data. Multi-purpose data is generally generated from systems with different structures and languages. For example, heart rate data is in the form of a continuous time series, while LMS interactions are recorded as discrete events. Creating a "common semantic framework" using semantic languages (such as RDF, OWL) or common embedding models (such as BERT or multimodal transformers) enables the co-interpretation of this data (Nozari, 2023).

Furthermore, in advanced systems, the orchestration layer is able to make predictive decisions based on previous predictions and data trend analysis about which data is likely to be of greater importance in the future. For example, if the system detects that a learner is on the path to performance decline, it may send resources such as sleep patterns, physical activity levels, or psychological data to the analyst with higher priority. These intelligent decisions are reminiscent of the central role of orchestration in adaptive and personalized learning systems (Kaddouri et al., 2025).

Finally, the ethical dimension and transparency of the orchestration process should also be considered. Although intelligent orchestration can increase the accuracy of predictions, if it is not properly documented or explainable, it may lead to ambiguous or unfair automated decisions. Therefore, orchestration systems need to support explainable AI and human oversight mechanisms to enable review, regulation, and trust (Nozari, 2024).

In summary, intelligent orchestration of multi-purpose data is the link between "data-centricity" and "cognitive decision-making" in modern educational systems. This process empowers analytical models to detect, predict, and intervene by consciously selecting and combining data sources. In the era of data-driven learning, orchestration is not a technical layer, but a strategic element in the architecture of intelligent education.

## 7. CONCLUSION

In today's fast-paced world, education is rapidly moving away from traditional formats and towards intelligent, dynamic and data-driven ecosystems. Focusing on predictive learning environments, this research shows that seamless data integration, along with leveraging the capabilities of artificial intelligence and the Internet of Things, can create a fundamental transformation in the teaching-learning process. In this direction, it is necessary that multi-purpose data (such as biological, behavioral, cognitive, environmental and interactional data) are not only collected, but also coordinated in a meaningful conceptual and analytical structure so that educational decisions are formed based on a comprehensive, real-time and reliable picture.

During this research, it became clear that the mere use of big data, without designing appropriate analytical infrastructures and architectures, will not only not be useful, but may also lead to analytical errors, misleading decisions and a decrease in the quality of education. For this reason, it was proposed to include different layers in the data structure: from data collection at the sensor level, to preprocessing at the edge layers, and finally advanced analytics in cloud cores. This layering not only increases the speed and accuracy of analysis, but also enables system scalability, stability, and flexibility.

On the other hand, the understanding that data is only valuable when it is meaningful in the appropriate context was repeated throughout the research. Analyzing data without knowledge of time, context, educational goal, and learner status is like issuing a medical prescription without examining the patient. For this reason, analytical models must be context-sensitive and be able to make different decisions based on changing contexts. This requires the development of intelligent data orchestration mechanisms that can dynamically and adaptively select and weight data.

The evidence presented in this study also emphasizes that predictive analytics, if properly designed and implemented, can significantly increase educational effectiveness. These analytics can not only identify academic failure, reduced participation, or mental fatigue before they occur, but can also suggest targeted, personalized, and immediate interventions. In fact, moving from reactive to predictive education is one of the key achievements of using AI in connected learning environments.

At the same time, the challenges of this path should not be overlooked. One of the main challenges is the issue of explainability and reliability of intelligent models. Although many deep learning models are highly accurate, it is difficult for teachers and policymakers to understand the internal logic of their decisions. Therefore, there is a need to design models that are not only accurate, but also interpretable and explainable. Only then can these systems be expected to be deployed in real educational environments and gain social acceptance.

From an ethical perspective, the use of personal, physiological, or cognitive data of learners requires serious considerations in terms of privacy, informed consent, and educational justice. Systems that analyze sensitive data without transparency are not only harmful, but will also lead to a decrease in public trust in educational technologies in the long run. Therefore, responsible design, along with process documentation, human review, and compliance with legal frameworks, must be an integral part of any data-driven educational architecture.

Furthermore, the research showed that the successful implementation of predictive learning environments does not depend only on technology, but also on culture building, teacher empowerment, curriculum redesign, and alignment of educational policies with data-driven requirements. Without supporting institutions, technological infrastructures alone will not be able to create transformation. In the meantime, the role of interdisciplinary researchers, technology-savvy policymakers, and flexible educational administrators will be more prominent than ever.

In conclusion, it can be said that the future of education is undoubtedly moving towards environments that use intelligent data synthesis, predictive analytics, and adaptive intervention to tailor learning for each individual, at each time, and according to their specific needs. This future is not far away, but is in the making, and what is now necessary is conscious participation, thoughtful design, and attention to the technical, human, and ethical dimensions of this transformation. The present research is only an initial step in this direction, but it is a step that can initiate major changes in the digital education system.

## REFERENCES


Aithal, P. S., & Aithal, S. (2023). Predictive analysis on future impact of ubiquitous education technology in higher education and research. [IJAEML]. *International Journal of Applied Engineering and Management Letters*, *7*(3), 88–108. DOI: 10.47992/IJAEML.2581.7000.0190

Aliahmadi, A., Ghahremani-Nahr, J., & Nozari, H. (2023). Pricing decisions in the closed-loop supply chain network, taking into account the queuing system in production centers. *Expert Systems with Applications*, *212*, 118741. DOI: 10.1016/j.eswa.2022.118741

Aliahmadi, A., & Nozari, H. (2023, January). Evaluation of security metrics in AIoT and blockchain-based supply chain by Neutrosophic decision-making method. In Supply chain forum: an international journal (Vol. 24, No. 1, pp. 31-42). Taylor & Francis. DOI: 10.1080/16258312.2022.2101898

Aliahmadi, A., Nozari, H., Ghahremani-Nahr, J., & Szmelter-Jarosz, A. (2022). Evaluation of key impression of resilient supply chain based on artificial intelligence of things (AIoT). arXiv preprint arXiv:2207.13174.

Andrews, M., Owen, A., & Oye, E. (2025). Integrating MuleSoft with Learning Management Systems (LMS): Enhancing Educational Experiences through Seamless Data Connectivity.

Bairy, V. (2025). AI-Driven Network Optimization Improving Connectivity and User Experience Through Intelligent Design in Smart Education. In Smart Education and Sustainable Learning Environments in Smart Cities (pp. 59-76). IGI Global Scientific Publishing.

Bathaee, M., Nozari, H., & Szmelter-Jarosz, A. (2023). Designing a new location-allocation and routing model with simultaneous pick-up and delivery in a closed-loop supply chain network under uncertainty. *Logistics (Basel)*, *7*(1), 3. DOI: 10.3390/logistics7010003

Bhosle, A. (2025). Real-Time Analytics and AI Transforming Data Engineering for Sustainable Learning in Cloud Environments. In Smart Education and Sustainable Learning Environments in Smart Cities (pp. 347-364). IGI Global Scientific Publishing.

Cavus, M., Dissanayake, D., & Bell, M. (2025). Next generation of electric vehicles: AI-driven approaches for predictive maintenance and battery management. *Energies*, *18*(5), 1041. DOI: 10.3390/en18051041

Damaševičius, R. (2025). Quantum Pedagogy: A 21st Century Framework for Education 5.0. In Impacts of AI on Students and Teachers in Education 5.0 (pp. 479-522). IGI Global Scientific Publishing.

Devan, K. (2025). Automating AI Infrastructure: A Guide to Scalable and Optimized Cloud Platforms for Smart Education. In Smart Education and Sustainable Learning Environments in Smart Cities (pp. 123-138). IGI Global Scientific Publishing.

Dhiman, V. (2025). Ensemble Learning Techniques for Advanced Threat Detection in Complex Data Environments for Smart Education. In Smart Education and Sustainable Learning Environments in Smart Cities (pp. 191-206). IGI Global Scientific Publishing.

Diameh, J. T., Oluwatobi, B. T., Daniels, C., Sunday, O. E., Nelson, C. A., & Quaye, M. (2025). Integrating AI-driven predictive analytics in project risk management to optimize decision-making and performance efficiency. *Int. J. Eng. Technol. Res. Manag*, *9*, 373–389.

Fallah, M., & Nozari, H. (2021). Neutrosophic mathematical programming for optimization of multi-objective sustainable biomass supply chain network design. *Computer Modeling in Engineering & Sciences*, *129*(2), 927–951. DOI: 10.32604/cmes.2021.017511

Greven, C., & Schroeder, U. (2015). 2SIMPLE-Symbiotic Interrelated Seamless Integrated Mobile Personalizable Learning Environments. In DeLFI WOrkshops (pp. 232-238).

Isaeva, R., Karasartova, N., Dznunusnalieva, K., Mirzoeva, K., & Mokliuk, M. (2025). Enhancing learning effectiveness through adaptive learning platforms and emerging computer technologies in education. *Jurnal Ilmiah Ilmu Terapan Universitas Jambi*, *9*(1), 144–160. DOI: 10.22437/jiituj.v9i1.37967

Kaddouri, M., Mhamdi, K., Chniete, I., Marhraoui, M., Khaldi, M., & Jmad, S. (2025). Adopting AI in Education: Technical Challenges and Ethical Constraints. In Fostering Inclusive Education With AI and Emerging Technologies (pp. 25-72). IGI Global.

Lee, C. S. (2007). Diagnostic, predictive and compositional modeling with data mining in integrated learning environments. *Computers & Education*, *49*(3), 562–580. DOI: 10.1016/j.compedu.2005.10.010

Lotfi, F. H. Z., Najafi, S. E., & Nozari, H. (Eds.). (2016). *Data envelopment analysis and effective performance assessment*. IGI Global.

Lu, W. (2025, January). Scalable and Interpretable Learning Tool Development within Game-based Learning Environment: A Case Study of Mission HydroSci. In *Companion Proceedings of the 2025 ACM International Conference on Supporting Group Work* (pp. 124-126). DOI: 10.1145/3688828.3699657

Mehta, P. S., Doshi, S. T., Butle, S. N., Inamdar, S. C., & Shinde, S. D. (2025). The Fusion of Academia and Industry via Cloud Integration in Education: Customized Learning and Adaptive Systems. In Bridging Academia and Industry Through Cloud Integration in Education (pp. 109-144). IGI Global Scientific Publishing.

Mills, M. A., & Khoei, T. T. (2024, September). Future-Proofing Computer Behavior: A Framework for Predictive Analytics and Seamless Device Integration. In 2024 2nd International Conference on Artificial Intelligence, Blockchain, and Internet of Things (AIBThings) (pp. 1-5). IEEE. DOI: 10.1109/AIBThings63359.2024.10863652

Mohammadi, H., Ghazanfari, M., Nozari, H., & Shafiezad, O. (2015). Combining the theory of constraints with system dynamics: A general model (case study of the subsidized milk industry). International journal of management science and engineering management, 10(2), 102-108.

Moon, J., Lee, D., Choi, G. W., Seo, J., Do, J., & Lim, T. (2024). Learning analytics in seamless learning environments: A systematic review. *Interactive Learning Environments*, *32*(7), 3208–3225.

Movahed, A. B., Aliahmadi, A., Parsanejad, M., & Nozari, H. (2023). A systematic review of collaboration in supply chain 4.0 with meta-synthesis method. *Supply Chain Analytics*, *4*, 100052. DOI: 10.1016/j.sca.2023.100052

Movahed, A. B., Movahed, A. B., & Nozari, H. (2024). Opportunities and challenges of marketing 5.0. Smart and Sustainable Interactive Marketing, 1-21.

Movahed, A. B., Movahed, A. B., & Nozari, H. (2024). Opportunities and challenges of smart supply chain in Industry 5.0. Information Logistics for Organizational Empowerment and Effective Supply Chain Management, 108-138.

Movahed, A. B., Movahed, A. B., & Nozari, H. (2024). Marketing 6.0 Conceptualization. In Advanced Businesses in Industry 6.0 (pp. 15-31). IGI Global.

Naithani, K., Raiwani, Y. P., & Tiwari, S. Analyzing the Seamless Integration of Machine Learning and Internet of Things in the Daily Dynamics of Contemporary Living. In Evolution of Machine Learning and Internet of Things Applications in Biomedical Engineering (pp. 201-217). CRC Press. DOI: 10.1201/9781003476207-13

Najafi, S. E., Nozari, H., & Edalatpanah, S. A. (2022). Artificial Intelligence of Things (AIoT) and Industry 4.0–Based Supply Chain (FMCG Industry). A roadmap for enabling industry 4.0 by artificial intelligence, 31-41.

Nozari, H. (Ed.). (2023). *Building Smart and Sustainable Businesses with Transformative Technologies*. IGI Global. DOI: 10.4018/979-8-3693-0210-1

Nozari, H. (2024). Supply chain 6.0 and moving towards hyper-intelligent processes. In *Information logistics for organizational empowerment and effective supply chain management* (pp. 1–13). IGI Global.

Nozari, H., & Chobar, A. P. (2024). The Dimensions and Components of Marketing 5.0: Introduction to Marketing 6.0. In Advanced Businesses in Industry 6.0 (pp. 75-86). IGI Global.

Nozari, H., & Edalatpanah, S. A. (2023). Smart systems risk management in IoT-based supply chain. In *Advances in reliability, failure and risk analysis* (pp. 251–268). Springer Nature Singapore. DOI: 10.1007/978-981-19-9909-3_11

Nozari, H., Fallah, M., Kazemipoor, H., & Najafi, S. E. (2021). Big data analysis of IoT-based supply chain management considering FMCG industries. *Бизнес-информатика*, *15*(1, 1 (eng)), 78–96. DOI: 10.17323/2587-814X.2021.1.78.96

Nozari, H., Fallah, M., Szmelter-Jarosz, A., & Krzemiński, M. (2021). Analysis of security criteria for IoT-based supply chain: a case study of FMCG industries. Central European Management Journal, 29(4).

Nozari, H., Ghahremani-Nahr, J., & Najafi, E. (2023). The role of Internet of things and Blockchain in the development of agile and sustainable supply chains. In Digital Supply Chain, Disruptive Environments, and the Impact on Retailers (pp. 271-282). IGI Global. DOI: 10.4018/978-1-6684-7298-9.ch015

Nozari, H., Ghahremani-Nahr, J., & Szmelter-Jarosz, A. (2023). A multi-stage stochastic inventory management model for transport companies including several different transport modes. *International Journal of Management Science and Engineering Management*, *18*(2), 134–144. DOI: 10.1080/17509653.2022.2042747

Nozari, H., Ghahremani-Nahr, J., & Szmelter-Jarosz, A. (2024). AI and machine learning for real-world problems. [), Elsevier.]. *Advances in Computers*, *134*, 1–12. DOI: 10.1016/bs.adcom.2023.02.001

Nozari, H., Szmelter-Jarosz, A., & Ghahremani-Nahr, J. (2021). The ideas of sustainable and green marketing based on the internet of everything—The case of the dairy industry. *Future Internet*, *13*(10), 266. DOI: 10.3390/fi13100266

Nozari, H., Szmelter-Jarosz, A., & Ghahremani-Nahr, J. (2022). Analysis of the challenges of artificial intelligence of things (AIoT) for the smart supply chain (case study: FMCG industries). *Sensors (Basel)*, *22*(8), 2931. DOI: 10.3390/s22082931 PMID: 35458916

Nozari, H., Szmelter-Jarosz, A., & Rahmaty, M. (2024). Smart marketing based on artificial intelligence of things (AIoT) and Blockchain and evaluating critical success factors. In *Smart and Sustainable Interactive Marketing* (pp. 68–82). IGI Global Scientific Publishing. DOI: 10.4018/979-8-3693-1339-8.ch005

Oloruntoba, N. O. (2025). AI-Driven autonomous database management: Self-tuning, predictive query optimization, and intelligent indexing in enterprise it environments. *World Journal of Advanced Research and Reviews*, *25*(2), 1558–1580. DOI: 10.30574/wjarr.2025.25.2.0534

Rafiq, J. E., Abdelali, Z., Amraouy, M., Nouh, S., & Bennane, A. (2025). Predicting academic performance: toward a model based on machine learning and learner's intelligences. International Journal of Electrical & Computer Engineering (2088-8708), 15(1).

Rahmaty, M., & Nozari, H. (2023). Optimization of the hierarchical supply chain in the pharmaceutical industry. *Edelweiss Applied Science and Technology*, *7*(2), 104–123. DOI: 10.55214/25768484.v7i2.376

Ranjan, R. (2025). AI-Powered Data Platforms Bridging the Gap Between Analytics and Action in Smart Education. In Smart Education and Sustainable Learning Environments in Smart Cities (pp. 107-122). IGI Global Scientific Publishing.

Rathee, R., Vats, H., & Sharma, S. (2025). AI-Enhanced Predictive Scheduling Optimizing Project Timelines for Blue-Green Infrastructure Deployment. In Integrating Blue-Green Infrastructure Into Urban Development (pp. 61-80). IGI Global Scientific Publishing.

Rehan, H. (2024). Advancing Cancer Treatment with AI-Driven Personalized Medicine and Cloud-Based Data Integration. *Journal of Machine Learning in Pharmaceutical Research*, *4*(2), 1–40.

Setyadi, A., Pawirosumarto, S., Damaris, A., & Dharma, R. (2025). Risk management, digital technology literacy, and modern learning environments in enhancing learning innovation performance: A framework for higher education. *Education and Information Technologies*, *30*(11), 1–29. DOI: 10.1007/s10639-025-13380-4

Shinde, R. (2025). Predictive Scheduling in the Age of AI: Optimizing Project Timelines for Sustainable Learning Environments. In Smart Education and Sustainable Learning Environments in Smart Cities (pp. 333-346). IGI Global Scientific Publishing.

Spaho, E., Çiço, B., & Shabani, I. (2025). IoT Integration Approaches into Personalized Online Learning: Systematic Review. *Computers*, *14*(2), 63. DOI: 10.3390/computers14020063

Sun, D., Looi, C. K., Yang, Y., & Jia, F. (2025). Exploring students' learning performance in computer-supported collaborative learning environment during and after pandemic: Cognition and interaction. *British Journal of Educational Technology*, *56*(1), 128–149. DOI: 10.1111/bjet.13492

Szmelter-Jarosz, A., Ghahremani-Nahr, J., & Nozari, H. (2021). A neutrosophic fuzzy optimisation model for optimal sustainable closed-loop supply chain network during COVID-19. *Journal of Risk and Financial Management*, *14*(11), 519. DOI: 10.3390/jrfm14110519

Teles, R. O., & Moreira, F. T. (2025). Integrating AI in Formative Assessment Under UDL Principles in Diverse Learning Environments. In Improving Student Assessment With Emerging AI Tools (pp. 95-122). IGI Global Scientific Publishing.

Udupi, P. K., Malali, P., & Noronha, H. (2016, March). Big data integration for transition from e-learning to smart learning framework. In 2016 3rd MEC international conference on big data and smart city (ICBDSC) (pp. 1-4). IEEE. DOI: 10.1109/ICBDSC.2016.7460379

Vemula, V. R. (2025). AI-Enhanced Self-Healing Cloud Architectures for Data Integrity, Privacy, and Sustainable Learning. In Smart Education and Sustainable Learning Environments in Smart Cities (pp. 93-106). IGI Global Scientific Publishing.

Venice, J. A., Vettriselvan, R., Rajesh, D., Suresh, N. V., & Abirami, P. (2025). Enabling Personalized Learning and Adaptive Systems Through Strategic Management: Cloud Integration in Education. In Bridging Academia and Industry Through Cloud Integration in Education (pp. 49-72). IGI Global Scientific Publishing.

Vetrivel, S. C., Vidhyapriya, P., & Arun, V. P. (2025). Data Science for Learning Analytics: Understanding and Improving Learning Processes. In Driving Quality Education Through AI and Data Science (pp. 409-432). IGI Global Scientific Publishing.

Widiyati, T. D. S. C., Setyosari, P., Praherdhiono, H., Nakaya, A., & Khotimah, K. (2024). Seamless Learning to Enhancing Resilience and Professional Ethics in Higher Education Students. *Journal of Ecohumanism*, *3*(8), 12227–12239.

Yeganeh, L. N., Fenty, N. S., Chen, Y., Simpson, A., & Hatami, M. (2025). The Future of Education: A Multi-Layered Metaverse Classroom Model for Immersive and Inclusive Learning. *Future Internet*, *17*(2), 63. DOI: 10.3390/fi17020063

# Compilation of References


Adedoyin, O. B., & Soykan, E. (2023). Covid-19 pandemic and online learning: The challenges and opportunities. *Interactive Learning Environments*, *31*(2), 863–875. DOI: 10.1080/10494820.2020.1813180

Ahmad, B., Zaman, S. U., & Alam, S. H. (2025). Role of AI-Based Marketing Activities in Shaping Brand Experience, Preference, and Loyalty. *Qlantic Journal of Social Sciences and Humanities*, *6*(1), 237–253. DOI: 10.55737/qjssh.vi-i.25320

Aithal, P. S., & Aithal, S. (2023). Predictive analysis on future impact of ubiquitous education technology in higher education and research. [IJAEML]. *International Journal of Applied Engineering and Management Letters*, *7*(3), 88–108. DOI: 10.47992/IJAEML.2581.7000.0190

Akcanca, N. (2020). 21st Century Skills: The Predictive Role of Attitudes Regarding STEM Education and Problem-Based Learning. *International Journal of Progressive Education*, *16*(5), 443–458. DOI: 10.29329/ijpe.2020.277.27

Akcapınar, G., & Bayazıt, A. (2018). Investigating Video Viewing Behaviors of Students with Different Learning Approaches Using Video Analytics. *Turkish Online Journal of Distance Education*, *19*(4), 116–125. DOI: 10.17718/tojde.471907

Alam, A., & Mohanty, A. (2022, December). Predicting students' performance employing educational data mining techniques, machine learning, and learning analytics. In International Conference on Communication, Networks and Computing (pp. 166-177). Cham: Springer Nature Switzerland.

Alangari, T. S. (2022). Online STEM education during COVID-19 period: A systematic review of perceptions in higher education. *Eurasia Journal of Mathematics, Science and Technology Education*, *18*(5), em2105. DOI: 10.29333/ejmste/11986

Albtosh, L. (2025). Challenges and Limitations of Using LLMs in Software Security. In *Application of Large Language Models (LLMs) for Software Vulnerability Detection* (pp. 439–464). IGI Global Scientific Publishing., DOI: 10.4018/979-8-3693-9311-6.ch012

Alfredo, R., Echeverria, V., Jin, Y., Yan, L., Swiecki, Z., Gašević, D., & Martinez-Maldonado, R. (2024). Human-centred learning analytics and AI in education: A systematic literature review. Computers and Education: Artificial Intelligence, 100215.

Algahtani, A. M. I. R. A. H. (2024). A Comparative Study of AI-Based Educational Tools: Evaluating User Interface Experience and Educational Impact. *Journal of Theoretical and Applied Information Technology, 102*(5).

Aliahmadi, A., & Nozari, H. (2023, January). Evaluation of security metrics in AIoT and blockchain-based supply chain by Neutrosophic decision-making method. In Supply chain forum: an international journal (Vol. 24, No. 1, pp. 31-42). Taylor & Francis. DOI: 10.1080/16258312.2022.2101898

Aliahmadi, A., Nozari, H., Ghahremani-Nahr, J., & Szmelter-Jarosz, A. (2022). Evaluation of key impression of resilient supply chain based on artificial intelligence of things (AIoT). arXiv preprint arXiv:2207.13174.

Aliahmadi, A., Ghahremani-Nahr, J., & Nozari, H. (2023). Pricing decisions in the closed-loop supply chain network, taking into account the queuing system in production centers. *Expert Systems with Applications, 212*, 118741. DOI: 10.1016/j.eswa.2022.118741

Aliahmadi, A., Movahed, A. B., & Nozari, H. (2024). Collaboration analysis in supply chain 4.0 for smart businesses. In *Building Smart and Sustainable Businesses With Transformative Technologies* (pp. 103–122). IGI Global Scientific Publishing.

Alsobhi, H. A., Alakhtar, R. A., Ubaid, A., Hussain, O. K., & Hussain, F. K. (2023). Blockchain-based micro-credentialing system in higher education institutions: Systematic literature review. *Knowledge-Based Systems, 265*, 110238. DOI: 10.1016/j.knosys.2022.110238

Analytic Steps. (2021). Top 10 Big Data Analytics Tools. https://www.analyticssteps.com/blogs/top-10-big-data-analytics-tools

Anderson, J. (2025). *Innovative Visual Merchandising Strategies in the Digital Era.* https://www.researchgate.net/publication/389272534

Andini, S. (n.d.). *PROJECT-BASED LEARNING MODEL TO PROMOTE STUDENTS CRITICAL AND CREATIVE THINKING SKILLS. 17.*

Andrews, M., Owen, A., & Oye, E. (2025). Integrating MuleSoft with Learning Management Systems (LMS): Enhancing Educational Experiences through Seamless Data Connectivity.

Andronie, M., Lăzăroiu, G., Iatagan, M., Hurloiu, I., & Dijmărescu, I. (2021). Sustainable cyber-physical production systems in big data-driven smart urban economy: A systematic literature review. *Sustainability (Basel)*, *13*(2), 751. DOI: 10.3390/su13020751

Andronie, M., Lăzăroiu, G., tefănescu, R., U ă, C., & Dijmărescu, I. (2021). Sustainable, smart, and sensing technologies for cyber-physical manufacturing systems: A systematic literature review. *Sustainability (Basel)*, *13*(10), 5495. DOI: 10.3390/su13105495

Annapareddy, V. N., Kumar, P. K., Sabeenian, R. S., Ambika, M., Balaram, A., & Kumararaja, K. (2025). *Artificial Intelligence Infused Real Time Interaction Systems for Next Generation Retail Experiences Personalized Consumer Insights and Augmented Shopping Journeys*., DOI: 10.2991/978-94-6463-718-2_19

Astawan, I. G., Suarjana, I. M., Werang, B. R., Asaloei, S. I., Sianturi, M., & Elele, E. C. (2023). STEM-Based Scientific Learning and Its Impact on Students' Critical and Creative Thinking Skills: An Empirical Study. *Jurnal Pendidikan IPA Indonesia*, *12*(3), 482–492. DOI: 10.15294/jpii.v12i3.46882

Attanasio, M., Mazza, M., Le Donne, I., Nigri, A., & Valenti, M. (2024). Salience Network in Autism: Preliminary results on functional connectivity analysis in resting state. *European Archives of Psychiatry and Clinical Neuroscience*, •••, 1–14. DOI: 10.1007/s00406-024-01949-y PMID: 39673625

Awaji, B., & Solaiman, E. (2022). Design, implementation, and evaluation of blockchain-based trusted achievement record system for students in higher education. arXiv preprint arXiv:2204.12547. DOI: 10.5220/0011044200003182

Ayub Khan, A., Laghari, A. A., Shaikh, A. A., Bourouis, S., Mamlouk, A. M., & Alshazly, H. (2021). Educational blockchain: A secure degree attestation and verification traceability architecture for higher education commission. *Applied Sciences (Basel, Switzerland)*, *11*(22), 10917. DOI: 10.3390/app112210917

Azmir, F. (2025). *Integration of Smart Technologies and Sustainable, Purpose-Driven Consumer Engagement: A Review Outline*. https://doi.org/DOI: 10.5281/zenodo.15735254

Bairy, V. (2025). AI-Driven Network Optimization Improving Connectivity and User Experience Through Intelligent Design in Smart Education. In Smart Education and Sustainable Learning Environments in Smart Cities (pp. 59-76). IGI Global Scientific Publishing.

Baleja, K. (2024, July). Exploring the Efficacy of Personalized Learning Pathways Utilizing Artificial Intelligence in Education. In EdMedia+ Innovate Learning (pp. 157-161). Association for the Advancement of Computing in Education (AACE).

Barron, K. E., & Powell, D. N. (2014). Options on how to organize and structure advising. *Academic advising: A handbook for advisors and students, 1*, 14-23.

Basu, T. (2013). Five pillars of prescriptive analytics success. *Analytics magazine, 8*,8-12.

Bathaee, M., Nozari, H., & Szmelter-Jarosz, A. (2023). Designing a new location-allocation and routing model with simultaneous pick-up and delivery in a closed-loop supply chain network under uncertainty. *Logistics (Basel)*, *7*(1), 3. DOI: 10.3390/logistics7010003

Baxter, S. L., Marks, C., Kuo, T. T., Ohno-Machado, L., & Weinreb, R. N. (2019). Machine learning-based predictive modeling of surgical intervention in glaucoma using systemic data from electronic health records. *American Journal of Ophthalmology*, *208*, 30–40. DOI: 10.1016/j.ajo.2019.07.005 PMID: 31323204

Beckman, S. (2002). The Nature of artifacts. In Dahlbom, B., Beckman, S., & Nilsson, G. B. (Eds.), *Artifacts and Artificial Science* (pp. 45–92). Almqvist & Wiksell International.

Bell, S. (2010). Project-Based Learning for the 21st Century: Skills for the Future. *The Clearing House: A Journal of Educational Strategies, Issues and Ideas*, *83*(2), 39–43. DOI: 10.1080/00098650903505415

Betsch, T. (2008). The nature of intuition and its neglect in research on judgment and decision making. *Intuition in judgment and decision making*, 3-22.

Betsch, T., & Glöckner, A. (2010). Intuition in judgment and decision making: Extensive thinking without effort. *Psychological Inquiry*, *21*(4), 279–294. DOI: 10.1080/1047840X.2010.517737

Bhimavarapu, U. (2026). Optimizing Sentiment Analysis in Legal Documents With BERT and GPT Integration. In *Reshaping Criminology with AI* (pp. 381–402). IGI Global Scientific Publishing., DOI: 10.4018/979-8-3693-8871-6.ch016

Bhosle, A. (2025). Real-Time Analytics and AI Transforming Data Engineering for Sustainable Learning in Cloud Environments. In Smart Education and Sustainable Learning Environments in Smart Cities (pp. 347-364). IGI Global Scientific Publishing.

Boyd, D., & Crawford, K. (2012). Critical questions for big data: Provocations for a cultural, technological, and scholarly phenomenon. *Information Communication and Society*, *15*(5), 662–679. DOI: 10.1080/1369118X.2012.678878

Brooks, C., & Greer, J. (2014, March). Explaining predictive models to learning specialists using personas. In *Proceedings of the fourth international conference on learning analytics and knowledge* (pp. 26-30). DOI: 10.1145/2567574.2567612

Bryson, J. (2004). What to do when stakeholders matter. *Public Management Review*, *6*(1), 21–53. DOI: 10.1080/14719030410001675722

Bujang, S. D. A., Selamat, A., & Krejcar, O. (2021, February). A predictive analytics model for students grade prediction by supervised machine learning. []. IOP Publishing.]. *IOP Conference Series. Materials Science and Engineering*, *1051*(1), 012005. DOI: 10.1088/1757-899X/1051/1/012005

Candelieri, A., & Archetti, F. (2019). Global optimization in machine learning: The design of a predictive analytics application. *Soft Computing*, *23*(9), 2969–2977. DOI: 10.1007/s00500-018-3597-8

Carella, G., & Conte, M. (2024). Supporting Problem-Solving skills through Strategic Design tools: an exploratory study. In *ICERI2024 Proceedings* (pp. 3937-3945). DOI: 10.21125/iceri.2024.0997

Carroll, J. M., & Swatman, P. A. (2000). Structured-case: A methodological framework for building theory in information systems research. *European Journal of Information Systems*, *9*(4), 235–242. DOI: 10.1057/palgrave.ejis.3000374

Cavus, M., Dissanayake, D., & Bell, M. (2025). Next generation of electric vehicles: AI-driven approaches for predictive maintenance and battery management. *Energies*, *18*(5), 1041. DOI: 10.3390/en18051041

Cerro Martinez, J. P., Guitert Catasus, M., & Romeu Fontanillas, T. (2020). Impact of using learning analytics in asynchronous online discussions in higher education. *International Journal of Educational Technology in Higher Education*, *17*(1), 1–19. DOI: 10.1186/s41239-020-00217-y

Chandramma, R., Babu, K. S., Ranjith, K. S., Sinha, A. K., Neerugatti, V., & Reddy, D. S. (2025, January). Enhancing E-learning Accessibility through AI (Artificial Intelligence) and Inclusive Design. In 2025 6th International Conference on Mobile Computing and Sustainable Informatics (ICMCSI) (pp. 1466-1471). IEEE.

Chang, Y., Wang, X., Wang, J., Wu, Y., Yang, L., Zhu, K., Chen, H., Yi, X., Wang, C., Wang, Y., Ye, W., Zhang, Y., Chang, Y., Yu, P. S., Yang, Q., & Xie, X. (2024). A Survey on Evaluation of Large Language Models. *ACM Transactions on Intelligent Systems and Technology*, *15*(3), 1–45. DOI: 10.1145/3641289

Chanthala, C., Santiboon, T., & Ponkham, K. (2018, January). Instructional designing the STEM education model for fostering creative thinking abilities in physics laboratory environment classes. In AIP Conference Proceedings (Vol. 1923, No. 1). AIP Publishing. DOI: 10.1063/1.5019501

Chen, J., Brandimarte, L., & Susarla, A. (2024). Does Increasing Reliance on Artificial Intelligence Boost Creativity? Assessing AI-Augmented Creativity with Large Language Models. Assessing AI-Augmented Creativity with Large Language Models (July 17, 2024).

Chen, S.-Y., Lai, C.-F., Lai, Y.-H., & Su, Y.-S. (2022). Effect of project-based learning on development of students' creative thinking. *International Journal of Electrical Engineering Education*, *59*(3), 232–250. DOI: 10.1177/0020720919846808

Chen, T. I., Lin, S. K., & Chung, H. C. (2023). Gamified Educational Robots Lead an Increase in Motivation and Creativity in STEM Education. *Journal of Baltic Science Education*, *22*(3), 427–438. DOI: 10.33225/jbse/23.22.427

Christopher, M., Payne, A., & Ballantyne, B. (2002). *Relationship Marketing: Creating Stakeholder Value* (2nd revised edition). Butterworth-Heinemann.

Clarke, J., Nelson, K., & Stoodley, I. (2013, January). The place of higher education institutions in assessing student engagement, success and retention: A maturity model to guide practice. In *Proceedings of the 36th Higher Education Research and Development Society of Australasia Conference (HERDSA 2013)*. University of Southern Queensland.

Clark, J. A., Liu, Y., & Isaias, P. (2020). Critical success factors for implementing learning analytics in higher education: A mixed-method inquiry. *Australasian Journal of Educational Technology*, *36*(6), 89–106. DOI: 10.14742/ajet.6164

Clarkson, M. E. (1995). A stakeholder framework for analyzing and evaluating corporate social performance. *Academy of Management Review*, *20*(1), 92–117. DOI: 10.2307/258888

Clow, D. (2013). An overview of learning analytics. *Teaching in Higher Education, 18*(6), 683–695. DOI: 10.1080/13562517.2013.827653

Cogliano, M., Bernacki, M. L., Hilpert, J. C., & Strong, C. L. (2022). A self-regulated learning analytics prediction-and-intervention design: Detecting and supporting struggling biology students. *Journal of Educational Psychology, 114*(8), 1801–1816. DOI: 10.1037/edu0000745

Cooper, R., & Heaverlo, C. (2013). Problem Solving and Creativity and Design: What Influence Do They Have on Girls' Interest in STEM Subject Areas? *American Journal of Engineering Education, 4*(1), 27–38. DOI: 10.19030/ajee.v4i1.7856

Creed, C., Al-Kalbani, M., Theil, A., Sarcar, S., & Williams, I. (2023). Inclusive Augmented and Virtual Reality: A Research Agenda. *International Journal of Human-Computer Interaction.* Advance online publication. DOI: 10.1080/10447318.2023.2247614

Cukurova, M. (2025). The interplay of learning, analytics and artificial intelligence in education: A vision for hybrid intelligence. *British Journal of Educational Technology, 56*(2), 469–488. DOI: 10.1111/bjet.13514

Dahlbom, B. (1996). The New informatics. *Scandinavian Journal of Information Systems, 8*, 29–48.

Damaševičius, R. (2025). Quantum Pedagogy: A 21st Century Framework for Education 5.0. In Impacts of AI on Students and Teachers in Education 5.0 (pp. 479-522). IGI Global Scientific Publishing.

Daniel, B. (2015). Big Data and analytics in higher education: Opportunities and challenges. *British Journal of Educational Technology, 46*(5), 904–920. DOI: 10.1111/bjet.12230

Darvishi, A., Khosravi, H., Sadiq, S., & Gašević, D. (2022). Incorporating AI and learning analytics to build trustworthy peer assessment systems. *British Journal of Educational Technology, 53*(4), 844–875. DOI: 10.1111/bjet.13233

De Laet, T., Millecamp, M., Ortiz-Rojas, M., Jimenez, A., Maya, R., & Verbert, K. (2020). Adoption and impact of a learning analytics dashboard supporting the advisor—Student dialogue in a higher education institute in Latin America. *British Journal of Educational Technology, 51*(4), 1002–1018. DOI: 10.1111/bjet.12962

Demartini, C. G., Sciascia, L., Bosso, A., & Manuri, F. (2024). Artificial intelligence bringing improvements to adaptive learning in education: A case study. *Sustainability (Basel), 16*(3), 1347. DOI: 10.3390/su16031347

Devan, K. (2025). Automating AI Infrastructure: A Guide to Scalable and Optimized Cloud Platforms for Smart Education. In Smart Education and Sustainable Learning Environments in Smart Cities (pp. 123-138). IGI Global Scientific Publishing.

Dewi, H. R., Mayasari, T., & Handhika, J. (2019). Increasing creative thinking skills and understanding of physics concepts through application of stem-based inquiry. [Jurnal Penelitian Pendidikan IPA]. *JPPIPA*, *4*(1), 25–30.

Dhiman, V. (2025). Ensemble Learning Techniques for Advanced Threat Detection in Complex Data Environments for Smart Education. In Smart Education and Sustainable Learning Environments in Smart Cities (pp. 191-206). IGI Global Scientific Publishing.

Diameh, J. T., Oluwatobi, B. T., Daniels, C., Sunday, O. E., Nelson, C. A., & Quaye, M. (2025). Integrating AI-driven predictive analytics in project risk management to optimize decision-making and performance efficiency. *Int. J. Eng. Technol. Res. Manag*, *9*, 373–389.

Doss, A. N., Krishnan, R., Karuppasamy, A. D., & Sam, B. (2024). Learning analytics model for predictive analysis of learners behavior for an indigenous MOOC platform (tadakhul system) in Oman. *International Journal of Information and Education Technology (IJIET)*, *14*(7), 961–967. DOI: 10.18178/ijiet.2024.14.7.2123

Duan, Y., Edwards, J. S., & Dwivedi, Y. K. (2019). Artificial intelligence for decision making in the era of Big Data–evolution, challenges and research agenda. *International Journal of Information Management*, *48*, 63–71. DOI: 10.1016/j.ijinfomgt.2019.01.021

Dwivedi, D. N., Mahanty, G., & nath Dwivedi, V. (2024). The role of predictive analytics in personalizing education: tailoring learning paths for individual student success. In Enhancing Education With Intelligent Systems and Data-Driven Instruction (pp. 44-59). IGI Global Scientific Publishing.

Dyagilev, K., & Saria, S. (2016). Learning (predictive) risk scores in the presence of censoring due to interventions. *Machine Learning*, *102*(3), 323–348. DOI: 10.1007/s10994-015-5527-7

Eager, B., & Brunton, R. (2023). Prompting higher education towards AI-augmented teaching and learning practice. *Journal of University Teaching & Learning Practice*, *20*(5), 1–19. DOI: 10.53761/1.20.5.02

Ejjami, R. (n.d.). Marketing 5.0: Harnessing AI and Emerging Technologies to Shape the Future of Business. In *IJFMR240426423* (Vol. 6, Issue 4). www.ijfmr.com

Elias, T. (2011). Learning analytics. *Learning*, 1-22.Retrieved June 16, 2025, from https://citeseerx.ist.psu.edu/document?repid=rep1&type=pdf&doi=732e452659685fe3950b0e515a28ce89d9c5592a

Ender, S. C., Winston, R. B.Jr, & Miller, T. K. (1982). Academic advising as student development. *New Directions for Student Services*, *1982*(17), 3–18. DOI: 10.1002/ss.37119821703

Evans, J. (2003). In two minds: Dual-process accounts of reasoning. *Trends in Cognitive Sciences*, *7*(10), 454–459. DOI: 10.1016/j.tics.2003.08.012 PMID: 14550493

Ezzaim, A., Dahbi, A., Haidine, A., & Aqqal, A. (2023). AI-based adaptive learning: A systematic mapping of the literature. *Journal of Universal Computer Science*, *29*(10), 1161–1198. DOI: 10.3897/jucs.90528

Fajrina, S., Lufri, L., & Ahda, Y. (2020). Science, technology, engineering, and mathematics (STEM) as a learning approach to improve 21st century skills: A review. *International Journal of Online & Biomedical Engineering*, *16*(7), 95–104. DOI: 10.3991/ijoe.v16i07.14101

Fallah, M., & Nozari, H. (2021). Neutrosophic mathematical programming for optimization of multi-objective sustainable biomass supply chain network design. *Computer Modeling in Engineering & Sciences*, *129*(2), 927–951. DOI: 10.32604/cmes.2021.017511

Fitri, R., Lufri, L., Alberida, H., Amran, A., & Fachry, R. (2024). The project-based learning model and its contribution to student creativity: A review. [Jurnal Pendidikan Biologi Indonesia]. *JPBI*, *10*(1), 1. Advance online publication. DOI: 10.22219/jpbi.v10i1.31499

Freeman, R. E. (2010). *Strategic management: A Stakeholder approach*. Cambridge University Press. DOI: 10.1017/CBO9781139192675

Gaftandzhieva, S., Docheva, M., & Doneva, R. (2021). A comprehensive approach to learning analytics in Bulgarian school education. *Education and Information Technologies*, *26*(1), 145–163. DOI: 10.1007/s10639-020-10261-w

Galaige, J., Steele, G. T., Binnewies, S., & Wang, K. (2022). A framework for designing student-facing learning analytics to support self-regulated learning. *IEEE Transactions on Learning Technologies*, *15*(3), 376–391. DOI: 10.1109/TLT.2022.3176968

Gao, B., Wang, Y., Xie, H., Hu, Y., & Hu, Y. (2023). Artificial Intelligence in Advertising: Advancements, Challenges, and Ethical Considerations in Targeting, Personalization, Content Creation, and Ad Optimization. In *SAGE Open* (Vol. 13, Issue 4). SAGE Publications Inc. https://doi.org/DOI: 10.1177/21582440231210759

García Aranda, C., Molina García, A., Morillo Balsera, M., Martínez Cuevas, S., Rodríguez Hurtado, M. E., Pérez Rodríguez, J., ... & Izquierdo García, P. C. (2020). Creativity and innovation skills in university stem education: The chet project approach.

Gašević, D., Tsai, Y. S., & Drachsler, H. (2022). Learning analytics in higher education–Stakeholders, strategy and scale. *The Internet and Higher Education, 52*, 1–5. DOI: 10.1016/j.iheduc.2021.100833

Ghahremani-Nahr, J., Najafi, S. E., & Nozari, H. (2022). A combined transportation model for the fruit and vegetable supply chain network. *Journal of Optimization in Industrial Engineering*, *15*(2), 131–145.

Ghahremani-Nahr, J., Nozari, H., & Aliahmadi, A. (2023). Contract Design for Return Products in a Cooperative Closed-Loop Supply Chain. *Global Business Review*. DOI: 10.1177/09721509221148892

Ghahremani-Nahr, J., Nozari, H., Rahmaty, M., Zeraati Foukolaei, P., & Sherejsharifi, A. (2023). Development of a novel fuzzy hierarchical location-routing optimization model considering reliability. *Logistics (Basel)*, *7*(3), 64. DOI: 10.3390/logistics7030064

Ghorbani, J., Aghdasi, S., Nazem, M., McCartney, J. S., & Kodikara, J. (2025). Augmented intelligence framework for real-time ground assessment under significant uncertainty. *Engineering with Computers*, 1–22. DOI: 10.1007/s00366-025-02108-0

Giang, N. T. C., Anh, N. T. Q., Dao, T. T., Tuan, P. A., Linh, C. T. H., & Chau, P. T. H. (2024). A systematic review of problem-solving skill development for students in STEM education. International Journal of Learning. *Teaching and Educational Research*, *23*(5), 1–20.

Gligorea, I., Cioca, M., Oancea, R., Gorski, A. T., Gorski, H., & Tudorache, P. (2023). Adaptive learning using artificial intelligence in e-learning: A literature review. *Education Sciences*, *13*(12), 1216. DOI: 10.3390/educsci13121216

Goes, P. B. (2014). Editor's comments: Big data and IS research. *Management Information Systems Quarterly*, *38*(3), 3–8.

Gokhan Nalbant, K., & Aydin, S. (2025). *AI-Powered Digital Marketing: Transforming Personalized Experiences*. www.arjhss.com

Gomes, R. C., & Liddle, J. (2009). The balanced scorecard as a performance management tool for third sector organizations: The case of the Arthur Bernardes Foundation, Brazil. *BAR - Brazilian Administration Review*, *6*(4), 354–366. DOI: 10.1590/S1807-76922009000400006

Gomes, S., Lopes, J. M., & Nogueira, E. (2025). Anthropomorphism in artificial intelligence: A game-changer for brand marketing. *Future Business Journal*, *11*(1). Advance online publication. DOI: 10.1186/s43093-025-00423-y

Gordon, V. N., Habley, W. R., & Grites, T. J. (Eds.). (2011). *Academic advising: A comprehensive handbook*. John Wiley & Sons.

Grabill, N., Wang, S., Olayinka, H. A., De Alwis, T. P., Khalil, Y. F., & Zou, J. (2024). AI-augmented failure modes, effects, and criticality analysis (AI-FMECA) for industrial applications. *Reliability Engineering & System Safety*, *250*, 110308. DOI: 10.1016/j.ress.2024.110308

Gray, G., Schalk, A. E., Cooke, G., Murnion, P., Rooney, P., & O'Rourke, K. C. (2022). Stakeholders' insights on learning analytics: Perspectives of students and staff. *Computers & Education*, *187*, 1–16. DOI: 10.1016/j.compedu.2022.104550

Gregor, S., Martin, M., Fernandez, W., Stern, S., & Vitale, M. (2006). The Transformational dimension in the realization of business value from information technology. *The Journal of Strategic Information Systems*, *15*(3), 249–270. DOI: 10.1016/j.jsis.2006.04.001

Greven, C., & Schroeder, U. (2015). 2SIMPLE-Symbiotic Interrelated Seamless Integrated Mobile Personalizable Learning Environments. In DeLFI WOrkshops (pp. 232-238).

Guaña-Moya, J., Ballesteros-Casco, T., Arteaga-Alcívar, Y., Antamba-Guasgua, J., Lutsak, E. V. A., & Morales, J. C. (2023, June). The New Educational Models Based on Information and Communication Technology and Education 4.0. In International Conference in Information Technology and Education (pp. 267-277). Singapore: Springer Nature Singapore. DOI: 10.1007/978-981-99-5414-8_26

Guo, X. (2022). A Study on Cross-Media Teaching Model for College English Classroom Based on Output-Driven Hypothetical Neural Network. *Computational Intelligence and Neuroscience*, *2022*(1), 5283439.

Gupta, S., Epiphaniou, G., & Maple, C. (2023). AI-augmented usability evaluation framework for software requirements specification in cyber physical human systems. *Internet of Things : Engineering Cyber Physical Human Systems*, *23*, 100841. DOI: 10.1016/j.iot.2023.100841

Guryanova, L. S., Yatsenko, R., Dubrovina, N. A., & Babenko, V. O. (2020). Machine learning methods and models, predictive analytics and applications. Academic Press.

Gutiérrez, F., Seipp, K., Ochoa, X., Chiluiza, K., De Laet, T., & Verbert, K. (2020). LADA: A learning analytics dashboard for academic advising. *Computers in Human Behavior, 107*, 105826. DOI: 10.1016/j.chb.2018.12.004

Gyonyoru, K. I. K., & Katona, J. (2025). Comprehensive Overview of the Concept and Applications of AI-based Adaptive Learning. *Acta Polytechnica Hungarica, 22*(3), 167–186. DOI: 10.12700/APH.22.3.2025.3.9

Hacıoğlu, Y., & Gülhan, F. (2021). The effects of STEM education on the students' critical thinking skills and STEM perceptions. *Journal of Education in Science, Environment and Health, 7*(2), 139–155. DOI: 10.21891/jeseh.771331

Hadi, M. U., Qureshi, R., Shah, A., Irfan, M., Zafar, A., Shaikh, M. B., Akhtar, N., Wu, J., & Mirjalili, S. (2023). A survey on large language models: Applications, challenges, limitations, and practical usage. *Authorea Preprints, 3*. https://techrxiv.figshare.com/articles/preprint/A_Survey_on_Large_Language_Models_Applications_Challenges_Limitations_and_Practical_Usage/23589741/1/files/41501037.pdf DOI: 10.36227/techrxiv.23589741.v1

Hanfy, H., Daleure, G., Abuquad, K., & Al Hosani, S. (2022). Enhancing critical and creative thinking skills in math at post-secondary level: Examining STEM versus STeM for efficiency and effectiveness. In *English language and general studies education in the united arab emirates: Theoretical, empirical and practical perspectives* (pp. 129–144). Springer Nature Singapore. DOI: 10.1007/978-981-16-8888-1_9

Hanif, S., Wijaya, A. F. C., & Winarno, N. (2019). Enhancing Students' Creativity through STEM Project-Based Learning. Journal of science Learning, 2(2), 50-57.

Han, J., Park, D., Hua, M., & Childs, P. R. (2022). Is group work beneficial for producing creative designs in STEM design education? *International Journal of Technology and Design Education, 32*(5), 2801–2826. DOI: 10.1007/s10798-021-09709-y

Hart, D., & Coates, N. (2011). International student complaint behaviour: Understanding how East-Asian business and management students respond to dissatisfaction during their university experience. *International Journal of Management Education, 9*(4), 57–66. DOI: 10.3794/ijme.94.380

Hasançebi, F., Güner, Ö., Kutru, C., & Hasancebi, M. (2021). Impact of STEM integrated argumentation-based inquiry applications on students' academic success, reflective thinking and creative thinking skills. *Participatory Educational Research*, *8*(4), 274–296. DOI: 10.17275/per.21.90.8.4

Hasibuan, M. P., Sari, R. P., Syahputra, R. A., & Nahadi, N. (2022). Application of integrated project-based and STEM-based E-learning tools to improve studentsâ€™ creative thinking and self-regulation skills. *Jurnal Penelitian Pendidikan IPA*, *8*(1), 51–56. DOI: 10.29303/jppipa.v8i1.1050

Hehakaya, W., Matdoan, M. N., & Rumahlatu, D. (2022). Integrating STEAM with PjBL and PBL on biology education: Improving students' cognitive learning results, creative thinking, and digital literacy. *Biosfer: Jurnal Pendidikan Biologi*, *15*(1), 76–84. DOI: 10.21009/biosferjpb.24468

Herodotou, C., Naydenova, G., Boroowa, A., Gilmour, A., & Rienties, B. (2020). How can predictive learning analytics and motivational interventions increase student retention and enhance administrative support in distance education? *Journal of Learning Analytics*, *7*(2), 72–83. DOI: 10.18608/jla.2020.72.4

Herodotou, C., Rienties, B., Boroowa, A., Zdrahal, Z., & Hlosta, M. (2019). A large-scale implementation of predictive learning analytics in higher education: The teachers' role and perspective. *Educational Technology Research and Development*, *67*(5), 1273–1306. DOI: 10.1007/s11423-019-09685-0

He, W., Yan, J., Wang, C., Liao, L., & Hu, X. (2023). Exploring the impact of the design thinking model on fifth graders' creative self-efficacy, situational interest, and individual interest in STEM education. *Thinking Skills and Creativity*, *50*, 101424. DOI: 10.1016/j.tsc.2023.101424

Hilliger, I., Ortiz-Rojas, M., Pesántez-Cabrera, P., Scheihing, E., Tsai, Y. S., Muñoz-Merino, P. J., Broos, T., Whitelock-Wainwright, A., & Pérez-Sanagustín, M. (2020). Identifying needs for learning analytics adoption in Latin American universities: A mixed-methods approach. *The Internet and Higher Education*, *45*, 100726. DOI: 10.1016/j.iheduc.2020.100726

Hlosta, M., Herodotou, C., Papathoma, T., Gillespie, A., & Bergamin, P. (2022). Predictive learning analytics in online education: A deeper understanding through explaining algorithmic errors. *Computers and Education: Artificial Intelligence*, *3*, 100108. DOI: 10.1016/j.caeai.2022.100108

Holik, I., & Sanda, I. D. (2023). The possibilities of developing STEM skills in higher education. *Athens Journal of Technology & Engineering*, *10*(1), 9–26. DOI: 10.30958/ajte.10-1-1

Hrabowski, F., Suess, J., & Fritz, J. (2011). *Assessment and analytics in institutional transformation*. UMBC Office of the Vice President of Information Technology.

Huang, C., Han, Z., Li, M., Wang, X., & Zhao, W. (2021). Sentiment evolution with interaction levels in blended learning environments: Using learning analytics and epistemic network analysis. *Australasian Journal of Educational Technology, 37*(2), 81–95. DOI: 10.14742/ajet.6749

Hu, L., Olivieri, M., Giovannetti, M., & Cedrola, E. (2025). The retail strategies of luxury fashion firms in the metaverse: Enhancing brand experiences. *Journal of Retailing and Consumer Services, 84*. Advance online publication. DOI: 10.1016/j.jretconser.2024.104202

Hussain, Z., Khan, A., Majeed, M. U., & Albattat, A. (2025). Metaverse and Sustainable Business Models in SMEs. In *Metaverse and Sustainable Business Models in SMEs*. IGI Global., DOI: 10.4018/979-8-3693-9005-4

Huysken, K., Olivey, H., McElmurry, K., Gao, M., & Avis, P. (2019). Assessing collaborative, project-based learning models in introductory science courses. *The Journal of Scholarship of Teaching and Learning, 19*(1). Advance online publication. https://scholarworks.iu.edu/journals/index.php/josotl/article/view/26777. DOI: 10.14434/josotl.v19i1.26777

Hwang, G. J., & Chien, S. Y. (2022). Definition, roles, and potential research issues of the metaverse in education: An artificial intelligence perspective. *Computers and Education: Artificial Intelligence, 3*. Advance online publication. DOI: 10.1016/j.caeai.2022.100082

Ifenthaler, D. (2017). Are higher education institutions prepared for learning analytics? *TechTrends, 61*(4), 366–371. DOI: 10.1007/s11528-016-0154-0

Inaganti, A. C., Ravichandran, N., Nersu, S. R. K., & Muppalaneni, R. (2021). AI-Augmented Workforce Planning: Leveraging Predictive Analytics for Talent Acquisition and Retention. *Artificial Intelligence and Machine Learning Review, 2*(1), 10–20.

Isabekov, A., & Sadyrova, G. (2018). Project-based learning to develop creative abilities in students. In *Vocational Teacher Education in Central Asia: Developing Skills and Facilitating Success* (pp. 43–49). Springer International Publishing Cham. https://library.oapen.org/bitstream/handle/20.500.12657/27694/1002312.pdf#page=60

Isaeva, R., Karasartova, N., Dznunusnalieva, K., Mirzoeva, K., & Mokliuk, M. (2025). Enhancing learning effectiveness through adaptive learning platforms and emerging computer technologies in education. *Jurnal Ilmiah Ilmu Terapan Universitas Jambi, 9*(1), 144–160. DOI: 10.22437/jiituj.v9i1.37967

Jin, M., Zhou, Z., Li, M., & Lu, T. (2024). A Deep Learning-based Predictive Analytics Model for Remote Patient Monitoring and Early Intervention in Diabetes Care. Journal of Artificial Intelligence General science (JAIGS) ISSN: 3006-4023, 6(1), 479-491.

Jones, R. K. (2024). Beyond Traditional Learning: Leveraging BERT for Enhanced Android Malware Detection. In *Multisector Insights in Healthcare, Social Sciences, Society, and Technology* (pp. 208–228). IGI Global Scientific Publishing. DOI: 10.4018/979-8-3693-3226-9.ch012

Joseph-Richard, P., Uhomoibhi, J., & Jaffrey, A. (2021). Predictive learning analytics and the creation of emotionally adaptive learning environments in higher education institutions: A study of students' affect responses. *The International Journal of Information and Learning Technology, 38*(2), 243–257. DOI: 10.1108/IJILT-05-2020-0077

Kaddouri, M., Mhamdi, K., Chniete, I., Marhraoui, M., Khaldi, M., & Jmad, S. (2025). Adopting AI in Education: Technical Challenges and Ethical Constraints. In Fostering Inclusive Education With AI and Emerging Technologies (pp. 25-72). IGI Global.

Kahneman, D., & Frederick, S. (2002). Representativeness revisited: Attribute substitution in intuitive judgment. *Heuristics and biases: The psychology of intuitive judgment, 49*(49-81), 74.

Kalogeras, S., Mejri, S., & Efthimiou, F. (2022). The neuroscience of student engagement: Case studies in narrative pedagogies in mathematics, science, and technology. [IJOPCD]. *International Journal of Online Pedagogy and Course Design, 12*(1), 1–19. DOI: 10.4018/IJOPCD.311440

Kasap, A. (2025). E-COMMERCE REDEFINED: HARNESSING EMERGING TECHNOLOGIES FOR THE FUTURE OF TRADE. In *International Journal of Economic and Administrative Academic Research* (Vol. 5, Issue 1). https://orcid.org/0000-0001-7231-2693

Kasneci, E., Seßler, K., Küchemann, S., Bannert, M., Dementieva, D., Fischer, F., Gasser, U., Groh, G., Günnemann, S., Hüllermeier, E., Krusche, S., Kutyniok, G., Michaeli, T., Nerdel, C., Pfeffer, J., Poquet, O., Sailer, M., Schmidt, A., Seidel, T., & Kasneci, G. (2023). ChatGPT for good? On opportunities and challenges of large language models for education. *Learning and Individual Differences, 103*, 102274. DOI: 10.1016/j.lindif.2023.102274

Kencana, M. A., & Syukri, M. (2020, February). The effect of science, technology, engineering, and mathematics (STEM) on students' creative thinking skills. [). IOP Publishing.]. *Journal of Physics: Conference Series, 1460*(1), 012141. DOI: 10.1088/1742-6596/1460/1/012141

Kew, S. N., & Tasir, Z. (2022). Learning analytics in online learning environment: A systematic review on the focuses and the types of student-related analytics data. *Technology, Knowledge and Learning*, 1-23. https://doi.org/DOI: 10.1007/s10758-021-09541-2

Khajah, M., Lindsey, R. V., & Mozer, M. C. (2016). How deep is knowledge tracing? *arXiv preprint arXiv:1604.02416*. https://doi.org//arXiv.1604.02416DOI: 10.48550

Kirchenbauer, J., Geiping, J., Wen, Y., Katz, J., Miers, I., & Goldstein, T. (2023). A watermark for large language models. *International Conference on Machine Learning*, 17061–17084. https://proceedings.mlr.press/v202/kirchenbauer23a.html

Klašnja-Milićević, A., Ivanović, M., & Budimac, Z. (2017). Data science in education: Big data and learning analytics. *Computer Applications in Engineering Education, 25*(6), 1066–1078. DOI: 10.1002/cae.21844

Klein, M., Carpentier, T., Jeanclaude, E., Kassab, R., Varelas, K., de Bruijn, N., & Aligne, F. (2020, September). AI-augmented multi function radar engineering with digital twin: Towards proactivity. In *2020 IEEE Radar Conference (RadarConf20)* (pp. 1-6). IEEE. DOI: 10.1109/RadarConf2043947.2020.9266455

Kollom, K., Tammets, K., Scheffel, M., Tsai, Y. S., Jivet, I., Muñoz-Merino, P. J., Moreno-Marcos, P. M., Whitelock-Wainwright, A., Calleja, A. R., Gasevic, D., Kloos, C. D., Drachsler, H., & Ley, T. (2021). A four-country cross-case analysis of academic staff expectations about learning analytics in higher education. *The Internet and Higher Education, 49*, 100788. DOI: 10.1016/j.iheduc.2020.100788

Koon, S. (2025). A Beautiful Mind: Principles and Strategies for AI-Augmented Human Reasoning. arXiv preprint arXiv:2503.15530.

Kortam, N., Basheer, A., Hofstein, A., & Hugerat, M. (2018). How project-based learning promotes 7th grade students' motivation and attitudes towards studying biology. *Action Research and Innovation in Science Education, 1*(2), 9–17. DOI: 10.51724/arise.10

Kotsiantis, S. B. (2012). Use of machine learning techniques for educational proposes: A decision support system for forecasting students' grades. *Artificial Intelligence Review, 37*(4), 331–344. DOI: 10.1007/s10462-011-9234-x

Kraftl, P., McKenzie, M., Gulson, K., Accioly, I., Blackmore, J., Burke, C., & Wood, A. (2022). Learning spaces: built, natural and digital considerations for learning and learners. In *Education and the learning experience in Reimagining education: The International Science and Evidence based Education Assessment* (pp. 452–547). UNESCO MGIEP. DOI: 10.56383/KWAW2002

Kumar Gubbala, A. LeelaVemula, H., singh, K., Tan Nguyen, N., & Hatole, S. (2025). *Strategic Marketing in the Digital Age: Bridging Consumer Behavior and Brand Innovation* (Vol. 2, Issue 2). https://acr-journal.com/

Kumar, M., Ang, L. T., Ho, C., Soh, S. E., Tan, K. H., Chan, J. K. Y., Godfrey, K. M., Chan, S.-Y., Chong, Y. S., Eriksson, J. G., Feng, M., & Karnani, N. (2022). Machine learning–derived prenatal predictive risk model to guide intervention and prevent the progression of gestational diabetes mellitus to type 2 diabetes: Prediction model development study. *JMIR Diabetes, 7*(3), e32366. DOI: 10.2196/32366 PMID: 35788016

Kurilovas, E. (2019). Advanced machine learning approaches to personalise learning: Learning analytics and decision making. *Behaviour & Information Technology, 38*(4), 410–421. DOI: 10.1080/0144929X.2018.1539517

Kwon, H., & Lee, Y. (2025). A meta-analysis of STEM project-based learning on creativity. *STEM Education, 5*(2), 275–290. DOI: 10.3934/steme.2025014

Larkin, T. L. (2015, September). Creativity in STEM education: Reshaping the creative project. In 2015 international conference on interactive collaborative learning (ICL) (pp. 1184-1189). IEEE.

Larmer, J., Mergendoller, J., & Boss, S. (2015). *Setting the standard for project based learning*. Ascd. https://books.google.com/books?hl=en&lr=&id=10XwCQAAQBAJ&oi=fnd&pg=PP1&dq=Setting+the+Standard+for+Project-Based+Learning:+A+Proven+Approach+to+Rigorous+Classroom+Instruction&ots=MF6bg8l6zE&sig=Nb6gb1RkpvNIMzsN1iaF3qwmOls

Lee, A. S., & Baskerville, R. L. (2003). Generalizing generalizability in information systems research. *Information Systems Research*, *14*(3), 221–243. DOI: 10.1287/isre.14.3.221.16560

Lee, C. S. (2007). Diagnostic, predictive and compositional modeling with data mining in integrated learning environments. *Computers & Education*, *49*(3), 562–580. DOI: 10.1016/j.compedu.2005.10.010

Lekan, K., & Pardos, Z. A. (2025). AI-Augmented Advising: A Comparative Study of GPT-4 and Advisor-Based Major Recommendations. *Journal of Learning Analytics*, *12*(1), 110–128. DOI: 10.18608/jla.2025.8593

Li, K. C., Lam, H. K., & Lam, S. S. (2015). A review of learning analytics in educational research. In *Technology in Education. Technology-Mediated Proactive Learning: Second International Conference, ICTE 2015, Hong Kong, China, July 2-4, 2015, Revised Selected Papers 2* (pp. 173-184). Springer Berlin Heidelberg. DOI: 10.1007/978-3-662-48978-9_17

Li, G., Deng, L., Tang, H., Pan, G., Tian, Y., Roy, K., & Maass, W. (2024). Brain-inspired computing: A systematic survey and future trends. *Proceedings of the IEEE.*

Li, Z. Z., Wang, H., Gasevic, D., Yu, J., & Liu, J. K. (2023). Enhancing blockchain adoption through tailored software engineering: An industrial-grounded study in education credentialing. *Distributed Ledger Technologies: Research and Practice*, *2*(4), 1–24. DOI: 10.1145/3632532

Longhi, M. T., & Behar, P. A. (2024). Socio-Affective Competence in Virtual Learning Environments: A View from the Empathetic. In Creative Approaches to Technology-Enhanced Learning for the Workplace and Higher Education: Proceedings of 'The Learning Ideas Conference' 2024, Volume 2 (Vol. 2, p. 350). Springer Nature. DOI: 10.1007/978-3-031-73427-4_34

Lopez, S. (2025). *Integrating Artificial Intelligence in Regional Education: A Holistic Framework for Inclusive, Adaptive, and Community-Centric Learning* (Vol. 6). Electronic Journal of Social and Strategic Studies.

Lotfi, F. H. Z., Najafi, S. E., & Nozari, H. (Eds.). (2016). *Data envelopment analysis and effective performance assessment.* IGI Global.

Lu, W. (2025, January). Scalable and Interpretable Learning Tool Development within Game-based Learning Environment: A Case Study of Mission HydroSci. In *Companion Proceedings of the 2025 ACM International Conference on Supporting Group Work* (pp. 124-126). DOI: 10.1145/3688828.3699657

Mangaroska, K., & Giannakos, M. (2018). Learning analytics for learning design: A systematic literature review of analytics-driven design to enhance learning. *IEEE Transactions on Learning Technologies, 12*(4), 516–534. DOI: 10.1109/TLT.2018.2868673

March, S. T., & Smith, G. F. (1995). Design and natural science research on information technology. *Decision Support Systems, 15*(4), 251–266. DOI: 10.1016/0167-9236(94)00041-2

Marciano, L., Dubicka, B., Magis-Weinberg, L., Morese, R., Viswanath, K., & Weber, R. (2025). Digital Media, Cognition, and Brain Development in Adolescence. In *Handbook of Children and Screens* (pp. 21–29). Springer. DOI: 10.1007/978-3-031-69362-5_4

Marsono, M., Khasanah, F., & Yoto, Y. (2019, January). Integrating STEM (Science Technology Engineering and Mathematics) education on advancing vocational student's creative thinking skills. In 2nd international conference on vocational education and training (ICOVET 2018) (pp. 170-173). Atlantis Press.

Mathrani, A., Susnjak, T., Ramaswami, G., & Barczak, A. (2021). Perspectives on the challenges of generalizability, transparency and ethics in predictive learning analytics. *Computers and Education Open, 2*, 100060. DOI: 10.1016/j.caeo.2021.100060

Mayer, M. (2009). *Innovation at Google: The physics of data [PARC forum]*. Retrieved 11 August, 2009, from https://www.slideshare.net/PARCInc/innovation-at-google-the-physics-of-data

McAfee, A., Brynjolfsson, E., Davenport, T. H., Patil, D. J., & Barton, D. (2012). Big data: The management revolution. *Harvard Business Review, 90*(10), 60–68. PMID: 23074865

Mehta, P. S., Doshi, S. T., Butle, S. N., Inamdar, S. C., & Shinde, S. D. (2025). The Fusion of Academia and Industry via Cloud Integration in Education: Customized Learning and Adaptive Systems. In Bridging Academia and Industry Through Cloud Integration in Education (pp. 109-144). IGI Global Scientific Publishing.

Memarian, B., & Doleck, T. (2023). Fairness, Accountability, Transparency, and Ethics (FATE) in Artificial Intelligence (AI) and higher education: A systematic review. *Computers and Education: Artificial Intelligence, 5*, 100152.

Meylani, R. (2024). A Critical Glance at Adaptive Learning Systems Using Artificial Intelligence: A Systematic Review and Qualitative Synthesis of Contemporary Research Literature. *Batı Anadolu Eğitim Bilimleri Dergisi, 15*(3), 3518–3546. DOI: 10.51460/baebd.1525452

Miller, L. (2021). *American Journal of Business, Commerce and Economics* australiansciencejournals.com/business *The Future of Retail: How Technology is Shaping Consumer Shopping Habits*

Mills, M. A., & Khoei, T. T. (2024, September). Future-Proofing Computer Behavior: A Framework for Predictive Analytics and Seamless Device Integration. In 2024 2nd International Conference on Artificial Intelligence, Blockchain, and Internet of Things (AIBThings) (pp. 1-5). IEEE. DOI: 10.1109/AIBThings63359.2024.10863652

Mitchell, R. K., Agle, B. R., & Wood, D. J. (1997). Toward a theory of stakeholder identification and salience: Defining the principle of who and what really counts. *Academy of Management Review*, *22*(4), 853–886. DOI: 10.2307/259247

Mohammadi, H., Ghazanfari, M., Nozari, H., & Shafiezad, O. (2015). Combining the theory of constraints with system dynamics: A general model (case study of the subsidized milk industry). International journal of management science and engineering management, 10(2), 102-108.

Mohammadi, H., Ghazanfari, M., Nozari, H., & Shafiezad, O. (2015). Combining the theory of constraints with system dynamics: A general model (case study of the subsidized milk industry). *International Journal of Management Science and Engineering Management, 10*(2), 102-108.

Mohinur, A. (2024). Project-based learning as a creative and innovative way of teaching english as a foreign language. *University Research Base*, 54–60.

Moon, J., Lee, D., Choi, G. W., Seo, J., Do, J., & Lim, T. (2024). Learning analytics in seamless learning environments: A systematic review. *Interactive Learning Environments*, *32*(7), 3208–3225.

Movahed, A. B., & Movahed, A. B. (2025). Sustainable Smart Economies: Green Technologies and Circular Business Models. In *Dynamic and Safe Economy in the Age of Smart Technologies* (pp. 73–90). IGI Global Scientific Publishing. https://www.igi-global.com/chapter/sustainable-smart-economies/377630

Movahed, A. B., Abyaneh, A. G., Khakbazan, M., & Movahed, A. B. (2025). Smart Economy Cybersecurity: AI-Driven Risk Management in Digital Markets. In *Dynamic and Safe Economy in the Age of Smart Technologies* (pp. 49–72). IGI Global Scientific Publishing. DOI: 10.4018/979-8-3693-4369-2.ch004

Movahed, A. B., Movahed, A. B., & Nozari, H. (2024). Marketing 6.0 Conceptualization. In Advanced Businesses in Industry 6.0 (pp. 15-31). IGI Global Scientific Publishing.

Movahed, A. B., Movahed, A. B., & Nozari, H. (2024). Marketing 6.0 Conceptualization. In Advanced Businesses in Industry 6.0 (pp. 15-31). IGI Global.

Movahed, A. B., Movahed, A. B., & Nozari, H. (2024). Opportunities and challenges of marketing 5.0. Smart and Sustainable Interactive Marketing, 1-21.

Movahed, A. B., Movahed, A. B., & Nozari, H. (2024). Opportunities and challenges of smart supply chain in Industry 5.0. Information Logistics for Organizational Empowerment and Effective Supply Chain Management, 108-138.

Movahed, A. B., Movahed, A. B., & Nozari, H. (2024a). Opportunities and challenges of smart supply chain in Industry 5.0. Information Logistics for Organizational Empowerment and Effective Supply Chain Management, 108-138.

Movahed, A. B., Movahed, A. B., & Nozari, H. (2024b). Marketing 6.0 Conceptualization. In Advanced Businesses in Industry 6.0 (pp. 15-31). IGI Global Scientific Publishing.

Movahed, A. B., Aliahmadi, A., Parsanejad, M., & Nozari, H. (2023). A systematic review of collaboration in supply chain 4.0 with meta-synthesis method. *Supply Chain Analytics*, *4*, 100052. DOI: 10.1016/j.sca.2023.100052

Mubarak, A. A., Cao, H., & Ahmed, S. A. (2021). Predictive learning analytics using deep learning model in MOOCs' courses videos. *Education and Information Technologies*, *26*(1), 371–392. DOI: 10.1007/s10639-020-10273-6

Mudawi, N. A., Pervaiz, M., Alabduallah, B. I., Alazeb, A., Alshahrani, A., Alotaibi, S. S., & Jalal, A. (2023). Predictive Analytics for Sustainable E-Learning: Tracking Student Behaviors. Sustainability (2071-1050), 15(20).

Mukaromah, S. H., & Wusqo, I. U. (2020, March). The influence of PjBL model with stem approach on global warming topic to students' creative thinking and communication skills. []. IOP Publishing.]. *Journal of Physics: Conference Series*, *1521*(4), 042052. DOI: 10.1088/1742-6596/1521/4/042052

Munguia, P., Brennan, A., Taylor, S., & Lee, D. (2020). A learning analytics journey: Bridging the gap between technology services and the academic need. *The Internet and Higher Education*, *46*, 100744. DOI: 10.1016/j.iheduc.2020.100744

Myers, D., Mohawesh, R., Chellaboina, V. I., Sathvik, A. L., Venkatesh, P., Ho, Y.-H., Henshaw, H., Alhawawreh, M., Berdik, D., & Jararweh, Y. (2024). Foundation and large language models: Fundamentals, challenges, opportunities, and social impacts. *Cluster Computing*, *27*(1), 1–26. DOI: 10.1007/s10586-023-04203-7

Nadkarni, P. M., Ohno-Machado, L., & Chapman, W. W. (2011). Natural language processing: An introduction. *Journal of the American Medical Informatics Association : JAMIA*, *18*(5), 544–551. DOI: 10.1136/amiajnl-2011-000464 PMID: 21846786

Naithani, K., Raiwani, Y. P., & Tiwari, S. Analyzing the Seamless Integration of Machine Learning and Internet of Things in the Daily Dynamics of Contemporary Living. In Evolution of Machine Learning and Internet of Things Applications in Biomedical Engineering (pp. 201-217). CRC Press. DOI: 10.1201/9781003476207-13

Najafi, S. E., Nozari, H., & Edalatpanah, S. A. (2022). Artificial Intelligence of Things (AIoT) and Industry 4.0–Based Supply Chain (FMCG Industry). A roadmap for enabling industry 4.0 by artificial intelligence, 31-41.

Najafi, S. E., Nozari, H., & Edalatpanah, S. A. (2022b). Artificial Intelligence of Things (AIoT) and Industry 4.0–Based Supply Chain (FMCG Industry). A roadmap for enabling industry 4.0 by artificial intelligence, 31-41.

Najafi, S. E., Nozari, H., & Edalatpanah, S. A. (2022). Investigating the key parameters affecting sustainable IoT-based marketing. In *Computational Intelligence Methodologies Applied to Sustainable Development Goals* (pp. 51–61). Springer International Publishing. DOI: 10.1007/978-3-030-97344-5_4

Naseer, F., Khan, M. N., Tahir, M., Addas, A., & Aejaz, S. H. (2024). Integrating deep learning techniques for personalized learning pathways in higher education. *Heliyon*, *10*(11), e32628. DOI: 10.1016/j.heliyon.2024.e32628 PMID: 38961899

Naveed, H., Khan, A. U., Qiu, S., Saqib, M., Anwar, S., Usman, M., Akhtar, N., Barnes, N., & Mian, A. (2025). A Comprehensive Overview of Large Language Models. *ACM Transactions on Intelligent Systems and Technology*, 3744746. Advance online publication. DOI: 10.1145/3744746

Ning, J., Ma, Z., Yao, J., Wang, Q., & Zhang, B. (2025). Personalized learning supported by learning analytics: A systematic review of functions, pathways, and educational outcomes. *Interactive Learning Environments*, •••, 1–23. DOI: 10.1080/10494820.2025.2478437

Nisah, N., Widiyono, A., Milkhaturrohman, M., & Lailiyah, N. N. (2021). Keefektifan Model Project Based Learning Terhadap Peningkatan Hasil Belajar IPA di Sekolah Dasar. *Pedagogi: Jurnal Penelitian Pendidikan, 8*(2). https://www.researchgate.net/profile/Aan-Widiyono/publication/357812316_Keefektifan_Model_Project_Based_Learning_terhadap_Peningkatan_Hasil_Belajar_IPA_di_Sekolah_Dasar/links/61e0affb9a753545e2cbca6c/Keefektifan-Model-Project-Based-Learning-terhadap-Peningkatan-Hasil-Belajar-IPA-di-Sekolah-Dasar.pdf

Nithya, B., & Ilango, V. (2017, June). Predictive analytics in health care using machine learning tools and techniques. In *2017 International Conference on Intelligent Computing and Control Systems (ICICCS)* (pp. 492-499). IEEE. DOI: 10.1109/ICCONS.2017.8250771

Nozari, H., & Chobar, A. P. (2024). The Dimensions and Components of Marketing 5.0: Introduction to Marketing 6.0. In Advanced Businesses in Industry 6.0 (pp. 75-86). IGI Global Scientific Publishing.

Nozari, H., & Chobar, A. P. (2024). The Dimensions and Components of Marketing 5.0: Introduction to Marketing 6.0. In Advanced Businesses in Industry 6.0 (pp. 75-86). IGI Global.

Nozari, H., & Samadi, S. (2025). Digital Twin-Enhanced Sentiment Analysis for Targeted Marketing Optimization. In Dynamic and Safe Economy in the Age of Smart Technologies (pp. 121-138). IGI Global Scientific Publishing. DOI: 10.4018/979-8-3693-4369-2.ch008

Nozari, H., Abdi, H., & Rafiei, K. (2025). Edge Computing and Marketing in the Smart Economy: Processing Consumer Data in Real-Time. In Dynamic and Safe Economy in the Age of Smart Technologies (pp. 191-208). IGI Global Scientific Publishing.

Nozari, H., Fallah, M., Szmelter-Jarosz, A., & Krzemiński, M. (2021). Analysis of security criteria for IoT-based supply chain: a case study of FMCG industries. Central European Management Journal, 29(4).

Nozari, H., Ghahremani-Nahr, J., & Najafi, E. (2023). The role of Internet of things and Blockchain in the development of agile and sustainable supply chains. In Digital Supply Chain, Disruptive Environments, and the Impact on Retailers (pp. 271-282). IGI Global. DOI: 10.4018/978-1-6684-7298-9.ch015

Nozari, H., Irani, H. R., & Rahmaty, M. (2023, November). Investigating Critical Success Factors in IoT-Based Marketing Systems. In International Conference on Optimization and Data Science in Industrial Engineering (pp. 259-271). Cham: Springer Nature Switzerland.

Nozari, H., Tavakkoli-Moghaddam, R., & Dolgui, A. (2024, September). Analysis of Critical Success Factors of Sustainable and Resilient Aioe-based Supply Chain in Industry 5.0. In IFIP International Conference on Advances in Production Management Systems (pp. 76-90). Cham: Springer Nature Switzerland. DOI: 10.1007/978-3-031-65894-5_6

Nozari, H., Tavakkoli-Moghaddam, R., Ghahremani-Nahr, J., & Najafi, E. (2023). A conceptual framework for Artificial Intelligence of Medical Things (AIoMT). In Computational Intelligence for Medical Internet of Things (MIoT) Applications (pp. 175-189). Academic Press.

Nozari, H., Tavakkoli-Moghaddam, R., Rohaninejad, M., & Hanzalek, Z. (2023, September). Artificial intelligence of things (AIoT) strategies for a smart sustainable-resilient supply chain. In IFIP International Conference on Advances in Production Management Systems (pp. 805-816). Cham: Springer Nature Switzerland. DOI: 10.1007/978-3-031-43670-3_56

Nozari, H. (2024a). Green supply chain management based on artificial intelligence of everything. *Journal of Economics and Management*, *46*, 171–188. DOI: 10.22367/jem.2024.46.07

Nozari, H. (2024b). Supply chain 6.0 and moving towards hyper-intelligent processes. In *Information logistics for organizational empowerment and effective supply chain management* (pp. 1–13). IGI Global Scientific Publishing.

Nozari, H. (2025a). NeuroTwinceutics™ as a Neuromorphic Digital Twin Model for Predictive and Personalized Pharmacotherapy. *Transformative Science*, *1*(1), 1–8.

Nozari, H. (2025b). Cognitive Targeting and Neuromarketing Applications in AI-Driven Digital Advertising. *Applied Innovations in Industrial Management*, *5*(2), 52–58. DOI: 10.63630/aiim.52.52

Nozari, H. (Ed.). (2023). *Building Smart and Sustainable Businesses with Transformative Technologies*. IGI Global. DOI: 10.4018/979-8-3693-0210-1

Nozari, H. (Ed.). (2025). *Dynamic and Safe Economy in the Age of Smart Technologies*. IGI Global. DOI: 10.4018/979-8-3693-4369-2

Nozari, H., Abdi, H., & Jahangard, S. (2025). Quantum Cognitive Intelligence Network Q-CIN as a Transformative Framework for Industry 6.0. *ALL Bioscience*, *1*(1), 27–37.

Nozari, H., Abdi, H., & Szmelter-Jarosz, A. (2025). A Neuromorphic and Bio-Inspired Framework for Optimization in Multi-Echelon Supply Networks. *Transformative Science*, *1*(1), 9–17.

Nozari, H., Abdi, H., Szmelter-Jarosz, A., & Motevalli, S. H. (2024). Design of dual-channel supply chain network based on the internet of things under uncertainty. *Mathematical & Computational Applications*, *29*(6), 118. DOI: 10.3390/mca29060118

Nozari, H., & Aliahmadi, A. (2023). Analysis of critical success factors in a food agile supply chain by a fuzzy hybrid decision-making method. [Formerly known as Iranian Journal of Management Studies]. *Interdisciplinary Journal of Management Studies*, *16*(4), 905–926.

Nozari, H., & Edalatpanah, S. A. (2023). Smart systems risk management in IoT-based supply chain. In *Advances in reliability, failure and risk analysis* (pp. 251–268). Springer Nature Singapore. DOI: 10.1007/978-981-19-9909-3_11

Nozari, H., Fallah, M., Kazemipoor, H., & Najafi, S. E. (2021). Big data analysis of IoT-based supply chain management considering FMCG industries. *Бизнес-информатика*, *15*(1, 1 (eng)), 78–96. DOI: 10.17323/2587-814X.2021.1.78.96

Nozari, H., & Ghahremani-Nahr, J. (2023). A comprehensive strategic-tactical multi-objective sustainable supply chain model with human resources considerations. *Supply Chain Analytics*, *4*, 100044. DOI: 10.1016/j.sca.2023.100044

Nozari, H., Ghahremani-Nahr, J., & Szmelter-Jarosz, A. (2023). A multi-stage stochastic inventory management model for transport companies including several different transport modes. *International Journal of Management Science and Engineering Management*, *18*(2), 134–144. DOI: 10.1080/17509653.2022.2042747

Nozari, H., Ghahremani-Nahr, J., & Szmelter-Jarosz, A. (2024). AI and machine learning for real-world problems. [). Elsevier.]. *Advances in Computers*, *134*, 1–12. DOI: 10.1016/bs.adcom.2023.02.001

Nozari, H., Najafi, E., Fallah, M., & Hosseinzadeh Lotfi, F. (2019). Quantitative analysis of key performance indicators of green supply chain in FMCG industries using non-linear fuzzy method. *Mathematics*, *7*(11), 1020. DOI: 10.3390/math7111020

Nozari, H., Najafi, S. E., Jafari-Eskandari, M., & Aliahmadi, A. (2016). Providing a model for virtual project management with an emphasis on IT projects. In *Strategic Management and Leadership for Systems Development in Virtual Spaces* (pp. 43–63). IGI Global Scientific Publishing. DOI: 10.4018/978-1-4666-9688-4.ch003

Nozari, H., & Rahmaty, M. (2023). Modeling the make-to-order problem considering the order queuing system under uncertainty. *International Journal of Industrial Engineering*, *34*(4), 1–20.

Nozari, H., Rahmaty, M., Foukolaei, P. Z., Movahed, H., & Bayanati, M. (2025). Optimizing Cold Chain Logistics with Artificial Intelligence of Things (AIoT): A Model for Reducing Operational and Transportation Costs. *Future Transportation*, *5*(1), 1. DOI: 10.3390/futuretransp5010001

Nozari, H., Rahmaty, M., & Szmelter-Jarosz, A. (2024). A framework for AIoT-based smart sustainable marketing system. In *Artificial Intelligence of Things for Achieving Sustainable Development Goals* (pp. 255–271). Springer Nature Switzerland. DOI: 10.1007/978-3-031-53433-1_13

Nozari, H., & Sadeghi, M. E. (2021). Artificial intelligence and Machine Learning for Real-world problems (A survey). *International Journal of Innovation in Engineering, 1*(3), 38–47.

Nozari, H., Szmelter-Jarosz, A., & Ghahremani-Nahr, J. (2021). The ideas of sustainable and green marketing based on the internet of everything—The case of the dairy industry. *Future Internet, 13*(10), 266. DOI: 10.3390/fi13100266

Nozari, H., Szmelter-Jarosz, A., & Ghahremani-Nahr, J. (2022). Analysis of the challenges of artificial intelligence of things (AIoT) for the smart supply chain (case study: FMCG industries). *Sensors (Basel), 22*(8), 2931. DOI: 10.3390/s22082931 PMID: 35458916

Nozari, H., Szmelter-Jarosz, A., & Rahmaty, M. (2024). Smart marketing based on artificial intelligence of things (AIoT) and Blockchain and evaluating critical success factors. In *Smart and Sustainable Interactive Marketing* (pp. 68–82). IGI Global Scientific Publishing. DOI: 10.4018/979-8-3693-1339-8.ch005

Nozari, H., Tavakkoli-Moghaddam, R., & Gharemani-Nahr, J. (2022). A neutrosophic fuzzy programming method to solve a multi-depot vehicle routing model under uncertainty during the covid-19 pandemic. *International Journal of Engineering, 35*(2), 360–371.

Nurhidayah, I. J., Wibowo, F. C., & Astra, I. M. (2021). Project Based Learning (PjBL) Learning Model in Science Learning: Literature Review. *Journal of Physics: Conference Series, 2019*(1), 012043. DOI: 10.1088/1742-6596/2019/1/012043

Nutt, P. C., & Robert, W. (1992). *Backoff. 1992. Strategic management of public and third sector organizations: A handbook for leaders*. JosseyBass.

OECD. (2013). *OECD Report: The State of Higher Education 2013*. Retrieved March 24, 2025, from http:// www.oecd.org/edu/imhe/thestateofhighereducation2013.htm

Okewu, E., & Daramola, O. (2017, October). Design of a learning analytics system for academic advising in Nigerian universities. In *2017 International Conference on Computing Networking and Informatics (ICCNI)* (pp. 1-8). IEEE. https://doi.org/ DOI: 10.1109/ICCNI.2017.8123785

Oloruntoba, N. O. (2025). AI-Driven autonomous database management: Self-tuning, predictive query optimization, and intelligent indexing in enterprise it environments. *World Journal of Advanced Research and Reviews*, *25*(2), 1558–1580. DOI: 10.30574/wjarr.2025.25.2.0534

Olson, P. (2024). *Supremacy: AI, ChatGPT, and the Race that Will Change the World*. St. Martin's Press. https://books.google.com/books?hl=en&lr=&id=9nLeEAAAQBAJ&oi=fnd&pg=PT144&dq=Supremacy:+AI,+ChatGPT,+and+the+Race+that+Will+Change+the+World&ots=8TWwMPRV8_&sig=Lk42QDh2rdzBCjtH9V9bs8l5kFs

Oner, A. T., Nite, S. B., Capraro, R. M., & Capraro, M. M. (2016). From STEM to STEAM: Students' beliefs about the use of their creativity. *The STEAM Journal*, *2*(2), 6. DOI: 10.5642/steam.20160202.06

Othman, O., Iksan, Z. H., & Yasin, R. M. (2022). Creative Teaching STEM Module: High School Students' Perception. *European Journal of Educational Research*, *11*(4), 2127–2137. DOI: 10.12973/eu-jer.11.4.2127

Ou, C., Thajchayapong, P., & Joyner, D. (2024, July). Open, collaborative, and AI-augmented peer assessment: Student participation, performance, and perceptions. In Proceedings of the Eleventh ACM Conference on Learning@ Scale (pp. 496-500).

Owan, V. J., Abang, K. B., Idika, D. O., Etta, E. O., & Bassey, B. A. (2023). Exploring the potential of artificial intelligence tools in educational measurement and assessment. *Eurasia Journal of Mathematics, Science and Technology Education*, *19*(8), em2307. DOI: 10.29333/ejmste/13428

Özsoy, N., & Özyer, S. (2018). Creative drama and example of activity plan in STEM. *European Journal of Education Studies*.

Papazafeiropoulou, A., Pouloudi, A., & Currie, W. L. (2001). Applying the stakeholder concept to electronic commerce: Extending previous research to guide government policy makers. In *Proceedings of the 34th Annual Hawaii International Conference on System Sciences* (pp. 1–10). https://doi.org/DOI: 10.1109/HICSS.2001.926521

Patel, K. K., Pal, A., Saurav, K., & Jain, P. (2022). Mental Health Detection Using Transformer BERT. In *Handbook of Research on Lifestyle Sustainability and Management Solutions Using AI, Big Data Analytics, and Visualization* (pp. 91–108). IGI Global Scientific Publishing. DOI: 10.4018/978-1-7998-8786-7.ch006

Patil, S. (2025). AI-driven personalized learning paths in MOOCS: Optimizing engagement and outcomes in digital education. In *Digital Transformation and Sustainability of Business* (pp. 387–395). CRC Press. DOI: 10.1201/9781003606185-90

Pattnaik, A., & Mohanty, M. (2025). *Innovate to Dominate: AI and Sustainability in Business.*

Pew Research Center. (2016), From universities to churches, Republicans and Democrats differ in views of major institutions. Retrieved from https://www.pewresearch.org/fact-tank/2016/09/26/from-universities-to-churches-republicans-and-democrats-differ-in-views-of-major-institutions/

Phillips, R., Freeman, R. E., & Wicks, A. C. (2003). What stakeholder theory is not. *Business Ethics Quarterly, 13*(4), 479–502. DOI: 10.5840/beq200313434

Picciano, A. G. (2012). The evolution of big data and learning analytics in American higher education. *Online Learning : the Official Journal of the Online Learning Consortium, 16*(3), 3, 9–20. DOI: 10.24059/olj.v16i3.267

Pinasa, S., Siripun, K., & Yuenyong, C. (2018, January). Developing design-based STEM education learning activities to enhance students' creative thinking. In AIP Conference Proceedings (Vol. 1923, No. 1). AIP Publishing.

Poh, Z. X., & Khor, E. T. (2024). Predictive Analytics for Student Online Learning Performance Using Machine Learning and Data Mining Techniques. In International Journal on E-Learning (pp. 269-283). Association for the Advancement of Computing in Education (AACE). DOI: 10.70725/686437bpltsf

Pramesti, D., Probosari, R. M., & Indriyanti, N. Y. (2022). Effectiveness of project based learning low carbon STEM and discovery learning to improve creative thinking skills. *Journal of Innovation in Educational and Cultural Research, 3*(3), 444–456. DOI: 10.46843/jiecr.v3i3.156

Rafiq, J. E., Abdelali, Z., Amraouy, M., Nouh, S., & Bennane, A. (2025). Predicting academic performance: toward a model based on machine learning and learner's intelligences. International Journal of Electrical & Computer Engineering (2088-8708), 15(1).

Rahimi, H., & Hosseini, M. G. (2025). The Mixed-Methods Study on the Impact of Augmented Reality on Brand Equity and Smart Decision-Making in Retail Industries. *New Marketing Research Journal, 14*(4), 149–182. DOI: 10.22108/nmrj.2025.144073.3143

Rahmaty, M. (2024). Presenting a conceptual model to identify the dimensions, components, and applications of a resilient green supply chain. *Journal of Industrial and Systems Engineering, 16*(1), 157–164.

Rahmaty, M., & Nozari, H. (2023). Optimization of the hierarchical supply chain in the pharmaceutical industry. *Edelweiss Applied Science and Technology*, *7*(2), 104–123. DOI: 10.55214/25768484.v7i2.376

Raj, N. S., & v G, R. (2022). Early prediction of student engagement in virtual learning environments using machine learning techniques. *E-Learning and Digital Media*, *19*(6), 537–554. DOI: 10.1177/20427530221108027

Raksapoln, K., & Suttiwan, W. (2021, November). Enhancing creativity and collaboration by learning management in STEM Education. In 2021 2nd SEA-STEM International Conference (SEA-STEM) (pp. 116-118). IEEE. DOI: 10.1109/SEA-STEM53614.2021.9667983

Ram, I., Rosenberg-Kima, R., Lewin, D. R., Barzilai, A., Chumtonov, O., & Roll, I. (2025). Active Learning and the Development of 21st Century Skills in Online STEM Education: A Large-Scale Survey. *Online Learning : the Official Journal of the Online Learning Consortium*, *29*(1), 4–29. DOI: 10.24059/olj.v29i1.3533

Ranjan, R. (2025). AI-Powered Data Platforms Bridging the Gap Between Analytics and Action in Smart Education. In Smart Education and Sustainable Learning Environments in Smart Cities (pp. 107-122). IGI Global Scientific Publishing.

Ratcliff, R., Smith, P. L., Brown, S. D., & McKoon, G. (2016). Diffusion decision model: Current issues and history. *Trends in Cognitive Sciences*, *20*(4), 260–281. DOI: 10.1016/j.tics.2016.01.007 PMID: 26952739

Rathee, R., Vats, H., & Sharma, S. (2025). AI-Enhanced Predictive Scheduling Optimizing Project Timelines for Blue-Green Infrastructure Deployment. In Integrating Blue-Green Infrastructure Into Urban Development (pp. 61-80). IGI Global Scientific Publishing.

Raza, A. (2025). Personalized Learning through AI: Opportunities and Challenges in Adaptive Educational Technologies. *Journal of AI Integration in Education*, *2*(1), 21–28.

Razali, M. N., Zakariah, H., Hanapi, R., & Rahim, E. A. (2022, May). Predictive model of undergraduate student grading using machine learning for learning analytics. In 2022 4th International Conference on Computer Science and Technologies in Education (CSTE) (pp. 260-264). IEEE. DOI: 10.1109/CSTE55932.2022.00055

Reddy Gadekallu, T., Huynh-The, T., Wang, W., Yenduri, G., Ranaweera, P., Pham, Q.-V., Benevides Da Costa, D., & Liyanage, M. (2022). Blockchain for the Metaverse. *RE:view*.

Reddy, V. K., Said, L., Sengupta, B., Chetlur, M., Costantino, J. P., Gopinath, A., Flynt, S., Balunaini, P., & Vedula, S. (2015). Personalized Learning Pathways: Enabling intervention creation and tracking. *IBM Journal of Research and Development*, *59*(6), 4–1. DOI: 10.1147/JRD.2015.2456711

Reed, M. S. (2008). Stakeholder participation for environmental management: A literature review. *Biological Conservation*, *141*(10), 2417–2431. DOI: 10.1016/j.biocon.2008.07.014

Rehan, H. (2024). Advancing Cancer Treatment with AI-Driven Personalized Medicine and Cloud-Based Data Integration. *Journal of Machine Learning in Pharmaceutical Research*, *4*(2), 1–40.

Rerhaye, L., Altun, D., Krauss, C., & Müller, C. (2021, July). Evaluation methods for an AI-supported learning management system: quantifying and qualifying added values for teaching and learning. In *International Conference on Human-Computer Interaction* (pp. 394-411). Cham: Springer International Publishing. DOI: 10.1007/978-3-030-77857-6_28

Rifandi, R., & Rahmi, Y. L. (2019, October). STEM education to fulfil the 21st century demand: A literature review. []. IOP Publishing.]. *Journal of Physics: Conference Series*, *1317*(1), 012208. DOI: 10.1088/1742-6596/1317/1/012208

Rodríguez, S. P. L., & Marquínez, O. P. B. (2024). Empathic Interactions in Multigrade Schools: A Strategy for Developing a Didactic Subject of Learning. *Migration Letters : An International Journal of Migration Studies*, *21*(S2), 180–206.

Russell, S., & Norvig, P. (2021). *Artificial Intelligence: A Modern Approach*. Pearson.

Rutterford, J., Upton, M., & Kodwani, D. (2006). *Financial Strategy: Adding Stakeholder Value* (2nd ed.). John Wiley & Sons.

Saad, E., Elekyaby, M. S., Ali, E. O., & Hassan, S. F. A. E. (2020). Double diamond strategy saves time of the design process. *International Design Journal*, *10*(3), 211–222. DOI: 10.21608/idj.2020.96345

Sagio, I., Prameswaro, I. S., & Ekasari, S. (2025). Artificial intelligence in the retail sector: Market and business model transformation. [INJOLE]. *International Journal of Economic Literature*, *3*(4), 133–146.

Sahibzada, S., Malik, F. S., Nasir, S., & Lodhi, S. K. (2025). AI-Augmented Turbulence and Aerodynamic Modelling: Accelerating High-Fidelity CFD Simulations with Physics-informed Neural Networks. *International Journal of Innovative Research in Computer Science and Technology*, *13*(1), 91–97. DOI: 10.55524/ijircst.2025.13.1.14

Sajja, R., Sermet, Y., Cikmaz, M., Cwiertny, D., & Demir, I. (2024). Artificial intelligence-enabled intelligent assistant for personalized and adaptive learning in higher education. *Information (Basel), 15*(10), 596. DOI: 10.3390/info15100596

Salas-Pilco, S. Z., Xiao, K., & Hu, X. (2022). Artificial intelligence and learning analytics in teacher education: A systematic review. *Education Sciences, 12*(8), 569. DOI: 10.3390/educsci12080569

Samanpour, A. R., Ruegenberg, A., & Ahlers, R. (2017). The future of machine learning and predictive analytics. In *Digital marketplaces unleashed* (pp. 297–309). Springer Berlin Heidelberg.

Sandre, A. (2022). *From risk to illness: Examining familial and environmental pathways to the development of depression via neural response to socio-affective information.* McGill University.

Saputri, M., Syukri, M., & Elisa, . (2022, February). Analysis of momentum and impulse on students' creative thinking skill through project based learning integrated STEM (science, technology, engineering, mathematics). []. IOP Publishing.]. *Journal of Physics: Conference Series, 2193*(1), 012066. DOI: 10.1088/1742-6596/2193/1/012066

Saqr, M., & Alamro, A. (2019). The role of social network analysis as a learning analytics tool in online problem based learning. *BMC Medical Education, 19*(160), 1–11. DOI: 10.1186/s12909-019-1599-6 PMID: 31113441

Sari, H. E., Tumanggor, B., & Efron, D. (2024). Improving educational outcomes through adaptive learning systems using ai. *International Transactions on Artificial Intelligence, 3*(1), 21–31. DOI: 10.33050/italic.v3i1.647

Sawu, M. R. F., Sukarso, A. A., Lestari, T. A., & Handayani, B. S. (2023). The effect of STEM learning in building creative dispositions and creative thinking skills of junior high school students. *Jurnal Penelitian Pendidikan IPA, 9*(8), 6219–6229. DOI: 10.29303/jppipa.v9i8.4180

Sayed, W. S., Noeman, A. M., Abdellatif, A., Abdelrazek, M., Badawy, M. G., Hamed, A., & El-Tantawy, S. (2023). AI-based adaptive personalized content presentation and exercises navigation for an effective and engaging E-learning platform. *Multimedia Tools and Applications, 82*(3), 3303–3333. DOI: 10.1007/s11042-022-13076-8 PMID: 35789938

Sciarrone, F. (2018, April). Machine learning and learning analytics: Integrating data with learning. In 2018 17th International conference on information technology based higher education and training (ITHET) (pp. 1-5). IEEE.

Setyadi, A., Pawirosumarto, S., Damaris, A., & Dharma, R. (2025). Risk management, digital technology literacy, and modern learning environments in enhancing learning innovation performance: A framework for higher education. *Education and Information Technologies*, *30*(11), 1–29. DOI: 10.1007/s10639-025-13380-4

Seyedtabib, M., Najafi-Vosough, R., & Kamyari, N. (2024). The predictive power of data: Machine learning analysis for Covid-19 mortality based on personal, clinical, preclinical, and laboratory variables in a case–control study. *BMC Infectious Diseases*, *24*(1), 411. DOI: 10.1186/s12879-024-09298-w PMID: 38637727

Sghir, N., Adadi, A., & Lahmer, M. (2023). Recent advances in Predictive Learning Analytics: A decade systematic review (2012–2022). *Education and Information Technologies*, *28*(7), 8299–8333. DOI: 10.1007/s10639-022-11536-0 PMID: 36571084

Sharkin, B. S. (2004). College counseling and student retention: Research findings and implications for counseling centers. *Journal of College Counseling*, *7*(2), 99–108. DOI: 10.1002/j.2161-1882.2004.tb00241.x

Shibani, A., Knight, S., & Shum, S. B. (2020). Educator perspectives on learning analytics in classroom practice. *The Internet and Higher Education*, *46*, 100730. DOI: 10.1016/j.iheduc.2020.100730

Shinde, R. (2025). Predictive Scheduling in the Age of AI: Optimizing Project Timelines for Sustainable Learning Environments. In Smart Education and Sustainable Learning Environments in Smart Cities (pp. 333-346). IGI Global Scientific Publishing.

Shridharan, M., Willingham, A., Spencer, J., Yang, T. Y., & Brinton, C. (2018, March). Predictive learning analytics for video-watching behavior in MOOCs. In 2018 52nd Annual Conference on Information Sciences and Systems (CISS) (pp. 1-6). IEEE. DOI: 10.1109/CISS.2018.8362323

Silvola, A., Näykki, P., Kaveri, A., & Muukkonen, H. (2021). Expectations for supporting student engagement with learning analytics: An academic path perspective. *Computers & Education*, *168*, 1–12. DOI: 10.1016/j.compedu.2021.104192

Simbeck, K. (2024). They shall be fair, transparent, and robust: Auditing learning analytics systems. *AI and Ethics*, *4*(2), 555–571. DOI: 10.1007/s43681-023-00292-7

Singh, B., Kaunert, C., Lal, S., & Arora, M. K. (2025). Enhancing AI-Augmented Classrooms: Teacher-Centric Integration of Intelligent Tutoring Systems and Adaptive Learning Environments. In Fostering Inclusive Education With AI and Emerging Technologies (pp. 99-130). IGI Global.

Sirajudin, N., Suratno, J., & Pamuti, . (2021, March). Developing creativity through STEM education. [). IOP Publishing.]. *Journal of Physics: Conference Series, 1806*(1), 012211. DOI: 10.1088/1742-6596/1806/1/012211

Smith, V. C., Lange, A., & Huston, D. R. (2012). Predictive modeling to forecast student outcomes and drive effective interventions in online community college courses. *Online Learning : the Official Journal of the Online Learning Consortium, 16*(3), 51–61. DOI: 10.24059/olj.v16i3.275

Spaho, E., Çiço, B., & Shabani, I. (2025). IoT Integration Approaches into Personalized Online Learning: Systematic Review. *Computers, 14*(2), 63. DOI: 10.3390/computers14020063

Stasolla, F., Zullo, A., Maniglio, R., Passaro, A., Di Gioia, M., Curcio, E., & Martini, E. (2025). Deep Learning and Reinforcement Learning for Assessing and Enhancing Academic Performance in University Students: A Scoping Review. *AI, 6*(2), 40. DOI: 10.3390/ai6020040

Steele, G. E. (2018). Student success: Academic advising, student learning data, and technology. *New Directions for Higher Education, 2018*(184), 59–68. DOI: 10.1002/he.20303

Strielkowski, W., Grebennikova, V., Lisovskiy, A., Rakhimova, G., & Vasileva, T. (2025). AI-driven adaptive learning for sustainable educational transformation. *Sustainable Development (Bradford), 33*(2), 1921–1947. DOI: 10.1002/sd.3221

Stylianidou, F., Glauert, E. B., Rossis, D., Compton, A., Cremin, T., Craft, A., & Havu-Nuutinen, S. (2018). Fostering inquiry and creativity in early years STEM education: Policy recommendations from the Creative Little Scientists Project. *European Journal of STEM Education, 3*(3). Advance online publication. DOI: 10.20897/ejsteme/3875

Sumathy, V., & Navamani, G. (2024). AI-Driven Personalized Learning: Enhancing Student Success through Adaptive Technologies. Library of Progress-Library Science, Information Technology & Computer, 44(3).

Sun, D., Looi, C. K., Yang, Y., & Jia, F. (2025). Exploring students' learning performance in computer-supported collaborative learning environment during and after pandemic: Cognition and interaction. *British Journal of Educational Technology, 56*(1), 128–149. DOI: 10.1111/bjet.13492

Susnjak, T. (2024). Beyond predictive learning analytics modelling and onto explainable artificial intelligence with prescriptive analytics and ChatGPT. *International Journal of Artificial Intelligence in Education*, *34*(2), 452–482. DOI: 10.1007/s40593-023-00336-3

Sutaphan, S., & Yuenyong, C. (2023). Enhancing grade eight students' creative thinking in the water stem education learning unit. Cakrawala Pendidikan. *Jurnal Ilmiah Pendidikan*, *42*(1), 120–135.

Szmelter-Jarosz, A., & Nozari, H. (2025). AI-Driven Decision Intelligence and Human-AI Collaboration in Economic Systems. In Dynamic and Safe Economy in the Age of Smart Technologies (pp. 171-190). IGI Global Scientific Publishing.

Szmelter-Jarosz, A., Ghahremani-Nahr, J., & Nozari, H. (2021). A neutrosophic fuzzy optimisation model for optimal sustainable closed-loop supply chain network during COVID-19. *Journal of Risk and Financial Management*, *14*(11), 519. DOI: 10.3390/jrfm14110519

Taheripour, E., Sadjadi, S. J., & Amiri, B. (2025). A Novel Approach to Portfolio Construction: An Application of FinBERT Sentiment Analysis and Credibilistic CVaR Criterion. *IEEE Access*. https://ieeexplore.ieee.org/abstract/document/10977954/

Tan, L. Y., Hu, S., Yeo, D. J., & Cheong, K. H. (2025). Artificial Intelligence-Enabled Adaptive Learning Platforms: A Review. Computers and Education: Artificial Intelligence, 100429.

Tavakkoli-Moghaddam, R., Nozari, H., Bakhshi-Movahed, A., & Bakhshi-Movahed, A. (2024). A Conceptual framework for the Smart Factory 6.0. In *Advanced Businesses in Industry 6.0* (pp. 1–14). IGI Global. DOI: 10.4018/979-8-3693-3108-8.ch001

Tavdgiridze, L., Didmanidze, I., KHASAIA, I., SHEROZIA, N., DOBORDGINIDZE, D., AKHVLEDIANI, D., & AKHVLEDIANI, Z. (2024). STEM teaching in contemporary education. Challenges to National Defence in Contemporary Geopolitical Situation, 1(1).

Taylor, R., Fakhimi, M., Ioannou, A., & Spanaki, K. (2024). Personalized learning in education: A machine learning and simulation approach. *Benchmarking*. Advance online publication. DOI: 10.1108/BIJ-06-2023-0380

Teles, R. O., & Moreira, F. T. (2025). Integrating AI in Formative Assessment Under UDL Principles in Diverse Learning Environments. In Improving Student Assessment With Emerging AI Tools (pp. 95-122). IGI Global Scientific Publishing.

Thangavel, S., Sharmila, K., & Sufina, K. (2025). Revolutionizing Education Through Augmented Reality (AR) and Virtual Reality (VR): Innovations, Challenges and Future Prospects. *Asian Journal of Interdisciplinary Research, 8*(1), 1–28. DOI: 10.54392/ajir2511

The Society for Learning Analytics Research (SoLAR). 2023. SoLAR Publications (https://www.solaresearch.org/)

Theng, D., & Theng, M. (2020, July). Machine learning algorithms for predictive analytics: A review and new perspectives. In Conf. High Technol. Lett (Vol. 26, No. 6, pp. 536-545).

Thingwiangthong, P., Termtachatipongsa, P., & Yuenyong, C. (2021, March). Status quo and needs of STEM Education curriculum to enhance creative problem solving competency. [). IOP Publishing.]. *Journal of Physics: Conference Series, 1835*(1), 012089. DOI: 10.1088/1742-6596/1835/1/012089

Thirunavukarasu, A. J., Ting, D. S. J., Elangovan, K., Gutierrez, L., Tan, T. F., & Ting, D. S. W. (2023). Large language models in medicine. *Nature Medicine, 29*(8), 1930–1940. DOI: 10.1038/s41591-023-02448-8 PMID: 37460753

Tiukhova, E., Vemuri, P., Flores, N. L., Islind, A. S., Óskarsdóttir, M., Poelmans, S., Baesens, B., & Snoeck, M. (2024). Explainable Learning Analytics: Assessing the stability of student success prediction models by means of explainable AI. *Decision Support Systems, 182*, 114229. DOI: 10.1016/j.dss.2024.114229

Tlili, A., Huang, R., Shehata, B., Liu, D., Zhao, J., Metwally, A. H. S., Wang, H., Denden, M., Bozkurt, A., Lee, L. H., Beyoglu, D., Altinay, F., Sharma, R. C., Altinay, Z., Li, Z., Liu, J., Ahmad, F., Hu, Y., Salha, S., . . . Burgos, D. (2022). Is Metaverse in education a blessing or a curse: a combined content and bibliometric analysis. In *Smart Learning Environments* (Vol. 9, Issue 1). Springer. https://doi.org/DOI: 10.1186/s40561-022-00205-x

Tsai, Y. S., Rates, D., Moreno-Marcos, P. M., Muñoz-Merino, P. J., Jivet, I., Scheffel, M., Drachsler, H., Delgado Kloos, C., & Gašević, D. (2020). Learning analytics in European higher education—Trends and barriers. *Computers & Education, 155*, 103933. DOI: 10.1016/j.compedu.2020.103933

Tytler, R. (2020). STEM education for the twenty-first century. Integrated approaches to STEM education: An international perspective, 21-43.

Tzimas, D., & Demetriadis, S. (2021). Ethical issues in learning analytics: A review of the field. *Educational Technology Research and Development, 69*(2), 1101–1133. DOI: 10.1007/s11423-021-09977-4

Udupi, P. K., Malali, P., & Noronha, H. (2016, March). Big data integration for transition from e-learning to smart learning framework. In 2016 3rd MEC international conference on big data and smart city (ICBDSC) (pp. 1-4). IEEE. DOI: 10.1109/ICBDSC.2016.7460379

Ullah, R. S., Hashim, F., Bandeali, M. M., & Akbar, A. (2025). Artificial Intelligence in Curriculum Design a Roadmap for Adaptive and Personalized Learning in Higher Education. *The Critical Review of Social Sciences Studies*, *3*(3), 304–322. DOI: 10.59075/8j71b437

Üret, A., & Ceylan, R. (2021). Exploring the effectiveness of STEM education on the creativity of 5-year-old kindergarten children. *European Early Childhood Education Research Journal*, *29*(6), 842–855. DOI: 10.1080/1350293X.2021.1913204

Uskov, V. L., Bakken, J. P., Putta, P., Krishnakumar, D., & Ganapathi, K. S. (2021, June). Smart education: predictive analytics of student academic performance using machine learning models in Weka and Dataiku systems. In International KES Conference on Smart Education and Smart E-Learning (pp. 3-17). Singapore: Springer Singapore. DOI: 10.1007/978-981-16-2834-4_1

Uvaneshwari, M., Nandagopal, K., Shrivastava, P., Senthil, K. A., Balakrishna, C., & Selvan, R. S. (2025). Enhancing Big Data Customer Sentiment Analysis With BERT-BiLSTM. In *Elevating Brand Loyalty With Optimized Marketing Analytics and AI* (pp. 1–18). IGI Global Scientific Publishing., DOI: 10.4018/979-8-3693-9954-5.ch001

Vadisetty, R., & Polamarasetti, A. (2024, December). AI-Augmented Skill Development Roadmaps: Tailoring 12-Month Learning Paths for Future-Ready Careers in Education 4.0 and Industry 4.0. In 2024 13th International Conference on System Modeling & Advancement in Research Trends (SMART) (pp. 655-661). IEEE.

Valavanidis, A. (2023). Artificial intelligence (ai) applications. *Department of Chemistry, National and Kapodistrian University of Athens, University Campus Zografou, 15784*. https://www.researchgate.net/profile/Athanasios-Valavanidis/publication/369914014_Artificial_Intelligence_AI_Applications_The_most_important_technology_we_ever_develop_and_we_must_ensure_it_is_safe_and_beneficial_to_human_civilization_I/links/6433f22c4e83cd0e2fa3aad1/Artificial-Intelligence-AI-Applications-The-most-important-technology-we-ever-develop-and-we-must-ensure-it-is-safe-and-beneficial-to-human-civilization-I.pdf

Vemula, V. R. (2025). AI-Enhanced Self-Healing Cloud Architectures for Data Integrity, Privacy, and Sustainable Learning. In Smart Education and Sustainable Learning Environments in Smart Cities (pp. 93-106). IGI Global Scientific Publishing.

Venice, J. A., Vettriselvan, R., Rajesh, D., Suresh, N. V., & Abirami, P. (2025). Enabling Personalized Learning and Adaptive Systems Through Strategic Management: Cloud Integration in Education. In Bridging Academia and Industry Through Cloud Integration in Education (pp. 49-72). IGI Global Scientific Publishing.

Vetrivel, S. C., Vidhyapriya, P., & Arun, V. P. (2025). Data Science for Learning Analytics: Understanding and Improving Learning Processes. In Driving Quality Education Through AI and Data Science (pp. 409-432). IGI Global Scientific Publishing.

Villán-Vallejo, A., Zitouni, A., García-Llamas, P., Fernández-Raga, M., Suárez-Corona, A., & Baelo, R. (2022). Soft Skills and STEM education: Vision of the European university EURECA-PRO. *BHM. Berg- und Hüttenmännische Monatshefte*, *167*(10), 485–488. DOI: 10.1007/s00501-022-01275-7 PMID: 36118302

Vincs, K., McCormick, J., & Balanzategui, J. (2022). *Artificial Intelligence Driven Non-Linear Narrative: An Extended Reality Application for Management Training*. https://doi.org/DOI: 10.13140/RG.2.2.26214.29767

Viswanath, K., & Weber, R. (2024). Digital Media, Cognition, and Brain Development. Handbook of Children and Screens: Digital Media, Development, and Well-Being from Birth Through Adolescence, 21.

Vuyyuru, S. R. (2025). Exploring the Convergence of Virtual and Physical Shopping Experiences in the Metaverse and Omnichannel Retail Through AI and Immersive Technologies. *Journal of Science and Technology*, *10*(6), 13–19. DOI: 10.46243/jst.2025.v10.i06.pp13-19

Wang, B., & Li, P. P. (2024). Digital creativity in STEM education: The impact of digital tools and pedagogical learning models on the students' creative thinking skills development. *Interactive Learning Environments*, *32*(6), 2633–2646.

Wang, H., Xu, Z., Fujita, H., & Liu, S. (2016). Towards felicitous decision making: An overview on challenges and trends of Big Data. *Information Sciences*, *367*, 747–765. DOI: 10.1016/j.ins.2016.07.007

Weng, W. H. (2020). Machine learning for clinical predictive analytics. In *Leveraging data science for global health* (pp. 199–217). Springer International Publishing. DOI: 10.1007/978-3-030-47994-7_12

Whitelock-Wainwright, A., Tsai, Y. S., Drachsler, H., Scheffel, M., & Gašević, D. (2021). An exploratory latent class analysis of student expectations towards learning analytics services. *The Internet and Higher Education*, *51*, 1–12. DOI: 10.1016/j.iheduc.2021.100818

Widiyati, T. D. S. C., Setyosari, P., Praherdhiono, H., Nakaya, A., & Khotimah, K. (2024). Seamless Learning to Enhancing Resilience and Professional Ethics in Higher Education Students. *Journal of Ecohumanism, 3*(8), 12227–12239.

Widyasmah, M., & Herlina, K. (2020, February). Implementation of STEM Approach Based on Project-based Learning to Improve Creative Thinking Skills of High School Students in Physics. [). IOP Publishing.]. *Journal of Physics: Conference Series, 1467*(1), 012072. DOI: 10.1088/1742-6596/1467/1/012072

Wilis, R., Prayitno, B. A., Sunarno, W., & Anjirawaroj, S. (2023). Improving students' metacognitive abilities and creative thinking skills through STEM-based in online learning. [Jurnal Pendidikan Biologi Indonesia]. *JPBI, 9*(1), 90–102. DOI: 10.22219/jpbi.v9i1.22994

Williams, J. (2016). Quality assurance and quality enhancement: Is there a relationship? *Quality in Higher Education, 22*(2), 97–102. DOI: 10.1080/13538322.2016.1227207

Winarko, G. C. (2024). Project-Based Learning with Scratch to Improve Students' Creative Thinking Ability: Systematic Literature Review. *Griya Journal of Mathematics Education and Application, 4*(2), 190–196. DOI: 10.29303/griya.v4i2.440

Wolff, A., Zdrahal, Z., Herrmannova, D., Kuzilek, J., & Hlosta, M. (2014). Developing predictive models for early detection of at-risk students on distance learning modules.

Wong, B. T. M., & Li, K. C. (2020). A review of learning analytics intervention in higher education (2011–2018). *Journal of Computers in Education, 7*(1), 7–28. DOI: 10.1007/s40692-019-00143-7

Xia, Y., Shin, S. Y., & Shin, K. S. (2024). Designing personalized learning paths for foreign language acquisition using big data: Theoretical and empirical analysis. *Applied Sciences (Basel, Switzerland), 14*(20), 9506. DOI: 10.3390/app14209506

Xu, M., Ng, W. C., Lim, W. Y. B., Kang, J., Xiong, Z., Niyato, D., Yang, Q., Shen, X. S., & Miao, C. (2022). *A Full Dive into Realizing the Edge-enabled Metaverse: Visions, Enabling Technologies,and Challenges*. http://arxiv.org/abs/2203.05471

Yeganeh, L. N., Fenty, N. S., Chen, Y., Simpson, A., & Hatami, M. (2025). The Future of Education: A Multi-Layered Metaverse Classroom Model for Immersive and Inclusive Learning. *Future Internet, 17*(2), 63. DOI: 10.3390/fi17020063

Yekollu, R. K., Bhimraj Ghuge, T., Sunil Biradar, S., Haldikar, S. V., & Farook Mohideen Abdul Kader, O. (2024, February). AI-driven personalized learning paths: Enhancing education through adaptive systems. In International Conference on Smart data intelligence (pp. 507-517). Singapore: Springer Nature Singapore. DOI: 10.1007/978-981-97-3191-6_38

Yıldırım, B., & Selvi, M. (2016). Examination of the effects of STEM education integratedas a part of science technology society and environmentcourses. *International Journal of Human Sciences*, *13*(3), 3684. DOI: 10.14687/jhs.v13i3.3876

Ylilehto, M., Komulainen, H., & Ulkuniemi, P. (2021). The critical factors shaping customer shopping experiences with innovative technologies. *Baltic Journal of Management*, *16*(5), 661–680. DOI: 10.1108/BJM-02-2021-0049

Yordanova, Z., & Nozari, H. (2025). Harnessing Cyber-Physical Systems and Digital Twins for Industrial Innovation and Economic Resilience. In Dynamic and Safe Economy in the Age of Smart Technologies (pp. 33-48). IGI Global Scientific Publishing. DOI: 10.4018/979-8-3693-4369-2.ch003

Young-Jones, A. D., Burt, T. D., Dixon, S., & Hawthorne, M. J. (2013). Academic advising: Does it really impact student success? *Quality Assurance in Education*, *21*(1), 7–19. DOI: 10.1108/09684881311293034

Yuan[1], L., Hou[1], B., Feng, D., & Rahman[1], S. S. A. (2025, June). Predictive Analytics in Education: Leveraging Al for Personalizing Student Learning Trajectories. In Proceedings of the 2nd International Conference on Educational Development and Social Sciences (EDSS 2025) (Vol. 924, p. 309). Springer Nature.

Zaheer, S. (2025a). *The Future of AR in Retail: Revolutionizing Online Shopping with Immersive Experiences International Journal of Engineering Technology Research & Management THE FUTURE OF AR IN RETAIL: REVOLUTIONIZING ONLINE SHOPPING WITH IMMERSIVE EXPERIENCES.* https://doi.org/DOI: 10.5281/zenodo.15250951

Zaheer, S. (2025b). Virtual reality and behavioural science: Harnessing immersive environments to influence user behaviors. *International Journal of Engineering Technology Research & Management*. https://doi.org/DOI: 10.5281/zenodo.15250907

Zhai, Y., Zhang, Y., Chu, Z., Geng, B., Almaawali, M., Fulmer, R., Lin, Y.-W. D., Xu, Z., Daniels, A. D., Liu, Y., Chen, Q., & Du, X. (2025). Machine learning predictive models to guide prevention and intervention allocation for anxiety and depressive disorders among college students. *Journal of Counseling and Development*, *103*(1), 110–125. DOI: 10.1002/jcad.12543

Zhou, Z.-H. (2021). *Machine learning*. Springer nature. https://books.google.com/books?hl=en&lr=&id=ctM-EAAAQBAJ&oi=fnd&pg=PR6&dq=machine+learning&ots=o_NjW8Uu5o&sig=2W9Jm8ACfRC0VDNlKa_YUb-8i2M

Zhou, C., Liu, X., Yu, C., Tao, Y., & Shao, Y. (2024). Trust in AI-augmented design: Applying structural equation modeling to AI-augmented design acceptance. *Heliyon*, *10*(1), e23305. DOI: 10.1016/j.heliyon.2023.e23305 PMID: 38192792

# About the Contributors

**Anikha Ahmed**, Marketing professional with 2 years of hands-on experience in consumer engagement, brand strategy and digital campaigns. Currently pursuing an MBA with a dual specialisation in Marketing and Finance, aiming to bridge creative insight with analytical depth. Skilled in market research, competitive analysis, and strategic planning, with a keen interest in translating data into actionable business decisions. Eager to apply a holistic approach of technical and research analytics to drive impactful strategies and excellence.

**Abdul Basith** is an MBA candidate at Woxsen University, Hyderabad, specializing in Marketing and Operations. His core areas of interest include AI in Marketing, Market Research, Brand Strategy, Consumer Behaviour, Digital Marketing, and the Evolving role of Artificial Intelligence in enhancing brand experiences. He is particularly focused on how AI-powered technologies such as augmented and virtual reality are reshaping consumer engagement through immersive and interactive brand environments. Currently, he is engaged in a field-based research internship that involves studying brand performance across high streets and shopping malls in metropolitan areas like Hyderabad. Alongside this, he is contributing to multiple research publications, with a strong emphasis on the intersection of AI, marketing innovation, and the future of consumer experience..

**Erman Coskun** is a full professor of Management Information Systems and Quantitative Methods. He has an academic career of over 25 years, having held positions in the United States, Turkiye, and Cyprus. Dr. Coskun's research is focused on Complexity of Information Systems, Digital Transformation, Human-Computer Interaction, Business Analytics, Business Intelligence, Enterprise Resource Planning, Supply Chain Management, Logistics, Port and Transportation System Efficiency, and Disaster and Crisis Management. His research has been published in journals including Government Information Quarterly, Systems and Software, Information and Software Technology, Journal of Homeland Security and Emergency Management and top conferences in MIS area such as International Conference on Information Systems (ICIS), Americas Conference on Information Systems (AMCIS), European Conference on Information Systems(ECIS). He has more than 30 journal publications and more than 75 conference papers. Dr. Coskun has held a variety of managerial and administrative positions in several institutions.

**Atajan Rovshenov** earned his Bachelor of Education (B.Ed) in CEIT (Computer & Instructional Technology Education) from Sakarya University and Master of Education (M.Ed) in CEIT from Ege University. He is a PhD Candidate at the Department of Management Information Systems of Izmir Bakircay University. His research area includes Information Systems and Educational Technology.

**Nida Shaikh** is an MBA candidate at Woxsen University, Hyderabad, specializing in Marketing and Operations. Her core areas of interest include digital marketing, brand strategy, consumer insights, and operations planning. She is currently working as an Operations Intern, where she manages CRM workflows and project tracking using ClickUp. With a strong passion for optimizing business processes and enhancing customer engagement, she is actively involved in cross-functional projects that blend operational efficiency with marketing impact.

**Agnieszka Szmelter-Jarosz** is an assistant professor at University of Gdańsk, Poland (Department of Logistics, Faculty of Economics). I am both a researcher and teacher. My research activities are lately focused on transport behaviour, mobility patterns and travel choices, mostly in urban and suburban zones, among all the generations. I am focused also on CSR in pharmaceutical logistics. In my teaching activities I am focused on Business Process Management, logistics management, also in ERP, CRM and WMS systems.

**Zornitsa Yordanova** is a leading expert in Business Information Systems, Innovation, and Digital Transformation at the University of National and World Economy (Bulgaria). She brings extensive teaching experience from various European universities and has authored over 100 academic publications.

# Index

## A



## B



## C



## D



## E